THE PSYCHOLOGICAL FOUNDATIONS OF CRIMINAL JUSTICE

THE PSYCHOLOGICAL FOUNDATIONS OF CRIMINAL JUSTICE

VOLUME II

Contemporary Perspectives on Forensic Psychiatry and Psychology

edited by
Harold J. Vetter
Department of Criminal Justice
University of South Florida

and

Robert W. Rieber
Department of Psychology
John Jay College of Criminal Justice

The John Jay Press
New York

First Edition, 1980

Copyright © 1980 The John Jay Press

All rights reserved. Published in the United States of America
by The John Jay Press, 444 West 56th Street,
New York, New York 10019

Library of Congress Cataloging in Publication Data (revised)
Main entry under title:

The Psychological foundations of criminal justice.

    Includes bibliographies and index.
    1. Insanity—Jurisprudence—United States—
Addresses, essays, lectures.   2. Psychology,
Forensic—Addresses, essays, lectures.   3. Forensic
psychiatry—United States—Addresses, essays,
lectures.
I. Rieber, Robert W.   II. Vetter,

Harold J., 1926–
KF9242.A5P77   345′.73′05019   78–18781
ISBN 0 – 89444–025X   ISBN 0–89444–026–8 (pb)

Manufactured in the United States of America

Table
of
Contents

Acknowledgments

We wish to acknowledge the authors and publishers below who have granted permission to use material in this book and who reserve all rights in their work:

Ennis and Litwack, "Psychiatry and the Presumption of Expertise," from *California Law Review*, Vol. 62, No. 693, 1974, pp. 694–751; revised for this volume. Guze, Goodwin, and Crane, "Criminality and Psychiatric Disorders," from *Archives of General Psychiatry*, Vol. 20, May, 1969, pp. 583–591. Halleck, "Rehabilitation of Criminal Offenders," from *Psychiatric Annals*, Vol. 4, No. 3, March, 1974, copyright, 1974 Psychiatric Annals Insight Publishing Co., Inc., pp. 61–85. Henn, Herjanic, and Vanderpearl, "Forensic Psychiatry," from *The Journal of Nervois and Mental Disease*, Vol. 162, No. 6, copyright © 1976 The Williams & Wilkins Co., pp. 423–429. Lipsitt, Paul D., "The Dilemma of Competency for Trial and Mental Illness," from *New England Journal of Medicine*, Vol. 282, No. 14, pp. 797–798. Nassi, "Therapy of the Absurd," from *Corrective and Social Psychiatry*, Vol. 21, No. 4, 1975, pp. 21–27. Roberts, "Some Observations on the Problems of the Forensic Psychiatrist," from *Wisconsin Law Review*, Spring, 1975, pp. 240–267. Rosenhan, "The Contextual Nature of Psychiatric Diagnosis," from *Jounral of Abnormal Psychology*, Vol. 84, No. 5, 1975, pp. 462–474. Rosenhan, "On Being Sane in Insane Places," from *Science*, Vol. 179, January, 1973, copyright, 1973 American Association for the Advancement of Science, pp. 250–258. Schulman, "Determination of Competency," from *Law, Psychiatry, and the Mentally Disordered*

THE PSYCHOLOGICAL FOUNDATIONS OF CRIMINAL JUSTICE

I.

Psychiatric and Psychological Interpretations of Criminality

Introduction

Responsibility for the management of a broad range of deviant behaviors—behaviors perceived by others as bizarre, threatening, or merely inexplicable—has been invested in the professional practitioner of psychiatry. Labeled "mental illnesses," deviant behaviors are ambiguously defined and may range from the "transient situational maladjustment" of an individual experiencing bereavement to the strange grimaces and antic behavior of a person labeled "schizophrenic." The psychiatrist, as a member of the medical profession, employs a vocabulary and set of concepts which constitute a series of elaborate metaphors and analogies that bear a tenuous, sometimes tortuous relationship to the physical disease models which they describe. Consequently, a deviant individual becomes a "patient;" the deviant behavior is referred to as "symptoms;" the determinants of the behavior become the "underlying pathology."

Many critics of psychiatry and the "medical model" approach to deviance have sharply questioned the applicability of the "medical model" range of behavioral phenomena broad enough to include transient situational maladjustment and schizophrenia. Others, including psychiatrists like Thomas Szasz, have objected to the "medical model" on moral and ethical grounds, claiming that the kind of pathological determinism assumed by the model deprives individuals of responsibility for their actions.

A further source of objections to the "medical model" approach is the *intrapsychic* conceptualization within which the traditional psychiatric approach has operated. The theoretical principals of American psychiatry have mainly been derived from psychoanalysis, the theories of conscious and unconscious processes formulated by Sigmund Freud. Psychoanalytic theory is identified as psychodynamic or intrapsychic, because the principal constructs of the theory are built around factors and forces within an individual's psyche that are largely hypothesized or inferred. Psychoanalytic theory is conceptual, and behavior is "explained" by specifying the relationships that occur between or among internal psychic structures.

Psychologists, who had not worked in applied psychology prior to World War II, were generally working in academic jobs. Following the war, the demand for trained professionals in clinical work gave enormous impetus to the field of clinical psychology. Psychologists received most of their training from psychiatrists and found jobs in clinics and institutions that were directed and administered by psychiatrists. Consequently, few differences in viewpoint between psychiatrists and clinical psychologists emerged until the late 1950s and early 1960s. In the 1960s, psychologists whose orientations and backgrounds differed considerably from those of their colleagues in clinical psychology and psychiatry began to move into clinical positions. Trained in the tradition of experimental psychology, with an emphasis upon objectivity, quantification, systematic research, and empirical verification, these psychologists emphasized a point of view toward deviance that had been shaped by models developed in laboratories rather than clinics. When they turned their attention to criminal behavior, inevitably psychologists would attempt to recast or reformulate the problems involved in accounting for criminality within a conceptual framework. To them, that framework assigned prominence to the social learning processes in an individual's acquisition and maintenance of criminal behavior.

INTRAPSYCHIC PERSPECTIVES ON CRIMINAL BEHAVIOR

Behavior, as viewed within the psychoanalytic framework, is *functional* in two ways: it operates to fulfill certain needs or drives, and it has consequences for other aspects of behavior. However, the importance that Freud attributed to *unconscious factors* adds a further complexity to the interpretation of behavior, for it requires acceptance of the proposition that much, if not most, of an individual's behavior possesses meaning which lies outside the range of awareness. Consequently, neurotic behavior is construed as the outward *symbolic manifestation of dynamic dysfunction*. To the psychoanalyst, neurotic behavior represents the unsuccessful attempt by one component of personality (the ego) to exercise control over another component (the id).

For an understanding of criminal behavior, the immediate and direct implication of motivational functionalism is that a focus on the criminal action itself (manifest function) defeats any attempt to understand the causes of the crime. Feldman (1969) states:

> . . . like any other behavior, criminal behavior is a form of self-expression, and what is intended to be expressed in the act of crime is not only observable in the act itself, but also may even be beyond the awareness of the criminal actor himself. So for example, an overt criminal act of stealing may be undertaken for the attainment of purposes which are far removed from, and even contrary to, that of simple illegal aggrandizement; indeed, it may even be, as shall be seen in the sequel, that the criminal, in stealing, seeks not material gain but self-punishment. The etiological basis of a criminal act can, therefore, be understood only in terms of the functions, latent as well as manifest, which the act was intended to accomplish.

Although specific functions of a given criminal act must be sought in the life history of the individual offender, the general etiological formula for psychoanalytic criminology asserts that criminal behavior is an attempt at maintaining a psychic balance or restoring a psychic balance which has been disrupted.

Despite a consensus of professional opinion among psychoanalytic criminologists concerning the general etiological formula or "psychic balance," considerably less unanimity is evident about the specific factors in an individual's socialization which dispose that person toward criminality in an effort to maintain psychic balance. Feldman (1969) identifies five variations of criminality: 1. criminality as neurosis, 2. the antisocial individual as a result of defective socialization, 3. criminal behavior as compensation for frustration of conventional psychic needs, 4. criminal behavior as a function of defective superego, and 5. criminal behavior as anomie. As Feldman notes, these variations range from a concentration on hypothesized internal factors to an emphasis upon external conditions which may exert a decisive influence on the individual.

The weakness of the etiological formula is readily apparent. In the case of "criminality as neurosis," empirical data simply fail to support the contention that a criminal is typically a neurotic individual compulsively driven toward self-punishment. Contrary to the formula, criminal offenders appear to make every effort to elude capture. Moreover, empirical evidence, discussed in Part V of this volume, suggests that "neurotic" personality characteristics are distributed within the criminal population in approximately the same proportion as that found in the noncriminal population.

Equally dubious is the view of the criminal as an antisocial character who seeks immediate gratification, lives entirely in the present, and is unable to withstand tedium and monotony. Many kinds of criminal behavior require extensive preparation by way of training in specific skills or in systematic planning. As Feldman observes, behavior in professional, organized, and white-collar crime seems to exemplify Freud's "reality principle."

In failing to assign appropriate emphasis to the fact that patterned criminality is not the spontaneous creation of the individual offender, psychoanalytic criminology minimizes the crucial importance of social learning. According to Feldman (1969):

> . . . this learning process requires the individual's participation in the formation and maintenance of relationships with others who dispose of the necessary knowledge and put it to use. It is in the context of these relationships that the individual learns his criminality and adopts for himself distinctive criminalistic attitudes and percepts. Presumably, the experiences of such a learning process must have an effect on the personality of the individual undergoing them. Yet, this reciprocating influence of criminal experience on the personality of the criminal appears to have no consideration in psychoanalytic criminology. Indeed, all of the interpretations of the basic etiology formula share this common implicit assumption that the personality differentials to which causal status is attributed are temporarily antecedent to the individual's participation in criminal activity. Nevertheless, it is at least a plausible alternative that such personality differentials are consequential precipitants of the individual's induction into criminality. And in failing to take this possibility into account, the entire structure of psychoanalytic criminology becomes vulnerable to the charge that it merely begs the question from the outset.

Finally, psychoanalytic criminology possesses some serious flaws when formally judged as a theory. Psychoanalytic constructs tend to be global and all-inclusive in nature and loaded with "surplus meaning"; rarely, if ever, do they describe explicit, observable events. Nevertheless, in time psychoanalytic constructs become the "facts" of psychoanalysis, and subsequently more speculatively elaborate concepts are based upon those "facts."

Most research generated by psychoanalytic theory does not seem to be directed toward the subsequent modification of theory in light of newly acquired information; instead it is used to demonstrate the essential validity of the basic postulates and assumptions of theory. Because of the ambiguity and lack of specific operations of the constructs in the theory, no hypothesis derived from psychoanalytic theory can be either clearly confirmed or clearly refuted. Consequently, critics of psychoanalysis have charged that the theory and its proponents do not conform to the widely accepted canons of empirical verification and refutation implicit in the scientific method.

REALITY THERAPY

Glasser's (1965) reality therapy is a reaction to psychoanalysis and its emphasis upon unconscious motives and "psychic balance." Glasser treats criminal behavior as "irresponsibility." To him a youthful car thief is not exhibiting "pathology" in traditional psychoanalytic terms; he is acting in an irresponsible manner which deprives others of the ability to fulfill *their* needs. Consequently, the thief's desire to ride forces someone else to walk. Because it deals in the present and avoids the terminology of psychoanalysis, reality therapy has had a good deal of popular appeal among people who work in corrections, especially those who perceive the vigorous application of the "Protestant ethic" as the eventual solution to the crime problem. As a scientific explanation of criminal behavior, Glasser's concepts are untested and perhaps untestable.

THE CRIMINAL PERSONALITY

A recent defection from the intrapsychic theory occurred with the publication of the first volume of a trilogy by Samuel Yochelson and Stanton E. Samenow, entitled *The Criminal Personality.* This book reported the results of a fifteen year project conducted under a federal grant at St. Elizabeths Hospital in Washington, D.C. It involved an intensive study of 255 criminals from a wide variety of backgrounds: rich, poor, white, black, young, old, Christian, Moslem, and Jew. Approximately 150,000 to 200,000 contact hours were spent with the subjects and they were tested with everything from EEG and EKG to finger dexterity examinations. In terms of magnitude, the study is probably without precedent in the history of criminological investigation.

Yochelson was a practicing psychoanalyst in Buffalo, New York, who ended his private practice to pursue his interest in criminality and its determinants. He was joined later in the project by Samenow, a clinical psychologist. Yochelson died in the summer of 1977 when the first volume of the projected three-volume title was in press, but Samenow has continued with the project.

During the first four years of the project, the data gathered was everything that a psychiatrist with a psychoanalytic orientation could have wanted: evidence of Oedipal conflicts, infantile strivings toward omnipotence, childhood traumas, and unconscious drives. Yochelson came to the conclusion, however, that he was being deceived by his subjects, who were using their participation in the project as a cover for continued burglaries, rapes, and robberies under the protection afforded by the guarantee of privileged communication. This realization led Yochelson to an agonizing reappraisal of his psychoanalytic orientation. He found himself compelled to abandon his career-long Freudian views and turned to a probe of thought and action patterns among his criminal subjects. He and his psychologist colleague, "reluctant converts" from psychoanalysis, identified 53 patterns of thinking and action that they claim to have found in all of the 255 subjects in the study.

Yochelson and Samenow identify their patterns under descriptions like Loner, Lying, Power Thrust, Anger, Pride, Failure to Assume Obligation and Lack of Time Perspective. It is interesting to compare these categories with the list of characteristics typical of the psychopath identified by Hervey Cleckley more than thirty years ago. Yochelson and Samenow present their conclusions in the manner of someone dispensing revelations of fundamental truth. Any criminal justice practitioner with first-hand contact with criminal offenders is apt to find their "discoveries" something less than momentous.

There is something about this extremely controversial project to dislike for nearly everyone. Traditional researchers with an orientation in behavioral science will either dismiss the project or will object to its methodological crudity: there were no control groups, little or no attempt at quantification, no pretense to having followed a research design that lends itself to tests of statistical significance, numerous contradictions in the descriptions, and a reliance throughout on subjectivity rather than objectivity. Psychiatrists will be pained by the authors' account of the frustration and failures that led Yochelson and Samenow to abandon the entire medical model because it had proved a hindrance rather than a help. As the authors put it:

> Once we discarded "mental illness" as a factor we began to understand more about a patient's reality. The concept of mental illness had been the greatest barrier to acquiring this knowledge.

Liberals will be distressed by the authors' summary rejection of environmentalism as a valid approach to understanding the criminal offender. Yochelson and Samenow write:

> . . . the criminal is not a victim of circumstances. He makes

choices early in life, regardless of his socioeconomic status, race, or parents' child-rearing practices. A large segment of society has continued to believe that a person becomes a criminal because of environmental influences. Several factors account for the persistence of this conclusion. Parents who have criminal offspring deny that there is something inherent in the individual that surfaces as criminality. They desperately look for a cause and, in the effort to explain, they latch on to some event or series of events in a person's life for which he is not responsible. Many social scientists have promulgated a deterministic view of man and for years have been explaining criminality largely in terms of environmental influences. Government programs have operated on this basis. The media have espoused this attitude. In efforts to eradicate crime, society has tried to do something, rather than nothing. Attacking environmental sources has been considered one positive step. However, these efforts have met with failure for reasons that the reader will understand as he reads this volume. Changing the environment does not change the man. Finally, the criminal is ever ready to present himself as a victim once he is apprehended. He feeds society what he at best only half believes himself. Actually, he knows that circumstances have nothing to do with his violations, but he uses that rhetoric if he thinks it will lead others to view him more sympathetically.

No matter how irritating their judgments, Yochelson and Samenow cannot be ignored. In challenging the traditional viewpoints of criminology, the authors have provided a stimulus to other investigators to refute or confirm the conclusions in *The Criminal Personality* by means of conventional research.

SOCIAL LEARNING INTERPRETATIONS

In 1937, in a work entitled *The Professional Thief*, the criminologist Edwin H. Sutherland provided what has come to be regarded as the classic statement of a theory concerning the genesis of criminal behavior. He called his theory *differential association*. Sutherland attempted to account for the etiology of criminal behavior in the group-based learning experiences of the individual in terms of the following postulates:

1. Criminal behavior is learned.

2. Criminal behavior is learned in interaction with other persons in a process of communication.

3. The principal part of the learning of criminal behavior occurs within intimate personal groups.

4. When criminal behavior is learned, the learning includes: techniques of committing the crime, which are sometimes very complicated, sometimes very simple, and the specific direction of motives, drives, rationalizations, and attitudes.

5. The specific direction of motives and drives is learned from definitions of the legal codes as favorable or unfavorable.

6. A person becomes delinquent because of an excess of definitions favorable to violation of the law over definitions unfavorable to violation of the law.

7. Differential associations may vary in frequency, duration, priority, and intensity.

8. The process of learning criminal behavior by association with criminal and anticriminal patterns involves all of the mechanisms that are involved in any other learning.

9. While criminal behavior is an expression of general needs and values, it is not explained by those general needs and values since non-criminal behavior is an expression of the same needs and values.

Differential association remained untested, primarily because of difficulties involved in operationalizing the fundamental concepts on which the theory rested. Criminological investigators were unable to resolve the difficulties posed by mentalistic constructs like "attitudes" and "motives." Since Sutherland's time, considerable progress has been made in the understanding of the complex factors involved in learning. In particular, the work of B. F. Skinner and his followers in operant conditioning has emphasized the importance of *reinforcement* in the acquisition and maintenance of behavior. Aware of this work, several theorists have felt that differential association needed revision in light of contemporary knowledge of the learning process.

C.R. Jeffery (1965), a sociologist who studied under Sutherland, first attempted to modernize the theory of differential association by applying its language and concepts to those of operant conditioning. Jeffery stated that criminal or delinquent behavior is acquired through a process of *differential reinforcement.* Consequently, a person is more likely to repeat behavior which results in positive consequences (reward or removal of an aversive stimulus) than behavior culminating in negative conditioners (punishment or removal of a positive stimulus) or ending in neutral consequences. Criminal behavior, like any other behavior, is maintained by its consequences. A theft may result in the positive reinforcement elicted by a stolen item. A murder or assault can produce positive reinforcement through biochemical change in the aggressor. An addict taking a drug removes the aversive conditions of withdrawal.

According to Jeffery (1965), differential reinforcement theory makes several important assumptions:

> 1. The reinforcing quality of differential stimuli differs for different actors depending on the past conditioning history of each;
> 2. Some individuals have been reinforced for criminal behavior whereas other individuals have not been;
> 3. Some individuals have been punished for criminal behavior whereas other individuals have not been;
> 4. An individual will be intermittently reinforced and/or punished for criminal behavior; that is, he will not be reinforced every time he commits a criminal act.

To Jeffery, no two people are identical, and everyone has a different history of conditioning. When one of two individuals with identical families, backgrounds, and association steals, the criminal behavior is explained by the fact that it is dependent upon the reinforcing quality of the stolen item, past stealing responses which have been reinforced and past stealing responses which have been punished. These three variables will differ between any pair of individuals despite any similarities in their backgrounds or associations. Consequently, Jeffery uses the term *differential* reinforcement because different conditioning histories exist for different individuals. Differential association theory cannot account for this phenomenon. Thus, through Jeffery's application of reinforcement contingencies, a serious weakness of Sutherland's original theory is eliminated.

Of primary importance in Sutherland's theory is his belief that social reinforcement maintains criminal behavior. To Sutherland, other people reinforce criminal behavior either through verbal adulation or active confederation. People also serve as discriminative stimuli which provide to the individual valuable information on the potential for reward or punishment. For example, it is highly unlikely that delinquent behavior will occur in the presence of a uniformed police officer. The officer indicates that the potential for reward is highly limited and that criminal behavior will likely result in punishment. Conversely, a juvenile in the presence of a typical juvenile gang is likely to misbehave, because the potential for the rewards of social acceptance and praise is quite high.

People also can act as aversive stimuli through reprimanding, arresting, or even shooting an offender. All of these behaviors represent Sutherland's concept of "attitudes" favorable or unfavorable to criminal behavior.

Jeffery, questioning the sole importance of social reinforcement, states that some criminal behavior reinforces itself. Stolen goods serve as positive reinforcement whether or not anyone other than the thief is aware of them. By demonstrating a model of criminal behavior without social reinforcement, Jeffery threatens the very foundations of differential association and current sociological ideas, all of which have emphasized the primary importance of social forces in the determination of behavior. The question of reinforcement contingencies must be empirically resolved, and theory must be restructured to account for results.

Robert Burgess and Ronald Akers (1966) completely reformulated Sutherland's differential association theory. They applied the principles of operant learning as outlined by Jeffery and verified propriety of the principles through the presentation of experimental evidence. They reformed Sutherland's original nine proposals into seven statements, incorporating modern learning theory into the original concepts. Reed Adams (1973) critically evaluated the Burgess and Akers propositions and revised them into a cohesive, up-to-date theoretical presentation. Adams (1974) contrasted the effects of social and non-social determinants of behavior. Results demonstrated that non-social factors *did* play a major role in the determination of misbehavior. Adams concludes that once acquired, criminal behavior is maintained by non-social reinforcement, social factors being involved only to a small extent. Consequently, Adams has demonstrated the absolute necessity to modernize Sutherland's theory to include his results.

CRIMINALITY AND THE DEVIANCE PERSPECTIVE

As Saleem A. Shah (1969) states, mental health professionals "tend generally to conceptualize deviance in terms of certain characteristics of the person while ignoring or underemphasizing the societal contexts within which deviant roles are defined and confirmed." His article analyzes the deviancy labeling process with regard to behaviors defined as crimes and those defined as mental illness, decision rules in law and medicine and some research findings regarding court-ordered mental examinations, and certain consequences of mental health labels and opinions with regard to legal issues.

David E. Silber (1974) explores some consequences of psychiatric conceptualizations of criminality. When criminal behavior is defined as psychological disturbance, thereby making treatment rather than punishment the appropriate societal sanction, important issues are raised concerning the civil liberties of the offender. For the mental health worker in the punitive environment of a correctional institution, the prospects of treatment are extremely bleak:

. . . the custodial staffs of prisons usually view the professional staff with ambivalence or outright hostility. They worry about the possibility of riots, believe that prisoners are generally incorrigible, and suspect that therapy is a form of mollycoddling. . . . They therefore are often reluctant to encourage the expansion or initiation of treatment programs within the correctional setting and may passively oppose ones already present.

Leigh M. Roberts (1965) discusses the professional preparation of the psychiatrist to function in the legal setting and some of the problems likely to be encountered, ranging from the assessment of a defendant's ability to stand trial to predicting the possible effect of incarceration on an alleged offender. He stresses the necessity for the psychiatrist who intends to operate as a forensic specialist to acquire an understanding of, and familiarity with, legal concepts and procedures. Roberts pays special attention to the rules of evidence under which the forensic specialist is expected to provide testimony as an expert witness in court.

REFERENCES

Adams, R. "Differential Association and Learning Principles Revisited." *Social Problems*, 1973, 20, 458–470.

Adams, R. "The Adequacy of Differential Association Theory." *Journal of Research in Crime and Delinquency*, 1974, 11, 1–8.

Burgess, R. L., and Akers, R. A. "A Differential Association-reinforcement Theory of Criminal Behavior. *Social Problems*, 1966, 14, 128–147.

Feldman, D. "Psychoanalysis and Crime." In D. R. Cressey and D. Ward (Eds.), *Delinquency, Crime, and Social Process*. New York: Harper and Row, 1969.

Glasser, W. *Reality Therapy*. New York: Harper and Row, 1965.

Jeffery, C. R. "Criminal Behavior and Learning Theory." *Journal of Criminal Law, Criminology, and Police Science*, 1965, 56, 294–300.

Roberts, L. M. "Some Observations on the Problems of the Forensic Psychiatrist." *Wisconsin Law Review*, 1965, 240–267.

Shah, S. A. "Crime and Mental Illness: Some Problems in Defining and Labeling Deviant Behavior." *Mental Hygiene*, 1969, 53, 21–33.

Silber, D. E. "Controversy Surrounding the Criminal Justice System and Its Implications for the Role of Mental Health Workers." *American Psychologist*, 1974, 30, 239–244.

Sutherland, E. H. *The Professional Thief*. Chicago: University of Chicago Press, 1937.

Yochelson, S., and Samenow, S. E. *The Criminal Personality*. New York: J. Aronson, 1977.

Crime and Mental Illness: Some Problems in Defining and Labeling Deviant Behavior

Saleem A. Shah

Efforts to understand and deal with problems of crime and mental illness should be preceded by an examination of the societal processes by which deviant behavior is defined and labeled. It is important to know about the kinds of behavior declared to be so objectionable to the community, so irritating to segments of the population, or so threatening to social order and stability that they are defined as deviant and are subject to various sanctions. The process of defining and labeling social deviance is complex and requires consideration of several factors. Mental health professionals tend generally to conceptualize deviance in terms of certain characteristics of the person, while ignoring or underemphasizing the societal contexts within which deviant roles are defined and confirmed.

This article deals with three broad issues: 1. the deviancy labeling process with regard to behaviors defined as crimes and those defined as mental illness; 2. decision rules in law and medicine, and some research findings regarding court-ordered mental examinations; and 3. certain consequences of mental health labels and opinions with regard to legal issues.

BEHAVIOR AND SOCIAL DEVIANCE

Various problems of definition arise in assessing social deviance. In part this is because all behavior occurs within specific group contexts, and the frames of reference of the evaluators are not always comparable. Furthermore, since the evaluators of the behavior may be located at different points of interaction with the person, the behavior they see may differ significantly. Thus, how a particular form of deviant behavior is to be evaluated—in fact, whether the behavior is even to be viewed as deviant—depends largely on the evaluator's frame of reference; and whether the deviant behavior is seen as evidence of crime, perversion, drunkenness, bad manners, corruption, laziness, genius, or mental illness is contingent on the criteria according to which the evaluator operates and how these criteria are applied.

It should therefore be evident that forms of behavior per se do not differentiate deviants from non-deviants. It is the response of the more conventional, conforming, and influential members of the society who identify and interpret behavior that—at least in sociological terms—transforms persons into deviants. (1–4)

THE CRIMINAL LABELING PROCESS

In examining the criminal labeling process, we can start with the presence of various social norms designed to regulate social relations and behavior. Some social norms have considerable force and sanctions to support compliance whereas others have little such force. Among the more universal and permanent social norms are many associated with social institutions. Institutional norms tend to be supported by high degrees of consensus and usually elicit intense reactions when they are violated. Related to social norms are the central goals of a culture, i.e., *social values*. Not only are *social values* shared widely in the culture, but they are regarded as matters of collective welfare, and often involve strong emotional belief in their importance. Social norms often involve some basic goals or values held in high regard in the culture. Thus, murder, manslaughter, rape, robbery, and theft are violations not just of legal norms, but also of social norms involving basic values in the protection of human life, sexual and family life, and property, respectively.(5)

Criminal laws may be seen as laws regulating behavior that are enforced by coercion of the state. Although some criminal laws may obviously relate to the protection of important social values, others are not so related, but instead reflect the attitudes, values, and expectations of predominant and influential culture groups. In general, when violations of certain social norms tend to exceed the tolerance limits of the community, legal regulations may be brought into being to control such behavior. Understandably, there are few absolute standards for the regulation of social behavior. Behavior not previously labeled "criminal" may come to be so designated; on the other hand, behavior so defined may eventually lose this label.

Discussion of social deviance often appears based on the assumption that the behavior in question reflects something inherently different, and that the deviant act occurs because of some special characteristic of the person committing it. However, since different groups judge different things to be deviant, it becomes obvious that the determination of deviance very much involves the person or group making the judgment, the particular process by which the judgment is reached, and the situation in which the determination is made. To ignore this complex and variable aspect of the labeling process would logically tend to limit the kinds of theories developed and the understanding obtained about deviant behavior.

There is also a tendency to assume that those who violate criminal laws constitute a somewhat homogeneous group. Such a view provides a very inadequate conceptualization of the phenomenon of social deviance. Becker(1) points out that deviance is, in a sense, *created* by society in that society establishes various rules whose infraction constitutes deviation. It becomes apparent, therefore, that deviance is not simply a quality of the act a person commits, but more a consequence of the application by others of rules and sanctions to the norm-violators or "offenders." The deviant, then, may be viewed as one to whom that label has successfully been applied; and deviant behavior is behavior that the social group so labels.

Since the above labeling process—involving as it does a number of interacting variables—is certainly not infallible, it cannot be assumed that the category of offenders includes all those who actually have violated laws. Indeed, there are numerous studies to suggest that only a very small proportion of all law-violating behavior in the community comes to official attention. Various law violations may be committed, but the person may suffer no official sanction unless someone brings the matter to the attention of law enforcement agencies or the behavior is detected by such agencies.

Further, persons believed to have committed deviant acts may at certain times or in certain situations be handled more leniently, or more severely, than at other times. For example, during festive occasions drunkenness and disorderly behavior may be treated rather tolerantly. Likewise, such behavior in middle- and upper-class neighborhoods may be handled more permissively than it is in poorer areas. In contrast, during periods of "all-out attack" by law enforcement agencies on particular types of crimes, e.g., homosexuality, narcotics addiction, and gambling, many persons previously ignored or tolerated may be given official attention, criminal labeling, and other sanctions.

The degree to which an act may be treated as deviant also depends on who commits the act and who feels he has been harmed by it. Studies of juvenile delinquency make the point that boys from middle- and upper-class areas, even when apprehended, do not get as far into the legal processes as do boys from lower-class areas. Similarly, the law may tend to be applied differentially to members of minority groups. Such findings suggest that various social-class variables are deeply embedded in the legislative, law enforcement, and administration-of-justice processes pertaining to law-violating behavior.

Many factors operate to determine whether the law-violator will move forward into the criminal process or will be diverted from the process. Thus, many law-violations may not be brought to official attention because they may not be viewed as serious or irritating enough. It may also happen that the family may be able to make restitution for damages or other loss, or may seek remedial assistance from social and mental health agencies or professionals, and thus avoid official sanctions under the criminal law. It may also be that the complaint regarding the deviant behavior may be brought to the attention of mental health rather than law enforcement agencies; as a result, the deviant behavior may be regarded as "sick" and be handled along therapeutic lines.

Similarly, many of the factors operating at the earlier stages of the criminal process may well determine to varying degrees the disposition and outcome at later stages. For example, prompt availability of counsel may often be a significant variable; also, an accused person at large on bail is better able to assist counsel in locating witnesses and helping to prepare other aspects of his defense than a person confined to jail because of inability to make bail.

CONCEPTUALIZATION OF MENTAL DISEASE

The concept of mental disease has long been used in various ways in the legal process for dealing with social deviants who not only are law-violators but who, in addition, display characteristics viewed as "odd." There is a variety of situations in which mental health concepts, definitions, opinions, and even social value judgments interact with the legal process. A number of rather serious and complex problems arise when the differing concepts, labels, and philosophical and ideological orientations of law and mental health interact.

Before discussing such problems, it seems appropriate to give some attention to the concept of mental disease and the processes involved in the labeling of behavior so identified. It has frequently been asserted that mental disease refers to a fairly specific and clearly diagnosable condition—at least by those with knowledge and expertise in mental health. The concept of *mental disease* has often been compared with the concept of disease as used in general medicine, with the explicit statement that use of the term in these two situations is very similar, if not exactly alike.

It would appear that, as a carryover from the search in medicine for various micro-organisms found to have a functional (causal) relationship with various symptoms related to a specific disease, in the case of mental disease the semantic shift has been to hypothesized defects or diseases of the nervous system. Hence persons are said to be suffering from "nervous breakdown," to be troubled by "nerves," and to have "mental disease." However, the search for defects or diseases of the nervous system has not yet yielded explanations for the vast range of problems and suffering commonly referred to as mental illness or mental disease. In medicine the term "illness" is used in a literal, non-figurative sense to denote an un-desirable alteration or change away from optimal levels of organic bodily functioning. In contrast, the term "mental illness" is applied to *patterns of behavior* judged to be maladaptive, inappropriate, or undesirable on the basis of various psychological, social, and legal norms.

It appears, then, that, in contrast to the fairly specific, objective, and precise criteria for determining *physical* disease, the criteria and norms used in defining *mental disease* are neither specific nor objective nor are they separable from a multitude of ethical and social considerations inherent in the labeling process. Not surprisingly therefore, the term "mental disease" is often applied in a somewhat indiscriminate way to a motley collection of interpersonal and social behaviors judged deviant according to varying psychological and cultural norms used by the persons applying such labels. Understandably, therefore, the definitions tend to be vague and are often remarkably circular and lacking in uniformity and reliability. It would seem that the term "mental disease" is actually used in a metaphorical sense to refer to a variety of social and psychological maladjustments and related human problems. (6–8)

Not only is the term "mental disease" used to describe (label) a variety of deviant behaviors, it is often also used to explain a veritable host of psychosocial problems, e.g., crime, promiscuity, marital infidelity, political fanaticism, general unhappiness and discontent, and, one might add, sometimes even the behavior of those whom we happen not to like. The term seems at times to be used as a ready explanation for almost any type of behavior that does not make sense, reveals no clear or reasonable motivation, or distrubs our sensibilities.

Davidson(9) has cautioned against the loose and indiscriminate use of the label *mental disease:*

. . . As doctors, we see any major deviation from the norm as unhealthy; and, therefore, any such deviation is ill-health or sickness. Thus, in our book we include as mental disorders such deviations as learning difficulties, stress reactions, sexual deviations, mental deficiency, antisocial behavior. By *book*, I mean the volume called *Diagnostic and Statistical Manual of Mental Disorders*, published by this Association [American Psychiatric Association]. Now mark this well—it is going to haunt us. This is a list of *mental disorders*. It says so on the cover. Therefore, "Transient situational disturbances"—so listed—must be mental disorders; so are alcoholism, habit disturbances, mental deficiencies, speech disturbances, and so on . . . .

Our categories are so broad that we could squeeze into them such concepts as hostility to an employer, or marital discord over money.

Later in this same article, Davidson goes on to emphasize further his warnings about such expanding use of the *mental disease* label to an ever-increasing number of social deviations and problems:

. . . As the word is generally used, "sickness" does not include such deviations as stress reactions, personality disorders, and learning disturbances. We are practising magic if we think that we can make these deviations into sicknesses merely by listing them in our own little book.

It would be fair to say that, by and large, the kind of sensitivity shown by this writer to numerous problems and consequences stemming from loose application of the label *mental disease* is distinguished by its infrequency. Many mental health professionals seem unappreciative, if not even unaware, of the logical and conceptual issues involved in the labeling of deviation. This would, in general, be even more true of the many lawyers and judges who tend rather uncritically to accept and to make free use of the concept of mental disease, believing it to have the same meaning as the concept of disease used in physical medicine.

A SOCIOLOGICAL PERSPECTIVE

The above discussion of the concept of mental disease is largely in terms of a clinical model, in which primary focus is on the deviant individual and his particular psychological and intrapsychic characteristics. However, it is important to note that in recent years it has rather convincingly been argued that mental illness may perhaps more usefully be considered as a *social status* rather than as a disease. This would be because the symptoms of mental illness are vaguely defined and widely distributed, and because the definition of behavior symptomatic of mental illness is usually dependent on *social* rather than *medical* contingencies. Furthermore, the argument continues, the status of the mental patient is more often an *ascribed status*, conditions for entry into that status being external to him, than it is an *achieved status*, with conditions for status entry dependent on the patient's own behavior. According to this sociological argument, the societal reaction is a fundamentally important variable in all stages of a deviant career.(4)

Sociologists have also pointed out that the early selection and screening of persons with regard to mental illness are done by various members of the community—not by mental health professionals. Thus certain persons displaying deviant behavior may be selected by members of their family, friends, neighbors, or law enforcement and other personnel and brought to attention for official evaluation of their "mental illness." It is clear that such early selection is based on social criteria, not on psychiatric or mental health ones.(3, 7, 10)

There are also occasions when a person's behavior, although tolerated in his primary group, becomes visible to authorities in secondary groups who have different values and standards for evaluating behavior. There are different tolerance levels for various behaviors, and those who define certain types of deviance as signs of "mental illness" may forcefully bring the person to a treatment center or for other official labeling or handling. We might recall that the data collected by Hollingshead and Redlich(11) indicated that members of the lower social strata were more likely to take this path to treatment centers.

DECISION RULES IN LAW AND MEDICINE

In decision-making, problems typically arise when situations of uncertainty have to be dealt with. Complications are also introduced by the particular consequences of the decision choices. The kind of rules used for dealing with uncertainty in such decision-making situations therefore assumes considerable importance in understanding and predicting the likely responses of decision-makers.(12)

DECISION RULE IN LAW

In the case of criminal trials, both in England and in the United States, there is an explicit rule for arriving at decisions in the face of uncertainty: "A man is innocent until proven guilty." The basic legal decision rule in criminal law states: "When in doubt, acquit"—that is, the judge and jury must *not* be equally wary of erroneously convicting or acquitting: the error that is most important to avoid is erroneous conviction. This legal rule is also very explicitly expressed in the maxim "Better a thousand guilty men go free than one innocent man be convicted."

There are rather obvious reasons why, in a democratic society, with its emphasis on safeguarding the individual from improper use of the power of the state, the above decision rule is important. It is felt that the harm to society of having a number of guilty persons go free is not quite as great as the considerable harm to the person who is the victim of erroneous conviction.

DECISION RULE IN MEDICINE

Although the rule for resolving uncertainty in medicine is not stated as explicitly as the rule in law and there is probably less rigidity in applying it, nevertheless, is would appear that such a decision rule is just as imperative in many respects as the legal rule. The general rule in medicine may be stated as follows: "When in doubt continue to suspect illness"— that is, for a physician to dismiss a patient as being well when he actually is ill is a more serious error than to assume illness when such may not in fact exist.

Most physicians learn very early in their training that they are far more culpable if they dismiss a sick patient than if they retain a well one. It should be pointed out, however, that it is not just physicians who feel this way. This rule seems to be grounded both in legal proceedings and in popular sentiment. Therefore, a physician who dismisses a patient as being well who subsequently dies of some illness that might have been, or should have been, detected may be subject not only to legal action, but also to moral condemnation by colleagues and by other patients. This suggests that, in the main, physicians tend to follow a decision rule that may be expressed, "When in doubt, lean in favor of suspecting illness." Of course, one is immediately reminded of a related maxim that would be highly pertinent for physicians: "Better safe than sorry."(12)

With regard to the matter of *mental illness*, it seems reasonable to assume that psychiatrists' medical training and the ingrained attitudes and rules with respect to the detection of pathological conditions would carry over to their work in mental health. There is a fairly common set, not only in psychiatrists, but also in clinical psychologists, psychiatric social workers and psychiatric nurses, to look for signs of psychopathology and maladjustment.

The general assumption in medical practice that the harm in not recognizing illness would often be far greater than that in suspecting illness where it may not exist does make very good sense and relates to rather clear differential consequences. It also gives proper consideration to the kinds of consequences that would follow from the two possible types of error: 1. accepting the hypothesis that the patient is sick when he is not, and 2. rejecting the hypothesis that the patient is sick when in fact there is sickness. Although there is some sentiment against the first kind of error, as in cases of unnecessary surgery, it has none of the force or urgency attendant on the second kind of error, which could lead to serious harm and possibly even the death of the patient.

However, in mental health the argument can quite reasonably be made that the error of judging a well person sick is *at least as much* to be avoided as the error of judging the sick person well. Yet often examinations by mental health professionals seem guided by the medical rather than the legal type of decision rule. From what has been said earlier, and also on the basis of some research on this subject(3, 4, 13) it appears that, in conducting mental examinations, psychiatrists often tend to err in terms of presuming mental illness.

COURT-ORDERED MENTAL EXAMINATIONS

Scheff(4) studied the psychiatric screening and civil commitment proceedings for mental patients in a Midwestern state. His study revealed several important and even disturbing findings. The psychiatric interviews ranged in length from 5 to 17 minutes, with a *mean time of 10.2 minutes*. Given the fact that the examiners were faced with borderline cases, that they took little time in the examinations, and that they usually recommended commitment, the investigator concluded that their decisions were based largely on presumption of illness in the patients. From his study of the examination process itself, Scheff concluded that the "evidence" on which the examiners based their decisions to retain patients in a mental hospital often seemed arbitrary.

Observations of the judicial hearings on the civil commitment of the above patients raised even more serious questions about the adequacy and equity of such proceedings. The hearings were conducted profunctorily and with lightning rapidity. The mean time, calculated for 22 hearings observed in one court, was *1.6 minutes*.

On the basis of his study, Scheff(4) arrived at the following conclusions:

> The data presented here suggest that the screening is usually perfunctory, and that in the crucial screening examination by the court-appointed psychiatrists, there is a presumption of illness. Since most court decisions appear to hinge on the recommendations of these psychiatrists, there appears to be a

large element of status ascription in the official societal reaction to persons alleged to be mentally ill, as exemplified by the court's actions. This finding points to the importance of lay definitions of mental illness in the community, since the "diagnosis" of mental illness by laymen in the community initiates the official societal reaction, and to the necessity of analyzing social processes connected with their recognition and reaction to the deviant behavior that is called mental illness in our society.

There have been other studies that also raise serious questions about the adequacy of such mental examinations and the way in which such information is used by the courts. Even more serious questions are raised concerning the knowledge and understanding of mental health professionals about the legal questions to which their examinations and conclusions are addressed.

Hess and Thomas(14) did a study of incompetency to stand trial involving examinations conducted at a major state hospital in Michigan. They studied the psychiatrist's role, the legal role, the role of the hospital, and the role of the patient in such examinations and legal proceedings.

(It should be noted that the legal issue of competency to stand trial consists of a determination of the accused's mental condition, *not* in relation to the crime, but in relation to his ability to stand trial. The legal criteria require that the accused 1. have sufficient mental capacity to understand the nature and object of the proceedings against him, 2. understand his own position with reference to such proceedings, and 3. be able to assist counsel in his defense.)

The following are some findings of the study done by these psychiatric investigators(14):

> . . . It should be noted that the merits of such [expert psychiatric] testimony and their relevance to the legal question of incompetency is a matter to be decided by the judge and jury. In this study we found that almost without exception the psychiatrist's role was grossly distorted. The vast majority of the records studied indicated that the psychiatrist confused the legal standards for incompetency with those of responsibility. Often part of the psychiatrist's report to the court would contain reference to standards of incompetency, and another part would refer to standards of responsibility. For example, one record stated, "This man does not know right from wrong, he is incompetent, he is not able to assist his counsel, he should be committed to an institution because he is insane and should be released only when he is found to be sane." It should be stated

that the preceding example is in no way an unusual or unique statement.

. . . Material from patients' records, including physicians' progress notes, reports of staff conferences, and discharge and parole certificates, left no doubt that the hospital staff was applying very high and invariant standards of mental health to these patients . . . At no time was any reference noted to the actual standards legally required for competency . . . .

. . . There is no question but that the requirements made of patients and parolees go far beyond those necessitated by the legal test for competency and, indeed, would tax the psychological capacities of many "normal" persons.

McGarry(15) did a related study of competency to stand trial, in Massachusetts. His findings in many respects were remarkably similar to those of Hess and Thomas. For example, McGarry states:

The observations cited above support the hypothesis that one judgment is made, a medical judgment with regard to diagnosis. The legal questions of criminal responsibility and competence for trial presumably are subsumed, in the eyes of the psychiatrist, under the medical diagnosis and follow uniformly under the psychosis—non-psychosis criterion. It is not at all clear that the psychiatrists involved were aware of the distinction between the two quite separate issues of criminal responsibility and competence to stand trial.

On the basis of his study, McGarry arrived at the following conclusions:

1. Psychiatrists appear to view psychotics as uniformly incompetent to stand trial and criminally irresponsible, reflecting an exclusively medical frame of reference.
2. The courts usually accept the psychiatrist's judgment with regard to the need for hospitalization and, in effect, the patient's incompetence to stand trial on a criminal complaint.
3. Indefinite pre-trial commitments probably are detrimental to rehabilitation and discharge from the state hospitals. Such commitments arising out of misdemeanors are probably unjustified.
4. Due process of law may be compromised when the meaning and importance of competence to stand trial is not understood by the examining psychiatrist, in that the constitutional right to a speedy trial may be denied to a competent defendant.

5. In Massachusetts, due process of law is probably additionally compromised in pre-trial commitments in that notice of the right to contest commitments at a hearing is not provided.

SOME CONSEQUENCES OF LABELING

The findings of many of the studies of court-ordered mental examinations(4, 13–15) indicate clearly, even glaringly, that the process of official labeling and dispositions of certain categories of social deviants involves much confusion of definitions, concepts, and criteria among mental health professionals and lawyers—including judges.

It is evident that quite often mental health professionals conducting examinations with regard to various legal issues such as pre-trial competency, criminal responsibility, sexual psychopathy, and the like do *not* know the precise legal questions and criteria involved. Lacking such information and appropriate and essential legal consultation and guidance, the examiners tend to fall back on various rules of thumb derived from clinical experience. Thus, psychosis is taken to be synonymous with pre-trial incompetency and criminal irresponsibility, whereas the absence of psychosis is viewed as indicating competency and responsibility.

The aforementioned problems become further complicated and compounded when attention is turned to the criteria used by many mental hospitals for returning the patient to court following his commitment as a pre-trial incompetent. All too often, if appears, the staff—lacking information and guidance regarding legal criteria and standards—falls back on the usual psychiatric criteria for release of patients from the hospital. Hence, it may use standards for returning the patient to court that far surpass any envisioned by the courts for competency to stand trial. It may be noted that the basic issue with respect to pre-trial incompetency is clearly a *legal* one.

Similar problems arise even in the use and meaning of the term "mental disease." This term is commonly and even loosely used by many mental health professionals and also appears in certain statutes and legal tests for determining criminal responsibility. For example, the *Durham* rule in the District of Columbia uses the terms "mental disease" and "mental defect." (*Durham v. United States*, 214 F. 2d 847 (D.C. Cir. 1954)) As used in this appellate decision those terms have acquired a specific *legal meaning* relating to the test for determination of criminal responsibility. For a while after the *Durham* decision had been reached, it was apparent that frequently judges and juries were using this legal concept as it was being *defined for them* by mental health experts testifying in court.

It was following much confusion and uncertainty on this issue that, in 1962, the United States Court of Appeals for the District of Columbia wrote an *en banc* opinion, in the *McDonald* decision *(McDonald v. United States*, 312 F. 2d 847 (D.C. Cir. 1962) *(en banc))*, making quite explicit the distinction between psychiatric and legal meanings and usage of the term "mental disease." The relevant section of the *McDonald* opinion reads as follows:

> What psychiatrists may consider a "mental disease or defect" for clinical purposes, where their concern is treatment, may or may not be the same as mental disease or defect for the jury's purpose in determining criminal responsibility . . . . We emphasize that, since the question of whether the defendant has a disease or defect is ultimately for the triers of fact, obviously its resolution cannot be controlled by expert opinion.

In a recent opinion, in *Washington v. United States*, 390 F. 2d 444 (D.C. Cir. 1968), the same appellate court expressed deep concern over the persistent use of labels by expert witnesses and the paucity of meaningful information presented to the jury. The majority opinion stated that such persistent use of labels not only was uninformative, but also distracted the jury's attention from the few underlying facts that were mentioned. The opinion stated: "Again and again the jury was diverted from evidence of the defendant's underlying mental and emotional difficulties by the emphasis on conclusory labels." (page 9)

The other and even more significant point made in this opinion related to the possible confusion in expert testimony of medical and psychiatric issues with the *legal issue* of ascertaining blameworthiness, i.e., making a moral judgment. It was pointed out that experts may often not distinguish sufficiently between their medical and psychiatric judgments and the legal and moral judgments to be made by the jury.

> With the relevant information about the defendant, and guided by the legal principles enunciated by the court, the jury must decide, in effect, whether or not the defendant is blameworthy. Undoubtedly, the decision is often painfully difficult, and perhaps its very difficulty accounts for the readiness with which we have encouraged the expert to decide the question. *But our society has chosen not to give this decision to psychiatrists or to any other professional elite but rather to twelve lay representatives of the community.* (emphasis added)

The same opinion goes on to recommend that trial judges limit the experts' use of medical and diagnostic labels. It was recognized that it would be undesirable to eliminate all technical labels completely since they sometimes did provide a convenient and meaningful method of communication. It was pointed out, however, that trial judges had the responsibility for assuring that the meaning of technical terms was explained to the jury—and this in such a fashion as to relate their meaning to the defendant.

To deal with the aforementioned problems of confusing medical-psychiatric terms with legal-moral judgments, the court made the following significant declaration:

> A strong minority of this court has consistently advocated that psychiatrists be prohibited from testifying whether the alleged offense was the "product" of mental illness, since this is part of the ultimate issue to be decided by the jury. We now adopt that view. The term "product" has no clinical significance for psychiatrists. Thus, there is no justification for permitting psychiatrists to testify on the ultimate issue. Psychiatrists should explain how the defendant's disease or defect relates to his alleged offense, that is, how the development, adaptation and functioning of the defendant's behavioral processes may have influenced his conditions. But psychiatrists should not speak directly in terms of "product," or even "result" or "cause."

It has been noted earlier that the frame of reference, the official deviance labeling process, and the consequences of such labeling differ markedly, depending on whether a legal or a medical orientation is involved. In light of the foregoing discussion of legal and medical decision rules for resolving uncertainty, it becomes apparent that, in interactions between law and mental health, some serious conceptual, ideological, and practical problems arise.

It seems glaringly clear, at least to this writer, that the use of medically oriented decision rules, viz., those tending to presume illness, may work to the serious detriment of the persons involved in the labeling process, despite the good intentions of the professionals involved. As noted earlier medical decision rules do *not* have valid application and usefulness in the mental health field. Indeed, the use of decision rules involving the presumption of illness is very much to be cautioned against when involuntary confinement of persons is concerned. The possible harm to the person becomes even greater when similar presumptive tendencies and loose terminology are used in the labeling and adjudication of persons classified as "sexual psychopaths." Despite the description of these statutes as "civil" and "remedial" and their stated therapeutic intent, the indeterminate confinement to institutions often markedly lacking adequate treatment resources cannot easily be rationalized as being therapeutic rather than punitive experiences for the persons so confined.(16–23)

THE ISSUE OF "DANGEROUSNESS"

Concern about the "dangerousness" of a person is often raised in cases in which involuntary commitment to a mental hospital is being considered. This question is also raised in the adjudication of "sexual psychopaths." Although concern about a person's dangerousness to the community seems reasonable enough, it is important to note two critical factors involved in determining a person's "dangerousness." First, the issue of dangerousness as involved in such legal proceedings involves *essentially issues of social policy.* Second, it should be evident from the previous discussion that the definition of deviance and the official labeling process involve not only the deviant, but also the groups in the community responsible for such definitions and labels.

It has been pointed out that what constitutes dangerousness is frequently left unspecified and thus allows for various administrative decisions by lawyers, psychiatrists, and others.(23) The basic issue, it appears, is not simply whether or not a person is viewed as being dangerous; rather, it depends upon *who* the person is, *in what ways* he is dangerous, and the social context of his behavior. Many persons are allowed by the community to be dangerous; others are allowed to be dangerous in some ways but not in others; and some forms of dangerous behavior may legally be allowed, e.g., automobile track racing, sky diving, and "death-defying" circus acts. Drunken drivers, for example, are dangerous both to themselves and to others. It could very readily be shown that the number of people killed and injured by drunken drivers is many times more than persons harmed by paranoid schizophrenics, other psychotics, and various sex offenders. Nevertheless, persons labeled schizophrenic and many sex offenders are often quite readily committed for indeterminate periods in view of their *possible dangerousness,* whereas drunk drivers are not. Likewise, it is difficult to see how exhibitionists—covered by "sexual psychopath" and related statutes—are to be viewed as being more "dangerous" to the community than, say, bank robbers, persons committing assaults with guns and knives, drunk drivers, or those involved in the manufacture and sale of "dangerous" and defective drugs.

There is another very critical issue involved here. In our system of criminal justice we suspend judgments as to whether a particular kind of behavior may be dangerous when such behavior is anticipated or deemed possible but has not yet taken place. To confine persons on the basis of *what they might do some time in the future* would raise very serious constitutional issues pertaining to preventive detention. However, when the deviant behavior happens to be one attributed to a "mental disorder," the judgment concerning possible dangerousness is *not* suspended, but is made under various "civil" commitment statutes.

It appears that this is another example in which *medical* rather than *legal* decision rules are used with the tacit consent of both professions.

In any event, the point being made is that these complex issues have essentially to be resolved in terms of community norms and broad social policy judgments—*not* on the basis of medical, psychiatric, psychological, or other such criteria. It is critically important that, in the definition and control of dangerous behavior through indeterminate confinement, very meticulous care be taken to use decision rules and burden-of-proof criteria that approximate *legal rules* and that carefully consider the consequences of such labeling.

SOME RECOMMENDATIONS

In light of the foregoing, some broad recommendations can be made to mental health professionals who may be involved in court-ordered mental examinations and related situations:

1. Since the various questions to be resolved by the court are basically and essentially legal and involve social policy matters, it is imperative that mental health professionals take pains to determine the precise legal questions and criteria involved and consider how the data derived from their examinations may relate to such legal issues. It is quite presumptuous, to say the least, to give the court opinions and recommendations on issues of pre-trial competency, criminal responsibility, civil commitment, or release from the hospital when the legal issues and legal criteria are *not* properly understood. Indeed, in view of the serious consequences and possible harm to the person, obtaining information about the legal questions is not just desirable but, to my mind, is a *professional and ethical obligation.* The advice and guidance of regular legal consultants may well be essential to understand the legal issues properly.

2. When conducting court-ordered and related examinations, the mental health professional should take care to use decision rules closely related to *legal requirements* for burden of proof, *not* the medical rules discussed earlier in this presentation. That is to say, the presence of mental illness should *not* be presumed on the basis of lay opinions. Further, such labels should not be hastily applied. The legal rulings on this point by higher courts are quite clear. It has repeatedly been held that there should be a presumption of normality or sanity. Furthermore, the burden of proof of insanity is on the petitioners, there must be a *preponderance of evidence,* and the evidence should be of a "clear and

unexceptionable" nature.

3. In view of the increasing community demands for newer service roles and facilities for a variety of deviants and persons with problems, mental health professionals need to be appropriately realistic and modest with regard both to the availability and to the effectiveness of therapeutic methods. It should be remembered that the use of certain labels is not simply a question of semantics; rather, the labels reflect specific ways of conceptualizing problems, the conceptualization used relates to specific treatment models, and the labels applied tend to determine the ways in which the deviant will be handled and the particular agencies to be involved in his care. More openness is needed in considering a variety of treatment models, with careful assessments of their relative effectiveness, cost, and manpower implications.

4. Finally, since legal sanctions and controls do reflect broad social policy, care should be taken to ensure that mental health terms and criteria *not* be used to decide issues that basically require social and moral judgments. Such moral judgments are to be made only by the "triers of fact" in the courtroom—the judge and jury.

NOTES

(1) Becker, H. S.: *Outsiders: Studies in the Sociology of Deviance.* New York, The Free Press, 1963.

(2) Kitsuse, J. I.: *Social Problems*, 9:247 (Winter) 1962.

(3) Mechanic, D.: *Mental Hygiene*, 46:66 (January), 1962.

(4) Scheff, T. J.: *Social Problems*, 11:401 (Spring) 1964.

(5) Clinard, M. B.: *Sociology of Deviant Behavior.* New York, Rinehart & Co., 1958.

(6) Adams, H.: *American Psychologist*, 19:191 (March), 1964.

(7) Scheff, T. J.: *Sociometry*, 23:436, 1963.

(8) Szasz, T. S.: *The Myth of Mental Illness.* New York, Hoeber-Harper, 1961.

(9) Davidson, H. A.: *American Journal of Psychiatry*, 115:411 (November), 1958.

(10) Erikson, K. T.: *Psychiatry*, 20:263 (August), 1957.

(11) Hollingshead, A. B., and Redlich, F. C.: *Social Class and Mental Illness.* New York, John Wiley & Sons, 1958.

(12) Scheff, T. J.: *Behavioral Science*, 8:97 (April), 1963.

(13) Kutner, L.: *Northwestern University Law Review*, 57:383 (September), 1962.

(14) Hess, J. A., and Thomas, T. E.: *American Journal of Psychiatry*, 119:715 (December), 1963.

(15) McGarry, A. L.: *American Journal of Psychiatry*, 122:623 (December), 1965.

(16) Birnbaum, M.: *New England Journal of Medicine*, 261:1220, 1959.

(17) Birnbaum, M.: *American Bar Association Journal*, 52:69 (January), 1966.

(18) Goldstein, A. S.: *American Journal of Orthopsychiatry*, 33:123, 1963.

(19) Goldstein, J., and Katz, J.: *Yale Law Journal*, 70:225, 1960.

(20) Lindman, F. T., and McIntyre, D. M. (eds.): *The Mentally Disabled and the Law*. Chicago, University of Chicago Press, 1961.

(21) Shah, S. A.: *Some Issues Related to the Official Labeling and Handling of Criminal Behavior*. In: Kittrie, N. (ed.): *Of Crime and Criminals in America.*

(22) Shah, S. A.: *The Mentally Disordered Offender: A Consideration of Some Aspects of the Criminal-Judicial-Correctional Process*. In: Allen, R., Ferster, E. Z., and Rubin, J. (eds.): *Readings in Law and Psychiatry*. Baltimore, Johns Hopkins University Press, 1968.

(23) Szasz, T. S.: *Law, Liberty and Psychiatry*. New York, Macmillan, 1963.

Controversy Concerning the Criminal Justice System and Its Implications for the Role of Mental Health Workers

David E. Silber

The old debate over how to view criminal offenders, always lively and occasionally acrimonious, has taken a new turn in the past decade or so. The argument used to be over whether criminals were sick (and thus ought to be treated instead of punished) or bad. The new dimension is concerned with the consequences of a psychiatric conception: Is it an encroachment of civil liberties? and Is the treatment conception psychologically sound? The issues are complicated and interlocked, emotionally charged, and important to society. Before going to the question of treatment and roles for treatment workers, it would be worthwhile to review the arguments; what follows is an attempt to separate the main hypotheses of both camps.

Criminal behavior is symptomatic of psychological disturbance *was* the enlightened liberal position. Many psychiatric writers (Abrahamsen, 1967; Alexander & Healy, 1935; Alexander & Staub, 1956; Halleck, 1967; and Lindner, 1946; among others) have characterized criminals as having the same traumatic developmental difficulties, leading to similar deficient personalities, as neurotic individuals. Often the explanations hypothesize the same psychosexual connections between adult criminal behavior and infantile fixations as are assumed to operate in the formation of neurotic behaviors: "We direct our regard back to the fog-enshrouded days of infancy and early childhood, when were laid down the irrevocable patterns of our lives [Lindner, 1946, p. 58]." The most passionate advocate of the psychoanalytic-psychodynamic interpretation of criminals as "mentally ill" is probably Menninger (1968). Menninger argued that society's response to criminals (as evil and immoral persons) is as misguided as earlier notions that mental illness is a sign of satanic possession.

Most interpretations of criminal behavior as disturbed are made in a reformist spirit, usually coupled with appeals to radically change the criminal justice system. Proposals usually include changing the court system, changing the role of mental health worker, and transforming the prison system: "We [the public] commit the crime of damning some of our fellow citizens with the label 'criminal' and having done this, we force them through an experience that is soul searing and dehumanizing [Menninger, 1968, p. 9]." Their alternative proposals may be summarized as follows:

1. *Precriminal detection.* Delinquency-prone youths should be detected prior to contact with the police, to allow preventative measures (unspecified) to be instituted. Presumably this might entail enforced treatment for uncooperative juveniles and/or their families.

2. *The substitution, in most cases, of informal nonadversary proceedings (either civil or criminal) for the formal adversary proceedings now characteristic of criminal trials.* Others (e.g., Glueck, 1962) have argued for some informal method of determining guilt or innocence that would not take *mens rea* ("evil intent") into account, in much the same way that juvenile court is supposed to work.

3. *The substitution of indefinite sentences for fixed or indeterminate sentences.* The indefinite sentence lasts until the person is pronounced "cured" as in the case of civil commitments to a mental hospital. The indeterminate sentence is a penalty sentence, usually with a maximum and minimum time specified. Along with an indefinite sentence, the person would be remanded to a treatment center rather than to prison for incarceration. Institutionalization would be mandatory, but the aim would be correction of psychological disturbance and social rehabilitation.

4. *Treatment.* Psychotherapy in one form or another would be widely used, along with environmental manipulation, guidance, and education. It is recognized that some persons might have to remain in such confinement programs on a more or less permanent basis. Interestingly, most commentators do not mention using the newer behavior modification techniques in their proposals for such treatment centers, although psychologists in prison settings often do (Brodsky, 1972).

In short, the general purpose of these proposals would be to provide settings where the man, rather than the deed, is adjudicated and treated.

THE NEW OPPOSITION

To a growing body of civil libertarians, these proposals are appalling and pose a challenge to personal freedom occasioned by the growth of what they call the "Therapeutic State." Kittrie (1971) has admirably clarified the threats to traditional legal safeguards posed by nonadversary civil commitment proceedings. Szasz (1963) has attacked the intrusion of psychiatric thought into the legal arena as a curtailment of liberty. Treatment in specialized corrective facilities and mental hospitals has been attacked by Spece (1972) on the same grounds. In the process, the concept of the mental health worker as a helper of persons takes a dreadful beating. We come off, instead, as wanting a piece of the legal action (Christie, 1971), ill-informed and judgmental (Szasz, 1963), sloppy in thought and hasty in action (Kittrie, 1971), or unreflective and mildly sadistic (Spece, 1972). It would be wise to take close heed of the main points raised by these writers.

1. Informal, civil proceedings jeopardize a person's basic rights ordinarily guaranteed under criminal law. Such rights include the right to counsel, specified indictment, time to prepare a defense, trial by jury, be present during the proceedings, confront adversary witnesses directly, and be judged solely on the basis of innocence or guilt.

2. Civil commitment for indefinite periods is a judgment against the person, not the deed, and as such represents a step toward totalitarian social control. Indefinite sentences also unfairly penalize the person accused of crimes which normally carry light sentences.

3. Once committed, a person loses all civil liberties and is even more vulnerable to enforced treatment and mistreatment than the incarcerated prisoners.

4. Psychiatry and clinical psychology contain inconsistent, contradictory views of human functioning, so that any psychiatric stance in a legal proceeding is capable (in good faith) of being opposed by another psychiatric stance.

5. Treatment programs are widely carried out without theoretical rationale, or solid empirical support. Little is known concerning the relative efficacy of various treatment programs, if, indeed, they even work. An especially problematic area is physical intrusion into the body as a way of changing behavior, such as occurs with electroconvulsive shock treatment, electrical stimulation of the brain, injections of noxious substances during aversive conditioning, and psychosurgery of one kind or another.

6. "Mental health" concepts, as uncritically applied to convicted persons, are not based on medical considerations, but rather on social and ethical value systems.

7. Coercive treatment programs stand little chance of success precisely because they are coercive.

8. Psychiatrically oriented institutionalized treatment programs extant have failed dismally, yet are "total institutions," as are prisons, and are often even more degrading and dehumanizing than prisons. The social stigma of the label *mentally ill* is at least as bad and enduring as being labeled *criminal*.

These objectives leave unsolved the problem of what to do with and for the convicted offender so as to provide correctional rather than retributive experiences during imprisonment. And they completely ignore the question of whether the individual criminal is in a position to perceive what is best for himself.

An indirect result of these arguments, however, is that they make it appear that treatment and therapy are the order of the day in correctional facilities. Professionals and the general public alike tend to believe, as does Antilla (1972), that "treatment ideology has achieved a kind of breakthrough within the last few decades [p. 287]." Bazelon (1972) has criticized psychologists for failing to change the majority of offenders, after making the explicit assumption that "the experts—you—are minding the store [p. 151]." This is not a fair attack because it is not true. Mental health workers in the adult correctional system are few and far between, and treatment is the exception, rather than the rule. The rest of this article will examine what ought to be the role of the mental health worker in the criminal justice system, what activities might be expanded, and what avenues for staffing might prove fruitful.

MENTAL HEALTH WORKERS IN CRIMINAL JUSTICE

In view of the foregoing, it is quite clear that mental health workers in the criminal justice system must examine and question what their role ought to be. This section proposes limits and reiterates some areas where increased efforts and programs can be developed.

First, mental health workers should become very leery about testifying in court. Almost all writers, including Menninger, have complained about psychiatric testimony, yet psychologists and psychiatrists continue to march to the witness box with increasing frequency. Interestingly, the pressure may come more from the prosecution than the defense. Kittrie (1971) quoted a study done in the criminal courts of the District of Columbia which found this to be the case. In such instances, where psychiatric workers are directed to testify, reports ought to be limited to the current mental status of the defendant. If the defendant is suspected of being acutely psychotic (and thus unable to participate in his own defense), the determination ought to follow from a formal civil commitment procedure. In other situations, the mental health worker ought to avoid doing what he patently cannot: that is, render a post hoc judgment of psychological status. Since the major grounds of exculpation are now via the M'Naughton rule, evidence in support of it should come from people who observed the defendant at the time of the offense. To qualify as a defense under M'Naughton, a person would have to be so overtly psychotic as to appear so even to untrained observers. Another reason for allowing adjudication to follow from legal considerations has been stressed by Rubin (1965): Treatment can be as meaningful and successful in a prison facility as a mental hospital or special treatment program. Mental hospitals have the wrong "set" for treating felons; they perceive the patient as helpless and disturbed. Most criminals are not out of contact with reality, but rather are deviant in social values and behaviors.

Similarly, mental health workers ought to invoke extreme caution before suggesting mandatory treatment programs as substitutes for imprisonment. Removal from society is punishment, and mandatory treatment programs, with indefinite commitments, constitute potentially greater punishment to the individual than determinate imprisonment. Even the fact that such treatment programs would be controlled by the state health or social welfare agency is a questionable advantage, because abuses to patients could more easily masquerade as "treatment" and elude legal detection. An example of the dangers to civil liberty is the project outlined in the American Psychological Association *Monitor* of August 1972 ("Treatment Camps for Addicts"). The plan would call for a mandatory treatment of addicts in special camps, in order to protect society from drug-occasioned crime and speed the addict's "recovery." There was no mention of how the incorrigible addict would be identified or adjudicated, what legal safeguards would be present during or after commitment proceedings, or what treatment modalities would be used. It is clear from the article that the recalcitrant or negative inmate would face long-term confinement indistinguishable from a prison setting except for the lack of an expiration date.

Research into effective methods of treatment ought to be encouraged, but the research personnel should be drawn from staff outside of the correctional setting. The mental health worker in the correctional institution ought to function as an ethical watchdog to discourage dangerous programs. There are enough innocuous techniques available which have not received adequate scrutiny so that such methods as, for example, aversive conditioning using anectine (Spece, 1972), can be eschewed for a very long time.

Finally, in deciding where the role of the mental health worker ought to be, it can be argued that prisons are not necessarily any more static than other institutions of society. In addition, correctional programs have the practical advantages of being already in existence, having avowedly rehabilitative goals, and having (in most states) a central coordinating office. In general, the mental health worker ought to stay out of the adjudication process and in the correctional system. However, there is a valuable service that mental health workers can render without infringing civil liberties: to protest against laws which define psychologically abnormal or unusual behavior as criminal, for example, laws against homosexual behavior between consenting adults.

TREATMENT IN CORRECTIONAL SETTINGS

Most prisoners receive little or no systematic treatment of any kind. Even in the Lewisburg Federal Penitentiary, this has been found to be so (Rother & Ervin, 1971). There seems to be three major reasons for this: First, the staffs of most correctional facilities are woefully inadequate. In 1967, it was estimated that the ratio of professional staff to prisoners was 1:179 nationally (Task Force on Corrections, 1967). Smith (1971) quoted a survey that listed only 60 full-time psychiatrists for 230 adult correctional facilities in the United States. Clearly, the experts are not "minding the store."

Second, most prisoners do not manifest "traditional" forms of psychopathology. Using data quoted by Brodsky and Vandiver (Brodsky, 1972), Smith (1971), plus Brodsky's survey (1970), it is clear that the percentage of psychotic and neurotic individuals is quite low (ranges of 1%–3% and 4%–7%, respectively). The major diagnostic category was some variation of the character disorder/psychopathic personality label. Such prisoners are hostile, suspicious, and immature and tend to identify with subcultural values that are legally proscribed. They usually perceive their personality functioning to be acceptable. They are not, in general, likely to clamor for individual psychotherapy and usually are seen on referral. Thus, there is no strong sustained interest on the part of prisoners themselves for treatment. The opposite view is that prisoners recognize the low quality of treatment services and stay away for that reason (American Friends Service Committee, 1971).

Finally, the custodial staffs of prisons usually view the professional staff with ambivalence or outright hostility. They worry about the possibility of riots, believe that prisoners are generally incorrigible, and suspect that therapy is a form of mollycoddling. Guards usually have little or no formal training in psychology or human relations, often fear and dislike the prisoners they are charged with guarding, and may resent the professional because of his higher status. They therefore are often reluctant to encourage the expansion or initiation of treatment programs within the correctional setting and may passively oppose ones already present.

Thus, it is one of life's little ironies that treatment is attacked because it does not help prisoners (Antilla, 1972; Bazelon, 1972), when in fact the prisoner's chance of receiving treatment is almost zero. Therapy has not been given the chance to work, and it ought to have that chance before being written off as worthless. Treatment has been identified with psychoanalytically oriented individual psychotherapy, an error that has gone largely unchallenged; obviously, there are more and newer techniques in use. Let me now suggest some specifics concerning treatment in corrections.

THE DIAGNOSTIC AND RECEPTION CENTER

Increasingly, prisoners are being sent first to these centers. To have an impact on the prison career of the inmate, diagnosis and classification should occur as soon as the offender is incarcerated. The same panoply of professionals as in a well-run mental hospital should have contact with the prisoner, and the results should be discussed at a case conference. Major decisions concerning diagnosis, therapy, and placement with the system would be made there, and a particular "package" tailored to the individual would be arrived at. The inmate should be given feedback; diagnosis is too often a one-way street. This is a particular danger in corrections, where hostility and suspicion are excessively present anyhow. The center staff ought to use the feedback technique to motivate the prisoner to get involved in his own rehabilitation. Enough general evidence exists to conclude that if a prisoner is treated as a dignified and reasonable human being, he will more often than not respond in a like manner. A similar procedure has been in operation in North Carolina, which seems to offer some sort of crisis intervention aid, such as found in a neighborhood community mental health center, for prisoners with acute disturbances.

THE TRADITIONAL PRISON SETTING

Within the penitentiary and reformatory, the mental health worker can be a treatment source and "system challenger" (Brodsky, 1972). As a system challenger, he ought to goad the administration to eliminate retrogressive and abusive regulations; as a positive contribution, he should intervene to work on the attitudes and behaviors of the custodial staff toward the offender. Such activities would include in-service training for current staff, human relations instructions to new guards, role-playing sessions, and psychological instruction. To explicate the viewpoint implied above: The mental health worker stands outside the institutional hierarchy. I would argue that the first concern of the therapist is the client, and by staying on the periphery the mental health worker can make his contribution most effectively. This is neither "radical" nor antiestablishment, but simply the recognition that treatment works best when the therapist is not identified as a cog of the system by the inmate. Thus, activities such as sitting on disciplinary boards, writing parole recommendations, or acting as an information conduit to the administration are not properly within the treatment worker's purview.

The backbone of the mental health worker's activities ought to be as a purveyor of therapeutic services. The immediate questions that arise are, What sort of therapy and with whom? Usual guidelines applied to nonincarcerated patients are meaningless, given the behaviors and personality configurations of prisoners. Practical considerations dictate that the cheapest and most intensive methods be used most often, such as group therapy, behavioral techniques, and marathon therapy groups. The few published reports available suggest that intensive therapy can be effective (Sindhu, 1970), as can therapeutic community organization (Miles, 1969), marathon-type retreats (Carrol & McCormick, 1970), and behavior techniques and token economies (DeRisi, 1971; Wright, 1968). Experience suggests that intensive, Synanon-type marathon groups are particularly effective when embedded in the context of regular group sessions.

Simply reducing defenses or eliminating undesirable attitudes and symptoms is not enough, considering the environment to which the prisoner usually returns. Treatment legitimately includes teaching the prisoner ways of putting the institutions of society to work for him (a point suggested by Warden R. Williams, 1970, of the Maryland House of Corrections) and ways to either change or avoid negative environmental influences.

Ideally, the report of the diagnostic center will accompany the prisoner, so treatment—if desirable—can start immediately. If, however, we really take seriously the issue of individual civil rights, prisoners should not be coerced directly or indirectly into participating. Thoughtful explanations of method and desirability are indicated, especially in instances where noxious stimuli or stress methods are used (e.g., in Synanon-type encounters).

Mental health workers can serve as informal counselors to self-help groups such as Alcoholics Anonymous or the Black Muslims. Ethnic-pride groups such as the Black Muslims can have a profound effect on prisoners, and mental health workers should feel free to offer aid. There are two other activities that the treatment worker should do, but probably will not be allowed to do: arrange human relations seminars between inmates and guards, and arrange couples groups in the prison which include both inmates and their spouses (or fiancees).

PARTIAL-RELEASE AND POSTRELEASE SETTINGS

The need to confront the social realities and pressures on ex-offenders in their readjustment to street life marks the partial-release and postrelease efforts as perhaps the most important correctional and treatment settings. Two important innovations in the recent past have been the halfway house (usually in an urban setting) for nondangerous offenders and the work-release program (usually operated out of an honor camp). Counseling, and especially experientially oriented group therapy, can be crucial here in alleviating the great strain placed on someone who is *in* a free environment, but not *of* it. The therapist will have to handle complaints and frustrations, help control impulsiveness, defuse defenses, and serve as a stable model—all without appearing smug or saintly. Immediate family members can be brought into the treatment at this point, in combined family groups.

Currently there are almost no programs of post release treatment. This is extraordinarily unfortunate, as the first postrelease year is apparently the hardest; something on the order of 40 % are rearrested within the first year (Federal Bureau of Investigation, 1970). Aftercare programs run by the correctional system should be quickly established, so that treatment can either be continued or be available if needed. I stress the need for these to be under the aegis of the correctional system because its professionals are probably most qualified to perceive the special problems of ex-offenders in making a satisfactory postrelease adjustment.

All of the foregoing makes no sense at all, given the current staff situation in the correctional system. In addition, it is no secret that many are incompletely trained or marking time until something better comes along. Recruitment is hampered because salaries are relatively low (Task Force on Corrections, 1967), prestige is low, and prisons are frequently away from the urban scene, where professionals like to locate. There are, however, a number of pragmatic, relatively inexpensive remedies available. Perhaps the single most neglected resource is the university-based professional training program. All programs in clinical psychology, social work, and psychiatry require significant amounts of field experience. There is no reason why correctional facilities cannot function as training centers (as, for example, does Jackson State Prison in Michigan). State universities in particular ought to be approached, given their common funding source. To give the correctional-system professional more status as a supervisor, those who meet licensing requirements could be appointed as adjunct clinical staff (a current practice for hospital staff supervisors). An even more innovative plan is in practice in North Carolina, where mental hospital psychologists are hired by the University of North Carolina itself, then assigned to field placements in hospitals and clinics. Something like this could be done with correctional staff as well, thus providing them with perceived prestige, as well as resolving some staffing problems.

A second possibility is for departments of corrections to underwrite the cost of professional education in return for a commitment to work for a number of years following graduation. This system seems to work for the armed forces and the Veteran's Administration, many of whose career professionals were recruited that way. Within the system itself, employment would be more attractive if the duties of the mental health worker were split between various institutions. Or, if not practical, some sort of biyearly rotation between institutions could be offered. Finally, professionals could be enticed by the offer of five-fourths pay; that is, they would be allowed to take one full day per week for outside consulting while receiving full pay and benefits.

Interrupting the cycle of arrest, conviction, and rearrest is crucial; as New York City Police Commissioner Murphy (1972) said, the correctional systems must be changed and changed rapidly. Offering full mental health services at every stage of the prison experience—from sentencing to and after release—can help achieve this goal while offering satisfying roles for mental health professionals within the criminal justice system.

REFERENCES

ABRAHAMSEN, D. *The Psychology of Crime.* New York: Columbia University Press, 1967.

ALEXANDER, F., & HEALY, W. *The Roots of Crime.* New York: Knopf, 1935.

ALEXANDER, F., & STAUB, H. *The Criminal, the Judge, and the Public.* (Rev. ed.) Glencoe, Ill.: Free Press, 1956.

AMERICAN FRIENDS SERVICE COMMITTEE. *Struggle for Justice.* New York: Hill & Wang, 1971.

ANTILLA, I. Punishment versus Treatment—Is There a Third Alternative? *Abstracts on Criminology and Penology,* 1972, 12, 287–290.

BAZELON, D. L. *Psychologists in Corrections. Are They Doing Good for the Offender or Well for Themselves? In* S. L. Brodsky (Ed.), *Psychologists in the Criminal-Justice System.* Marysville, Ohio: American Association of Correctional Psychologists, 1972.

BRODSKY, S. L. Mental Disease and Mental Ability. In: S. L. Brodsky & N. E. Eggleston (Eds.), *The Military Prison: Theory, Practice and Research.* Carbondale: Southern Illinois University Press, 1970.

BRODSKY, S. L. *Psychologists in the Criminal Justice-System.* Marysville, Ohio: American Association of Correctional Psychologists, 1972.

CARROLL, J. L., & McCORMICK, C. G. The Cursillo Movement in a Penal Setting: An Introduction. *Canadian Journal of Corrections*, 1970, 12, 151–160.

CHRISTIE, N. Law and Medicine: The Case against Role Blurring. *Law and Society Review*, 1971, 5, 357–366.

DeRISI, W. J. Performance Contingent Parole: A Behavior Modification System for Juvenile Offenders. Paper presented at the meeting of the American Psychological Association, Washington, D.C., September 1971.

FEDERAL BUREAU OF INVESTIGATION. *Uniform Crime Reports—1970.* Washington, D.C.: U.S. Government Printing Office, 1971.

GLUECK, S. *Law and Psychiatry: Cold War or Entente Cordiale?* Baltimore, Md.: Johns Hopkins University Press, 1962.

HALLECK, S. *Psychiatry and the Dilemma of Crime.* New York: Harper, 1967.

KITTRIE, N. *The Right to Be Different.* Baltimore, Md.: Johns Hopkins University Press, 1971.

LINDNER, R. M. *Stone Walls and Men.* New York: Odyssey, 1946.

MENNINGER, K. *The Crime of Punishment.* New York: Viking, 1968.

MILES, A. E. The Effects of a Therapeutic Community on the Interpersonal Relationships of a Group of Psychopaths. *British Journal of Criminology.* 1969, 9, 22–38.

MURPHY, P. V. America Must Learn Correction Needs. *American Journal of Corrections*, 1972, 34, 22–24, 47.

ROTHER, L. H., & ERVIN, F. R. Psychiatric Care of Federal Prisoners. *American Journal of Psychiatry*, 1971, 128, 424–430.

RUBIN, S. *Psychiatry and Criminal Law.* Dobbs Ferry, N.Y.: Oceana, 1965.

SINDHU, H. S. Therapy with Violent Psychopaths in an Indian Prison Community. *International Journal of Offender Therapy*, 1970, 14, 138–144.

SMITH, C. E. Recognizing and Sentencing the Exceptional and Dangerous Offender. *Federal Probation*, 1971, 4, 3–12.

SPECE, R. J. Conditioning and Other Technologies Used to "Treat?" "Rehabilitate?" "Demolish?" Prisoners and Mental Patients. *Southern California Law Review*, 1972, 45, 616–684.

SZASZ, T. S. *Law, Liberty and Psychiatry.* New York: Macmillan 1963.

TASK FORCE ON CORRECTIONS. *President's Commission on Law Enforcement and Administration of Justice.* Washington, D.C.: U.S. Government Printing Office, 1967.

WILLIAMS, R. L. The Effects of Social Change and Community Involvement on Modern Day Correctional Practices and Processes. In D. E. Silber (Chm.), The Personality of the Offender and the Correctional System: Are the Right Needs Being Met? Symposium presented at the meeting of the American Psychological Association, Miami Beach, Florida, September 1970.

WRIGHT, W. F. Treatment Program at the Reception, Diagnostic, and Treatment Centre, Grandview School, Galt, Ont. *Canadian Journal of Corrections*, 1968, 10, 337–345.

Some Observations
on the Problems
of the Forensic Psychiatrist

Leigh M. Roberts

The professions of law and psychiatry currently interact with greater intensity and frequency than at any prior point in time. The opinion of the psychiatrist may be sought in widely ranging legal areas. He may become concerned with civil cases involving personal injuries, wills, contracts, deeds, annulments, divorce, guardianship, and commitment to mental institutions. The psychiatrist's opinion is also crucial in criminal cases involving the alleged offender's mental state at the time of trial and at the time of commission of the alleged offense. His recommendations are sought regarding the possible rehabilitation of a criminal offender. Furthermore, juvenile delinquents and sex offenders are often referred for diagnosis or treatment.

Yet the professions of psychiatry and law frequently engage in vitriolic exchanges involving matters of mutual concern. The issues which have developed involve differences in theory, values, and practices. It is evident that although some significant issues remain unresolved between the two professions, many relatively minor differences are magnified in the heated debates. There is no doubt that basic methods of cooperation must be evolved if the needs of society are to be served.

It is my belief that points of misunderstanding between the two professions may be more easily eliminated once these problems are comprehended. First, the areas of conflict will be examined. Then a functional approach to the solution of some existing problems will be offered. Finally, some of the areas of current debate will be presented, in an attempt to clarify the issues or to propose solutions to these more specific problems.

Numerous problems are present for the psychiatrist as he deals with the legal profession. Some of these are caused primarily by the psychiatrist. For example, frequently minimal psychiatric evaluation is presented as a full evaluation, or less than optimally competent psychiatric practitioners are selected to work with attorneys. There may be a failure in active cooperation by the psychiatrist or he may expect remarkably high remuneration for his forensic psychiatric services. Many psychiatrists try to avoid dealing with legal problems, and others participate as partisan advocates to the point they become poor witnesses. A general emotional flavor of hostility toward lawyers is held by some psychiatrists. These concerns create difficulties for the legal profession, but there are many other areas that create difficulties for the psychiatrist.

THE ADVERSARY SYSTEM

There are occasions when the attorney seeks to make the psychiatrist a partisan witness for his client. While such an approach is part of the adversary system, it is a type of approach that psychiatrists may not understand. The adversary approach may well lead to a "battle of psychiatric experts." This may lead to expression of lack of respect by fellow physicians and even public abuse. A good example of such abuse is seen when a psychiatrist testifies in a proceeding involving a brutal crime. The public usually demands punishment for such offenders, and a verdict of not guilty by reason of insanity is subject to extreme public criticism.

More importantly, the psychiatrist may not understand the adversary system of justice itself. To him the courtroom battle may appear only to obstruct justice. A source of this confusion is the various rules of procedure and evidence, such as, for example, the hearsay exclusionary rule. These rules seem only to obstruct the search for truth in the psychiatrist's eyes. Furthermore, many psychiatrists object to substantive rules of law which they feel do not accurately reflect advances made in the field of psychiatry. An example of this is the current debate involving the *correct* definition of "legal insanity."

THE UNFAVORABLE APPEAL OF FORENSIC PSYCHIATRY

One of the most significant limitations of current psychiatric practice is that relatively few psychiatrists are willing to participate in medical-legal problems.(1) This is demonstrated when many of the most highly respected psychiatrists refuse to testify in court. Forensic psychiatry is therefore left to less qualified psychiatrists by default. This is particularly unfortunate at a time when psychiatric testimony is more in demand than ever before. (2)

Part of the problem stems from the psychiatrist's current position in society. The possible areas of involvement for the psychiatrist are vast, with great public and private demands for mental health information and care. This places the psychiatrist in the privileged position of being in a "seller's market." Thus he is able to select those aspects of psychiatric practice in which he wishes to engage. He selects those patients with whom he chooses to work and avoids those who are less rewarding, often in terms of emotional and monetary satisfaction. He is able to work in conjunction with large public mental hospitals or to establish a private practice. He participates in those professional activities which he enjoys and which reward him, while abstaining from pursuits which he feels make less suitable use of his skills or which are substantially unpleasant in their conduct.

These are some of the aspects of the professional seller's market in which the psychiatrist finds himself. All of this does not mean that the psychiatrist does not donate substantial skills, energy, and time to the betterment of society, with minimal or no economic compensation. It has meant, however, that up to this point a majority of psychiatrists have had relatively minimal contact with legal-psychiatric problems.

Some of the reasons for this lack of involvement, such as personal abuse and public criticism, have previously been noted. Yet there are additional reasons. It is difficult for the psychiatrist to schedule his time for courtroom testimony. Such testimony is a time-consuming process and, additionally, must be fitted into the total proceedings of the trial rather than being primarily for the convenience of the physician. The relatively low compensation for his time in legal proceedings also takes a psychiatrist away from legal-medical work. Equally important is his rather poor relationship with the legal profession. The association of some members of the legal profession with unfounded malpractice claims has caused, in part, this poor relationship.

Yet, the major threat posed by the legal system to the psychiatrist is his imagined loss of dignity and status if he testifies in court. This stereotyped picture finds him in the midst of a dramatic criminal trial. (3) He visualizes himself as the victim of sharp-tongued lawyers who distort his testimony. He envisions the rapture of a hostile gathering of judge, attorneys, jurors, press, spectators, and the community at large. The distortion in such a view is, of course, obvious. Yet the psychiatrist is driven away from legal involvement to the extent that he believes in the truth of this stereotype.

The courtroom or the attorney's office is therefore viewed as a place of uneasiness and unfamiliarity by the psychiatrist. The legal proceedings do not prove accommodating to the psychiatrist, quite in contrast to his position of status and prominence. He greatly prefers the customary work setting of the office, hospital, or agency in which he determines events in his own way. He finds it particularly difficult to accustom himself to being dealt with as an adversary in cross-examination and to being cut off in presentation of testimony he believes essential to presenting a relatively complete picture of an individual. It is hard for him to repress data he is never asked to reveal and to have questions phrased for him in ways which are poorly translatable into his own technical jargon.

There is no easy solution to this problem. But it is safe to say that as long as a psychiatrist feels abuses he will continue to avoid legal-medical involvements. Yet it is certain that a clearer understanding of his function may eliminate this and many of the other problems outlined above.

THE PROBLEMS OF CONFLICT

Psychiatrists misunderstand how the legal system works, and their role in it. And this is compounded because lawyers fail to realize that psychiatrists so misunderstand, and thus do nothing to eliminate this lack of understanding. Conflicts are increased in proportion to the degree of this mutual misunderstanding. What I offer here is a practical and realistic approach to the solution of many of these problems.

THE TRAINING OF THE PSYCHIATRIST

Is it essential for lawyers to recognize how much they may rely upon a psychiatrist's advice and conclusions. Correlatively, it is important for psychiatrists to understand how far they may go in giving such advice and stating such conclusions. I believe that this understanding may be furthered by a discussion of the kind of training a psychiatrist receives, for this training shapes to a great extent the psychiatrist's views.

The psychiatrist emerges in his professional role as the product of two differing types of professional education. He first enters medical school with a background of pre-medical college preparation. At this point his primary assets are a high level of intelligence and a motivation to be of service to fellow human beings.(4) He also brings with him a background of personal life experiences and values. Then for four years he is molded by a concentrated curriculum of basic science and clinical experience with medical disease entities.

Following completion of medical school, the physician enters a period of internship in a hospital. It is only after completion of this training that he enters the three-or-more-year period of training to become a psychiatrist. Further training may be taken in an institute for psychoanalysis or in specialized areas such as community psychiatry, child psychiatry, psychiatric research, or crime and delinquency. It should be noted that a major transition occurs from the scientific orientation of the physician in medical school to the more humanistic orientation in specialized psychiatric training.

The training patterns are of relatively recent origin. Medical schools have shifted markedly within the past half century, and the present model of psychiatric residency training programs dates back only three decades. Major current trends in psychiatric orientation are dynamic psychiatry and community psychiatry.(5) Dynamic psychiatry has emerged as a synthesis or psychoanalysis and psychobiology. Community psychiatry has provided an extension of psychiatric services into smaller urban and rural areas. It has resulted in availability of psychiatrists to a greater extent for legal problems in such areas than has ever been true in the past.

The core of clinical psychiatry is the doctor-patient interaction. In that relationship the psychiatrist comes to intimately know, understand, accept, and treat the individual who has come to him. This one-to-one treatment relationship is the central area of psychiatric practice and is the place in which the psychiatrist is most uniquely expert. A psychiatrist has a degree of expertness which is substantial in the clinical evaluation of individuals and their treatment, in the treatment of groups of emotionally disturbed persons, in the understanding of individual human behavior and its motivations, and, further, in the conscious and unconscious processes and related human problems.

It is important for the lawyer to remember that the psychiatrist is on less firm ground when he moves farther afield from the clinical setting, such as when he is asked to diagnose society's problems or when he is asked to apply his knowledge to more hypothetical questions. In these areas his knowledge and competence should be demonstrated before they are given automatic recognition.

THE SELECTION OF THE PSYCHIATRIST

Some of the lawyer's problems may be solved by trying to retain a psychiatrist who already understands the problems of the legal system. The lawyer should make a preliminary investigation of available psychiatrists. After he has several, tentatively, he should arrange a conference with each of them. This conference serves two purposes. First, the attorney can explain many of the problem areas of the law to the psychiatrist. This, as I have stated before, should go a long way toward solving problems. Secondly, the way that the psychiatrist responds to the attorney's explanation will help the attorney decide if he should employ the psychiatrist. One point should be emphasized here. The attorney's needs for a psychiatrist are, in many cases, two-fold: he must select a psychiatrist who is competent to evaluate his client, and one who is qualified to offer supporting testimony in court.

Certain criteria are helpful in the selection of an expert:(6)

> 1. Membership in local and national professional organizations—American Psychiatric Association, American Medical Association.
> 2. Certification by the professional specialty organization—Americn Board of Psychiatry and Neurology.
> 3. Academic sources of information regarding the specialty, such as the nearest university medical school department of psychiatry. Assistance may be obtained from such faculty members; at least information may be obtained from them regarding competent professionals in the area of forensic psychiatry.

The forensic psychiatrist who may be best suited for the attorney's purpose is one who rates well in the opinion of his professional colleagues, is a member of the national professional organization,(7) and has a number of publications in his field.

Once the psychiatrist is selected, the attorney should arrange a conference with him before he examines the client. It should begin with an explanation of the legal procedures which will be followed in the case. The role of the judge and the jury should be clearly explained to the psychiatrist. Relevant substantive law ought to be explained. For example, the distinction between mental illness and legal insanity should be clarified.(8) It must be made clear that the psychiatrist's testimony will be considered in relation to legal, and not medical, standards.

I have said before that the adversary system is perhaps the most confusing aspect of the legal process for the psychiatrist. It would be well for the lawyer to explain in great detail the aspects of the adversary system. The attorney should point out that the power of the state can only be exerted within clearly defined legal limits and procedures. This includes the right of each of the parties to challenge the evidence and the witnesses testifying against him and to introduce counter-evidence and witnesses. The attorney should try to clarify the reasons for this procedure. While many psychiatrists may not agree, at least they will understand, and through understanding they may be able to cooperate more effectively.

Relevant rules of evidence must also be explained to the psychiatrist at the pre-examination conference. In particular, the requirements of the hearsay rule should be carefully explained. Legal problems involving the hearsay rule require close cooperation between the two professions, and it is absolutely necessary that the psychiatrist be aware of the problems before the examination of the client is undertaken.

The attorney should also tell the psychiatrist exactly what is required from the evaluation—the psychiatric process is multi-faceted and can accomplish a number of different things. The nature of the particular legal problem, the legal standards involved, and the specific questions for which answers are required help to determine the information the psychiatrist will try to obtain.

The following situations are illustrative of the type of legal problems which the psychiatrist may be asked to help solve. In each instance the types of questions to be answered by the psychiatrist should be presented to him in advance of the examination and related to the prevailing legal standards pertinent in the particular situation.

In a criminal case the opinion of the psychiatrist may be sought with respect to issues of the defendant's ability to stand trial; the presence of a mental disorder and its nature, both currently and at the time of the alleged offense; the degree of danger of the individual to himself or others; the relationship of a mental disorder to the alleged offense; the possible benefit from available psychiatric therapy; and the predicted effect of incarceration on the alleged offender. With respect to alleged sex offenders the presence of a mental disorder and its nature, the relationship of the disorder to the alleged offense, the danger to others posed by the alleged offender, the degree of benefit anticipated from available outpatient or institutional psychiatric therapy and the likelihood of the repetition of the alleged offense may be questions asked of the psychiatrist.

In an annulment or divorce case the opinion of the psychiatrist may be sought to determine the presence and nature of a mental disorder in one or both of the parties. His opinion may be used to assess the possible benefit of available psychiatric therapy; the impact of divorce upon the parties' mental health, and the retrospective determination of mental health prior to marriage. In contested custody hearings the psychiatrist may be asked to assess the mental health of one or both parents with respect to their fitness for the custody of the children, the presence of mental disorder and its nature, and the degree of danger, physical or mental, posed by a parent toward the children.

In a will contest the psychiatrist may be asked to evaluate retro-spectively the mental health of the testator, the presence of a mental disorder and its nature at the time of the making of the will, and relationship of the mental disorder to the making of specific provisions of the will. In a civil suit for damages based on psychiatric disability the attorney may seek psychiatric expert opinion on the nature of the mental disorder and its relationship to an alleged event, as well as the degree of benefit anticipated from available psychiatric therapy, and the permanence of the disability.

Through the use of the conference technique it is hoped the attorney will be able to select a psychiatrist with whom he can work. At the same time some of the problems the psychiatrist notes as inherent in the legal system will be clarified. One warning should be made at this point: it is important to reexplain and emphasize all aspects of the legal process continually throughout the interprofessional relationship to a point that they are clearly understood by the participating psychiatrist. I shall return to this topic later.

THE EXAMINATION OF THE CLIENT

During the evaluation of a client referred by a lawyer the psychiatrist is confronted by legal, psychological, and ethical considerations beyond the usual scope of his psychiatric practice. The preceding clarification of the type of examination desired and the legal questions to be answered facilitates the examination. Standards of the examination will now be discussed; both the attorney and the psychiatrist must agree on what is desired if optimal results are to be obtained from the psychiatric evaluation.

It is important that both professionals be fully cognizant of the need for an adequate evaluation of the client. It is undesirable to impose significant time limitations, either through pressure of events or because of inadequate funds. Sufficient time must be devoted by the psychiatrist if his evaluation is to be meaningful. In certain matters a single interview may be sufficient, though for most cases a more intensive evaluation is desirable. Frequently two separate interviews, constituting a minimum of approximately two hours, produce more adequate data upon which to base the evaluation. In fact, it can develop that in cases involving highly complex psychiatric problems the required evaluation time may extend to several days or even weeks in an in-patient institutional setting.

The clinical psychiatric evaluation should lead to both a clinical diagnosis and a psychodynamic diagnosis.(9) Psychological testing also provides useful data to corroborate the findings of the psychiatrist. It also assists him in extending the scope of his inquiry with the client. However, psychological testing without a clinical psychiatric evaluation is usually less meaningful in providing answers to the types of questions the attorney wants answered.(10)

The evaluation in most cases should include a complete psychiatric evaluation with a full past and present history of the client. It should also include a mental status examination. This includes assessment of intelligence, competence of organic brain functioning, symptoms of mental disorder, patterns of coping with stressful situations, and levels of anxiety and depression. The determination of ability to respond to treatment requires detailed knowledge of the specific person, his mental disorder, motivation for therapy, responsivity of the particular disorder to known treatment techniques and available treatment resources. With alleged sex offenders, the detailed history of prior sexual activity, relationship of sexual problems to the alleged offense, and assessment of danger to past victims are all important. In each instance the psychiatric evaluation is highly individualized, but within a broad framework which is similar each time.

The performance of a physical examination may or may not be required in a particular psychiatric evaluation. In many instances the physical examination may be performed by another physician. Whenever organic brain functioning is a question, it is necessary that the physical examination, including a complete neurological examination, be performed. Indicated laboratory procedure should also be used to supplement the examination. Such laboratory procedure includes serological testing, skull x-rays, electroencephalogram, spinal fluid examination, and other specialized tests on clinical indication. Hospitalization for these detailed neurological tests may be necessary in order to study adequately the functioning of the central nervous system.

A detailed history is essential as part of a psychiatric evaluation. Such a complete history may be difficult to obtain from a client because of his concern about revealing certain information which might be relayed to either his attorney or to the court. It is therefore very helpful for the psychiatrist to obtain information from outside sources in order to broaden the scope of his inquiry during the interview. The opinions of significant persons in the individual's life such as spouse, parents, teachers, and religious leaders may be helpful. In the area of criminal law, confessions, police statements, and various statements made to other persons may be very useful. The psychiatrist should be cautioned that such material frequently constitutes hearsay evidence. He should be aware that he cannot, therefore, use such data as the specific basis for forming his opinion. This evidence is still important, however, in helping the psychiatrist focus on areas which otherwise might be overlooked and which can serve as corroborative data in forming an opinion, if the opinion is based on statements made by the client which confirm information obtained from other sources.

The method of conducting the examination is also an important consideration. It is always preferable to conduct the examination in privacy. An alleged criminal offender should not be restrained by handcuffs or the like during any portion of the interview, if at all possible. The likelihood of obtaining more meaningful interview material is significantly enhanced by these measures.

Introductory comments by the psychiatrist to the client should state the reason for the examination and the relationship of the psychiatrist to the client.(11) The absence of confidentiality in this relationship should be revealed at the outset. It is common in psychiatric evaluations that a great deal of private and highly personalized material is revealed. Since any information revealed by the client to the psychiatrist becomes possible content for subsequent public revelation in a document or in a court proceeding, he should be fully informed about this prior to making any such statements. In a criminal proceeding, for example, further revelation regarding the alleged offense may be forthcoming in the context of the psychiatric evaluation. Rapport for the relationship between the psychiatrist and the client is also enhanced by a straightforward, honest approach on the part of the psychiatrist.

During the course of his examination the psychiatrist arrives at a clinical diagnosis in accordance with the standard psychiatric nomenclature. In addition to his clinical diagnosis, he also formulates a psychodynamic diagnosis. The latter includes a description of the personality factors in the individual which are operative in daily living, including his thoughts and impulses and their attached emotions. At times it is difficult to complete this type of evaluation due to limitations in the examination situation. On the other hand, the stress of the examination may assist in providing much information which is useful in making such a dynamic diagnosis.

A concluding statement is rendered by the psychiatrist which represents his medical-legal opinion. This is based upon his total examination in relation to the specific problems presented by the client in his legal situation. Questions posed by the attorney prior to the examination are answered as fully as possible in this opinion. The report must be lucid, concise, and contain minimal technical language. Such technical terms as may be used should be fully defined.(12)

PRE-TRIAL CONFERENCES OF ATTORNEY AND PSYCHIATRIST

Upon completion of the examination it is advisable for the psychiatrist to meet again with the attorney. This is useful because it helps to redefine the basic issues in terms of what the evaluation has shown. The specific legal issues should be outlined for the psychiatrist, and he should present the specific psychiatric findings to the attorney. The chief benefit of the conference is the clarification of the basic issues in addition to reaffirming for the psychiatrist his exact role in any anticipated courtroom proceedings. If this is adequately done, the psychiatrist feels more free to testify and will likely present more effective testimony.

Adequate cross-examination requires significant knowledge on the attorney's part in relation to the specialized field in question. The expert witness testifying for a party in the adversary proceeding can be of significant assistance in acquainting the attorney with information about the client's specific illness. He can also provide the attorney with material to further enhance his understanding of the issues involved. We will see that this same co-operation can be used when the attorney prepares his hypothetical questions for the adverse expert witness. With the psychiatrist's help the questions can be intelligible and focused on the specific psychiatric issues involved in the case.

One other important factor should be discussed at this meeting. This involves the fee which the psychiatrist is to receive for his courtroom appearance. It should be on a fixed and not on a contingent basis. A contingent fee tends to deprive the witness of his objectivity and raises questions about the validity of his testimony. However, at the same time the fee should be adequate. As noted before, the psychiatrist is, for the most part, in a seller's market. While it is nice to argue that the psychiatrist should recognize his duty, all too often he will not participate unless paid sufficiently. In the case of the poor client, it is recognized that unpaid psychiatric evaluation and testimony may have to be sought. Even here, contingent fees should not be resorted to. In a criminal case where the defendant is indigent, however, some states provide for the appointment of an impartial expert witness.(13)

PSYCHIATRIC EXPERT TESTIMONY

The general area of psychiatric expert testimony probably creates more problems for the psychiatrist than any other aspect of his involvement with the legal system. Many psychiatrists have firm notions on how the legal system operates and some feel that it operates poorly, particularly insofar as it deals with psychiatric matters in the criminal area. They are perturbed by what they feel are unnecessary legal restrictions. But a basic point is that they do not adequately understand why these restrictions exist. And the psychiatrist may not understand what role he is to play in the total process of the trial. Needless to say the expert testimony will be found lacking to the extent that any of these problems exist.

The psychiatrist's objections to various rules of procedure and evidence may be alleviated if he can be made to understand either the purpose of the rules, or why they exist, even if outmoded. Thus the purpose of each relevant rule should be explained. And if a rule is outmoded, the attorney should explain why it has not been changed. For example, the fact that the legal system moves slowly in initiating change and that present-day thought generally recognizes that a certain rule is poor will create a feeling of understanding upon the psychiatrist's part. To the extent he understands the reasons, his whole attitude may change, and thus his testimony will be far more effective.

As pointed out before, many psychiatrists are disturbed by substantive rules of law which they believe are not in harmony with current psychiatric knowledge.(14) A prime example of this attitude may be seen in the current debate over the proper definition of "legal insanity." However, the attorney must impress the psychiatrist with the fact that testimony is given within a legal framework. The psychiatrist's basic role is to provide information which only he can give. He is not to try the case, and his interests are not legal interests.

There is an additional point that lawyers should consider when briefing their expert witnesses on trial procedure. I should state, however, that this consideration has been gained through practical experience with some trial courts and is by no means an absolute proposition. The consideration is that some courts tend to be more flexible than the laws under which they function. For example, courts may tend to give the psychiatrist great leeway in his testimony; I find this to be especially true with a psychiatrist who presents testimony that demonstrates an adequate psychiatric examination and an understanding of the necessary legal procedures involved in the case. Thus, the lawyer should, if possible, try to brief the psychiatric witness as to the attitudes of the trial judge who will try the case.

EXPECTED TESTIMONY FROM THE PSYCHIATRIST

Attorneys frequently have little idea of the standard they should require a psychiatrist to fulfill when he testifies. Before discussing standards, however, it is necessary to raise a preliminary point. Psychiatrists may feel, either consciously or unconsciously, that their testimony must be guarded. This is because they fail to distinguish the two situations concerning the confidences of the client. There is, first the very important consideration of confidentiality when a person *voluntarily* consults a psychiatrist for treatment. On the other hand, there is no confidentiality barrier when a psychiatrist examines a person as part of a procedure to determine legal rights and liabilities. This distinction must be clarified before the attorney can get optimum testimony from the psychiatrist. And a failure to do so will, in many cases, color the testimony of the expert witness.

The attorney should advise the psychiatrist on the most meaningful method of presenting testimony. For example, the demeanor of the witness is usually not stressed by the attorney as a factor that the jury seriously considers in evaluating testimony. He should explain that bombastic comments are far less well received than an earnest "soft sell" approach. The testimony should be concise and lucid. And it is of the utmost importance that the psychiatrist be constantly advised not to use technical terms in his testimony, since a very meaningful point may not be comprehended by the jury if couched in the psychiatrist's jargon.

Both professions should recognize that psychiatric testimony will be most effective if it is presented in an impartial and unbiased manner. Findings which tend to support an opposite point of view should be readily conceded, rather than grudgingly admitted. Yet it should be understood that psychiatrists cannot be impartial in the sense of having no allegiance to a school of thought or point of view. The personal biases and prejudices of the psychiatrist which are evident in his daily activities are also difficult to exclude from his testimony. For example, one expert may be more optimistic than another. These biases are components of the human personality and must be accepted as such. Yet the expert should not be partial in the sense of an allegiance to either party in a law suit. As one observer has stated:

> In legal proceedings he should be jealous of the prerogatives of the profession and appear always as an advisor rather than as an advocate, telling the truth as he sees it to the best of his ability, unmoved by the prospect of gain or fame. He should, in the legal field particularly, avoid so far as possible any controversies with his colleagues and seek opportunity for joint examination and report in contested cases. (15)

Lawyers and psychiatrists are frequently confused on the exact content of the expert's testimony. Basically, it is the function of the psychiatrist to present the mental state of the examined party at the relevant times in issue. The psychodynamic basis of any relevant behavior, including both conscious and unconscious processes, should be described. This will include presentation of the mental processes, forces, and motivations which result in specific behavior. Although different situations will call for different kinds of testimony, the following quotations will be illustrative. It should be noted that they are confined to the criminal law context.

When a psychiatrist who has examined the defendant testifies concerning his mental condition, he shall be permitted to make a statement as to the nature of his examination, his diagnosis of the mental condition of the defendant at the time of commission of the offense charged. . . . He shall be permitted to make any explanation reasonably serving to clarify his diagnosis and opinion. . . .(16)

Guttmacher, discussing the psychiatrist's role in testifying on the responsibility issue in a criminal case, becomes even more specific as to what questions the psychiatrist should address himself to:

1. Whether the defendant was suffering from a definite and generally recognized mental disorder and why and how this conclusion was reached;

2. The name, the chief characteristics and symptoms of the disorder, with particular emphasis on its effect on judgment, social behavior, and self-control of the affected individual;

3. The way and the degree to which the malady has affected the particular defendant's behavior, especially in regard to his judgment, social behavior and self-control;

4. Whether the alleged act could be considered symptomatic of the disorder.(17)

HYPOTHETICAL QUESTIONS FOR THE PSYCHIATRIST

The psychiatrist must understand that in his role as expert he usually serves as advisor to one of the advocates in the court proceedings. In this role he may be asked a hypothetical question which is framed to permit consideration of all pertinent "facts" in the case useful to the advocate's position. This commonly presents difficulty for the psychiatrist since he may be confronted with "facts" which are contrary to his own experience with the client whom he has examined.(18) If often appears to the psychiatrist that the hypothetical question fails to present a fair summary of the facts in the case. The question may assume some facts which appear wholly inconsistent with those actually known to the psychiatrist through his evaluation of the client. He may be confused when a differing set of facts about another hypothetical individual is introduced by the opposing lawyer to establish an opposite point of view.

The psychiatrist needs to understand that responses to hypothetical questions must be based solely on the "facts" of the hypothetical question itself, and must not reflect any other information about the client possessed by the psychiatrist. This point is usually not made clear to the psychiatric expert by either the lawyer or the court. He should know that his position as an expert in responding to a hypothetical question is not to determine the existence or non-existence of the facts posed in the question but to assume those facts to be true and respond accordingly.

He is similarly troubled by the great length of the hypothetical question. It may become somewhat clearer to him, if it is explained as being analogous to the medical model of a case presentation at a clinical-pathological conference.

The framing of the hypothetical question may be best done cooperatively by the lawyer and the psychiatrist. It becomes much easier for the psychiatrist to testify if the facts contained in the hypothetical question are essentially in agreement with his own findings. Since the hypothetical question may play a significant role in some legal proceedings, the psychiatrist's familiarity with it prior to his court appearance is very beneficial to his total testimony.

THE PSYCHIATRIST AND CROSS-EXAMINATION

The cross-examination phase of a trial presents many problems for the psychiatrist. Frequently he anticipates cross-examination as an ordeal to which he feels he should not be subjected. The possibility of personal abuse at the hands of the cross-examining attorney frequently results in his refusal to participate in courtroom activities. On the other hand, the attorney should explain that with adequate preparation, frank objectivity, and familiarity with legal procedures, cross-examination can be a stimulating experience. The pontifications of positions and reification of theoretical concepts will be challenged in court. Undocumented or speculative views will be exposed as being of little merit.

The attorney must explain the actual function of the cross-examination to the psychiatrist. While some trial attorneys feel that "ordinarily the best cross-examination of medical experts is no cross-examination," it is clear that the cross-examination will not always be eliminated.(19) For example, everyone should realize that a person, even though an expert witness, may inadvertently testify outside the realm of his particular training or experience. Such consequences can be avoided by the use of a vigorous cross-examination.

Specific techniques used by a cross-examining attorney should be explained to the psychiatrist. Testimony may be discredited by trying to impeach the expert's testimony. One method is to attempt to show that the psychiatrist is biased because he has a relationship with the hiring attorney under which he will receive substantial fees for the testimony that he gives. Another method is to challenge the psychiatrist's educational background to show that he is unqualified to give testimony on the particular issue in question. While the psychiatrist may view this as a personal attack, it is probable that the psychiatrist will be a more meaningful participant if the legal validity and purpose of this technique are made clear to him.

Specific detailed information may be sought during cross-examination to test the witness's knowledge. The attorney should brief his expert on the types of questions that are likely to be asked and advise him on the proper way to answer these questions. Some of the more important aspects of this phase of the preparation for cross-examination should be outlined.

If the detailed information requested is beyond the immediate recall of the witness, and outside the scope of material which he ordinarily uses for recall, he should be advised to state that medical reference sources are used for such information, and not to rely upon his memory. Particular reference sources may be used by the cross-examining attorney in an effort to cite conflicting points of view in the literature. An appropriate response by the expert to this line of questioning is a statement that his knowledge is based upon many sources, including his training and experience; the psychiatrist should state that he is not relying upon any particular single source book in forming his opinion. In the event specific books are recognized as authorities in the field, it is important to review statements in their proper context and to be sure that the most recent publication of the particular volume is being cited.

The psychiatrist should be advised to acknowledge rationally and unemotionally differences with other experts. Errors in previous testimony, if these are noted during later testimony or on cross-examination, should be recognized. The meaning of earlier statements may be distorted, misquoted, or taken out of context during the course of cross-examination. If such is the case, this should be brought to the attention of the court by the expert. This may be effectively done by asking the court reporter to quote from the earlier testimony.

The expert witness should not attempt to engage in legal debate with the cross-examining attorney while on the witness stand, since his skilled adversary is likely to be far more expert in this arena. Questions should not be answered with a categorical "yes" or "no" if qualification is necessary for a complete answer. Efforts by the attorney to limit the answer to "yes" or "no" may be resisted by the witness who needs to clarify his response to make it complete, and this will ordinarily be sustained by the court.

Thorough examination of the alleged offender, careful preparation for testimony, knowledge of the legal procedure, and a helpful impartial demeanor in the courtroom will ordinarily lead to good testimony on both direct and cross-examination, and with this pattern as a base the psychiatric expert can be assured that he need not fear cross-examination.

NOTES

(1) Watson, "Communication between Psychiatrists and Lawyers," *International Psychiatry Clinics*, 1 (1964): 186.

(2) Cf. Oleck, "A Cure for Doctor-Lawyer Frictions," *Clev.-Mar. L. Rev.*, 7 (1958): 473, 474.

(3) Dr. Watson verbalizes this view in a dramatic manner: "When most psychiatrists contemplate communicating with lawyers, they visualize the witness stand—which in their fantasies appears to have been wired for execution, or, at least, torture." Watson, "Communication between Psychiatrists and Lawyers," p. 193.

(4) American Psychiatric Association, *Psychiatry and Medical Education*, Vol. II (1952).

(5) Dynamic psychiatry is concerned with the multiple interacting mental forces which result in human behavior, thought, and emotion. Treatment is based on modifying these factors to reduce symptoms of a mentally disordered individual (Hinsie and Campbell, *Psychiatric Dictionary* [3d ed., 1960]).

Community psychiatry is a newly emerging type of psychiatric theory and practice. It is defined in several ways by different psychiatrists. A common definition states that it provides for prevention, recognition, treatment, and rehabilitation of the mentally ill and emotionally troubled in a given population. The development of positive mental health, as defined by Jahoda, within that given population, is another aspect of community psychiatry. Jahoda, *Current Concepts of Positive Mental Health* (1958). See also Roberts, Halleck, and Loeb, eds., *Community Psychiatry: What It Is and What It Isn't* (1965).

Psychobiology is the study of the functioning of the mind and the behavior of a person in relation to his environment.

(6) See generally, Davies, "Finding an Expert in the Sciences," *Clev.-Mar. L. Rev.*, 13 (1964): 309.

(7) The type of membership in the American Psychiatric Association, the major national professional organization for psychiatrists, is one useful criterion for the attorney in selecting a psychiatrist. Particular qualification standards must be met to achieve membership in this organization. Full membership is given only to psychiatrists who have three years of training or experience. Fellowship is bestowed upon members with outstanding contributions in particular areas of psychiatric practice. The bibliographic directory of the APA provides further useful preliminary data on which to base a decision to engage a particular psychiatrist.

(8) See generally, Stein, "Mental Competency and the Law," *Med. Trial Tech. Q.*, 10 (1964): 155.

(9) A psychodynamic diagnosis includes a description of individual personality factors which are operative in daily living, including thoughts and behavior, and their attached emotions. This type of diagnosis, in non-technical language, provides the best means of describing human behavior and its causation.

A clinical diagnosis is a descriptive "shortcut" which 1. provides a brief means of characterizing a specific person in relation to the symptoms of a particular mental disorder and 2. gives a rough basis of predicting future behavioral patterns for members of the group of persons so labeled. A clinical diagnosis is frequently more succinct but less useful in portraying a specific individual than is a psychodynamic diagnosis.

(10) Psychological testing provides a useful tool for evaluating an individual. Such tests may assess such things as intelligence, intellectual functioning of the central nervous system, and possible impairment in organic brain functioning, personality components, and disordered thinking and emotions. Administration of a number of different tests by the clinical psychologist provides additional data useful to the psychiatrist who clinically evaluates the individual. The psychological test results, in the absence of clinical evaluation, do not usually conclusively answer the attorney's questions. This is true even in the case of the determination of a level of intelligence, the area in which psychological testing affords the greatest precision.

(11) See generally, McDonald, *Psychiatry and the Criminal* (1958), p. 39.

(12) See generally, Watson, "Communication between Psychiatrists and Lawyers," pp. 191–92.

(13) See, e.g., Cal. Civ. Proc. Code & 1871; Wis. Stat. & 957.27 (1963).

(14) *State v. Esser*, 16 Wis. 2d 567, 115 N.W. 2d 505 (1962), is a nice illustration of this point.

(15) Overholser, "Presidential Address," *American J. of Psychiatry*, 105 (1948): 5.

(16) Model Penal Code § 4.07 (Tent. Draft No. 5, 1955).

(17) Guttmacher, "What Can the Psychiatrist Contribute to the Issue of Criminal Responsibility?," *J. of Nervous Mental Disorders*, 136 (1963): 103, 107.

(18) See generally, "The Physicians' Testimony, Including the Hypothetical Question," *N.Y.S.J. of Medicine*, 63 (1963): 2056.

(19) Goldstein, "Cross-examination of Expert Medical Witnesses," in *American Medical Association, Medical Legal Symposium Proceedings* (1959), p. 241.

II.

Psychodiagnosis
and
Pseudodiagnosis

Introduction

David L. Rosenhan (1973) conducted a study in which eight people—a psychiatrist, a graduate student, a painter, a housewife, a pediatrician, and three psychologists gained admittance as pseudopatients to twelve public and private mental hospitals at various locations in the United States. Each individual contacted a hospital and complained of hearing voices that seemed to say "empty," "hollow," and "thud." Although they were somewhat nervous and ill at ease during the initial interview, the behavior of the pseudopatients displayed normal behavior. Each gave a fictitious name and occupation to the diagnostician; the rest of the information in each life history was authentic.

Eleven of the twelve admissions received a diagnosis of schizophrenia, and one was identified as manic-depressive psychotic. These diagnostic assessments were determined primarily on the basis of the reported auditory hallucinations. The pseudopatients spent an average period of 19 days in the hospital with a range of from 7 to 52 days. During their hospitalization, all of the pseudopatients received more than 2,100 pills according to Rosenhan. At discharge, the diagnosis was "schizophrenia in remission."

Reiss and his associates (1977) have identified the following issues in the debate on the Rosenhan study: 1. validity of the distinction between abnormal and normal behavior, 2. validity of psychiatric diagnoses, 3. careless diagnostic practices, 4. contribution of context to diagnosis, 5. exclusion criteria, and 6. stickiness of psychiatric diagnosis. A careful consideration of these issues is essential to an understanding of Rosenhan's original study, Spitzer's critique of the Rosenhan research, and

Rosenhan's rebuttal of the points raised by Spitzer and other critics.

Validity of the distinction between abnormal and normal behavior. If Rosenhan had merely reported that his study had found low validity for psychiatric judgments of mental illness, his article probably would not have attracted much attention professionally. However, by making the very extreme claim that the judgments of mental illness are totally invalid, his article was given an extraordinary reception. Reiss et al., (1977) claim that Rosenhan's conclusion cannot be supported by Rosenhan's study:

> At most, a pseudopatient study could show that it is sometimes possible to feign mental illness, a fact known to scientists for at least several centuries. Judgments of abnormality are based on the patient's behavior and on the patient's self-report of behavior; if the information supplied is inaccurate, it should not be surprising that the diagnosis is also likely to be inaccurate. In Rosenhan's study, the diagnosticians had little reason to suspect that the pseudopatients were falsely reporting auditory hallucinations in order to conduct psychological research; hence they understandably accepted the pseudopatients' complaints at face value. *The issue of whether we can tell the difference between normal and abnormal behavior is whether we can do so when the information concerning symptoms is accurate and when the diagnosticians are highly trained and competent* (italics added). Because the information supplied to the diagnosticians in Rosenhan's study was in part fabricated, the study is largely irrelevant to the validity of the distinction between abnormal and normal behavior.

Robert L. Spitzer (1975) believes that the pseudopatients were, in fact, not fully perceived as real patients. He notes that the pseudopatients were released from the hospital after an average stay of approximately two weeks—a short period of hospitalization for patients diagnosed as psychotic. He suggests that the brief hospitalization period might indicate some awareness that the pseudopatients differed from real patients.

In his later publication Rosenhan (1975) moderated his extreme position that abnormal behavior is indistinguishable from normal behavior. In a more defensible revision, he claims that the pseudopatients could and should have been admitted to hospitals without having been diagnosed as schizophrenic.

Validity of psychiatric diagnosis. In admitting that the diagnosticians had no compelling reason to believe that the pseudopatients were faking symptoms, Rosenhan (1975) acknowledges that the hospitals were acting in an appropriate and humane manner by admitting the pseudopatients. In his revised account, he charges the hospitals with a significant error: diagnosing the pseudopatients as schizophrenic without sufficient evidence to support the diagnosis. Reiss and his co-authors (1977) observe that:

> The major symptom [of schizophrenia] is the presence of thought disorder (a serious defect of reason; delusions; or disorganization of thought processes). Withdrawal and a rich fantasy life are other prominent symptoms. There may be a fear of experiencing intense emotions. Hallucinations alone do not, and never did, serve as the only symptom defining schizophrenia.

In Rosenhan's opinion, the complaints of auditory hallucinations by his pseudopatients should have led, at best, to a diagnosis of hallucination or to a deferred diagnosis.

Reiss et al., (1977) do not disagree with Spitzer's conclusion that, given the symptoms reported and observed in the pseudopatients, schizophrenia was a reasonable diagnosis. They do, however, question why further clinical tests were not conducted to determine the possibility of organic brain damage. They also maintain that schizophrenia was equally inappropriate as a diagnosis in terms of the absence of indications of thought disorder, withdrawal, or delusional formations during the initial interviews. In their view, if schizophrenia had to be diagnosed to justify admitting the pseudopatients, it was necessary and proper that the initial diagnosis be followed with further careful clinical investigation.

Careless diagnostic practices. Farber (1975) also questions the failure of the diagnosticians to seek confirmation of their diagnoses by conducting adequate procedures subsequently. The administration of more than 2,100 pills to the pseudopatients without further confirmation of the original diagnoses raises serious, disturbing issues relating to psychiatric practices in hospitals. However, according to Rosenhan (1975), the diagnostic system is more at fault than the diagnosticians.

Contribution of context to diagnosis. The major point that Rosenhan (1975) makes in his later article is that the hospital setting tends to create a predisposition toward the perception of normal behavior as indicative of mental illness. The question of what constitutes normal behavior in a hospital is arguable. Spitzer, quoting one of Rosenhan's critics, offers the following argument:

> The pseudopatients did *not* behave normally in the hospital. Had their behavior been normal, they would have walked to the nurses' station and said, "Look, I am a normal person who tried

to see if I could get into the hospital by behaving in a crazy way and saying crazy things. It worked and I was admitted to the hospital, but now I would like to be discharged from the hospital."

Rosenhan effectively rebuts Spitzer's contention, pointing out that the pseudopatients' statement would probably be regarded as further evidence that the individual was, in fact, a real patient. He refers to the memorable film on mental hospital conditions, *Titticut Follies*, in which a patient insisted on being discharged and was humored by nurses and attendants.

Rosenhan's study never made clear how the hospital staff actually perceived the pseudopatients. The staff was never asked whether behavior at a particular time was considered normal or abnormal. Pseudopatients sat quietly, cooperated with staff and patients, answered "Fine" in response to questions about how they were doing, and occasionally asked how soon they would be eligible for grounds privileges. Would quiet cooperation be perceived as abnormal or normal? It appears that Rosenhan believed that the behavior of his pseudopatients was perceived as normal because they were confined for a period of almost three weeks in the hospital. A period of nineteen days for hospitalization does not seem to be excessive for someone who has sought admission on the basis of hallucinatory experiences.

Exclusion criteria. Farber's (1975) critique of Rosenhan's study directs attention to the author's criteria for judging recovery from mental illness. Rosenhan's original (1973) conveyed his surprise that, once the pseudopatients had stopped feigning abnormality, they were not diagnosed as having recovered and released soon after their admission. However, the mere absence of obvious kinds of abnormal behavior like grimaces, exaggerated postures, and incoherent speech for a relatively brief period of time is not sufficient to lead to a diagnosis of recovery. Most forms of mental illness or serious emotional disturbance tend to be episodic. Reiss et al., (1977) succinctly state: "If a schizophrenic patient hallucinates on Monday, is there anything that person can do on Tuesday to convince us that he or she will not hallucinate again in the near future?" They emphasize that the American Psychiatric Association Diagnostic and Statistical Manual (DSM-II) "does not provide either an empirical or conventional basis for judging when a person has recovered from a mental illness." A need exists to specify what kind of abnormal behavior must be absent and for how long in order to provide an objective basis for diagnosing recovery.

Stickiness of psychiatric diagnosis. When they were discharged, the pseudopatients were diagnosed as having "schizophrenia in remission," an interesting and rather rare appraisal. Spitzer (1975) believes that the diagnosis suggests the possibility that the pseudopatients had been detected as not being genuinely psychotic. Rosenhan, however, notes that "in remission" or "without symptoms" and "normal" are not synonymous and that "schizophrenia in remission" connotes a stigma. The U.S. Court of Appeals (*in re Ballay*, 1973) referred to the "general rule that a person adjudged to be insane is presumed to so continue until it is shown that sanity has returned." The Court observed that an individual released as "cured" might avoid a risk of being called insane or cured. Unfortunately, as the Court noted, "it has been demonstrated empirically that such a designation upon release is seldom forthcoming, even in the most probable cases."

Finally, any introduction to diagnosis would be incomplete without mentioning the revision of the *Psychiatric Diagnostic and Statistical Manual* being conducted by the American Psychiatric Association. The editors of this volume are deeply indebited to Maurice R. Green of Columbia University and St. Luke's Hospital Center for providing the following material.

FROM *DSM-II* TO *DSM-III*

Since 1978 some psychiatrists, as participants in the field trials—Phase One and Phase Two—have had limited use of the *Psychiatric Diagnostic and Statistical Manual III (DSM-III)* in collaboration with Janet Forman and Robert Spitzer of the A.P.A. Task Force on Nomenclature and Statistics. Attempting to refine, elaborate and test the psychiatric nomenclature, psychiatrists have used the *DSM-III* over the entire range of diagnostic categories. They have experienced great enthusiasm and satisfaction with it and with the refinements and improvements they contributed to the Micro-D revision (February, 1979) and to the final draft which appeared later in 1979.

The behavioristic phenomenological style of the classification system is refreshingly useful and clear, although it demands in many ways a fairly rigorous, painstaking inquiry. One must obtain the actual data for meeting or not meeting the specific criteria in the terse but authoritative definitions given for each diagnosis. The field trials for *DSM-III* helped a great deal to clarify many issues that have been somewhat ambiguous in the past, and they will enhance among diverse observers the manual's reliability, an asymptote all psychiatrists can aspire toward but never reach completely.

In the courtroom where the *DSM-II* coding is still used because of administrative policy, the *DSM-II* categories have been most useful for organizing data for cross examination. Because the *DSM-III* is free of the theoretical and ideological biases of the *DSM-II*, it is futile and confusing to find the equivalent *DSM-II* category in the *DSM-III*. As Barry and Ciccone also emphasize, one must be familiar with the whole work of the *DSM-III* and think through the appropriate diagnostic label from *that* particular frame of reference. However, I disagree with Barry and Ciccone(1) in their rejection of axis four and five—the nature and degree of severity of life stresses affecting the patient, and the highest level of adoptive functioning the patient has achieved in the past year before the initial visit to the psychiatrist. These axis are just as essential to a full understanding and appropriate planning of treatment for a psychiatric disorder as they are for most physical disorders, as Adolf Meyer pointed out again and again fifty years ago.

In the courtroom, the data from axis four and five are especially useful in giving the judge and the jury the full range of *facts* for a compassionate understanding of the person at judgment. The data are also valuable in guiding the decisions regarding punishment and disposition. Disregarding this material would encourage the mechanistic, impersonal approach decribed today at all levels of medical education.

When there is no evidence of impairment of any function nor of any distress that qualifies as an "illness," the *DSM-III* provides useful labeling and coding for precise descriptions of a variety of behaviors that must be dealt with in the courts. For psychiatrists who work in the court system, the descriptions are most valuable both in preparing psychiatric reports for the court and in removing the pathological bias that so many jurists and even forensic psychiatrists have long protested.

Alvin Feinstein's classic work, *Clinical Judgment*(2), helped pave the way for the *DSM-III*, because the author insisted on rigorous explications and operational statements for what many clinicians from all specialities of medicine tended to gloss over as intuitive but infallible decisions. The greatest contribution of the *DSM-III* is not so much in the validity and reliability studies that have gone into the choice of diagnostic terms and their criteria, but in the demands it makes on psychiatrists for having *their* facts in hand before they go begging for a judgment. Thereby, psychiatrists should, it is hoped, be able to meet the requirements of the judiciary more ably with detailed descriptions which the law requires of the origin, development, and complex nature of the person before them.

REFERENCES

Farber, I. E. "Sane and Insane: Constructions and Misconstructions." *Journal of Abnormal Psychology*, 1975, 84, 589–62.
Reiss, S., Peterson, R. A., Eron, L. D., and Reiss, M. M. *Abnormality: Ex-*

perimental and Clinical Approaches. New York: Macmillan, 1977.

Rosenhan, D. L. "On Being Sane in Insane Places." *Science,* 1973, 19, 250–258.

Rosenhan, D. L. "The Contextual Nature of Psychiatric Diagnosis." *Journal of Abnormal Psychology,* 1975, 84, 462–474.

Spitzer, R. L. "On Pseudoscience in Science, Logic in Remission, and Psychiatric Diagnosis: A Critique of Rosenhan's "On Being Sane in Insane Places." *Journal of Abnormal Psychology,* 1975, 84, 442–452.

NOTES

(1) Ciccone, J. Richard and Barry, J. David. The Experience of Using DSM-III in a Court-Clinic Setting: Basic Changes in the Methodology of Psychiatric Diagnosis. *Bulletin of the American Academy of Psychiatry and Law* (1978) 6:1, pp. 23–25.

(2) Feinstein, Alvin. *Clinical Judgment.* Williams & Wilkins. Baltimore, 1967.

On Being Sane in Insane Places

D.L. Rosenhan

If sanity and insanity exist, how shall we know them?

The question is neither capricious nor itself insane. However much we may be personally convinced that we can tell the normal from the abnormal, the evidence is simply not compelling. It is commonplace, for example, to read about murder trials wherein eminent psychiatrists for the defense are contradicted by equally eminent psychiatrists for the prosecution on the matter of the defendant's sanity. More generally, there are a great deal of conflicting data on the reliability, utility, and meaning of such terms as "sanity," "insanity," "mental illness," and "schizophrenia"(1). Finally, as early as 1934, Benedict suggested that normality and abnormality are not universal(2). What is viewed as normal in one culture may be seen as quite aberrant in another. Thus, notions of normality and abnormality may not be quite as accurate as people believe they are.

To raise questions regarding normality and abnormality is in no way to question the fact that some behaviors are deviant or odd. Murder is deviant. So, too, are hallucinations. Nor does raising such questions deny the existence of the personal anguish that is often associated with "mental illness." Anxiety and depression exist. Psychological suffering exists. But normality and abnormality, sanity and insanity, and the diagnoses that flow from them may be less substantive than many believe them to be.

At its heart, the question of whether the sane can be distinguished from the insane (and whether degrees of insanity can be distinguished from each other) is a simple matter: do the salient characteristics that lead to diagnoses reside in the patients themselves or in the environments and contexts in which observers find them? From Bleuler, through Kretchmer, through the formulators of the recently revised *Diagnostic and Statistical Manual* of the American Psychiatric Association, the belief has been strong that patients present symptoms, that those symptoms can be categorized, and, implicitly, that the sane are distinguishable from the insane. More recently, however, this belief has been questioned. Based in part on theoretical and anthropological considerations, but also on philosophical, legal, and therapeutic ones, the view has grown that psychological categorization of mental illness is useless at best and downright harmful, misleading, and pejorative at worst. Psychiatric diagnoses, in this view, are in the minds of the observers and are not valid summaries of characteristics displayed by the observed(3–5).

Gains can be made in deciding which of these is more nearly accurate by getting normal people (that is, people who do not have, and have never suffered, symptoms of serious psychiatric disorders) admitted to psychiatric hospitals and then determining whether they were discovered to be sane and, if so, how. If the sanity of such pseudo-patients were always detected, there would be prima facie evidence that a sane individual can be distinguished from the insane context in which he is found. Normality (and presumably abnormality, is distinct enough that it can be recognized wherever it occurs, for it is carried within the person. If, on the other hand, the sanity of the pseudopatients were never discovered, serious difficulties would arise for those who support traditional modes of psychiatric diagnosis. Given that the hospital staff was not incompetent, that the pseudopatient had been behaving as sanely as he had been outside of the hospital, and that it had never been previously suggested that he belonged in a psychiatric hospital, such an unlikely outcome would support the view that psychiatric diagnosis betrays little about the patient but much about the environment in which an observer finds him.

This article describes such an experiment. Eight sane people gained secret admission to 12 different hospitals(6). Their diagnostic experiences constitute the data of the first part of this article; the remainder is devoted to a description of their experiences in psychiatric institutions. Too few psychiatrists and psychologists, even those who have worked in such hospitals, know what the experience is like. They rarely talk about it with former patients, perhaps because they distrust information coming from the previously insane. Those who have worked in psychiatric hospitals are likely to have adapted so thoroughly to the settings that they are insensitive to the impact of that experience. And while there have been occasional reports of researchers who submitted themselves to psychiatric hospitalization(7), these researchers have commonly remained in the hospitals for short periods of time, often with the knowledge of the hospital staff. It is difficult to know the extent to which they were treated like patients or like research colleagues. Nevertheless, their reports about the inside of the psychiatric hospital have been valuable. This article extends those efforts.

PSEUDOPATIENTS AND THEIR SETTINGS

The eight pseudopatients were a varied group. One was a psychology graduate student in his 20's. The remaining seven were older and "established." Among them were three psychologists, a pediatrician, a psychiatrist, a painter, and a housewife. Three pseudopatients were women, five were men. All of them employed pseudonyms, lest their alleged diagnoses embarrass them later. Those who were in mental health professions alleged another occupation in order to avoid the special attentions that might be accorded by staff, as a matter of courtesy or caution, to ailing colleagues(8). With the exception of myself (I was the first pseudopatient and my presence was known to the hospital administrator and chief psychologist and, so far as I can tell, to them alone), the presence of pseudopatients and the nature of the research program was not known to the hospital staffs(9).

The settings were similarly varied. In order to generalize the findings, admission into a variety of hospitals was sought. The 12 hospitals in the sample were located in five different states on the East and West coasts. Some were old and shabby, some were quite new. Some were research-oriented, others not. Some had good staff-patient ratios, others were quite understaffed. Only one was a strictly private hospital. All of the others were supported by state or federal funds or, in one instance, by university funds.

After calling the hospital for an appointment, the pseudopatient arrived at the admissions office complaining that he had been hearing voices. Asked what the voices said, he replied that they were often unclear, but as far as he could tell they said "empty," "hollow," and "thud." The voices were unfamiliar and were of the same sex as the pseudopatient. The choice of these symptoms was occasioned by their apparent similarity to existential symptoms. Such symptoms are alleged to arise from painful concerns about the perceived meaninglessness of one's life. It is as if the hallucinating person were saying, "My life is empty and hollow." The choice of these symptoms was also determined by the *absence* of a single report of existential psychoses in the literature.

Beyond alleging the symptoms and falsifying name, vocation, and employment, no further alterations of person, history, or circumstances were made. The significant events of the pseudopatient's life history were presented as they had actually occurred. Relationships with parents and siblings, with spouse and children, with people at work and in school, consistent with the aforementioned exceptions, were described as they were or had been. Frustrations and upsets were described along with joys and satisfactions. These facts are important to remember. If anything, they strongly biased the subsequent results in favor of detecting sanity, since none of their histories or current behaviors were seriously pathological in any way.

Immediately upon admission to the psychiatric ward, the pseudopatient ceased simulating *any* symptoms of abnormality. In some cases, there was a brief period of mild nervousness and anxiety, since none of the pseudopatients really believed that they would be admitted so easily. Indeed, their shared fear was that they would be immediately exposed as frauds and greatly embarrassed. Moreover, many of them had never visited a psychiatric ward; even those who had, nevertheless had some genuine fears about what might happen to them. Their nervousness, then, was quite appropriate to the novelty of the hospital setting, and it abated rapidly.

Apart from that short-lived nervousness, the pseudopatient behaved on the ward as he "normally" behaved. The pseudopatient spoke to patients and staff as he might ordinarily. Because there is uncommonly little to do on a psychiatric ward, he attempted to engage others in conversation. When asked by staff how he was feeling, he indicated that he was fine, that he no longer experienced symptoms. He responded to instructions from attendants, to calls for medication (which was not swallowed), and to dining-hall instructions. Beyond such activities as were available to him on the admissions ward, he spent his time writing down his observations about the ward, its patients, and the staff. Initially these notes were written "secretly," but as it soon became clear that no one much cared, they were subsequently written on standard tablets of paper in such public places as the dayroom. No secret was made of these activities.

The pseudopatient, very much as a true psychiatric patient, entered a hospital with no foreknowledge of when he would be discharged. Each was told that he would have to get out by his own devices, essentially by convincing the staff that he was sane. The psychological stresses associated with hospitalization were considerable, and all but one of the pseudopatients desired to be discharged almost immediately after being admitted. They were, therefore, motivated not only to behave sanely, but to be paragons of cooperation. That their behavior was in no way disruptive is confirmed by nursing reports, which have been obtained on most of the patients. These reports uniformly indicate that the patients were "friendly," "cooperative," and "exhibited no abnormal indications."

THE NORMAL ARE NOT DETECTABLY SANE

Despite their public "show" of sanity, the pseudopatients were never detected. Admitted, except in one case, with a diagnosis of schizophrenia(10), each was discharged with a diagnosis of schizophrenia "in remission." The label "in remission" should in no way be dismissed as a formality, for at no time during any hospitalization had any question been raised about any pseudopatient's simulation. Nor are there any indications in the hospital records that the pseudopatient's status was suspect. Rather, the evidence is strong that, once labeled schizophrenic, the pseudopatient was stuck with that label. If the pseudopatient was to be discharged, he must naturally be "in remission" but he was not sane, nor, in the institution's view, had he ever been sane.

The uniform failure to recognize sanity cannot be attributed to the quality of the hospitals, for, although there were considerable variations among them, several are considered excellent. Nor can it be alleged that there was simply not enough time to observe the pseudopatients. Length of hospitalization ranged from 7 to 52 days, with an average of 19 days. The pseudopatients were not, in fact, carefully observed, but this failure clearly speaks more to traditions within psychiatric hospitals than to lack of opportunity.

Finally, it cannot be said that the failure to recognize the pseudopatients' sanity was due to the fact that they were not behaving sanely. While there was clearly some tension present in all of them, their daily visitors could detect no serious behavioral consequences—nor, indeed, could other patients. It was quite common for the patients to "detect" the pseudopatients' sanity. During the first three hospitalizations, when accurate counts were kept, 35 of a total of 118 patients on the admissions ward voiced their suspicions, some vigorously. "You're not crazy. You're a journalist, or a professor [referring to the continual note-taking]. You're checking up on the hospital." While most of the patients were reassured by the pseudopatient's insistence that he had been sick before he came in but was fine now, some continued to believe that the pseudopatient was sane throughout his hospitalization(11). The fact that the patients often recognized normality when staff did not raises important questions.

Failure to detect sanity during the course of hospitalization may be due to the fact that physicians operate with a strong bias toward what statisticians call the type 2 error(5). This is to say that physicians are more inclined to call a healthy person sick (a false positive, type 2) than a sick person healthy (a false negative, type 1). The reasons for this are not hard to find: it is clearly more dangerous to mis-diagnose illness than health. Better to err on the side of caution, to suspect illness even among the healthy.

But what holds for medicine does not hold equally well for psychiatry. Medical illnesses, while unfortunate, are not commonly pejorative. Psychiatric diagnoses, on the contrary, carry with them personal, legal, and social stigmas(12). It was therefore important to see whether the tendency toward diagnosing the sane insane could be reversed. The following experiment was arranged at a research and teaching hospital whose staff had heard these findings but doubted that such an error could occur in their hospital. The staff was informed that at some time during the following 3 months, one or more pseudopatients would attempt to be admitted into the psychiatric hospital. Each staff member was asked to rate each patient who presented himself at admissions or on the ward according to the likelihood that the patient was a pseudopatient. A 10-point scale was used, with a 1 and 2 reflecting high confidence that the patient was a pseudopatient.

Judgments were obtained on 193 patients who were admitted for psychiatric treatment. All staff who had had sustained contact with or primary responsibility for the patient—attendants, nurses, psychiatrists, physicians, and psychologists—were asked to make judgments. Forty-one patients were alleged, with high confidence, to be pseudopatients by at least one member of the staff. Twenty-three were considered suspect by at least one psychiatrist. Nineteen were suspected by one psychiatrist *and* one other staff member. Actually, no genuine pseudopatient (at least from my group) presented himself during this period.

The experiment is instructive. It indicates that the tendency to designate sane people as insane can be reversed when the stakes (in this case, prestige and diagnostic acumen) are high. But what can be said of the 19 people who were suspected of being "sane" by one psychiatrist and another staff member? Were these people truly "sane," or was it rather the case that in the course of avoiding the type 2 error the staff tended to make more errors of the first sort—calling the crazy "sane"? There is no way of knowing. But one thing is certain: any diagnostic process that lends itself so readily to massive errors of this sort cannot be a very reliable one.

PSYCHODIAGNOSTIC LABELS

Beyond the tendency to call the healthy sick—a tendency that accounts better for diagnostic behavior on admission than it does for such behavior after a lengthy period of exposure—the data speak to the massive role of labeling in psychiatric assessment. Having once been labeled schizophrenic, there is nothing the pseudopatient can do to overcome the tag. The tag profoundly colors others' perceptions of him and his behavior.

From one viewpoint, these data are hardly surprising, for it has long been known that elements are given meaning by the context in which they occur. Gestalt psychology made this point vigorously, and Asch(13) demonstrated that there are "central" personality traits (such as "warm" versus "cold") which are so powerful that they markedly color the meaning of other information in forming an impression of a given personality(14). "Insane," "schizophrenic," "manic-depressive," and "crazy" are probably among the most powerful of such central traits. Once a person is designated abnormal, all of his other behaviors and characteristics are colored by that label. Indeed, that label is so powerful that many of the pseudopatients' normal behaviors were overlooked entirely or profoundly misinterpreted. Some examples may clarify this issue.

Earlier I indicated that there were no changes in the pseudopatient's personal history and current status beyond those of name, employment, and, where necessary, vocation. Otherwise, a veridical description of personal history and circumstances was offered. Those circumstances were not psychotic. How were they made consonant with the diagnosis of psychosis? Or were those diagnoses modified in such a way as to bring them into accord with the circumstances of the pseudopatient's life, as described by him?

As far as I can determine, diagnoses were in no way affected by the relative health of the circumstances of a pseudopatient's life. Rather, the reverse occurred: the perception of his circumstances was shaped entirely by the diagnosis. A clear example of such translation is found in the case of a pseudopatient who had had a close relationship with his mother but was rather remote from his father during his early childhood. During adolescence and beyond, however, his father became a close friend, while his relationship with his mother cooled. His present relationship with his wife was characteristically close and warm. Apart from occasional angry exchanges, friction was minimal. The children had rarely been spanked. Surely there is nothing especially pathological about such a history. Indeed, many readers may see a similar pattern in their own experiences, with no markedly deleterious consequences. Observe, however, how such a history was translated in the psychopathological context, this from the case summary prepared after the patient was discharged.

> This white 39-year-old male . . . manifests a long history of considerable ambivalence in close relationships, which begins in

early childhood. A warm relationship with his mother cools during his adolescence. A distant relationship to his father is described as becoming very intense. Affective stability is absent. His attempts to control emotionality with his wife and children are punctuated by angry outbursts and in the case of the children spankings. And while he says that he has several good friends, one senses considerable ambivalence embedded in those relationships also. . . .

The facts of the case were unintentionally distorted by the staff to achieve consistency with a popular theory of the dynamics of a schizophrenic reaction(15). Nothing of an ambivalent nature had been described in relations with parents, spouse, or friends. To the extent that ambivalence could be inferred, it was probably not greater than is found in all human relationships. It is true the pseudopatient's relationships with his parents changed over time, but in the ordinary context that would hardly be remarkable—indeed, it might very well be expected. Clearly, the meaning ascribed to his verbalizations (that is, ambivalence, affective instability) was determined by the diagnosis: schizophrenia. An entirely different meaning would have been ascribed if it were known that the man was "normal."

All pseudopatients took extensive notes publicly. Under ordinary circumstances, such behavior would have raised questions in the minds of observers, as, in fact, it did among patients. Indeed, it seemed so certain that the notes would elicit suspicion that elaborate precautions were taken to remove them from the ward each day. But the precautions proved needless. The closest any staff member came to questioning these notes occurred when one pseudopatient asked his physician what kind of medication he was receiving and began to write down the response. "You needn't write it," he was told gently. "If you have trouble remembering, just ask me again."

If no questions were asked of the pseudopatients, how was their writing interpreted? Nursing records for three patients indicate that the writing was seen as an aspect of their pathological behavior, "Patient engages in writing behavior" was the daily nursing comment on one of the pseudopatients who was never questioned about his writing. Given that the patient is in the hospital, he must be psychologically disturbed. And given that he is disturbed, continuous writing must be a behavioral manifestation of that disturbance, perhaps a subset of the compulsive behaviors that are sometimes correlated with schizophrenia.

One tacit characteristic of psychiatric diagnosis is that it locates the sources of aberration within the individual and only rarely within the complex of stimuli that surrounds him. Consequently, behaviors that are stimulated by the environment are commonly misattributed to the patient's disorder. For example, one kindly nurse found a pseudopatient pacing the long hospital corridors. "Nervous, Mr. X?" she asked. "No, bored," he said.

The notes kept by pseudopatients are full of patient behaviors that were misinterpreted by well-intentioned staff. Often enough, a patient would go "berserk" because he had, wittingly or unwittingly, been mistreated by, say, an attendant. A nurse coming upon the scene would rarely inquire even cursorily into the environmental stimuli of the patient's behavior. Rather, she assumed that his upset derived from his pathology, not from his present interactions with other staff members. Occasionally, the staff might assume that the patient's family (especially when they had recently visited) or other patients had stimulated the outburst. But never were the staff found to assume that one of themselves or the structure of the hospital had anything to do with a patient's behavior. One psychiatrist pointed to a group of patients who were sitting outside the cafeteria entrance half an hour before lunchtime. To a group of young residents he indicated that such behavior was characteristic of the oral-acquisitive nature of the syndrome. It seemed not to occur to him that there were very few things to anticipate in a psychiatric hospital besides eating.

A psychiatric label has a life and an influence of its own. Once the impression has been formed that the patient is schizophrenic, the expectation is that he will continue to be schizophrenic. When a sufficient amount of time has passed, during which the patient has done nothing bizarre, he is considered to be in remission and available for discharge. But the label endures beyond discharge, with the unconfirmed expectation that he will behave as a schizophrenic again. Such labels, conferred by mental health professionals, are as influential on the patient as they are on his relatives and friends, and it should not surprise anyone that the diagnosis acts on all of them as a self-fulfilling prophecy. Eventually, the patient himself accepts the diagnosis, with all of its surplus meanings and expectations, and behaves accordingly(5).

The inferences to be made from these matters are quite simple. Much as Zigler and Phillips have demonstrated that there is enormous overlap in the symptoms presented by patients who have been variously diagnosed(16), so there is enormous overlap in the behaviors of the sane and the insane. The sane are not "sane" all of the time. We lose our tempers "for no good reason." We are occasionally depressed or anxious, again for no good reason. And we may find it difficult to get along with one or another person—again for no reason that we can specify. Similarly, the insane are not always insane. Indeed, it was the impression of the pseudopatients while living with them that they were sane for long periods of time—that the bizarre behaviors upon which their diagnoses were allegedly predicated constituted only a small fraction of their total behavior. If it makes no sense to label ourselves permanently depressed on the basis of an occasional depression, then it takes better evidence than is presently available to label all patients insane or schizophrenic on the basis of bizarre behaviors or cognitions. It seems more useful, as Mischel(17) has pointed out, to limit our discussions to *behaviors*, the stimuli that provoke them, and their correlates.

It is not known why powerful impressions of personality traits, such as "crazy" or "insane," arise. Conceivably, when the origins of and stimuli that give rise to a behavior are remote or unknown, or when the behavior strikes us as immutable, trait labels regarding the *behaver* arise. When, on the other hand, the origins and stimuli are known and available, discourse is limited to the behavior itself. Thus, I may hallucinate because I am sleeping, or I may hallucinate because I have ingested a peculiar drug. These are termed sleep-induced hallucinations, or dreams, and drug-induced hallucinations, respectively. But when the stimuli to my hallucinations are unknown, that is called craziness, or schizophrenia—as if that inference were somehow as illuminating as the others.

PSYCHIATRIC HOSPITALIZATION

The term "mental illness" is of recent origin. It was coined by people who were humane in their inclinations and who wanted very much to raise the station of (and the public's sympathies toward) the psychologically disturbed from that of witches and "crazies" to one that was akin to the physically ill. And they were at least partially successful, for the treatment of the mentally ill *has* improved considerably over the years. But while treatment has improved, it is doubtful that people really regard the mentally ill in the same way that they view the physically ill. A broken leg is something one recovers from, but mental illness allegedly endures forever(18). A broken leg does not threaten the observer, but a crazy schizophrenic? There is by now a host of evidence that attitudes toward the mentally ill are characterized by fear, hostility, aloofness, suspicion, and dread (19). The mentally ill are society's lepers.

That such attitudes infect the general population is perhaps not surprising, only upsetting. But that they affect the professionals— attendants, nurses, physicians, psychologists, and social workers—who treat and deal with the mentally ill is more disconcerting, both because such attitudes are self-evidently pernicious and because they are un- witting. Most mental health professionals would insist that they are sympathetic toward the mentally ill, that they are neither avoidant nor hostile. But it is more likely that an exquisite ambivalence characterizes their relations with psychiatric patients, such that their avowed impulses are only part of their entire attitude. Negative attitudes are there too and can easily be detected. Such attitudes should not surprise us. They are the natural offspring of the labels patients wear and the places in which they are found.

Consider the structure of the typical psychiatric hospital. Staff and patients are strictly segregated. Staff have their own living space, including their dining facilities, bathrooms, and assembly places. The glassed quarters that contain the professional staff, which the pseudopatients came to call "the cage," sit out on every dayroom. The staff emerge primarily for caretaking purposes—to give medication, to conduct a therapy or group meeting, to instruct or reprimand a patient. Otherwise, staff keep to themselves, almost as if the disorder that afflicts their charges is somehow catching.

So much is patient-staff segregation the rule that, for four public hospitals in which an attempt was made to measure the degree to which staff and patients mingle, it was necessary to use "time out of the staff cage" as the operational measure. While it was not the case that all time spent out of the cage was spent mingling with patients (attendants, for example, would occasionally emerge to watch television in the dayroom), it was the only way in which one could gather reliable data on time for measuring.

The average amount of time spent by attendants outside of the cage was 11.3 percent (range, 3 to 52 percent). This figure does not represent only time spent mingling with patients, but also includes time spent on such chores as folding laundry, supervising patients while they shave, directing ward cleanup, and sending patients to off-ward activities. It was the relatively rare attendant who spent time talking with patients or playing games with them. It proved impossible to obtain a "percent mingling time" for nurses, since the amount of time they spent out of the cage was too brief. Rather, we counted instances of emergence from the cage. On the average, daytime nurses emerged from the cage 11.5 times per shift, including instances when they left the ward entirely (range, 4 to 39 times). Late afternoon and night nurses were even less available, emerging on the average 9.4 times per shift (range, 4 to 41 times). Data on early morning nurses, who arrived usually after midnight and departed at 8 a.m., are not available because patients were asleep during most of this period.

Physicians, especially psychiatrists, were even less available. They were rarely seen on the wards. Quite commonly, they would be seen only when they arrived and departed, with the remaining time being spent in their offices or in the cage. On the average, physicians emerged on the ward 6.7 times per day (range, 1 to 17 times). It proved difficult to make an accurate estimate in this regard, since physicians often maintained hours that allowed them to come and go at different times.

The hierarchical organization of the psychiatric hospital has been commented on before(20), but the latent meaning of that kind of organization is worth noting again. Those with the most power have least to do with patients, and those with the least power are most involved with them. Recall, however, that the acquisition of role-appropriate behaviors occurs mainly through the observation of others, with the most powerful having the most influence. Consequently, it is understandable that attendants not only spend more time with patients than do any other members of the staff—that is required by their station in the hierarchy—but also, insofar as they learn from their superiors' behavior, spend as little time with patients as they can. Attendants are seen mainly in the cage, which is where the models, the action, and the power are.

I turn now to a different set of studies, these dealing with staff response to patient-initiated contact. It has long been known that the amount of time a person spends with you can be an index of your significance to him. If he initiates and maintains eye contact, there is reason to believe that he is considering your requests and needs. If he pauses to chat or actually stops and talks, there is added reason to infer that he is individuating you. In four hospitals, the pseudopatient approached the staff member with a request which took the following form: "Pardon me, Mr. [or Dr. or Mrs.] X, could you tell me when I will be eligible for grounds privileges?" (or ". . .when I will be presented at the staff meeting?" or ". . .when I am likely to be discharged?"). While the content of the question varied according to the appropriateness of the target and the pseudopatient's (apparent) current needs the form was always a courteous and relevant request for information. Care was taken never to approach a particular member of the staff more than once a day, lest the staff member become suspicious or irritated. In examining these data, remember that the behavior of the pseudopatients was neither bizarre nor disruptive. One could indeed engage in good conversation with them.

The data for these experiments are shown in Table 1, separately for physicians (column 1) and for nurses and attendants (column 2). Minor differences between these four institutions were overwhelmed by the degree to which staff avoided continuing contacts that patients had initiated. By far, their most common response consisted of either a brief response to the question, offered while they were "on the move" and with head averted, or no response at all.

The encounter frequently took the following bizarre form: (pseudopatient) "Pardon me, Dr. X. Could you tell me when I am eligible for grounds privileges?" (physician) "Good morning, Dave. How are you

TABLE 1. Self-initiated contact by pseudopatients with psychiatrists and nurses and attendants, compared to contact with other groups.

Contact	Psychiatric hospitals		University campus (nonmedical)	University medical center — Physicians		
	(1) Psychiatrists	(2) Nurses and attendants	(3) Faculty	(4) "Looking for psychiatrist"	(5) "Looking for an internist"	(6) No additional comment
Responses						
Moves on, head averted (%)	71	88	0	0	0	0
Makes eye contact (%)	23	10	0	11	0	0
Pauses and chats (%)	2	2	0	11	0	0
Stops and talks (%)	4	0.5	100	78	100	90
Mean number of questions answered (out of 6)	*	*	6	3.8	4.8	4.5
Respondents (No.)	13	47	14	18	15	10
Attempts (No.)	185	1283	14	18	15	10

*Not applicable.

today?" (Moves off without waiting for a response.)

It is instructive to compare these data with data recently obtained at Stanford University. It has been alleged that large and eminent universities are characterized by faculty who are so busy that they have no time for students. For this comparison, a young lady approached individual faculty members who seemed to be walking purposefully to some meeting or teaching engagement and asked them the following six questions.

1. "Pardon me, could you direct me to Encina Hall?" (at the medical school: ". . .to the Clinical Research Center?")

2. "Do you know where Fish Annex is?" (there is no Fish Annex at Stanford).

3. "Do you teach here?"

4. "How does one apply for admission to the college?" (at the medical school: ". . .to the medical school?").

5. "Is it difficult to get in?"

6. "Is there financial aid?"

Without exception, as can be seen in Table 1 (column 3), all of the questions were answered. No matter how rushed they were, all respondents not only maintained eye contact, but stopped to talk. Indeed, many of the respondents went out of their way to direct or take the questioner to the office she was seeking, to try to locate "Fish Annex," or to discuss with her the possibilities of being admitted to the university.

Similar data, also shown in Table 1 (columns 4, 5, and 6), were obtained in the hospital. Here too, the young lady came prepared with six questions. After the first question, however, she remarked to 18 of her respondents (column 4), "I'm looking for a psychiatrist," and to 15 others (column 5), "I'm looking for an internist." Ten other respondents received no inserted comment (column 6). The general degree of cooperative responses is considerably higher for these university groups than it was for pseudopatients in psychiatric hospitals. Even so, differences are apparent within the medical school setting. Once having indicated that she was looking for a psychiatrist, the degree of cooperation elicited was less than when she sought an internist.

POWERLESSNESS AND DEPERSONALIZATION

Eye contact and verbal contact reflect concern and individuation; their absence, avoidance and depersonalization. The data I have presented do not do justice to the rich daily encounters that grew up around matters of depersonalization and avoidance. I have records of patients who were beaten by staff for the sin of having initiated verbal contact. During my own experience, for example, one patient was beaten in the presence of other patients for having approached an attendant and told him, "I like you." Occasionally, punishment meted out to patients for misdemeanors seemed so excessive that it could not be justified by the most radical interpretations of psychiatric canon. Nevertheless, they appeared to go unquestioned. Tempers were often short. A patient who had not heard a call for medication would be roundly excoriated, and the morning attendants would often wake patients with, "Come on, you m—f—s, out of bed!"

Neither anecdotal nor "hard" data can convey the overwhelming sense of powerlessness which invades the individual as he is continually exposed to the depersonalization of the psychiatric hospital. It hardly matters *which* psychiatric hospital—the execellent public ones and the very plush private hospital were better than the rural and shabby ones in this regard, but, again, the features that psychiatric hospitals had in common overwhelmed by far their apparent differences.

Powerlessness was evident everywhere. The patient is deprived of many of his legal rights by dint of this psychiatric commitment(21). He is shorn of credibility by virtue of his psychiatric label. His freedom of movement is restricted. He cannot initiate contact with the staff, but may only respond to such overtures as they make. Personal privacy is minimal. Patient quarters and possessions can be entered and examined by any staff member, for whatever reason. His personal history and anguish is available to any staff member (often including the "grey lady" and "candy striper" volunteer) who chooses to read his folder, regardless of their therapeutic relationship to him. His personal hygiene and waste evacuation are often monitored. The water closets may have no doors.

At times, depersonalization reached such proportions that pseudopatients had the sense that they were invisible, or at least unworthy of account. Upon being admitted, I and other pseudopatients took the initial physical examinations in a semipublic room, where staff members went about their own business as if we were not there.

On the ward, attendants delivered verbal and occasionally serious physical abuse to patients in the presence of other observing patients, some of whom (the pseudopatients) were writing it all down. Abusive behavior, on the other hand, terminated quite abruptly when other staff members were known to be coming. Staff are credible witnesses. Patients are not.

A nurse unbuttoned her uniform to adjust her brassiere in the presence of an entire ward of viewing men. One did not have the sense that she was being seductive. Rather, she didn't notice us. A group of staff persons might point to a patient in the dayroom and discuss him animatedly, as if he were not there.

One illuminating instance of depersonalization and invisibility occurred with regard to medications. All told, the pseudopatients were administered nearly 2100 pills, including Elavil, Stelazine, Compazine, and Thorazine, to name but a few. (That such a variety of medications should have been administered to patients presenting identical symptoms is itself worthy of note.) Only two were swallowed. The rest were either pocketed or deposited in the toilet. The pseudopatients were not alone in this. Although I have no precise records on how many patients rejected their medications, the pseudopatients frequently found the medications of other patients in the toilet before they deposited their own. As long as they were cooperative, their behavior and the pseudopatients' own in this matter, as in other important matters, went unnoticed throughout.

Reactions to such depersonalization among pseudopatients were intense. Although they had come to the hospital as participant observers and were fully aware that they did not "belong," they nevertheless found themselves caught up in and fighting the process of depersonalization. Some examples: a graduate student in psychology asked his wife to bring his textbooks to the hospital so he could "catch up on his homework"—this despite the elaborate precautions taken to conceal his professional association. The same student, who had trained for quite some time to get into the hospital, and who had looked forward to the experience, "remembered" some drag races that he had wanted to see on the weekend and insisted that he be discharged by that time. Another pseudopatient attempted a romance with a nurse. Subsequently, he informed the staff that he was applying for admission to graduate school in psychology and was very likely to be admitted, since a graduate professor was one of his regular hospital visitors. The same person began to engage in psychotherapy with other patients—all of this as a way of becoming a person in an impersonal environment.

THE SOURCES OF DEPERSONALIZATION

What are the origins of depersonalization? I have already mentioned two. First are attitudes held by all of us toward the mentally ill—including those who treat them—attitudes characterized by fear, distrust, and horrible expectations on the one hand, and benevolent intentions on the other. Our ambivalence leads, in this instance as in others, to avoidance.

Second, and not entirely separate, the hierarchical structure of the psychiatric hospital facilitates depersonalization. Those who are at the top have least to do with patients, and their behavior inspires the rest of the staff. Average daily contact with psychiatrists, psychologists, residents, and physicians combined ranged from 3.9 to 25.1 minutes, with an overall mean of 6.8 (six pseudopatients over a total of 129 days of hospitalization). Included in this average are time spent in the admissions interview, ward meetings in the presence of a senior staff member, group and individual psychotherapy contacts, case presentation conferences, and discharge meetings. Clearly, patients do not spend much time in interpersonal contact with doctoral staff. And doctoral staff serve as models for nurses and attendants.

There are probably other sources. Psychiatric installations are presently in serious financial straits. Staff shortages are pervasive, staff time at a premium. Something has to give, and that something is patient contact. Yet, while financial stresses are realities, too much can be made of them. I have the impression that the psychological forces that result in depersonalization are much stronger than the fiscal ones and that the addition of more staff would not correspondingly improve patient care in this regard. The incidence of staff meetings and the enormous amount of record-keeping on patients, for example, have not been as substantially reduced as has patient contact. Priorities exist, even during hard times. Patient contact is not a significant priority in the traditional psychiatric hospital, and fiscal pressures do not account for this. Avoidance and depersonalization may.

Heavy reliance upon psychotropic medication tacitly contributes to depersonalization by convincing staff that treatment is indeed being conducted and that further patient contact may not be necessary. Even here, however, caution needs to be exercised in understanding the role of psychotropic drugs. If patients were powerful rather than powerless, if they were viewed as interesting individuals rather than diagnostic entities, if they were socially significant rather than social lepers, if their anguish truly and wholly compelled our sympathies and concerns, would we not *seek* contact with them, despite the availability of medications? Perhaps for the pleasure of it all?

LABELING AND DEPERSONALIZATION

Whenever the ratio of what is known to what needs to be known approaches zero, we tend to invent "knowledge" and assume that we understand more than we actually do. We seem unable to acknowledge that we simply don't know. The needs for diagnosis and remediation of behavioral and emotional problems are enormous. But rather than acknowledge that we are just embarking on understanding, we continue to label patients "schizophrenic," "manic-depressive," and "insane," as if in those words we had captured the essence of understanding. The facts of the matter are that we have known for a long time that diagnoses are often not useful or reliable, but we have nevertheless continued to use them. We now know that we cannot distinguish insanity from sanity. It is depressing to consider how that information will be used.

Not merely depressing, but frightening. How many people, one wonders, are sane but not recognized as such in our psychiatric institutions? How many have been needlessly stripped of their privileges of citizenship, from the right to vote and drive to that of handling their own accounts? How many have feigned insanity in order to avoid the criminal consequences of their behavior, and, conversely, how many would rather stand trial than live interminably in a psychiatric hospital—but are wrongly thought to be mentally ill? How many have been stigmatized by well-intentioned, but nevertheless erroneous, diagnoses? On the last point, recall again that a "type 2 error" in psychiatric diagnosis does not have the same consequences it does in medical diagnosis. A diagnosis of cancer that has been found to be in error is cause for celebration. But psychiatric diagnoses are rarely found to be in error. The label sticks, a mark of inadequacy forever.

Finally, how many patients might be "sane" outside the psychiatric hospital but seem insane in it—not because craziness resides in them, as it were, but because they are responding to a bizarre setting, one that may be unique to institutions which harbor nether people? Goffman(4) calls the process of socialization to such institutions "mortification"—an apt metaphor that includes the processes of depersonalization that have been described here. And while it is impossible to know whether the pseudopatients' responses to these processes are characteristic of all inmates—they were, after all, not real patients—it is difficult to believe that these processes of socialization to a psychiatric hospital provide useful attitudes or habits of response for living in the "real world."

SUMMARY AND CONCLUSIONS

It is clear that we cannot distinguish the sane from the insane in psychiatric hospitals. The hospital itself imposes a special environment in which the meanings of behavior can easily be misunderstood. The consequences to patients hospitalized in such an environment—the powerlessness, depersonalization, segregation, mortification, and self-labeling—seem undoubtedly counter-therapeutic.

I do not, even now, understand this problem well enough to perceive solutions. But two matters seem to have some promise. The first concerns the proliferation of community mental health facilities, of crisis intervention centers, of the human potential movement, and of behavior therapies that, for all of their own problems, tend to avoid psychiatric labels, to focus on specific problems and behaviors, and to retain the individual in a relatively nonpejorative environment. Clearly, to the extent that we refrain from sending the distressed to insane places, our impressions of them are less likely to be distorted. (The risk of distorted perceptions, it seems to me, is always present, since we are much more sensitive to an individual's behaviors and verbalizations than we are to the subtle contextual stimuli that often promote them. At issue here is a matter of magnitude. And, as I have shown, the magnitude of distortion is exceedingly high in the extreme context that is a psychiatric hospital.)

The second matter that might prove promising speaks to the need to increase the sensitivity of mental health workers and researchers to the *Catch 22* position of psychiatric patients. Simply reading materials in this area will be of help to some such workers and researchers. For others, directly experiencing the impact of psychiatric hospitalization will be of enormous use. Clearly, further research into the social psychology of such total institutions will both facilitate treatment and deepen understanding.

I and the other pseudopatients in the psychiatric setting had distinctly negative reactions. We do not pretend to describe the subjective experiences of true patients. Theirs may be different from ours, particularly with the passage of time and the necessary process of adaptation to one's environment. But we can and do speak to the relatively more objective indices of treatment within the hospital. It could be a mistake, and a very unfortunate one, to consider that what happened to us derived from malice or stupidity on the part of the staff. Quite the contrary, our overwhelming impression of them was of people who really cared, who were committed and who were uncommonly intelligent. Where they failed, as they sometimes did painfully, it would be more accurate to attribute those failures to the environment in which they, too, found themselves than to personal callousness. Their perceptions and behavior were controlled by the situation, rather than being motivated by a malicious disposition. In a more benign environment, one that was less attached to global diagnosis, their behaviors and judgments might have been more benign and effective.

NOTES

(1) P. Ash, *J. Abnorm. Soc. Psychol.* 44, 272 (1949); A. T. Beck, *Amer. J. Psychiat.* 119, 210 (1962); A. T. Boisen, *Psychiatry* 2, 233 (1938); N. Kreitman, *J. Ment. Sci.* 107, 876 (1961); N. Kreitman, P. Sainsbury, J. Morrisey, J. Towers, J. Scrivener, *ibid.*, p. 887; H. O. Schmitt and C. P. Fonda, *J. Abnorm. Soc. Psychol.* 52, 262 (1956); W. Seeman, *J. Nerv. Ment. Dis.* 118, 541 (1953). For an analysis of these artifacts and summaries of the disputes, see J. Zubin, *Annu. Rev. Psychol.* 18, 373 (1967); L. Phillips and J. G. Draguns, *ibid.* 22, 447 (1971).

(2) R. Benedict, *J. Gen. Psychol.* 10, 59 (1934).

(3) See in this regard H. Becker, *Outsiders: Studies in the Sociology of Deviance* (Free Press, New York, 1963); B. M. Braginsky, D. D. Braginsky, K. Ring, *Methods of Madness: The Mental Hospital as a Last Resort* (Holt, Rinehart & Winston, New York, 1969); G. M. Crocetti and P. V. Lemkau, *Amer. Sociol. Rev.* 30, 577 (1965); E. Goffman, *Behavior in Public Places* (Free Press, New York, 1964); R. D. Laing, *The Divided Self: A Study of Sanity and Madness* (Quadrangle, Chicago, 1960); D. L. Phillips, *Amer. Sociol. Rev.* 28, 963 (1963); T. R. Sarbin, *Psychol. Today* 6, 18 (1972); E. Schur, *Amer. J. Sociol.* 75, 309 (1969); T. Szasz, *Law, Liberty and Psychiatry* (Macmillan, New York, 1963); *The Myth of Mental Illness: Foundations of a Theory of Mental Illness* (Hoeber-Harper, New York, 1963). For a critique of some of these views, see W. R. Gove. *Amer. Sociol. Rev.* 35, 873 (1970).

(4) E. Goffman, *Asylums* (Doubleday, Garden City, N.Y., 1961).

(5) T. J. Scheff, *Being Mentally Ill: A Sociological Theory* (Aldine, Chicago, 1966).

(6) Data from a ninth pseudopatient are not incorporated in this report because, although his sanity went undetected, he falsified aspects of his personal history, including his marital status and parental relationships. His experimental behaviors therefore were not identical to those of the other pseudopatients.

(7) A. Barry, *Bellevue Is a State of Mind* (Harcourt Brace Jovanovich, New York, 1971); I. Belknap, *Human Problems of a State Mental Hospital* (McGraw-Hill, New York, 1956); W. Caudill, F. C. Redlich, H. R. Gilmore, E. B. Brody, *Amer. J. Orthopsychiat.* 22, 314 (1952); A. R. Goldman, R. H. Bohr, T. A. Steinberg, *Prof. Psychol.* 1, 427 (1970); unauthored, *Roche Report* 1 (No. 13), 8 (1971).

(8) Beyond the personal difficulties that the pseudopatient is likely to experience in the hospital, there are legal and social ones that, combined, require considerable attention before entry. For example, once admitted to a psychiatric institution, it is difficult, if not impossible, to be discharged on short notice, state law to the contrary notwithstanding. I was not sensitive to these dificulties at the outset of the project nor to the personal and situational emergencies that can arise, but later a writ of habeas corpus was prepared for each of the entering pseudopatients and an attorney was kept "on call" during every hospitalization. I am grateful to John Kaplan and Robert Bartels for legal advice and assistance in these matters.

(9) However distasteful such concealment is, it was a necessary first step to examining these questions. Without concealment, there would have been no way to know how valid these experiences were; nor was there any way of knowing whether whatever detections occurred were a tribute to the diagnostic acumen of the staff or to the hospital's rumor

network. Obviously, since my concerns are general ones that cut across individual hospitals and staffs, I have respected their anonymity and have eliminated clues that might lead to their identification.

(10) Interestingly, of the 12 admissions, 11 were diagnosed as schizophrenic and one, with the identical symptomatology, as manic-depressive psychosis. This diagnosis has a more favorable prognosis, and it was given by the only private hospital in our sample. On the relations between social class and psychiatric diagnosis, see A. deB. Hollingshead and F. C. Redlich, *Social Class and Mental Illness: A Community Study* (Wiley, New York, 1958).

(11) It is possible, of course, that patients have quite broad latitudes in diagnosis and therefore are inclined to call many people sane, even those whose behavior is patently aberrant. However, although we have no hard data on this matter, it was our distinct impression that this was not the case. In many instances, patients not only singled us out for attention, but came to imitate our behaviors and styles.

(12) J. Cumming and E. Cumming, *Community Ment. Health* 1, 135 (1965); A. Farina and K. Ring, *J. Abnorm. Psychol.* 70, 47 (1965); H. E. Freeman and O. G. Simmons, *The Mental Patient Comes Home* (Wiley, New York, 1963); W. J. Johannsen, *Ment. Hygiene* 53, 218 (1969); A. S. Linsky, *Soc. Psychiat.* 5, 166 (1970).

(13) S. E. Asch. *J. Abnorm. Soc. Psychol.* 41, 258 (1946); *Social Psychology* (Prentice-Hall, New York, 1952).

(14) See also I. N. Mensh and J. Wishner, *J. Personality* 16, 188 (1947); J. Wishner, *Psychol. Rev.* 67, 96 (1960); J. S. Bruner and R. Tagiuri, in *Handbook of Social Psychology*, G. Lindzey, Ed. (Addison-Wesley, Cambridge. Mass., 1954), vol. 2, pp. 634–654; J. S. Bruner, D. Shapiro, R. Tagiuri, in *Person Perception and Interpersonal Behavior*, R. Tagiuri and L. Petrullo, Eds. (Stanford Univ. Press, Stanford, Calif., 1958), pp. 277–288.

(15) For an example of a similar self-fulfilling prophecy, in this instance dealing with the "central" trait of intelligence, see R. Rosenthal and L. Jacobson, *Pygmalion in the Classroom* (Holt, Rinehart & Winston, New York, 1968).

(16) E. Zigler and L. Phillips, *J. Abnorm. Soc. Psychol.* 63, 69 (1961). See also R. K. Freudenberg and J. P. Robertson, *A.M.A. Arch, Neurol. Psychiatr.* 76, 14 (1956).

(17) W. Mischel, *Personality and Assessment* (Wiley, New York, 1968).

(18) The most recent and unfortunate instance of this tenet is that of Senator Thomas Eagleton.

(19) T. R. Sarbin and J. C. Mancuso, *J. Clin. Consult. Psychol.* 35, 159 (1970); T. R. Sarbin, *ibid.* 31, 447 (1967); J. C. Nunnally, Jr. *Popular*

Conceptions of Mental Health (Holt, Rinehart & Winston, New York, 1961).

(20) A. H. Stanton and M. S. Schwartz, *The Mental Hospital: A Study of Institutional Participation in Psychiatric Illness and Treatment* (Basic, New York, 1954).

(21) D. B. Wexler and S. E. Scoville, *Ariz. Law Rev.* 13, 1 (1971).

(22) I thank W. Mischel, E. Orne, and M. S. Rosenhan for comments on an earlier draft of this manuscript.

On Pseudoscience in Science, Logic in Remission, and Psychiatric Diagnosis: A Critique of Rosenhan's "On Being Sane In Insane Places"

Robert L. Spitzer

Some foods taste delicious but leave a bad aftertaste. So it is with Rosenhan's study, "On Being Sane in Insane Places" (Rosenhan, 1973a), which by virtue of the prestige and wide distribution of *Science,* the journal in which it appeared, provoked a furor in the scientific community. That the *Journal of Abnormal Psychology,* at this late date, chooses to explore the study's strengths and weaknesses is a testament not only to the importance of the issues that the study purports to deal with but to the impact that the study has had in the mental health community.

Rosenhan apparently believes that psychiatric diagnosis is of no value. There is nothing wrong with his designing a study the results of which might dramatically support this view. However, "On Being Sane in Insane Places" is pseudoscience presented as science. Just as his pseudopatients were diagnosed at discharge as "schizophrenia, in remission," so a careful examination of this study's methods, results, and conclusions leads me to a diagnosis of "logic, in remission."

Let us summarize the study's central question, the methods used, the results reported, and Rosenhan's conclusions. Rosenhan (1973a) states the basic issue simply: "Do the salient characteristics that lead to diagnoses reside in the patients themselves or in the environments and contexts in which observers find them?" Rosenhan proposed that by getting normal people who had never had symptoms of serious psychiatric disorders admitted to psychiatric hospitals "and then determining whether they were discovered to be sane" was an adequate method of studying this question. Therefore, eight "sane" people, pseudopatients, gained secret admission to 12 different hospitals with a single complaint of hearing voices. Upon admission to the psychiatric ward, the pseudopatients ceased simulating any symptoms of abnormality.

The diagnostic results were that 11 of the 12 diagnoses on admission were schizophrenia and 1 was manic-depressive psychosis. At discharge, all of the patients were given the same diagnosis, but were qualified as "in remission."(1) Despite their "show of sanity" the pseudopatients were never detected by any of the professional staff, nor were any questions raised about their authenticity during the entire hospitalization.

Rosenhan (1973a) concluded: "It is clear that we cannot distinguish the sane from the insane in psychiatric hospitals" (p. 257). According to him, what is needed is the avoidance of "global diagnosis," as exemplified by such diagnoses as schizophrenia or manic-depressive psychosis, and attention should be directed instead to "behaviors, the stimuli that provoke them, and their correlates."

THE CENTRAL QUESTION

One hardly knows where to begin. Let us first acknowledge the potential importance of the study's central research question. Surely, if psychiatric diagnoses are, to quote Rosenhan, "only in the minds of the observers," and do not reflect any characteristics inherent in the patient, then they obviously can be of no use in helping patients. However, the study immediately becomes confused when Rosenhan suggests that this research question can be answered by studying whether or not the "sanity" of pseudopatients in a mental hospital can be discovered. Rosenhan, a professor of law and psychology, knows that the terms "sane" and "insane" are legal, not psychiatric, concepts. He knows that no psychiatrist makes a diagnosis of "sanity" or "insanity" and that the true meaning of these terms, which varies from state to state, involves the inability to appreciate right from wrong—an issue that is totally irrelevant to this study.

DETECTING THE SANITY OF A PSEUDOPATIENT

However, if we are forced to use the terms "insane" (to mean roughly showing signs of serious mental disturbance) and "sane" (the absence of such signs), then clearly there are three possible meanings to the concept of "detecting the sanity" of a pseudopatient who feigns mental illness on entry to a hospital, but then acts "normal" throughout his hospital stay. The first is the recognition, when he is first seen, that the pseudopatient is feigning insanity as he attempts to gain admission to the hospital. This would be detecting sanity in a sane person simulating insanity. The second would be the recognition, after having observed him acting normally during his hospitalization, that the pseudopatient was initially feigning insanity. This would be detecting that the currently sane never was insane. Finally, the third possible meaning would be the recognition, during hospitalization, that the pseudopatient, though initially appearing to be "insane," was no longer showing signs of psychiatric disturbance.

These elementary distinctions of "detecting sanity in the insane" are crucial to properly interpreting the results of the study. The reader is misled by Rosenhan's implication that the first two meanings of detecting the sanity of the pseudopatients, which involve determining the pseudopatient to be a fraud, are at all relevant to the central research question. Furthermore, he obscures the true results of his study—because they fail to support his conclusion—when the third meaning of detecting sanity is considered, that is, a recognition that after their admission as "insane," the pseudopatients were not psychiatrically disturbed while in the hospital.

Let us examine these three possible meanings of detecting the sanity of the pseudopatient, their logical relation to the central question of the study, and the actual results obtained and the validity of Rosenhan's conclusions.

THE PATIENT IS NO LONGER "INSANE"

We begin with the third meaning of detecting sanity. It is obvious that if the psychiatrists judged the pseudopatients as seriously disturbed while they acted "normal" in the hospital, this would be strong evidence that their assessments were being influenced by the context in which they were making their examination rather than the actual behavior of the patient, which is the central research question. I suspect that many readers will agree with Hunter who, in a letter to *Science* [Hunter, 1973], pointed out that,

> The pseudopatients did *not* behave normally in the hospital. Had their behavior been normal, they would have walked to the nurses' station and said, 'Look, I am a normal person who tried to see if I could get into the hospital by behaving in a crazy way or saying crazy things. It worked and I was admitted to the hospital, but now I would like to be discharged from the hospital' [p. 361].

What were the results? According to Rosenhan, all the patients were diagnosed at discharge as "in remission." (2) The meaning of "in remission" is clear: It means without signs of illness. Thus, all of the psychiatrists apparently recognized that all of the pseudopatients were, to use Rosenhan's term, "sane." However, lest the reader appreciate the significance of these findings, Rosenhan (1973a) quickly gives a completely incorrect interpretation: "If the pseudopatient was to be discharged, he must naturally be 'in remission'; but he was not sane, nor, in the institution's view, had he ever been sane" (p. 252). Rosenhan's implication is clear: The patient was diagnosed "in remission" not because the psychiatrist correctly assessed the patient's hospital behavior but only because the patient had to be discharged. Is this interpretation warranted?

I am sure that most readers who are not familiar with the details of psychiatric diagnostic practice assume, from Rosenhan's account, that it is common for schizophrenic patients to be diagnosed "in remission" when discharged from a hospital. As a matter of fact, it is extremely unusual. The reason is that a schizophrenic is rarely completely asymptomatic at discharge. Rosenhan does not report any data concerning the discharge diagnoses of the real schizophrenic patients in the 12 hospitals used in his study. However, I can report on the frequency of a discharge diagnosis of schizophrenia "in remission" at my hospital, the New York State Psychiatric Institute, a research, teaching, and community hospital where diagnoses are made in a routine fashion, undoubtedly no different from the 12 hospitals of Rosenhan's study. I examined the official book that the record room uses to record the discharge diagnoses and their statistical codes for all patients. Of the over 300 patients discharged in the last year with a diagnosis of schizophrenia, not one was diagnosed "in remission." It is only possible to code a diagnosis of "in remission" by adding a fifth digit to the 4-digit code number for the subtype of schizophrenia (e.g., paranoid schizophrenia is coded as 295.3, but paranoid schizophrenia "in remission" is coded as 295.35). I therefore realized that a psychiatrist might intend to make a discharge diagnosis of "in remission" but fail to use the fifth digit, so that the official recording of the diagnosis would not reflect his full assessment. I therefore had research assistants read the discharge summaries of the last 100 patients whose discharge diagnosis was schizophrenia to see how often the term "in remission," "recovered," "no longer ill," or "asymptomatic" was used, even if not recorded by use of the fifth digit in the code number. The result was that only one patient, who was diagnosed paranoid schizophrenia, was described in the summary as being "in remission" at discharge. The fifth digit code was not used.

To substantiate my view that the practice at my hospital of rarely giving a discharge diagnosis of schizophrenia "in remission" is not unique, I had a research assistant call the record room librarians of 12 psychiatric hospitals, chosen catch as catch can.(3) They were told that we were interested in knowing their estimate of how often, at their hospital, schizophrenics were discharged "in remission" (or "no longer ill" or "asymptomatic"). The calls revealed that 11 of the 12 hospitals indicated that the term was either never used or, at most, used for only a handful of patients in a year. The remaining hospital, a private hospital, estimated that the term was used in roughly 7 % of the discharge diagnoses.

This leaves us with the conclusion that, because 11 of the 12 pseudopatients were discharged as "schizophrenia in remission," a discharge diagnosis that is rarely given to real schizophrenics, the diagnoses given to the pseudopatients were a function of the patients' behaviors and not of the setting (psychiatric hospital) in which the diagnoses were made. In fact, we must marvel that 11 psychiatrists all acted so rationally as to use at discharge the category of "in remission" or its equivalent, a category that is rarely used with real schizophrenic patients.

It is not only in his discharge diagnosis that the psychiatrist had an opportunity to assess the patient's true condition incorrectly. In the admission mental status examination, during a progress note or in his discharge note the psychiatrist could have described any of the pseudopatients as "still psychotic," "probably still hallucinating but denies it now," "loose associations," or "inappropriate affect." Because Rosenhan had access to all of this material, his failure to report such judgments of continuing serious psychopathology strongly suggests that they were never made.

All pseudopatients took extensive notes publicly to obtain data on staff and patient behavior. Rosenhan claims that the nursing records indicate that "the writing was seen as an aspect of their pathological behavior." The only datum presented to support this claim is that the daily nursing comment on one of the pseudopatients was, "Patient engages in writing behavior." Because nursing notes frequently and intentionally comment on nonpathological activities that patients engage in so that other staff members have some knowledge of how the patient spends his time, this particular nursing note in no way supports Rosenhan's thesis. Once again, the failure of Rosenhan to provide data regarding instances where normal hospital behavior was categorized as pathological is remarkable. The closest that Rosenhan comes to providing such data is his report of an instance where a kindly nurse asked if a pseudopatient, who was pacing the long hospital corridors because of boredom, was "nervous." It was, after all, a question and not a final judgment.

Let us now examine the relation between the other two meanings of detecting sanity in the pseudopatients: the recognition that the pseudopatient was a fraud, either when he sought admission to the hospital or during this hospital stay, and the central research question.

DETECTING "SANITY" BEFORE ADMISSION

Whether or not psychiatrists are able to detect individuals who feign psychiatric symptoms is an interesting question but clearly of no relevance to the issue of whether or not the salient characteristics that lead to diagnoses reside in the patient's behavior or in the minds of the observers. After all, a psychiatrist who believes a pseudopatient who feigns a symptom *is* responding to the pseudopatient's behavior. And Rosenhan does not blame the psychiatrist for believing the pseudopatient's fake symptom of hallucinations. He blames him for the diagnosis of schizophrenia. Rosenhan (1973b) states:

> The issue is not that the psychiatrist believed him. Neither is it whether the pseudopatient should have been admitted to the psychiatric hospital in the first place. . . . The issue is the diagnostic leap that was made between the single presenting symptom, hallucinations, and the diagnosis schizophrenia (or in one case, manic-depressive psychosis). Had the pseudopatients been diagnosed "hallucinating," there would have been no further need to examine the diagnosis issue. The diagnosis of hallucinations implies only that: no more. The presence of hallucinations does not itself define the presence of "schizophrenia." And schizophrenia may or may not include hallucinations. (p. 366)

Unfortunately, as judged by many of the letters to *Science* commenting on the study (Letters to the editor, 1973), many readers, including psychiatrists, accepted Rosenhan's thesis that it was irrational for the psychiatrists to have made an initial diagnosis of schizophrenia as *the most likely condition* on the basis of a single symptom. In my judgment, these readers were wrong. Their acceptance of Rosenhan's thesis was aided by the content of the pseudopatients' auditory hallucinations, which were voices that said "empty," "hollow," and "thud." According to Rosenhan (1973a), these symptoms were chosen because of "their apparent similarity to existential symptoms [and] the *absence* of a single report of existential psychoses in the literature" (p. 251). The implication is that if the content of specific symptoms has never been reported in the literature, then a psychiatrist should somehow know that the symptom is fake. Why then, according to Rosenhan, should the psychiatrist have made a diagnosis of hallucinating? This is absurd. Recently I saw a patient who kept hearing a voice that said, "It's O.K. It's O.K." I know of no such report in the literature. So what? I agree with Rosenhan that there has never been a report of an "existential psychosis." However, the diagnoses made were schizophrenia and manic-depressive psychosis, not existential psychosis.

DIFFERENTIAL DIAGNOSIS OF AUDITORY HALLUCINATIONS

Rosenhan is entitled to believe that psychiatric diagnoses are of no use and therefore should not have been given to the pseudopatients. However, it makes no sense for him to claim that within a diagnostic framework it was irrational to consider schizophrenia seriously as the most likely condition without his presenting a consideration of the differential diagnosis. Let me briefly give what I think is a reasonable differential diagnosis, based on the presenting picture of the pseudopatient when he applied for admission to the hospital.

Rosenhan says that "beyond alleging the symptoms and falsifying name, vocation, and employment, no further alterations of person, history, or circumstances were made" (p. 251). However, clearly the clinical picture includes not only the symptom (auditory hallucinations) but also the desire to enter a psychiatric hospital, from which it is reasonable to conclude that the symptom is a source of significant distress. (How often did the admitting psychiatrist suggest what would seem to be reasonable care: outpatient treatment? Did the pseudopatient have to add other complaints to justify inpatient treatment?) This, plus the knowledge that the auditory hallucinations are of 3 weeks duration, (4) establishes the hallucinations as significant symptoms of psychopathology as distinguished from so-called "pseudohallucinations" (hallucinations while falling asleep or awakening from sleep, or intense imagination with the voice heard from inside of the head).

Auditory hallucinations can occur in several kinds of mental disorders. The absence of a history of alcohol, drug abuse, or some other toxin, the absence of any signs of physical illness (such as high fever), and the absence of evidence of distractibility, impairment in concentration, memory or orientation, and a negative neurological examination all make an organic psychosis extremely unlikely. The absence of a recent precipitating stress rules out a transient situational disturbance of psychotic intensity or (to use a nonofficial category) hysterical psychosis. The absence of a profound disturbance in mood rules out an affective psychosis (we are not given the mental status findings for the patient who was diagnosed manic-depressive psychosis).

What about simulating mental illness? Psychiatrists know that occasionally an individual who has something to gain from being admitted into a psychiatric hospital will exaggerate or even feign psychiatric symptoms. This is a genuine diagnostic problem that psychiatrists and other physicians occasionally confront and is called "malingering." However, with the pseudopatients there was no reason to believe that any of them had anything to gain from being admitted into a psychiatric hospital except relief from their alleged complaint, and therefore no reason to suspect that the illness was feigned. Dear reader: There is only one remaining diagnosis for the presenting symptom of hallucinations under these conditions in the classification of mental disorders used in this country, and that is schizophrenia.

Admittedly, there is a hitch to a definitive diagnosis of schizophrenia: Almost invariably there are other signs of the disorder present, such as poor premorbid adjustment, affective blunting, delusions, or signs of thought disorder. I would hope that if I had been one of the 12 psychiatrists presented with such a patient, I would have been struck by the lack of other signs of the disorder, but I am rather sure that having no reason to doubt the authenticity of the patients' claim of auditory hallucinations, I also would have been fooled into noting schizophrenia as the most likely diagnosis.

What does Rosenhan really mean when he objects to the diagnosis of schizophrenia because it was based on a "single symptom?" Does he believe that there are real patients with the single symptom of auditory hallucinations who are misdiagnosed as schizophrenic when they actually have some other condition? If so, what is the nature of that condition? Is Rosenhan's point that the psychiatrist should have used "diagnosis deferred," a category that is available but rarely used? I would have no argument with this conclusion. Furthermore, if he had presented data from real patients indicating how often patients are erroneously diagnosed on the basis of inadequate information and what the consequences were, it would have been a real contribution.

Until now, I have assumed that the pseudopatients presented only one symptom of psychiatric disorder. Actually, we know very little about how the pseudopatients presented themselves. What did the pseudopatients say in the study reported in *Science*, when asked, as they must have been, what effect the hallucinations were having on their lives and why they were seeking admission into a hospital? The reader would be much more confident that a single presenting symptom was involved if Rosenhan had made available for each pseudopatient the actual admission work-up from the hospital record.

DETECTING SANITY AFTER ADMISSION

Let us now examine the last meaning of detecting sanity in the pseudopatients, namely, the psychiatrist's recognition, *after* observing him act normally during his hospitalization, that the pseudopatient was initially feigning insanity and its relation to the central research question. If a diagnostic condition, by definition, is always chronic and never remits, it would be irrational not to question the original diagnosis if a patient were later found to be asymptomatic. As applied to this study, if the concept of schizophrenia did not admit the possibility of recovery, then failure to question the original diagnosis when the pseudopatients were no longer overtly ill would be relevant to the central research question. It would be an example of the psychiatrist allowing the context of the hospital environment to influence his diagnostic behavior. But neither any psychiatric textbook nor the American Psychiatric Association's *Diagnostic and Statistical Manual of Mental Disorders* (American Psychiatric Association, 1968) suggests that mental illnesses endure forever. Oddly enough, it is Rosenhan (1973a) who, without any reference to the psychiatric literature, says: "A broken leg is something one recovers from, but mental illness allegedly endures forever" (p.254). Who, other than Rosenhan, alleges it?

As Rosenhan should know, although some American psychiatrists restrict the label of schizophrenia to mean chronic or process schizophrenia, most American psychiatrists include an acute subtype from which there often is a remission. Thus, the *Diagnostic and Statistical Manual*, in describing the subtype, acute schizophrenic episode, states that "in many cases the patient recovers within weeks."

A similar straw man is created when Rosenhan (1973a) says,

> The insane are not always insane . . . the bizarre behaviors upon which their [the pseudopatients] behaviors were allegedly predicated constituted only a small fraction of their total behavior. If it makes no sense to label ourselves permanently depressed on the basis of an occasional depression, then it takes better evidence than is presently available to label all patients insane or schizophrenic on the basis of behaviors or cognitions. (p. 254)

Who ever said that the behaviors that indicate schizophrenia or any other diagnostic category comprise the total of a patient's behavior? A diagnosis of schizophrenia does not mean that all of the patient's behavior is schizophrenic anymore than a diagnosis of carcinoma of the liver means that all of the patient's body is diseased.

Does Rosenhan at least score a point by demonstrating that, although the professional staff never considered the possibility that the pseudopatient was a fraud, this possibility was often considered by other patients? Perhaps, but I am not so sure. Let us not forget that all of the pseudopatients "took extensive notes publicly." Obviously this was highly unusual patient behavior and Rosenhan's quote from a suspicious patient suggests the importance it had in focusing the other patients' attention on the pseudopatients: "You're not crazy. You're a journalist or a professor [referring to the continual notetaking]. You're checking up on the hospital" (Rosenhan, 1973a, p. 252)

Rosenhan presents ample evidence, which I find no reason to dispute, that the professional staff spent little time actually with the pseudopatients. The note-taking may easily have been overlooked, and therefore they developed no suspicion that the pseudopatients had simulated illness to gain entry into the hospital. Because there were no pseudopatients who did not engage in such unusual behaviors, the reader cannot assess the significance of the patients' suspicions of fraud when the professional staff did not. I would predict, however, that a pseudopatient in a ward of patients with mixed diagnostic conditions would have no difficulty in masquerading convincingly as a true patient to both staff and patients if he did nothing unusual to draw attention to himself.

Rosenhan presents one way in which the diagnosis affected the psychiatrist's perception of the patient's circumstances: Historical facts of the case were often distorted by the staff to achieve consistency with psychodynamic theories. Here, for the first time, I believe Rosenhan has hit the mark. What he described happens all the time and often makes attendance at clinical case conferences extremely painful, especially for those with a logical mind and a research orientation. Although his observation is correct, it would seem to be more a consequence of individuals attempting to rearrange facts to comply with an unproven etiological theory than a consequence of diagnostic labeling. One could as easily imagine a similar process occurring when a weak-minded, behaviorally-oriented clinician attempts to rewrite the patient's history to account for "hallucinations reinforced by attention paid to patient by family members when patient complains of hearing voices." Such is the human condition.

One final finding requires comment. In order to determine whether "the tendency toward diagnosing the sane insane could be reversed," the staff of a research and teaching hospital was informed that at some time during the following three months, one or more pseudopatients would attempt to be admitted. No such attempt was actually made. Yet approximately 10 % of 193 real patients were suspected by two or more staff members (we are not told how many made judgments) to be pseudopatients. Rosenhan (1973a) concluded: "Any diagnostic process that lends itself so readily to massive errors of this sort cannot be a very reliable one" (p. 179). My conclusion is that this experimental design practically assures only one outcome.

RELIABILITY OF CLASSIFICATION

Some very important principles that are relevant to the design of Rosenhan's study are taught in elementary psychology courses and should not be forgotten. One of them is that a measurement or classification procedure is not reliable or unreliable in itself but only in its application to a specific population. There are serious problems in the reliability of psychiatric diagnosis as it is applied to the population to which psychiatric diagnoses are ordinarily given. However, I fail to see, and Rosenhan does not even attempt to show, how the reliability of psychiatric diagnoses applied to a population of individuals seeking help is at all relevant to the reliability of psychiatric diagnoses applied to a population of pseudopatients (or one including the threat of pseudopatients). The two populations are just not the same. Kety (1974) has expressed it dramatically:

> If I were to drink a quart of blood and, concealing what I had done, come to the emergency room of any hospital vomiting blood, the behavior of the staff would be quite predictable. If they labeled and treated me as having a bleeding peptic ulcer, I doubt that I could argue convincingly that medical science does not know how to diagnose that condition. (p. 959)

(I have no doubt that if the condition known as pseudopatient ever assumed epidemic proportions among admittants to psychiatric hospitals, psychiatrists would in time become adept at identifying them, though at what risk to real patients, I do not know.)

ATTITUDES TOWARD THE INSANE

I shall not dwell on the latter part of Rosenhan's study, which deals with the experience of psychiatric hospitalization. Because some of the hospitals participated in residency training programs and were research oriented, I find it hard to believe that conditions were quite as bad as depicted, but they may well be. I have always believed that psychiatrists should spend more time on psychiatric wards to appreciate how mind dulling the experience must be for patients. However, Rosenhan does not stop at documenting the horrors of life on a psychiatric ward. He asserts, without a shred of evidence from his study, that "negative attitudes [towards psychiatric patients] are the natural offspring of the labels patients wear and the places in which they are found." This is nonsense. In recent years large numbers of chronic psychiatric patients, many of them chronic schizophrenics and geriatric patients with organic brain syndromes, have been discharged from state hospitals and placed in communities that have no facilities to deal with them. The affected communities are up in arms not primarily because they are mental patients labeled with psychiatric diagnoses (because the majority are not recognized as ex-patients) but because the behavior of some of them is sometimes incomprehensible, deviant, strange, and annoying.

There are at least two psychiatric diagnoses that are defined by the presence of single behaviors, much as Rosenhan would prefer a diagnosis of hallucinations to a diagnosis of schizophrenia. They are alcoholism and drug abuse. Does society have negative attitudes toward these individuals because of the diagnostic label attached to them by psychiatrists or because of their behavior?

THE USES OF DIAGNOSIS

Rosenhan believes that the pseudopatients should have been diagnosed as having hallucinations of unknown origin. It is not clear what he thinks the diagnosis should have been if the pseudopatients had been sufficiently trained to talk, at times, incoherently, and had complained of difficulty in thinking clearly, lack of emotion, and that their thoughts were being broadcast so that strangers knew what they were thinking. Is Rosenhan perhaps suggesting multiple diagnoses of hallucinations, difficulty thinking clearly, lack of emotion, and incoherent speech . . . all of unknown origin?

It is no secret that we lack a full understanding of such conditions as schizophrenia and manic-depressive illness, but are we quite as ignorant as Rosenhan would have us believe? Do we not know, for example, that hallucinations, in the context just described, are symptomatic of a different condition than are hallucinations of voices accusing the patient of sin when associated with depressed affect, diurnal mood variation, loss of appetite, and insomnia? What about hallucinations of God's voice issuing commandments, associated with euphoric affect, psychomotor excitement, and accelerated and disconnected speech? Is this not also an entirely different condition?

There is a purpose to psychiatric diagnosis (Spitzer & Wilson, 1975). It is to enable mental health professionals to communicate with each other about the subject matter of their concern, comprehend the pathological processes involved in psychiatric illness, and control psychiatric disorders.

Control consists of the ability to predict outcome, prevent the disorder from developing, and treat it once it has developed. Any serious discussion of the validity of psychiatric diagnosis, or suggestions for alternative systems of classifying psychological disturbance, must address itself to these purposes of psychiatric diagnosis.

In terms of its ability to accomplish these purposes, I would say that psychiatric diagnosis is moderately effective as a shorthand way of communicating the presence of constellations of signs and symptoms that tend to cluster together, is woefully inadequate in helping us understand the pathological processes of psychiatric disorders, but does offer considerable help in the control of many mental disorders. Control is possible because psychiatric diagnosis often yields information of value in predicting the likely course of illness (e.g., an early recovery, chronicity, or recurrent episodes) and because for many mental disorders it is useful in suggesting the best available treatment.

Let us return to the three different clinical conditions that I described, each of which had auditory hallucinations as one of its manifestations. The reader will have no difficulty in identifying the three hypothetical conditions as schizophrenia, psychotic depression, and mania. Anyone familiar with the literature on psychiatric treatment will know that there are numerous well controlled studies (Klein & Davis, 1969) indicating the superiority of the major tranquilizers for the treatment of schizophrenia, of electroconvulsive therapy for the treatment of psychotic depression and, more recently, of lithium carbonate for the treatment of mania. Furthermore, there is convincing evidence that these three conditions, each of which is often accompanied by hallucinations, are influenced by separate genetic factors. As Kety (1974) said, "If schizophrenia is a myth, it is a myth with a strong genetic component."

Should psychiatric diagnosis be abandoned for a purely descriptive system that focuses on simple phenotypic behaviors before it has been demonstrated that such an approach is more useful as a guide to successful treatment or for understanding the role of genetic factors? I think not. (I have a vision. Traditional psychiatric diagnosis has long been forgotten. At a conference on behavioral classification, a keen research investigator proposes that the category "hallucinations of unknown etiology" be subdivided into three different groups based on associated symptomatology. The first group is characterized by depressed affect, diurnal mood variation, and so on, the second group by euphoric mood, psychomotor excitement . . . .)

If psychiatric diagnosis is not quite as bad as Rosenhan would have us believe, that does not mean that it is all that good. What is the reliability of psychiatric diagnosis? A review of the major studies of the reliability of psychiatric diagnosis prior to 1972 (Spitzer & Fleiss, 1974) revealed that "reliability is only satisfactory for three categories: mental deficiencies, organic brain syndrome, and alcoholism. The level of reliability is no better than fair for psychosis and schizophrenia, and is poor for the remaining categories." So be it. But where did Rosenhan get the idea that psychiatry is the only medical specialty that is plagued by inaccurate diagnosis? Studies have shown serious unreliability in the diagnosis of pulmonary disorders (Fletcher, 1952), in the interpretation of electrocardiograms (Davies, 1958), in the interpretation of X-rays, (Cochrane & Garland, 1952; Yerushalmy, 1947), and in the certification of causes of death (Markush, Schaaf, & Siegel, 1967). A review of diagnostic unreliability in other branches of physical medicine is given by Garland (1960) and the problem of the vagueness of medical criteria for diagnosis is thoroughly discussed by Feinstein (1967). The poor reliability of medical diagnosis, even when assisted by objective laboratory tests, does not mean that medical diagnosis is of no value. So it is with psychiatric diagnosis.

Recognition of the serious problems of the reliability of psychiatric diagnosis has resulted in a new approach to psychiatric diagnosis—the use of specific inclusion and exclusion criteria, as contrasted with the usually vague and ill-defined general description found in the psychiatric literature and in the standard psychiatric glossary of the American Psychiatric Association. This approach was started by the St. Louis group associated with the Department of Psychiatry of Washington University (Feighner, Robins, Guze, Woodruff, Winokur, & Munoz, 1972) and has been further developed by Spitzer, Endicott, and Robins (1974) as a set of criteria for a selected group of functional psychiatric disorders, called the Research Diagnostic Criteria (RDC). The Display shows the specific criteria for a diagnosis of schizophrenia from the latest version of the RDS.(5)

DIAGNOSTIC CRITERIA FOR SCHIZOPHRENIA FROM THE
RESEARCH DIAGNOSTIC CRITERIA

1. At least two of the following are required for definite diagnosis and one for probable diagnosis
   (a) Thought broadcasting, insertion, or withdrawal (as defined in the RDC).
   (b) Delusions of control, other bizarre delusions, or multiple delusions (as defined in the RDC), of any duration as long as definitely present.
   (c) Delusions other than persecutory or jealousy, lasting at least 1 week.
   (d) Delusions of any type if accompanied by hallucinations of any type for at least 1 week.
   (e) Auditory hallucinations in which either a voice keeps up a running commentary on the patient's behaviors or thoughts as they occur, or two

or more voices converse with each other (of any duration as long as definitely present).

(f) Nonaffective verbal hallucinations spoken to the subject (as defined in this manual).

(g) Hallucinations of any type throughout the day for several days or intermittently for at least 1 month.

(h) Definite instances of formal thought disorder (as defined in the RDC).

(j) Obvious catatonic motor behavior (as defined in the RDC).

2. A period of illness lasting at least 2 weeks.

3. At no time during the active period of illness being considered did the patient meet the criteria for either probable or definite manic or depressive syndrome (Criteria 1 and 2 under Major Depressive or Manic Disorders) to such a degree that it was a prominent part of the illness.

Reliability studies utilizing the RDC with case record material (from which all cues as to diagnosis and treatment were removed), as well as with live patients, indicate high reliability for all of the major categories and reliability coefficients generally higher than have ever been reported (Spitzer, Endicott, Robins, Kuriansky, & Gurland, in press). It is therefore clear that the reliability of psychiatric diagnosis can be greatly increased by the use of specific criteria. (The interjudge reliability [chance corrected agreement, K] for the diagnosis of schizophrenia using an earlier version of RDC criteria with 68 newly admitted psychiatric inpatients at the New York State Psychiatric Institute was .88, which is a thoroughly respectable level of reliability.) It is very likely that the next edition of the American Psychiatric Association's *Diagnostic and Statistical Manual* will contain similar specific criteria.

There are other problems with current psychiatric diagnosis. The recent controversy over whether or not homosexuality per se should be considered a mental disorder highlighted the lack of agreement within the psychiatric profession as to the definition of a mental disorder. A definition has been proposed by Spitzer (Spitzer & Wilson, 1975), but it is not at all clear whether a consensus will develop supporting it.

There are serious problems of validity. Many of the traditional diagnostic categories, such as some of the subtypes of schizophrenia and of major affective illness, and several of the personality disorders, have not been demonstrated to be distinct entities or to be useful for prognosis or treatment assignment. In addition, despite considerable evidence supporting the distinctness of such conditions as schizophrenia and manic-depressive illness, the boundaries separating these conditions from other conditions are certainly not clear. Finally, the categories of the traditional psychiatric nomenclature are of least value when applied to the large numbers of outpatients who are not seriously ill. It is for these patients that a more behaviorally or problem-oriented approach might be particularly useful.

I have not dealt at all with the myriad ways in which psychiatric diagnostic labels can be, and are, misused to hurt patients rather than to help them. This is a problem requiring serious research which, unfortunately, Rosenhan's study does not help illuminate. However, whatever the solutions to that problem, the misuse of psychiatric diagnostic labels is not a sufficient reason to abandon their use because they have been shown to be of value when properly used.

In conclusion, there are serious problems with psychiatric diagnosis, as there are with other medical diagnoses. Recent developments indicate that the reliability of psychiatric diagnosis can be considerably improved. However, even with the poor reliability of current psychiatric diagnosis, it is not so poor that it cannot be an aid in the treatment of the seriously disturbed psychiatric patient. Rosenhan's study, "On Being Sane in Insane Places," proves that pseudopatients are not detected by psychiatrists as having simulated signs of mental illness. This rather unremarkable finding is not relevant to the real problems of the reliability and validity of psychiatric diagnosis and only serves to obscure them. A correct interpretation of his own data contradicts his conclusions. In the setting of a psychiatric hospital, psychiatrists are remarkably able to distinguish the "sane" from the "insane.

REFERENCES

American Psychiatric Association. *Diagnostic and Statistical Manual of Mental Disorders* (2nd ed.). Washington, D.C.: American Psychiatric Association, 1968.

Cochrane, A. L., & Garland, L. H. Observer Error in Interpretation of Chest Films: International Investigation. *Lancet*, 1952, 2, 505–509.

Davies, L. G. Observer Variation in Reports on Electrocardiograms. *British Heart Journal*, 1958, 20, 153–161.

Feighner, J. P., Robins, E., Guze, S. B., Woodruff, R. A. Winokur, G., & Munoz, R. Diagnostic Criteria for Use in Psychiatric Research. *Archives of General Psychiatry*, 1972, 26, 57–63.

Feinstein, A. *Clinical Judgment*. Baltimore, Md.: Williams & Wilkins, 1967.

Fletcher, C. M. Clinical Diagnosis of Pulmonary Emphysema—An Experimental Study. *Proceedings of the Royal Society of Medicine*, 1952, 45, 577–584.

Garland, L. H. The Problem of Observer Error. *Bulletin of the New York Academy of Medicine*, 1960, 36, 570–584.

Hunter, F. M. Letters to the Editor. *Science*, 1973, 180, 361.

Kety, S. S. From Rationalization to Reason. *American Journal of Psychiatry*, 1974, 131, 957–963.

Klein, D., & Davis, J. *Diagnosis and Drug Treatment of Psychiatric Disorders*. Baltimore, Md.: Williams & Wilkins, 1969.

Letters to the Editor. *Science*, 1973, 180, 356–365.

Markush, R. E., Schaaf, W. E., & Siegel, D. G. The Influence of the Death Certifier on the Results of Epidemiologic Studies. *Journal of the National Medical Association*, 1967, 59, 105–113.

Rosenhan, D. L. On Being Sane in Insane Places. *Science*, 1973, 179, 250–258. (a)
Rosenhan, D. L. Reply to Letters to the Editor, *Science*, 1973, 180, 365–369. (b)
Spitzer, R. L., Endicott, J., & Robins, E. *Research Diagnostic Criteria*. New York: Biometrics Research, New York State Department of Mental Hygiene, 1974.
Spitzer, R. L., Endicott, J., Robins, E., Kuriansky J., & Gurland, B. Preliminary Report of the Reliability of Research Diagnostic Criteria Applied to Psychiatric Case Records. In A. Sudilofsky, B. Beer & S. Gershon (Eds.), *Prediction in Psychopharmacology*. New York: Raven Press, in press.
Spitzer, R. L., & Fleiss, J. L. A Reanalysis of the Reliability of Psychiatric Diagnosis. *British Journal of Psychiatry*, 1974, 125, 341–347.
Spitzer, R. L., & Wilson, P. T. Nosology and the Official Psychiatric Nomenclature. In A. Freedman & H. Kaplan (Eds.) *Comprehensive Textbook of Psychiatry*. New York: Williams & Wilkins, 1975.
Yerushalmy, J. Statistical Problems in Assessing Methods of Medical Diagnosis, with Special Reference to X-ray Techniques. *Public Health Reports*, 1947, 62, 1432–1449.

NOTES

(1) The original article only mentions that the 11 schizophrenics were diagnosed "in remission." Personal communication from D. L. Rosenhan indicates that this also applied to the single pseudopatient diagnosed as manic-depressive psychosis.

(2) In personal communication D. L. Rosenhan said that "in remission" referred to a use of that term or one of its equivalents, such as recovered or no longer ill.

(3) Rosenhan has not identified the hospitals used in this study because of his concern with issues of confidentiality and the potential for ad hominem attack. However, this does make it impossible for anyone at those hospitals to corroborate or challenge his account of how the pseudopatients acted and how they were perceived. The 12 hospitals used in my ministudy were: Long Island Jewish-Hillside Medical Center, New York; Massachusetts General Hospital, Massachusetts; St. Elizabeth's Hospital, Washington, D.C.; McLean Hospital, Massachusetts; UCLA, Neuropsychiatric Institute, California; Meyer-Manhattan Hospital (Manhattan State), New York; Vermont State Hospital, Vermont; Medical College of Virginia, Virginia; Emory University Hospital, Georgia; High Point Hospital, New York; Hudson River State Hospital, New York, and New York Hospital-Cornell Medical Center, Westchester Division, New York.

(4) This was not in the article but was mentioned to me in personal communication by D. L. Rosenhan.

(5) For what it is worth, the pseudopatient would have been diagnosed as "probable" schizophrenia using these criteria because of 1(f).

In personal communication, Rosenhan said that when the pseudopatients were asked how frequently the hallucinations occurred, they said "I don't know." Therefore, Criterion 1(g) is not met.

The Contextual Nature
of Psychiatric Diagnosis

David L. Rosenhan

One might imagine that the criticisms of "On Being Sane in Insane Places" (Rosenhan, 1973a) that have appeared here and elsewhere had quite exhausted the matter, but that is not the case. There is, in my view, yet another criticism that can be offered of that work, one that may be harsher than those printed here, and one that sets the current reaction into a comprehensible context. Stated vigorously, it is this:

"On Being Sane in Insane Places" is a negative work. It tells what is wrong with treatment and diagnosis, without telling how it might be improved. It asks us to abandon traditional psychiatric diagnosis without telling us what will replace it. It tells those who have labored to improve psychiatric care that their efforts are grossly insufficient, without offering alternatives of demonstrated value. It tells the mental health professional, on whose overworked back the burdens of mankind's anguishes fall, that even the little he can do by way of diagnosis and treatment is unworthy and wrong. It even suggests that, given our current state of knowledge, symptom diagnoses may be better than syndrome diagnoses, although that suggestion is no better supported by research data than are traditional diagnoses. It suggests that the context created by the psychiatric hospital colors our perception of psychiatric patients, but it does not tell us in what way we can deal with that problem. It leaves scientists and practitioners in the lurch, urging them to abandon the little they have by way of hospital treatment and diagnosis, without providing them alternative tools. It would destroy a paradigm without providing an alternative. In short, it is work half done.

There is little defense against that criticism, little comfort for the anguish it expresses and the anger it conveys. That the implications of context are presently revamping large segments of personality theory, social psychology, psycholinguistics, memory and perception is barely solace to the working clinician. The fact that my colleagues and I recognize that the work is not yet done, the fact that we have not rested, nor do we intend to rest, is again no consolation for the clinician who needs tools now. Until compelling alternatives are found, one can have little difficulty understanding those who fight mightily, even angrily, to retain current beliefs. Those beliefs were not earned without sweat in training, research, and on the clinical firing line.

Transitional eras are difficult. That seemingly endless period of time that lies between our awareness of serious shortcomings in our current views and the discovery and application of more fruitful conceptions is a breeding time for intense and conflictful emotions. But the fact is that our growing appreciation of the role that contexts play in a variety of psychological areas—a role that I will elaborate on shortly—promises improvement for the understanding, diagnosis, and treatment of psychological distress. In the final analysis, it is with that improvement that our aspirations lie. More than that, our personal appreciation of the role of context may serve to insulate us against the needless defensiveness that naturally arises during this transition period. It was with this understanding in mind that I earlier wrote:

> It would be a mistake and a very unfortunate one, to consider that what happened to us derived from malice or stupidity on the part of the staff. Quite the contrary, our overwhelming impression of them was of people who really cared, who were committed, and who were uncommonly intelligent. Where they failed, as they sometimes did painfully, it would be more accurate to attribute those failures to the environment in which they, too, found themselves than to personal callousness. Their perceptions and behavior were controlled by the situation, rather than being motivated by malicious disposition. In a more benign environment, one that was less attached to global diagnosis, their behaviors and judgments might have been more benign and effective. (Rosenhan, 1973a, p. 257)

THE CONTEXT OF PSYCHIATRIC DIAGNOSIS

The studies of diagnosis with which we are concerned are best understood in terms of the influence of contexts on perceptions. Contexts shade and color meaning; in fact, they often determine meaning. A short person among pygmies may seem to be a giant. One who is 15 pounds overweight seems stuffed on a beach but svelte at an obesity clinic. A person whose hand is missing may look tragic among factory workers but nearly unimpaired among paraplegics. Thus, contexts are powerful.

The influence of contexts of mind (sets) and contexts of natural objects and behaviors (settings) on perception and action has been a constant theme of psychological research over the decades. Gestalt psychologists were concerned with them. Kurt Lewin and his intellectual heirs were absorbed by them. And modern psychologists in such diverse fields as psycholinguistics, memory, social psychology, and personology have pursued matters of context with considerable intellectual profit. Suffice it to say that the contexts created by such matters as person, place, gender, status, and era, not to speak of relational and analytic contexts, have enormous impact on the way stimuli are perceived.

A few examples will make these matters clear to those whose interests have not been in this area. Psycholinguists observe that even the words we use create significant contexts. The question "How short are you?" carries a different presuppositional load than the question "How tall are you?", even though both have identical concrete meaning (Clark, 1969). Loftus and Palmer (1974) have shown that the very questions we use in interrogating someone may determine the kinds of answers we get, not merely regarding opinion but to the very details of fact. Researchers in memory and cognition find that the latency for detecting "0" and "1" in a string of letters is considerably shorter if those stimuli are defined as numbers (zero and one) rather than letters (Jonides & Gleitman, 1972; see also Jenkins, 1974).

All stimuli seem amenable to contextual influence, but some are more amenable than others. Contextual influence is particularly strong when stimuli are ambiguous. Stimuli that are well articulated seem much more able to defy the influence of a surrounding field than those that are ill-defined. By way of example, Figure 1, adapted from Selfridge (1955), makes the matter very clear in the area of visual perception. Most people have no difficulty in recognizing the upper part of the figure as THE CAT, even though the A and the H are identically shaped. Indeed, some readers respond so rapidly to context that they are surprised when the similarity of the shape of the middle letter is pointed out. That does not occur in the lower half of the figure. There, the A is so well articulated that perceivers see the phrase as a spelling error, and may spend some considerable amount of time figuring out what the phrase was really supposed to say.

These powerful effects occur because neither memory nor perception are passive processes. They are active, constructive ones in which the individual is swiftly and unwittingly processing, interpreting, construing,

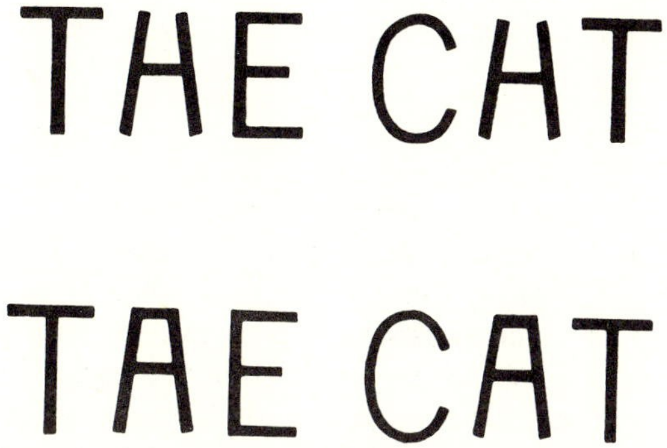

THE CHT

TAE CAT

FIGURE 1: The influence of context on visual perception.

and reconstruing events that are observed. Seemingly small changes in context, conveyed by a word, an instruction, a setting, or even a gesture, greatly alter understanding. They affect what is retrieved from memory. They affect judgment. They affect perception. And they affect psychiatric judgment and perception no less than judgment and perception in other areas.

Psychiatric diagnoses imply that what the diagnostician sees is descriptive of the patient's condition. Much as a cancer patient has cancer, the psychiatric patient is schizophrenic or manic-depressive, no matter where he is seen. But human behavior, even distressed human behavior, is no less ambiguous than other ambiguous stimuli, and no less amenable to context-dependent interpretation. Moreover, with regard to distressed behavior, there is particular reason to believe that however deep one's belief that what is perceived is schizophrenia, that belief is by no means compelling. Another diagnostician, equally sure of his skill, may arrive at a quite different diagnosis. Indeed, if 35 years of studies on agreement among diagnosticians have taught us anything, it is that, despite subjective conviction and regardless of skill and training, coefficients of diagnostic agreement (κ) between psychiatrists viewing the same behavior rarely exceed .8 which, for purposes of individual diagnosis, is quite low(1), are commonly in the range of .5, and can descend as low as .2. (For a recent summary of such studies, see Spitzer & Fleiss, 1974.) If anything attests to the ambiguity of such behavior and suggests the possibility that such behavior can be colored by contextual cues, these studies of agreement do.

There is yet another reason for believing that psychiatric diagnoses might be strongly influenced by contexts. Unlike most medical diagnoses, which can be validated in numerous ways, psychiatric diagnoses are maintained by consensus alone. This is not commonly known to either the consumer or the mental health profession. Spitzer and Wilson (in press) clarify the matter:

> In 1965 the American Psychiatric Association . . . assigned its Committee on Nomenclature and Statistics . . . the task of preparing for the APA a new diagnostic manual of disorders. . . . A draft of the new manual, DSM II, was circulated in 1967 to 120 psychiatrists known to have special interests in the area of diagnosis and was revised on the basis of their criticisms and suggestions. After further study it was adopted by the APA in 1967, and published and officially accepted throughout the country in 1968.

Nothing underscores the consensual nature of psychiatric disorders more than the recent action by the American Psychiatric Association to delete homosexuality from the *Diagnostic and Statistical Manual on Mental Disorders* (DSM-II, 1968). Whatever one's opinion regarding the nature of homosexuality, the fact that a professional association could vote on whether or not homosexuality should be considered a disorder surely underscores both the differences between psychiatric/mental disorders and the context-susceptibility of psychiatric ones. Changes in informed public attitudes toward homosexuality have brought about corresponding changes in the psychiatric perception of it.

SANE IN INSANE PLACES

Turning now to the studies under review, it should be clear that if the contexts created by setting influence psychiatric perception, then sane people who enter a psychiatric hospital should be diagnosed with the common psychiatric designation for hospitalized patients (schizophrenia) even though their presenting symptoms in no way describe that disorder. Correspondingly, if the contexts created by set color psychiatric perception, then mental health professionals who expect to find pseudopatients on their ward should diagnose many true patients as pseudopatients.

PRESENTING SYMPTOMS

Eight sane people(2) gained admission to 12 psychiatric hospitals by simulating a single symptom, hallucinations. These hallucinations had a special character. Their content had never been reported in the psychological literature. They were, by design, interesting auditory hallucinations that were perceived as a voice that said "empty," "dull," and "thud." It was intended that these hallucinations might lead an observer to suspect an interesting existential problem, as if these people were looking back over their lives and characterizing them as empty and dull. They were designed primarily to get the pseudopatients into the hospital.

Hallucinations, however, were not the only symptom that was presented. Behavioral nervousness was another. Some of the pseudopatients had had only fleeting prior contact with psychiatric hospitals. Others, even though they had been employed there, were nevertheless nervous. Some of the nervousness appeared to arise from a fear of being unmasked. Some of it had its source in a fear of the familiar unknown: Although several had worked in psychiatric hospitals, they had neither been there as patients nor spent much time there at night or during the weekends. Their vantage point was commonly from behind the desk or in the nurses' station. Nothing underscored their vulnerability to forces outside their control more than their impending hospitalization as pseudopatients. Nervousness, then, was unintended but also unavoidable.

For most of the pseudopatients, then, these two symptoms—plus the fact that they showed up at the hospital in the first place—constitute the entirety of their deception. These symptoms, of course, do not in any way constitute schizophrenia. That was not the intention. They were simply intended to be sufficient to get them into the hospital. Beyond the simulation of hallucinations and some concomitant nervousness, no further alteration of history or circumstances was made. The significant events of the pseudopatients' life histories were presented as they had occurred. Relationships with parents and siblings, with spouse and children, and with people at work and in school were described as they were or had been. Despite the absence of abnormal indications beyond those described, 11 of the pseudopatients were diagnosed, initially and finally, paranoid schizophrenia, and the 12th was diagnosed manic depressive psychosis.

Thus, set and setting, the contexts of mind and environment, heavily determine psychiatric diagnosis. But insofar as set is heavily permeated with expectation, it should prove at least partially reversible. An experiment was arranged at a hospital where the staff had heard these findings but doubted that such an error could occur in their institution.

Each staff member rated every patient who appeared at admissions or on the ward according to the likelihood that the patient was a pseudopatient. Judgments were obtained on 193 patients who were admitted for psychiatric treatment. Forty-one patients were alleged, with high confidence, to be pseudopatients by at least one member of the staff, 23 patients were considered suspect by at least one psychiatrist, and 19 were suspected by one psychiatrist and one other staff member. The pseudopatient who was designated for this hospital became ill and never entered. Thus the obtained data are for real patients.

Both studies confirm the view that the contexts of mind and setting color psychiatric perceptions, and there are others that make the same point. Temerlin (1968), for example, has shown that comments about a patient from a prestigious source have remarkable effects on how he is perceived. From a tape recorded interview, a doctor described a patient as interesting "because he looks neurotic, but actually is quite psychotic." The group of psychiatrists, clinical psychologists, and graduate clinical psychology students who heard this comment rated the interviewee as emotionally ill significantly more often than the controls who had either not heard the suggestion or had heard it reversed.

A study by Langer and Abelson (1974) deals with the same issue. A videotaped interview of a young man describing his job history and difficulties was presented to clinicians who were known to have either a behavioral or a traditional psychodynamic viewpoint. Half of the clinicians were told that the young man was a job applicant, whereas the remaining half were told that he was a patient. The clinicians' evaluations of the subject were quantified on a scale that ranged from 1 (very disturbed), through a midpoint, to 10 (very well adjusted). Those words, job applicant and patient, formed entirely different contexts for these judgments among traditional diagnosticians. Enormous differences were found in their judgment of the subject's adjustment according to whether the identical tape was presented as a patient interview (X = 3.47) or a job interview (X = 6.2). The more traditional the orientation of the clinician, the larger the difference was.

PROPER DIAGNOSES

What are the proper diagnoses for people who manifest some nervousness, complain of hallucinations, and nothing else, whose personal histories betray no sign of severe psychological distress, whose relationships are basically unimpaired, who have never in the past given evidence of severe psychological disorders, and who apparently have nothing to gain from malingering and for whom there is no evidence of malingering?

It should be noted that no party to this debate denies that the diagnoses that were actually given to the pseudopatients were erroneous. Spitzer (1975) directly expresses the hope that, had he examined one of the pseudopatients, "I would have been struck by the lack of other signs of the disorder." Both Spitzer (1975) and Weiner (1975) go to great lengths to exonerate the diagnosticians, but all agree that the diagnoses were wrong. I agree with them and with Millon (1975) that the fault lies not with the diagnosticians but elsewhere. We shall take up this matter at greater length later. For the moment, let us note our agreement that the diagnoses were wrong.

The central issue regarding diagnosis needs to be understood (see Rosenhan, 1973b, 1973c). The issue is not that the pseudopatients lied or that the psychiatrists believed them. The pseudopatients should not have been diagnosed Munchausen disease or Ganser syndrome—diagnoses that imply that the psychiatrists understood that the patients were feigning a symptom. Such diagnoses take much more evidence than can typically be assembled in an admissions interview. The issue is not whether the pseudopatients should have been admitted to the psychiatric hospital in the first place. If there were beds, admitting the pseudopatients was the only humane thing to do.

The issue is the diagnostic leap that was made between a single presenting symptom, hallucination, and the diagnosis, schizophrenia (or, in one case, manic-depressive psychosis). That is the heart of the matter. Had the pseudopatient been diagnosed hallucinating, there would have been no further need to examine the diagnostic issue. The diagnosis of hallucinations implies only that: no more. The presence of a hallucination does not itself define the presence of schizophrenia, and schizophrenia may or may not include hallucinations.

Lest the matter reduce to one scientist's word against others', let us examine the standard for diagnosis in psychiatry, the DSM II.

DSM– II

295. Schizophrenia. This large category includes a group of disorders manifested by characteristic disturbances of thinking, mood, and behavior. Disturbances in thinking are marked by alterations of concept formation which may lead to misinterpretation of reality and sometimes to delusions and hallucinations, which frequently appear psychologically self-protective. Corollary mood changes include ambivalence, constricted and inappropriate emotional responsiveness and loss of empathy with others. Behavior may be withdrawn, regressive and bizarre.

295.3 Schizophrenia, paranoid type . . . characterized

primarily by the presence of persecutory or grandiose delusions, often associated with hallucinations. Excessive religiosity is sometimes seen. The patient's attitude is frequently hostile and aggressive, and his behavior tends to be consistent with his delusions. (pp. 33–34)

But what then is the proper diagnosis for such complaints as the pseudopatients presented? I suggest the following: Hallucinations, hallucinations of unknown origin, ?, or DD (diagnosis deferred). Millon points out that the diagnosis of hallucinations of unknown origin is fraught with contextual difficulties. There is merit in his view, and I hold no special brief for that diagnosis. 'Certainly it is not the ultimate diagnosis. But it may very well be the one that reflects the present state of our knowledge better than traditional nosology does. Indeed, at present, my own preference runs to omitting diagnoses entirely, for it is far better from a scientific and treatment point of view to acknowledge ignorance than to mystify it with diagnoses that are unreliable, overly broad, and pejoratively connotative.

CRITICISMS

Much of Spitzer's (1975) critique consists of the justification of the diagnosis of schizophrenia.

> Unfortunately . . . many readers, including psychiatrists, were, in my judgment, wrong in accepting Rosenhan's thesis that it was irrational for the psychiatrists to have made an initial diagnosis of schizophrenia as *the most likely condition* on the basis of a single symptom. (p. 445)

He rules out alcohol, drug abuse, organic causes, or toxic psychosis as the cause of the hallucination. He rules out affective psychosis. The evidence, he says, does not support "hysterical psychosis," and there was no reason to believe that the illness was feigned. Spitzer writes:

> Dear reader: There is only one remaining diagnosis for the presenting symptom of hallucinations under these conditions in the classification of mental disorders used in this country and that is schizophrenia. (p. 446)

This is, of course, diagnosis by exclusion. And it makes schizophrenia a wastebasket diagnosis, a designation to be applied when nothing else fits. One would not have judged as much from the quotation offered above from the DSM–II, but perhaps in practice (and with sanction) it is. If that is the case, readers will judge for themselves whether the designation is useful, whether it constitutes a diagnosis in any sense of that term, and how likely it is for misdiagnoses to occur under such conditions.

It should now be clear that it is not the psychiatrists who diagnosed the pseudopatients but "the classification of mental disorders used in this country" (Spitzer, 1975) that is being questioned by these data. That question is supported by data from others. Ward, Beck, Mendelson, Mock, and Erbaugh (1962), in a study of diagnostic disagreement, found that inadequacy of the diagnostic nosology accounted for 62.5% of the reasons for disagreement, and another 32.5% was accounted for by inconsistency on the part of the diagnostician. Despite the attempts of the DSM–II to elaborate the symptomology associated with each presumed disorder, behaviors are too variable and their meanings too dependent on contextual perception for them to be captured under the rubrics proposed by the DSM–II. The very ambiguity of behavior, the fact that its meanings are not automatically transparent, defeats such attempts at classification from the outset, at least within the psychiatric hospital.

If anything, Spitzer's comments regarding schizophrenia as "the most likely condition," support the general views that were propounded in "On Being Sane in Insane Places" (Rosenhan, 1973a). Acknowledging that the diagnosis of paranoid schizophrenia was an error in 11 out of 11 instances (recall that the 12th was diagnosed manic depressive psychosis, a diagnosis that amounts to the same error for these purposes), Spitzer offers some illuminating insights regarding how such a patient error might nevertheless have been made. I have no disagreement with him on this score. Indeed, I concur heartily. But I emphasize, as I did in the original article, that "any diagnostic process that lends itself so readily to massive errors of this sort cannot be a very reliable one" (Rosenhan, 1973a, p. 252).

Attribution and logical analyses. The foregoing should clarify why neither attribution theory nor logical analysis (Weiner, 1975) justify the observed findings. Attribution theory is a theory of error. It is, as Heider (1958) stated, a naive psychology, one that accounts for why people might believe that the world is flat, that heavy stones fall faster than light ones, or that the sun rises in the east and sets in the west—even in the face of contrary evidence. But diagnosis should be based on scientific evidence and careful assessment of facts, not on the attributional inferences of naive observers. Indeed, Weiner's observations, like Spitzer's, support the view put forth in "On Being Sane in Insane Places" (Rosenhan, 1973a) by telling us precisely how (and how easily) psychiatric diagnosis goes astray. The present system of psychiatric diagnosis lends itself too easily to attributional errors. It needs seriously to be questioned.

IN REMISSION DOES NOT MEAN SANE

Spitzer (1975) points out that the designation "in remission" is exceedingly rare. It occurs in only a handful of cases in the hospitals he surveyed, and my own cursory investigations that were stimulated by his, confirm these observations. His data are intrinsically interesting as well as interesting for the meaning they have for this particular study. How shall they be understood?

Once again we return to the influence of context on psychiatric perception. Consider two people who show no evidence of psychopathology. One is called sane and the other is called paranoid schizophrenic, in remission. Are both characterizations synonymous? Of course not. Would it matter to you if on one occasion you were designated normal, and on the other you were called psychotic, in remission, with both designations arising from the identical behavior? Of course it would matter. The perception of an asymptomatic status implies little by itself; it is the context in which that perception is embedded that tells the significant story.

It is useful to observe here that the term "in remission" was used as the most conservative designation for patients' discharge diagnoses. Actually, eight of the patients were discharged in remission, three as improved, and one as asymptomatic. The latter two designations imply less of a perception of change than does the phrase in remission. But all three descriptors reify the original diagnosis. They do not imply that the diagnosis was wrong or questionable, or that over the course of the hospitalization behaviors that are inconsistent with the diagnosis of schizophrenia were observed which suggested that the diagnosis might have been an error. Nothing altered the original diagnosis. Diagnostic labels, once applied, have a stickiness of their own.

It is, in fact, a very painful commentary on the state of this healing art that, at best, only a handful of patients are discharged from psychiatric hospitals in remission, no longer ill, recovered, or asymptomatic. Because if these designations are rarely used, how much rarer must the designation "cured" be? And yet, one wonders. The literature on reactive schizophrenia conveys the impression of far greater success than is implied by Spitzer's discharge data. Could it be that we are not seeing something? Could it be that the psychiatric hospital holds many more recovered, improved, and no longer ill people who have been designated schizophrenic than our context-bound perceptions allow us to see? It is not a question that I can answer here, but it surely is one that is worthy of careful consideration.

EXPERIMENTER BIAS

Is it possible that experimenter bias infected the admissions and hospitalization procedures in such a way as to guarantee one particular outcome over another? If that is the case, then both Millon and Spitzer may be correct in describing the findings as trivial. Millon states it directly:

> At best, it supports the following rather trivial finding: Confederates of an experimenter who know the hypothesis being tested and who feign being psychologically disturbed, consistent with that hypothesis, will temporarily deceive unsuspecting clinicians accustomed to working in mental institutions. (p. 457)

Spitzer says that the study:

> proves that pseudopatients are not detected by psychiatrists as having simulated signs of mental illness. This rather unremarkable finding is not relevant to the real problems of reliability and validity of psychiatric diagnosis and only serves to obscure them. (p. 451)

Are they correct?

The possibility of experimenter bias cannot be dismissed. Its manifestations are legion, and many of the subtle ways by which it is communicated are as yet unknown (cf. Rosenthal, 1966). But both the history and conduct of this project, as well as an examination of the notion of experimenter bias as it might apply here, is reassuring in this regard.

This project began as, and continues to be, an investigation of the care and perception of patients in the environments in which such care occurs. Utilizing the disciplined observation technologies of social psychology and anthropology, its concern is not primarily with diagnosis but only with diagnosis as it affects perception of patients and the nature and quality of their care.

In seeking admission to psychiatric hospitals, the pseudopatients did not simulate their single symptom to trap admission officers into making an erroneous diagnosis. Their use of a single symptom, and its abandonment after they were admitted, served the central purpose of minimizing their own psychological burdens. Recall that we were not the first people to utilize pseudopatienthood to investigate the treatment milieu of psychiatric hospitals. More than two decades earlier, Caudill (1958; Caudill, Redlich, Gilmore, & Brody, 1952) had spent considerable time in a psychiatric hospital simulating a florid pattern of symptomology throughout. He was consumed with guilt over deceiving his colleagues and his report of his experiences was an excruciating warning to subsequent scientific generations that such elaborate deceptions can have enormous personal consequences. All of the pseudopatients knew of Caudill's work and were told that the simulation of a single symptom would likely reduce these problems. Abandoning even that symptom immediately on admission would not only reduce further that potential source of stress but also allow them to move more freely on the ward and among the patients. Moreover, I was aware that the simulation of a single symptom would facilitate discharge, which was a matter of no small concern when these studies were initiated.

The history and current direction of the project then, make no presuppositions regarding the effects of any diagnosis on patient care. However, might there not have been incidental departures from protocol on the parts of the pseudopatients? Our inquiries, conducted immediately after the pseudopatients were admitted, revealed only one such incident. In that instance, a pseudopatient altered his personal history by denying that he was married and alleging that his parents were deceased. His data, however, were omitted from the study (see Rosenhan, 1973a, footnote 6), even though they were consistent with the data from another pseudopatient.

It is important, however, to ask some difficult questions of experimenter bias in this connection. Granting for the moment that experimenter bias did affect these procedures, could it possibly have accounted for these findings? I believe not, because although experimenter bias has been found to be an outcome determinant of some power, it is not overwhelmingly powerful. In the present case, 12 out of 12 sane admissions were accorded a severe psychiatric diagnosis. To insist that all of them were misdiagnosed on the bias of experimenter bias places considerably more weight on that variable than it possibly can bear. After all, not all of Rosenthal and Jacobson's (1968) late bloomers were subsequently tested in the superior intelligence range, which would have been necessary for experimenter bias to be as potent as Millon alleges.

Experimenter bias is a set, a member of the class of sets that I have subsumed under the notion of contexts. It is a context of mind, and as such it can cut two ways: It can favor or disfavor an hypothesis. Recall the challenge experiment that was arranged at a research and teaching hospital where the staff had heard these findings but doubted that such an error could occur in their hospital. There we saw an instance of bias cutting in the direction of overdiagnosing sanity, at least according to the base rate of that particular hospital. The staff were quite confident of their ability to use the DSM–II and the variants on it that they had invented, and indeed they engaged in this small study because they were certain we were wrong. However, given a set in favor of detection, they overdetected.

In this regard, I have been told that pseudopatients would have been detected in a military hospital, and quite possibly by forensic psychiatrists. And that may be the case. But observe that in the latter instances bias cuts in favor of detection. Clearly, it does not cut in that direction in the typical psychiatric institution.

Finally, discharge diagnoses are interesting because they occur after a lengthy period of observation, thus providing ample time for diagnostic errors to be corrected. Visitors' notes (including notes written by concerned members of the pseudopatients' families) provide no evidence that the pseudopatients were actively biasing their behavior in the direction of craziness. If anything, they were often attempting to impress the staff with their sanity, a complex matter to which I shall return. Moreover, true patients commonly recognized the pseudopatients as sane during their hospitalization. Nevertheless, the discharge diagnoses were consistent with the admission diagnoses. Admitted in the main with the diagnosis of schizophrenia, they were discharged with the same diagnosis, but in remission or improved. The argument for experimenter bias becomes much less convincing over the length of these hospitalizations.

Can it seriously be held with Millon (1975) that because of their biases patients prolonged their hospitalization? Anyone who has served as a pseudopatient, and most psychiatric patients, will find that view untenable. Psychiatric hospitals, even the best of them, are places as dull and difficult for people who do not belong there as they often are for true patients. It asks too much of ordinary people to remain locked into a psychiatric hospital for as long as 52 days merely to provide a diagnostic point that was made well on admission.

Demand characteristics. Millon (1975) questions whether, in addition to experimenter bias, demand characteristics might have played a role in the obtained outcome. Demand characteristics are powerful variables, as the history of hypnosis research attests (Orne, 1969). It is, however, difficult to discern from Millon's critique in what sense demand characteristics are being invoked here. Often, demand characteristics are seen to operate in the pact of ignorance that is made between an experimenter and his subjects, so that each will not reveal his secret understandings of the experiment. Surely, that could not have been the case here, at least from the admissions officer's viewpoint. Another meaning of demand characteristics refers to controlling the setting in such a way that a particular outcome is more assured than it might ordinarily be. This is unlikely in the present instance because we did not control the setting. No other meaning of demand characteristics seems relevant to this experiment. But the fact that the demand characteristics of psychiatric hospitals lead its personnel to believe that all those who are not staff are likely to be schizophrenic or manic-depressive is certainly consistent with our view of these data.

Could the experiment have been done differently? Undoubtedly, the experiment could have been conducted another way, and because no single experiment ever fully elucidates a phenomenon, surely there will be other work in this area that tightens these findings, illuminates them further, replicates, and extends them. The use of televised stimuli, such as those employed by Langer and Abelson (1974), offers clear control advantages that may offset what is lost in ecological validity. And as far as in vivo studies are concerned, the use of new and different symptom sets might establish the limits of contextual interpretations of behavior in these settings.

Both Millon and Weiner suggest that one might simply have people come to the admissions office and request hospitalization without falsifying a symptom. This is an interesting idea, but one that I doubt would work. Diagnosticians, like anyone else, are not passive in the face of stimulus ambiguity. They inquire. They search. They attempt to obtain more data to reduce stimulus ambiguity interpretively. And what might the pseudopatient say regarding his desire to be admitted? What justification could he present?

The same problem arises with the suggestion that sane people be directly placed on the ward to see if they can be distinguished from insane ones. If such a differentiation is intended to occur without talking to patients, there would very likely be low capacity to detect. It was the common experience of pseudopatients on wards where staff dressed casually that they could not determine who was staff and who patient for some time. (One gleans similar impressions from new interns and residents who enter an informal ward—it is difficult to tell the patients from the staff by merely looking.) Talking to the real and pseudopatients is a different matter. Again, one reduces stimulus ambiguity, but one also encounters the problem of justifying the pseudopatient's presence on the ward.

Spitzer (1975) deals directly with reduction of stimulus ambiguity in my study when he asks, "What did the pseudopatients say . . . when asked, as they must have been, what effect the hallucinations were having on their lives and why they were seeking admission in a hospital?" (p. 447). They responded that the hallucinations troubled them greatly at the outset, but less so now. They denied being greatly distracted by them, but seemed mainly puzzled and naturally concerned. They had been told by friends to come to the hospital (or mental health center). The latter response often alerted considerable surprise in the admitting psychiatrist, and several pseudopatients were carefully queried about why they had not first taken their problem to their personal physician or a psychiatrist in the community. Because the pseudopatients, with only one exception, were not hospitalized in their own communities, they indicated that they did not have a personal physician in the community. (The single exception did not, in fact, have a personal physician.) Moreover, they indicated that they had heard that "this is a good hospital" and had therefore come on their own initiative.

I have dealt with the problem of justifying the presence of the pseudopatients, either at the admissions office or on the ward, by employing a single symptom that does not qualify for a standard disgnosis. Such a symptom should, as I have earlier indicated, alert a paradox, an inquiry, or a deferral of diagnosis. Given that the admitting and attending staff are competently trained, the easy assignment of a standard diagnosis confirms the view that the diagnostic system is not working. Recall again that the central diagnostic issue is the imaginative leap that was made between a single presenting symptom and a global pejorative diagnosis.

Sanity on the ward. Did the pseudopatients' behaviors on the ward fall within an acceptable definition of sane behavior? The problem is fascinating, because it directly implicates the influence of context on meaning. Millon puts the challenge squarely. He asserts that they did not behave sanely at all.

> Quite the contrary. The behaviors they portrayed were "standard" hospital patient behaviors. Though reported in cryptic fashion, it appears that the pseudopatients sat around quietly, acted cooperatively, said they were fine in response to staff inquiries, and asked innocuous questions such as, "When will I be eligible for ground privileges?" None of these would characterize a sane person in that situation. (p. 457)

Spitzer, quoting Hunter (Letters, 1973), concurs enthusiastically in that view:

> The pseudopatients did *not* behave normally in the hospital. Had their behavior been normal, they would have walked to the nurses' station and said, "Look, I am a normal person who tried to see if I could get into the hospital by behaving in a crazy way and saying crazy things. It worked and I was admitted to the hospital, but now I would like to be discharged from the hospital." (p. 443)

These are interesting observations because they demonstrate the degree to which context colors both expectation and perception. Because patients are cooperative in a hospital, because they say "fine" in response to staff inquiries, because they are quiet and ask questions about their eligibility for ground privileges, those behaviors, ipso facto, become abnormal, without additional validation or further proof. How long might it take a true patient, behaving in this perfectly reasonable manner to convince staff that he is indeed sane? And at what point do both clinical staff and researchers take notice of the on-off behavior of true patients and begin to ask serious questions about it?

In this connection it is useful to record some of the actions of the pseudopatients and the staff responses. They occasionally intervened with staff on behalf of other patients. They were friendly toward other patients, helpful to them, active on the wards, comforting to patients in their distress, and therapeutic with patients, but because all of this occurred on the ward, it was never seen as normal behavior. Indeed, two pseudopatients who directly requested discharge from staff members were simply ignored, and treated as yet another annoying request from another annoying patient.

Given that patients are shorn of credibility and are commonly held suspect in such matters by staff, would it really have been normal to go up to the nurses' station and say, "Look, I'm a normal person?" Might that not be construed as precisely the insane thing to do? I suspect that it might, and genuine patients have the same impression. (Recall the poor soul in the film *Titticut Follies* who did insist on being discharged for these very reasons.) We commonly asked patients, "How do you get out of the hospital?" Never did a patient advise, "Just tell them you're fine now, and that you want to go home." They recognized that they would not be believed. More commonly they encouraged us to be cooperative, patient, and not make waves. Sometimes they recommended a special kind of indirection: "Don't tell them you're well. They won't believe you. Tell them you're sick, but getting better. That's called insight, and they'll discharge you!"

Much as set and setting determine what Spitzer (1975) and Millon (1975) view as abnormal behavior, so do they offer us an especially narrow view of what normal behavior in such circumstances should be. Which psychology of behavior suggests that there is one and only one normal response to a given situation? Is it abnormal to stay in a hospital because one finds it interesting (or because one has made friends, or has nowhere else to go), anymore than it is to stay at one's desk on a beautiful day because one is absorbed in one's work? How might you know whether such behavior is normal or abnormal if you didn't inquire carefully—and no one did. Is normal or abnormal behavior self-evident from outside the person? Does one not need to inquire into the reasons for staying in a hospital just as carefully as one inquires into the reasons for wanting to leave?

Finally, it was precisely on the basis of such behaviors (the normality of which Spitzer and Millon question) that the staff in the challenge experiment detected pseudopatients. Set in the direction of discovering pseudopatients, they now used those very same standard hospital behaviors to arrive at their conclusions. In isolation, such behaviors tell us little about patients' psychiatric status. They essentially serve to confirm staff biases. Identical behaviors have vastly different meanings according to staff preconceptions that are acquired through set and setting. That is precisely the meaning of context dependency in psychiatric diagnosis.

The problem of what is normal and what is abnormal behavior is a complicated one in any setting. Some would seriously question the epistemological utility of such categorizations. But regardless, Spitzer's and Millon's fairly arbitrary classification of these behaviors only further reveals their context dependency.

THE FUTURE

It is natural to infer that what I have written here argues against categorization of all kinds. But that is not the case. I have been careful to direct attention to the present system of diagnosis, the DSM–II. It may be useful to close this essay with a few words on the conditions under which diagnosis may prove useful and the requirements that we must set for those who would produce new diagnostic systems.

First, as long as differences exist between people, it is possible to classify and categorize. The thrust of any rational argument cannot be against classification, per se, but only against poor classification and misclassification as it occurs with certain systems and affects patients' welfare.

Second, scientific understanding, if not human understanding, proceeds on the basis of classification. Nothing that is said here is intended to deprive the researcher of his classificatory system. He cannot proceed without it, but as long as his diagnostic data remain in his file until they are fully validated, they can do patients and treatment no harm.

Third, with regard to new classification systems that are intended for clinical usage with patients, we can require that evidence for their utility precede its promulgation. That has not hitherto been the case. Unlike psychological tests, which need to be validated before they are distributed, the Diagnostic and Statistical Manuals have been promulgated by the American Psychiatric Association before being carefully validated. As I indicated earlier, they rest heavily on consensus, rather than fact.

What might we require of new diagnostic systems before they are published and officially accepted? First, we should ask that coefficients of agreements between diagnosticians in a variety of settings *commonly* reach or exceed .90. That figure, which is associated with a bit more than 80 % of the variance in diagnosis, is a liberal one in terms of the possible consequences of misdiagnosis and the reversibility of the diagnoses.(1) The full reasoning behind that figure takes us away from the central thrust of this paper, but interested readers can confirm it for themselves in Cronbach, Gleser, Harinder, and Nageswari (1972) and Cronbach and Gleser (1959).

Second, we should require that the proven utility of such a system exceed its liabilities for patients. Understand the issue. Syphilis and cancer both have negative social and emotional overtones, but the treatments that exist for them presumably exceed the personal liabilities associated with the diagnosis. We ask no less of psychiatric categorization: that the diagnoses lead to useful treatments that cannot be implemented without the diagnoses.

Under such conditions, I doubt that any reasonable person would protest psychiatric classification. And until such requirements are fulfilled, protests directed against classification will seem reasonable indeed.

REFERENCES

American Psychiatric Association. *Diagnostic and Statistical Manual of Mental Disorders* (DSM–II). Washington, D.C.: American Psychiatric Association, 1968.

Caudill, W. *The Psychiatric Hospital as a Small Society.* Cambridge, Mass.: Harvard University Press, 1958.

Caudill, W., Redlich, F. C., Gilmore, H. R., & Brody, E. B. Social Structure and Interaction Process on a Psychiatric Ward. *American Journal of Orthopsychiatry*, 1952, 22, 314–334.

Cronbach, L. J., & Gleser, C. C. Interpretation of Reliability and Validity Coefficients: Remarks on a Paper by Lord. *Journal of Educational Psychology*, 1959, 50, 230–237.

Cronbach, L. J., Gleser, G. C., Harinder, N., & Nageswari, R. *The Dependability of Behavioral Measurements: Theory of Generalizability for Scores and Profiles.* New York: Wiley, 1972.

Heider, F. *The Psychology of Interpersonal Relations.* New York: Wiley, 1958.

Hunter, F. M. Letters to the Editor. *Science*, 1973, 180, 361.

Jenkins, J. J. Remember That Old Theory of Memory? Well, Forget It! *American Psychologist*, 1974, 29, 785–795.

Jonides, J., & Gleitman, H. A. Conceptual Category Effect in Visual Search: O as Letter or as Digit. *Perception and Psychophysics*, 1972, 12, 457–460.

Langer, E. J., & Abelson, R. P. A Patient by Any Other Name . . . ! Clinician Group Differences in Labeling Bias. *Journal of Consulting and Clinical Psychology*, 1974, 42, 4–9.

Loftus, E. F., & Palmer, J. C. Reconstruction of an Automobile Destruction: An Example of the Interaction between Language and Memory. *Journal of Verbal Learning and Verbal Behavior*, 1974, 13, 585–589.

Millon, T. Reflections on Rosenhan's "On Being Sane in Insane Places." *Journal of Abnormal Psychology*, 1975, 84, 456–461.

Orne, M. T. Demand Characteristics and the Concept of Quasi-controls. In R. Rosenthal & R. Rosnow (Eds.), *Artifact in Behavioral Research*. New York: Academic Press, 1969.

Rosenhan, D. L. On Being Sane in Insane Places. *Science*, 1973, 179, 250–258. (a)

Rosenhan, D. L. Letters to the Editor. *Science*, 1973, 180, 365–369. (b)

Rosenhan, D. L. Letters to the Editor. *Journal of the American Medical Association*, 1973, 224, 1646–1647. (c)

Rosenthal, R. *Experimenter Effects in Behavioral Research*. New York: Appleton-Century-Crofts, 1966.

Rosenthal, R., & Jacobson, L. *Pygmalion in the Classroom: Teacher Expectation and Pupils' Intellectual Development*. New York: Holt, Rinehart & Winston, 1968.

Selfridge, O. G. *Pattern Recognition and Modern Computers*. Proceedings of the Western Joint Computer Conference, Los Angeles, Calif., 1955. Cited in Neisser, U., *Cognitive Psychology*. New York: Appleton-Century-Crofts, 1967.

Spitzer, R. L. On Pseudoscience in Science, Logic in Remission, and Psychiatric Diagnoses: A Critique of Rosenhan's "On Being Sane in Insane Places." *Journal of Abnormal Psychology*, 1975, 84, 442–452.

Spitzer, R. L., & Fleiss, J. L. A Reanalysis of the Reliability of Psychiatric Diagnosis. *British Journal of Psychiatry*, 1974, 125, 341–347.

Spitzer, R. L., & Wilson, P. T. Nosology and the Official Psychiatric Nomenclature. In A. Freedman & H. Kaplan (Eds.), *Comprehensive Textbook of Psychiatry*. New York: Williams & Wilkins, in press.

Temerlin, M. K. Suggestion Effects in Psychiatric Diagnosis. *Journal of Nervous and Mental Disease*, 1968, 147, 349–359.

Ward, C. H., Beck, A. T., Mendelson, M., Mock, J. E., & Erbaugh, J. K. The Psychiatric Nomenclature: Reasons for Diagnostic Disagreement. *Archives of General Psychiatry*, 1962, 7, 198–205.

Weiner, B. "On Being Sane in Insane Places": A Process (Attributional) Analysis and Critique. *Journal of Abnormal Psychology*, 1975, 84, 433–441.

NOTES

(1) "The acceptable risk depends on the type of decision being made. In individual decisions (particularly counseling), it is generally desirable to be conservative, seeking additional information rather than accepting a hazardous conclusion. When a terminal decision is under consideration, it appears reasonable to set the maximum risk as .10 or .05 meaning that 1 in 10, or 1 in 20 decisions could be wrong. An even lower level might be desired for an important decision that could not be reversed should it prove to be wrong in the light of later experience" (Cronbach & Gleser, 1959, p. 233).

(2) The ambiguity of the term, mental illness, makes it difficult to find an unambiguous term that denotes its opposite. Mentally healthy, normal, and without severe psychological anguish all have difficulties of their own. I have chosen the words sane and insane to approximate the conditions I would describe. Many writers have correctly observed that these terms have legal connotations. But to my knowledge, all other terms have greater disadvantages.

III.

Incompetency and Insanity

Introduction

The law on competency to stand trial provides that an individual accused of a crime may be tried only if that individual is able to understand the nature of the charge being made and is able to aid counsel in preparing a defense. As the U.S. Supreme Court ruled in *Dusky v. United States* (1960), it is not sufficient for the trial judge to find that the defendant is oriented in time and place or has some recollection of events. The test must be "whether he has sufficient present ability to consult with his lawyer with a reasonable degree of rational understanding—and whether he has a rational as well as a factual understanding of the proceedings against him."

Slovenko (1973) states that the rule on competency to stand trial originated in cases involving physical disability. If the accused were incapacitated by illness or injury, the trial would be postponed until the accused had regained the physical ability to appear in court. Subsequently, the notion developed "that a person so disoriented or removed from reality that he could not properly participate and aid in a meaningful defense ought not to be put to trial." However, in application, rules became a means of disposing of "undesirables" for indefinite periods of time.

The U.S. Supreme Court (*Pate v. Robinson*, 1966) requires the question of mental illness to be raised by any of the principal participants in the judicial process—the defense counsel, prosecutor, or judge— whenever they have any reason to believe that the defendant's mental or psychological status may interfere with his capacity to participate in the trial. As illustrated in Figure 1, the question of competency can—indeed,

FIGURE 1: Psychiatric interventions within the criminal process (highly schematic)

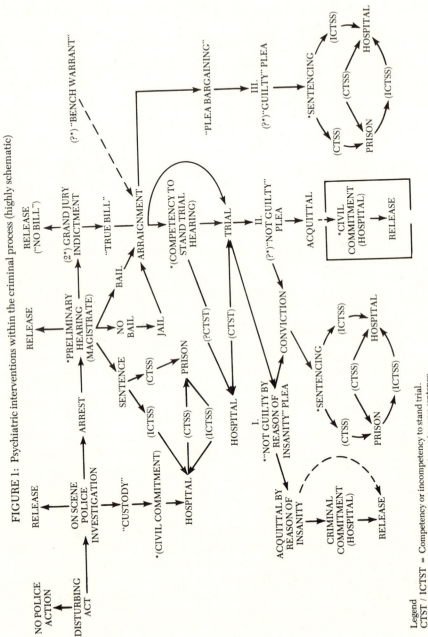

Legend
CTST / ICTST = Competency or incompetency to stand trial.
CTSS / ICTSS = Competency or incompetency to serve sentence.

must—be raised at any time during the criminal process. Unfortunately, Figure 1 refers to "competency to serve a sentence," a separate and complex issue not discussed here.

Alan A. Stone (1975) refers to the competency issue as "the most significant mental health inquiry pursued in the system of criminal law." The issue is crucially important because of: the numbers of persons to whom it is applied, the many times during the criminal trial process when it may be invoked, and the potential consequences for the defendant after its application. As a consequence of its application, the defendant may be denied bail; the defendant may be incarcerated for a period longer than the maximum sentence for the crime being charged; the defendant may be placed in an institution that combines the worst elements of jails and hospitals; and any pretrial mental examination poses serious questions about the defendant's rights under the Fifth Amendment. Although the commitment for incompetency remains in an individual's record, the individual may face state constitutional and statutory restrictions on this right to vote and on access to drivers' license. Moreover, an adjudication of incompetency commonly leads to a rebuttable presumption of continued incompetency (*Hurt v. United States*, 1964). As noted by the U.S. Court of Appeals (*Meoteris v. United States*, 1939): "The general rule seems to be that a person adjudged to be insane is presumed to so continue until it is shown that sanity has returned."

The procedures for determining competency vary considerably from jurisdiction to jurisdiction, but most jurisdictions require a court decision based on psychiatric testimony. In some states a jury may be impaneled if requested by the defendant, and in three states the court has the discretion to impanel a jury (Brakel and Rock, 1971). If a defendant is found incompetent to stand trial, the accused is usually committed to a mental institution until the medical or psychiatric authorities at the institution can certify competency to stand trial. During institutionalization, the defendant remains under court jurisdiction.

Stone (1975) stresses that the significance of the issue of competency has generally been obscured by confusing it with the defense of insanity:

> Consider the case of an obviously mentally ill person who commits some criminal act. Such an offender is typically arrested shortly after the crime. Since mental illness is apparent to everyone, two important legal questions arise. First, if this person is tried, will he be able to consult with his lawyers and participate in his defense? Second, was he responsible for the crime with which he is charged? The first is the question of competency to stand trial, the second is the question of insanity. Before a criminal trial can be held to answer the second question, the

defendant must be restored to competency. Thus, in the typical case it is the question of competency that arises first, and its resolution often determines the fate of the defendant.

Stone adds that many more persons are confined on the basis of incompetency than on the basis of a finding of "not guilty by reason of insanity" because of the readiness of courts to dispose of cases by any reasonable disposition: "Given the complexity and expense of a trial on the issue of not guilty by reason of insanity, and the congestion of the courts, a judge will often prefer to divert the patient from the criminal process in this way, particularly if he believes the hospital will provide either treatment or secure confinement." Consequently, as Robert E. Schulman (1973) observes in his selection, there is a "collusive collaboration between law and medicine (including the behavioral sciences) which effectively buries the patient alive." Although his language is more restrained and sedate, Paul D. Lipsitt (1970) makes essentially the same charge as Schulman makes. In his discussion of the implications of the Druken decision by the Supreme Judicial Court of Massachusetts (*Commonwealth v. Druken*, 254 N.E. 2d. 77), Lipsitt emphasizes the "confusion caused by the intermingling of issues of competency, insanity, and mental illness in the statutes." The concluding selection by Alan A. Stone is a valuable contribution to the clarification of the issues raised by the long and continuing attempts by the courts to find some compromise between the deterministic modern theory of the causes of action and the enduring free-will theory of the morality of action upon which our system of criminal jurisprudence is founded.

THE INSANITY DEFENSE

The concept of criminal responsibility implies that an individual has moral knowledge. It presumes an acknowledgement that the individual is required not to act in ways contrary to those sanctioned by social custom or tradition and embodied in the law. The concept of criminal responsibility also presupposes that the accused is capable of making functional distinctions between what is "right" and "wrong," as those terms are defined in codes of social conduct. Excluding the adverse effects of mental aberration or mental deficiency, the accused is "able to do what is right." The fundamental connection between moral knowledge and free choice is embodied in the legal principles which allow for the diminution or elimination of responsibility under certain conditions which lessen or destroy an individual's capacity for discriminating between "right" and "wrong" and acting in accordance with those discriminations.

The general and consistent view within the law has been that wrong doing must be conscious to be criminal. To define criminal responsibility, a variety of tests or formulae, which make no scientific claims, have been developed over the years for the instruction of juries.

The various rules and tests try to establish some relative gauge of criteria, based on numerous cases and upon moral, social and philosophical orientations of the community. The criteria provide society with guidelines to deal with a particular offender. The issues raised and tried before a jury are never simple; definitions which are both precise and inclusive are difficult to determine finally. Therefore, considerable confusion exists about the questions raised concerning expert testimony.

M'NAGHTEN

The M'Naghten ruling, which still prevails in England and thirty states in the United States, was pronounced in 1843. The ruling is discussed in detail in Volume I of *The Psychological Foundations of Criminal Justice*. Although England was believed to have been characterized by orderliness and complacency in 1843, Biggs (1955) observed that liberal ideals were beginning to penetrate the Victorian indifference to the suffering and poverty of the masses. During this time Daniel M'Naghten, a native of Scotland and a political fanatic, was found not guilty on grounds of insanity for the murder of Sir Robert Peel's secretary. M'Naghten had mistaken the secretary for Peel, who as Prime Minister was said to have been a highly conservative upholder of the status quo.

Although the form of M'Naghten's "insanity" was not designated at the trial, contemporary psychiatrists would probably have labeled him paranoid (Glueck, 1962). M'Naghten seemed to have been entangled in an elaborate web of delusions, including the belief that he was being pursued by spies and that the Tories and the Prime Minister were pursuing him because he had voted against them in the previous election (Robitscher, 1966).

Many segments of Victorian society and Queen Victoria herself were indignant at M'Naghten's acquittal. Glueck (1962) recounted, "In a delightful blend of wit, wisdom, and royal concern. . ." Victoria commented that she did not believe that anyone who wanted to murder a conservative Prime Minister could be insane. The House of Lords, as a result of the national indignation, asked the judges of England for an authoritative statement of existing law. Their basic answer was:

> To establish a defense on the grounds of insanity, it must be clearly proven that, at the time of committing the act . . . the party accused was labouring under such a defect of reason from disease of the mind, as not to know the nature and quality of the

act he was doing, or if he did know it . . . he did not know he was
doing what was wrong (Glueck, 1962).

Since the judges' pronouncement, the M'Naghten ruling has been a focal
point of legal and psychiatric controversy.

First, it has been charged that the ruling does not make clear whether
the judges were referring to legal or moral "wrong." Robitscher (1966)
illustrated the ambiguity with a hypothetical case quoted from Sir James
Stephen, English legal commentator:

> A kills B with knowledge of his act and its illegality, but under the
> insane delusion that the murder of B was directed by God and
> would result in the salvation of the human race. If the word
> 'wrong' means illegal, A's act is a crime. If the word 'wrong'
> means immoral, A would not be criminally responsible for the
> act.

The most recurring criticism of the M'Naghten ruling emanating from
psychiatric circles has been of the cognitive-moral emphasis of the ruling.
Goldstein (1967) has stated that M'Naghten is a restrictive rule which
reflects an outmoded, faulty psychology. It perceives thought processes as
separate cognitive, emotional, and control components and classes an
individual as insane only if that individual suffers from serious cognitive
or intellectual impairment. The ruling thereby limits the definition of
insanity to individuals who are extremely deteriorated psychotics. "As a
result," Goldstein continued, ". . . the elimination of M'Naghten and
willingness to adopt one of the newer rules had been treated as a liberal
test of faith."

Perhaps the most compelling objection to the M'Naghten ruling,
particularly from the point of view of the testifying psychopathologist,
has been stated by Roche (1958). Roche views the tests of responsibility as
expressed in the M'Naghten ruling when applied to cases other than those
cases of "disturbed consciousness" or "profound mental deficit'" as
"untenable propositions within the discipline of scientific medical
psychology." Leifer (1964) elaborates upon Roche's objection when he
argues that inferences pertaining to the verb "to know" can only be made
from behavior criteria. Leifer adds:

> It is not possible to infer behind that behavior to a private sphere
> of events, the mind . . . The psychiatrist has no special skills or
> tools which enable him to penetrate the mind much as the
> toxicologist has skills and tools for examining the blood.

PLUS "IRRESISTIBLE IMPULSE"

Dissatisfaction with the M'Naghten ruling, particularly with its emphasis upon the rational, has led to a series of attempts to add to, amend, or replace it. A supplement to the M'Naghten ruling exists in eighteen states; it was first adopted in Alabama in 1896, and in the federal system it is known as the "irresistible impulse" ruling. In English law the "irrestible impulse" ruling antedated the M'Naghten ruling which later overshadowed it. Recently, the "irrestible impulse" ruling has been applied to defendants who may perceive the quality of their acts and be aware that they are wrong, but who, nevertheless, are driven to commit their acts by an overpowering impulse resulting from a mental condition (Robitscher, 1966).

One assumption upon which the "irresistible impulse" ruling rests is that some mental diseases impair volition or self-control, even when cognition is relatively unimpaired (Goldstein, 1967). The assumption is made that there is such a thing as an irresistible impulse, as distinct from an unresisted impulse. Davidson (1958) challenged this assumption. Using then current psychiatric nosologies, he suggested that "irresistible impulse" might be applied to three categories of behavior: 1. explosive reactions in psychotics; 2. obsessive-compulsion in neurotics; and 3. rage reactions in individuals with no psychosis or neurosis. Davidson stated that as first contemplated by the law, "irrestible impulse" was intended to refer to the first of these categories. General agreement, he feels, exists that psychotics with explosive reactions should not be treated as guilty. He contends however, that these psychotics already receive adequate protection under the M'Naghten ruling because they would not appreciate the wrongfulness of the act. They therefore need no special doctrine for protection.

The basic problem with the "irresistable impulse," Davidson contends, is with the second category of behavior—individuals displaying neurotic compulsion, most frequently kleptomania or pyromania. Davidson asserts:

> It is technically incorrect. . . to say that such a person is in the helpless grip of an irresistible impulse. . . since the neurotic . . . can and usually does control it in the presence of a third party. True compulsions, he maintains, are always related to insignificant and harmless rituals like counting the cracks in the sidewalk or washing one's hands. No one, he states, "has to" commit a criminal act.

Cressey (1958) who essentially holds Davidson's point of view, states:

In most cases now labeled kleptomania, pyromania, etc., however, the actors appear to be motivated in the same way other criminals are motivated. Consequently they are, in the terminology of the criminal law, responsible. They select secluded places in which to perpetrate their acts, plan their activities in advance, realize that they will be arrested if detected, and do many other things indicative that there is a conscious normative referent in their behavior.

Cressey (1958) further questioned the assumption that larcenous behavior like shoplifting, is compulsive:

> The economic status of the observer, is of great importance in determining whether he thinks a person is not in economic need and is consequently compulsive. . . . If all psychiatrists were poverty-stricken the proportion of shoplifters called 'kleptomaniacs' would probably be higher than it is.

Concerning the neurotic compulsive, Davidson states that although abstinence may cause discomfort or anxiety, the neurotic compulsive individual can refrain from action and that it is "socially hazardous" to exempt these individuals from accountability (1958).

Concerning the third category of behavior by an otherwise normal person who commits a crime because of a rage reaction or acute alcoholism, Davidson argues that if their acts are not considered crimes then ". . . no one would ever be responsible for anything."

Implicit in the reluctance of English and most American courts to adopt an "irresistible impulse" clause seems to be the logic presented by Cressey and Davidson. There are doubts that any truly "irresistible impulse" exists; beliefs that if it does exist, it is too difficult to prove or disprove as a defense; and beliefs that such a defense is dangerous to society (Guttmacher and Weihofen, 1952).

THE NEW HAMPSHIRE DOCTRINE

New Hampshire was the only state which did not adopt the M'Naghten ruling. Influenced by the ideas of the influential forensic psychiatrist, Issac Ray, and by Judge Doe of New Hampshire, the courts in the state have been governed by an extremely "liberal" provision: if the criminal action were the "offspring or product of mental disease," then the accused may plead not guilty by reason of insanity (Robitscher, 1966). Perhaps the most important implication of the provision is that the question of responsibility is left to the discretion of the jury (Guttmacher and Weihofen, 1952).

DURHAM RULING

The New Hampshire provision had little influence elsewhere until 1954 when the United States Court of Appeals for the District of Columbia discarded M'Naghten and introduced the Durham ruling, apparently modeled after the liberal New Hampshire provision.

Monte Durham's crime, unlike that in most insanity defense trials, was not murder, but housebreaking. Durham, who was diagnosed as a psychopathic personality with psychosis, had a long history of mental disorder, had been hospitalized, and had attempted suicide several times. When the testifying psychiatrists were asked whether in their opinion, the defendant could distinguish right from wrong, they could not answer categorically. The jury was instructed according to the M'Naghten ruling, and Durham was found guilty. However, he was granted an appeal during which Judge David Bazelon abrogated the M'Naghten ruling for a new formula, which, like the New Hampshire provision, stated that a defendant must be held not guilty if the jury finds that his act was caused by mental disease or defect (Simon, 1967).

The Durham decision was widely hailed in most psychiatric and some legal circles as a very liberal ruling that reflected the "new psychology,"—it was felt that the Durham decision would permit a full range of psychiatric testimony to be presented in the courts. Most lawyers, however, were not enthusiastic about the Durham ruling. They felt, as expressed by Goldstein (1967), that it was a "non-rule"; it did not provide a jury with any standard by which to judge evidence, and it left to a group of non-professional individuals the additional burden of passing judgment on highly technical psychiatric testimony.

Leifer (1964), viewing the Durham ruling somewhat differently, stressed that a jury is rendered unable to make its own decision; it must agree with one of two teams of psychiatrists, each of which provides technical testimony in language that is not easily understandable.

Simon (1967) conducted an empirical study of the effects of the Durham ruling. She first provided descriptive statistics indicating that a fifteenfold increase had occurred in the proportion of defendants who were acquitted on grounds of insanity in the District of Columbia since the adoption of the Durham ruling. In a skillfully constructed experimental study in which "juries" listened to tape recorded trials, Simon attempted to determine the effects of the Durham ruling upon their deliberations. The high degree of congruence in verdicts between a jury instructed in accordance with the Durham ruling jury and an uninstructed jury led her to conclude that the Durham ruling is ". . .closer to the jury's natural sense of equity." However, one may question the need for any rule at all. That juries instructed in accordance with the Durham ruling deliberated significantly longer than those instructed in accordance with the M'Naghten ruling led her to conclude that the Durham rule ". . . serves to enhance the juror's responsibility." When the juries were asked what ruling they would recommend for future use, thirty-six percent of the jurors voted for the M'Naghten ruling, thirty-one percent for the Durham ruling, and thirty-one percent indicating no preference. Her results concerning jury preferences were therefore inconclusive.

The courts have been almost unanimous in their failure to follow the lead of the District of Columbia in adopting the Durham ruling. Moreover, the courts have, as Goldstein (1967) stated, attempted to . . . "reaffirm [their] faith in 'free will' and deterrence, [their] hostility to psychiatry and the 'deterministic' view of human behavior, [their] skepticism about psychiatry's status as a science, [their] fear that the concept of mental disease was so broad that it might encompass all or most serious crime, and especially the psychopath."

The Durham ruling received its share of criticism from the psychiatric field. Gaylin (1965) stated that arguing the holistic stress theory of behavior to its logical conclusion can lead to such absurdities as acquitting persons with psychosomatic ills like asthma, for crimes which they might commit. He adds that society could not afford to exempt from criminal responsibility all actions resulting from mental diseases like alcoholism, drug addiction, and sexual deviation. "Would we," he asks rhetorically, "grant immunity to the addict who steals to feed his habit, while we hold liable the pauper who steals to feed his hunger?"

An epitaph on the Durham ruling was written in June of 1972 when the U.S. Court of Appeals adopted the Model Penal Code (A.L.I.) in the case of *United States v. Brawner* (1972). In a concurring but separate opinion, Judge David Bazelon stated:

> *Durham* was designed to throw open the windows of the defense and ventilate a musty doctrine with all of the information acquired during a century's study of the intricacies of human behavior. It fueled a long and instructive debate which uncovered a vast range of perplexing and previously hidden questions. And the decision helped to move the question of responsibility from the realm of esoterica into the forefront of the critical issues of the criminal law.

MODEL PENAL CODE (A.L.I. RULE)

The Durham ruling had not been in existence a year when the

American Law Institute, in an attempt to clarify the ambiguity of the "product of mental disease or defect" clause, made its recommendations on insanity in its Model Penal Code (1962). Rejecting the advice of a psychiatric advisory committee which endorsed the Durham ruling, the A.L.I. proposed the following formulation:

> 1. A person is not responsible for criminal conduct if at the time of such conduct as a result of mental disease or defect he lacks substantial capacity either to appreciate the criminality of his conduct or to conform his conduct to the requirements of law.
> 2. As used in this Article, the terms "mental disease or defect" do not include an abnormality manifested only by repeated criminal or otherwise antisocial conduct.

The second provision is noteworthy in its obvious exclusion for consideration of the category of the "psychopathic personality." Glueck (1962) suggested that some complexities occur when the courts' deal with the psychopathic personality; in view of their resistance to treatment, acquittal of these individuals on grounds of insanity might not serve any purpose, and the high rate of recidivism among these individuals, when acquitted, presents the courts with the same problem that they attempted to solve.

In spite of their initial opposition, psychiatrists came to view the new Model Penal Code as an improvement over previous rulings because of the substitution of "appreciate" for "know," a seeming recognition of emotional as well as intellectual awareness of conduct. The substitution of "conform" for "control" was also deemed an improvement. The wide acceptance of the Model Penal Code was demonstrated empirically by Sadoff, Collins, and Keeler (1966), who asked military attorneys and psychiatrists to rank in order their preferences among the five most used tests of criminal responsibility. Psychiatrists ranked the Model Penal Code first. The attorneys preferred the M'Naghten ruling and the "irresistible impulse" ruling.

Although the Model Penal Code found acceptance, criticism was voiced concerning the vagueness of the terms, "appreciate" and "substantial." The question was also raised about the extent to which a lay jury could grasp the significance of the expression "to conform his conduct to the requirements of the law."

THE CURRENS TEST

Another major attempt to define insanity was pronounced by Chief Justice John Biggs who spoke for the majority of the United States Court of Appeals in the Currens Case (1961). The Currens test states that the jury may find the defendant not guilty on grounds of insanity if the accused ". . . as a result of mental disease or defect, lacked substantial capacity to conform his conduct to the requirements of the law which he is alleged to have violated." Although the "substantial capacity to conform" clause is like the Model Penal Code's formula, the Currens test omits what has been regarded as a cognitive criterion, "appreciate the criminality of his conduct" (Glueck, 1962). The Currens test has been criticized, however, because it would deny to jurors grounds for finding insanity when the capacity for self-control is unimpaired but, nevertheless, when the defendant did not "appreciate" the criminality of his conduct (Goldstein, 1967).

"DIMINISHED" RESPONSIBILITY

The legal concept of "diminished" or "partial" responsibility may be traced in English law. In the seventeenth century, Sir Matthew Hale, Lord Chief Justice of the Court of the King's Bench, differentiated two forms of insanity: "partial insanity of mind," and "a total insanity." Partial insanity, Hale prophetically observed, could excuse a crime but would be a matter of great difficulty (Biggs, 1955).

The Homicide Act of 1957 made the doctrine of diminished responsibility a part of English law (Robitscher, 1966). The plea has since 1957 become so popular in England that, in Goldstein's (1967) view, it threatens to replace the insanity defense entirely. In the United States, the doctrine of "partial responsibility" was first invoked in cases in which evidence of intoxication was admitted as defense against murder in the first degree. Unlike England, however, the United States has been slow in extending the plea to other types of mitigating evidence (Goldstein, 1967). Only about a dozen states recognize the doctrine of "partial responsibility."

Partial responsibility assumes partial importance when a question of capital punishment is involved; it offers the defense an alternative to the insanity defense which frequently brings with it indeterminate committment. Guttmacher (1963) expressed a reservation held by many of the critics of diminished responsibility when he warned against the uncritical assumption that partially responsible defendants merit shorter sentences than individuals pleading insanity. He adds that in many instances, the type of abnormality exhibited by partially responsible individuals requires *longer* periods of incarceration that that of other offenders in the interests of protecting society from their potential depredations. Confinement, however, should be within a benign and therapeutic environment.

REFERENCES

Biggs, J. *The Guilty Mind.* New York: Harcourt, Brace and Company, 1955.

Cressey, D. R. "The Differential Association Theory and Compulsive Crimes." In R. Nice (Ed.), *Crime and Insanity.* New York: Philosophical Library, 1958.

Davidson, H. A. "Irresistible Impulse and Criminal Responsibility. In R. Nice (Ed.), *Crime and Insanity.* New York: Philosophical Library, 1958.

Dusky v. United States, 362 U.S. 402; 80 S. Ct. 788 (1960).

Gaylin, W. M. "Psychiatry and the Law: Partners in Crime." *Columbia University Forum,* 1965, 8, 23–27.

Glueck, S. E. *Mental Disorder and the Criminal Law.* Boston: Little, Brown and Company, 1962.

Goldstein, A. S. *The Insanity Defense.* New Haven, Connecticut: Yale University Press, 1967.

Goldstein, J., and Katz, J. "Why an Insanity Defense?" *Daedalus,* 1963, 92, 549–563.

Guttmacher, M. S. "What Can the Psychiatrist Contribute to the Issue of Criminal Responsibility?" *Journal of Nervous and Mental Disorders,* 1963, 136, 103–117.

Guttmacher, M. S., and Weihofen, H. *Psychiatry and the Law.* New York: W. W. Norton, 1952.

Hurt v. United States, 327 F. 2d 978, 981 (8th Cir., 1964).

Leifer, R. "The Psychiatrist and Tests of Criminal Responsibility." *American Psychologist,* 1964, 19, 825–830.

Lipsitt, P. D. "The Dilemma of Competency for Trial and Mental Illness." *New England Journal of Medicine,* 1970, 282, 797–798.

Meoteris v. United States, 108 F. 2d 402, 405 (7th Cir., 1939)

Pate v. Robinson, 383 U.S. 375; 86 S. Ct. 836 (1966).

Roche, R. Q. *The Criminal Mind.* New York: Farrar, Straus and Cudahy, 1958.

Sadoff, R. L., Collins, D., and Keeler, W.J. "Psychiatric Testimony in Military Courts." *American Journal of Psychiatry,* 1966, 123, 1344–1348.

Schulman, R. E. "Determination of Competency: Burial at the Crossroads." In T. Brelje and L.M. Irvine (Eds.), *Law, Psychiatry and the Mentally Disabled.* Springfield, Illinois: Charles E. Thomas, 1973.

Simon, Rita J. *The Jury and the Defense of Insanity.* Boston: Little, Brown and Company, 1967.

Slovenko, R. *Psychiatry and Law.* Boston: Little, Brown and Company, 1973.

Stone, A. A. *Mental Health and the Law: A System in Transition.* Washington, D.C.: U.S. Government Printing Office, 1975.

Determination of Competency— Burial at the Crossroad

Robert E. Schulman

We all bring different experiences and biases to the issue of competency to stand trial. In an effort to insure that we all have some of the same basic information concerning this issue, I will begin with some definitions, propose a few legal and psychological issues, and endeavor to place the problem in a psycholegal framework.

The great number of people affected by the question of competency to stand trial is often not realized. A determination of incompetency is one of the most frequent reasons for hospitalization of persons involved in the criminal justice system. A large study of offenders (Scheidemandel and Kanno, 1969) admitted to more than 50 facilities across the country revealed that questions regarding competency were the reason for hospitalizing 52 percent of the offender-patient population. Among the same group, only 4 percent of the patients were individuals found not guilty by reason of insanity. On the basis of the sample in this study, it is speculated that across the nation at any given time, there are about 15,000 persons hospitalized who are waiting return for trial or discharge.

In terms of sheer numbers of individuals affected by questions of competency to stand trial, the problem is of substantial magnitude. Aside from the question of how many people are affected, the underlying psychological and legal issues present interesting and important questions. As a matter of fact, when one considers this issue, one needs to examine the underpinnings of the criminal law process and the relationship of this process to the behavioral sciences. Competency to stand trial is one of three points in the criminal justice system where behavioral science input has had an important, if confusing, impact. The issue of competency to stand trial is just as important as are questions regarding culpability or mental condition at the time of execution of sentence. Nevertheless, competency has received less attention and is less well understood by lawyers and behavioral science experts who serve the court.

Before considering these three intrusions into the legal system by behavioral science experts, a further preliminary statement must be made. The most difficult and confusing aspects of the issue of competency to stand trial are highlighted by trying to come to grips with the idea that mental illness per se is not the same as, or equal to, incompetency to stand trial. A finding that a person is mentally ill, even severely ill, does not answer the question of whether that person is capable of standing trial. On the other hand, the person who is not mentally ill may not be capable of standing trial either. The clearest case of a person incompetent to stand trial is the one where the patient is immobilized and totally unable to communicate with his attorney. He is, therefore, clearly unable to assist counsel in providing information necessary for the preparation of his case. Among the mentally ill group, the catatonic individual, for example, would fit this category. On the other hand, certain paranoid individuals with delimited and circumscribed delusional systems might be quite able to assist counsel in preparing a defense. Certainly, the patient's assistance to the attorney would be hampered if the paranoid delusional system intruded on reality to such an extent as to make the patient unreliable. Absence of mental illness does not necessarily mean that a person can or will assist in his defense. The person who willfully, stubbornly, and unwaiveringly refuses to communicate with his attorney may be incompetent to stand trial. Yet, that individual, while possibly being eccentric, might not be pigeonholed into any of our traditional psychiatric diagnostic categories. A finding of mental illness all too often has been equated with incompetency to stand trial. The primary reason for this confusion lies in the law which does not concretely spell out standards to be used in determining competency to stand trial and has left the criteria vague (Robey, 1965). Where the law has been definite, the behavioral science expert has distorted the criteria to fit an illness model.

The issue of competency to stand trial developed out of our English Common Law tradition which required that an accused person have the capability to adequately defend himself against his accusers in a court of law. Common law criteria for determining this was whether or not the defendant understood the nature of the legal process, recognized the consequences that could follow from the accusations made against him, and had the ability to assist his legal counsel in his own behalf.

INSANITY AT THE TIME OF TRIAL

Under contemporary law, and not much different from the common law tradition noted above, a person is eligible for trial if he is able to understand his position and to participate rationally and adequately in his defense. In part, this rule is formulated out of humane considerations and an extension of the prohibition against trials *in absentia*. The reason is that the mentally incompetent defendant, although physically present, is actually mentally absent and unable to help in his defense. The Illinois Code (Illinois Revised Statutes, Chapter 38) which is based on the American Law Institute's Model Penal Code is illustrative of the usual statutory provisions for competency:

A. If before a trial or after a judgment has been entered but before pronouncement of sentence, or after a death sentence has been imposed but before execution of that sentence, the court has reason to believe that the defendant is incompetent, the court shall suspend the proceedings and shall impanel a jury to determine the defendant's competency. If a jury is waived by the defendant, the court shall conduct a hearing to determine the defendant's competency.

B. If, during the trial, the court has reason to believe that the defendant is incompetent, the court shall suspend the proceedings and shall conduct a hearing to determine the defendant's competency and shall, at the election of the defendant, impanel a jury to determine that issue.

C. The burden of going forward with evidence of the defendant's incompetency shall be on the party, if any, requesting that determination.

D. The court may appoint qualified experts who shall be compensated by the county to examine the defendant with regard to his competency and to testify at the hearing. Any party may introduce, at the hearing, other evidence regarding the defendant's competency. No statement made by the accused in the course of any examination into his competency provided for by this Section, whether the examination shall be with or without the consent of the accused, shall be admitted in evidence against the accused on the issue of guilt in any criminal proceeding.

E. If the defendant is found to be competent, the proceedings which had been suspended shall be resumed.

If the defendant is found to be incompetent, he shall be committed or remain subject to the further order of the court in accordance with Section 104–3 of this Code.

The determination called for by the above procedural rule is guided by the following which, while purporting to define competency, sets out the general common law understanding of competency:

> For the purpose of this Article, "incompetent" means a person charged with an offense who is unable because of a mental condition:
>
> (a) To understand the nature and purpose of the proceedings against him; or
>
> (b) To assist in his defense; or
>
> (c) After a death sentence has been imposed, to understand the nature and purpose of such sentence.
>
> If before a trial, or after a judgment has been entered but before pronouncement of sentence, or after a death sentence has been imposed but before execution of that sentence, the court has reason to believe that the defendant is incompetent the court shall suspend the proceedings and shall impanel a jury to determine the defendant's competency.

The judicial interpretation of the test for competency to stand trial has presented inconsistencies. For example, in a case where an individual had, because of brain injuries, blunted affect and dulled emotional awareness, a Massachusetts court (*Commonwealth v. Harrison*, 1961) held that even if the defendant was emotionally blunted, if he was aware and understood cognitively his position relative to the accusations against him and was cognitively able to assist in his defense, then in spite of the absence of emotional elements, the individual would be deemed competent to stand trial. On the other hand, some cases (*U.S. v Chisholm*, 1904 and *Dusley v. U.S.*, 1960) hold that affective as well as cognitive appreciation is required for the individual to be deemed competent to stand trial.

The behavioral scientist's usefulness to the court may be facilitated by thorough understanding of the rule and implementation of the criteria Robey (1965) has suggested be used to gauge an individual's competency to stand trial. Under the general heading of comprehension of court proceedings, the behavioral scientist should consider the individual's awareness of his surroundings, procedure, principals, charges, possible verdicts, penalties, and legal rights. The individual should have the ability to advise counsel regarding facts, plea, and, in a limited way, legal strategy. The defendant should be able to maintain a relationship with the lawyer, maintain a consistent defense, should know when and which rights he is waiving, be able to interpret witnesses' testimony, and be able to testify if that were necessary. Another aspect which is important, but often overlooked, is the individual's susceptibility to decompensation while awaiting or standing trial. With regard to possible decompensation, Robey suggests that violent individuals, those suffering acute psychosis, suicidal depression, regressive withdrawal, or organic deterioration may be the ones most susceptible to decompensation prior to trial.

The behavioral scientist's *raison d'etre* in this framework can only be to furnish information to the court on these issues. Even this more limited involvement is questionable, but may be justified under special circumstances. The behavioral scientist should furnish facts upon which the court, with other information, may base its conclusion. If the behavioral scientist views his task in this light, Robey's guidelines may be helpful.

At this point, I want to briefly note the two other junctures in the criminal justice system where behavioral science input frequently is found. This, I believe, is important to do for clarity and to help us keep in mind the important distinction between these three legal tests.

INSANITY AT THE TIME OF THE OFFENSE

Simply put, the behavioral scientist, and again most often the psychiatrist, is asked to testify whether or not the accused knew that what he was doing was wrong. It is at this juncture and not the juncture where competency to stand trial is determined that the well-known tests of criminal responsibility are applied. There has been a great deal of quibbling and rhetoric over the M'Naghten Rule and the so-called refinements found in the Durham adaptation of the M'Naghten Rule. We are aware that well-informed and articulate behavioral scientists have criticized and taken serious issue with behavioral science input at this point in criminal proceedings (Szasz, 1963; Menninger, 1970).

The American Law Institute's Model Penal Code has proposed the following rule:

> 1. A person is not responsible for criminal conduct if at the time of such conduct as a result of mental disease or defect he lacks substantial capacity either to appreciate the criminality of his conduct or to conform his conduct to the requirements of the law.

INSANITY AT THE TIME OF EXECUTION

The law provides that an insane man cannot be executed, while a sane man can. The test is that the condemned person must realize that he is going to be punished for a crime he has committed. The behavioral scientist again is in a peculiar position in that if the man is not competent to be executed, then the task is to rehabilitate the individual so that he can be executed. This, of course, leads to a certain kind of nauseating absurdity and, to the best of this writer's knowledge, the issue of insanity at the time of execution is not raised frequently.

GAMESMANSHIP

Anyone, anytime, and in any manner may raise doubt concerning the individual's competency to stand trial. The degree of evidence required to proceed is minimal, and if any doubt at all is presented by either the defense or the prosecution, the court must then make some determination of the defendant's competency to stand trial. As a practical matter, ordinarily this issue is raised by the defense counsel and any simple statement to that effect is sufficient to raise the doubt. Once the issue is raised, whatever proceedings have been initiated are staid and a competency examination completed. Ordinarily, the cost of a competency examination is paid by the state.

Typically, defense counsel proceeds with a written motion asking for a competency examination. Following this motion, the court issues an order specifying that a particular physician or physicians who are disinterested and qualified experts determine the defendant's mental condition at the present time and report to the court regarding the individual's competency. The reports provided by the examining physician or physicians are frequently terse, unimaginative, and bland documents that would not pass critical scrutiny if it were not for the judge's acceptance and willingness to tolerate conclusions and lack of factual statements in the reports. Courts frequently do not pay close attention to the nature and extent of the examination that is completed. In most instances, the court asks the examiner to answer the ultimate question of responsibility. A well-documented psychiatric report may be criticized by the court if it does not directly answer the legal test. There is no clearer abdication of responsibility by the court than in this instance. All too often, the examiner believes that he is functioning under the M'Naghten Rule and confuses the determination of competency with the responsibility question. In addition, the examiner frequently does not clearly understand that mental illness in and of itself is not the criteria for the determination of competency to stand trial. If both of these confusions exist in the mind of the examiner, then he is more likely than not to find the individual incompetent; not because this is actually the case, but because the examiner's confusion leads him to err on the conservative side. The maxim is "when in doubt, hospitalize for longer period of examination." The examiner believes that there is little to lose in doing this and ordinarily does not envision himself as abridging the individual's constitutional rights. Indeed, frequently the defendant may wish to postpone the trial and determination of guilt or innocence.

The criminal law, as all law, is designed to dispose of cases and controversies. The question of competency to stand trial interferes with that goal. Competency examinations may be nothing more than a device for both sides to find out something more about the individual's personality. Supposedly, this additional information helps both sides in considering plea bargaining and reaching some disposition prior to trial. In this sense, a competency proceeding is a discovery procedure used by both sides to buttress respective plea bargaining positions. The defense attorney may resist competency examinations particularly where he believes that his client has an excellent insanity defense. In this situation, the defense attorney does not wish to have the client to stand trial at the present time even if his condition is less than adequate. Proceeding to trial when the defendant is not competent and the attorney is aware of the defendant's incompetency is tantamount to perpetrating a fraud on the court. If the client is incompetent but the attorney proceeds to trial, this violates the principle that a court does not want to proceed against an individual who is not mentally present. On the other hand, when the defense attorney anticipates the insanity defense case may be weak or not sufficiently persuasive, he may want a competency hearing as a way of buying time. During the delay, the prosecution, judge, and community may change their attitudes about the crime or defendant. Competency hearings, unfortunately, can move in the direction of becoming hearings to determine responsibility. In this summary procedure, the case is frequently heard before the judge without a jury and inappropriately goes beyond the limits to which it should be confined. Too often, the court decides too early that the defendant is not responsible. Convincing the court that the defendant is incompetent strengthens an otherwise weak insanity defense. This opening gambit is a device to have the court begin thinking about the defendant as a flesh and blood human being rather than just a felon. This is a softening-up tactic. When the defense maneuver is successful, the prosecution then is willing to have the client committed and often willing not to prosecute the case at all.

If the prosecuting attorney anticipates an insanity defense, he may raise the question of competency to stand trial to begin demonstrating that the psychiatric agruments about mental illness are without substance or merit. The prosecutor often knows that the individual will not submit to an examination conducted by prosecution psychiatrists when an insanity defense has been raised. Thus, the examination to determine competency to stand trial may give the prosecutor some information that he would not otherwise have.

The tactical and strategic movements by the attorneys on both sides can be justified or rationalized from a variety of different perspectives. It is critical, however, to recognize that the reasons for asking for any psychiatric examination often have nothing to do with the mental health of the individual, but are part of the gamesmanship employed in the prosecution and defense of criminal cases.

When the individual is found competent to stand trial the prosecution is resumed. This may result in an insanity defense, negotiated plea contingent upon treatment, or a conviction and sentence. If the individual is found incompetent to stand trial, ordinarily he is committed to a maximum security hospital for treatment until such a time that he is restored to competency. Commitment for custodial purposes only without attempts to rehabilitate and restore the individual to a competent state would be punishment without trial and is unconstitutional. Unfortunately, long custodial commitments frequently are the result of competency proceedings, not because of any malicious intent on anyone's part, but because most maximum security hospitals, or similar type institutions, while purporting and desiring to provide treatment, have few qualified staff to implement treatment.

When the individual is restored to competency, in the opinion of the hospital staff and treating physicians who are supposed to make that decision, he is to be returned to the court. Too often, however, it is not clear to the treating physician that he has this responsibility. Even if it were clear, the physician may be unwilling and unprepared to take the responsibility for returning the individual to court. First, the physician may be uncertain about what restored to competency really means. Secondly, if he does understand what restored to competency means, he may be unclear as to which condition the individual is supposed to be restored. Finally, if he understands the first and second of these problems, he may be reluctant to return the individual to the court because he realizes that if the individual is found guilty of the alleged act and placed in a prison, this is not going to do much for the individual's mental health which is probably tenuous anyway. It is easy then, for the physician to avoid taking any action and to believe that it is better to keep the individual in the hospital where he is being treated than do something that might result in a conviction and incarceration in a penal institution.

McGarry (1965) recently has reported findings which indicate how decisions concerning offender-patients are reached by the staff of psychiatric institutions. McGarry concluded that generally psychiatrists appear to view psychotics as incompetent to stand trial and reach their decision within an exclusively medical framework. He further notes that due process of law may be compromised where the importance of the issue is not understood by the examiner. Thus, certain constitutional rights like a speedy and prompt public trial may be denied the individual. McGarry also concluded on the basis of his limited sample that the courts ordinarily accepted a psychiatrist's judgment with regard to the issue of competency to stand trial and thus aid and abet the psychiatrists' use of a medical model for determining what indeed is a legal issue.

Generally, a person may be returned to court in two distinct manners. He may receive from the rehabilitating institution a bill of health stating that he is restored and he is now competent to stand trial. This route out of the hospital is contingent upon overcoming the many constraints of releasing and finding offender-patients restored. Institutions vary in their procedure for doing this. It may be one physician's responsibility or it may be delegated to a committee. The other way a person may obtain his release is via the route of *habeas corpus* through the courts. In such a proceeding, the patient, as the petitioner, asks the court to issue a writ of *habeas corpus* directing the hospital to show why the inmate should be continued in custody. If the hospital is unable to do that, then the individual must be returned to the court for trial or be released. The *habeas corpus* route for the individual is not easy and a great deal of pressure is put on him not to pursue this remedy. If the individual is able to execute his writ of *habeas corpus*, it is likely to be heard before a judge who is already influenced and guided by the hospital staff. This in turn makes it easy for the hospital staff to justify continued hospitalization.

Giving all sides the benefit of sound and ethical intentions, we nevertheless, regardless of how unwittingly it has come about, have a collusive collaboration between law and medicine (including the behavioral sciences) which effectively buries the patient alive. The grave diggers are the behavioral scientists. Just why the behavioral scientist is involved in the competency issue is not any clearer than why he is involved elsewhere in the criminal law process. At other junctures in the criminal justice system, however, the psychological issues seem more definite, even if camouflaged and distorted by the M'Naghten Rule or other tests of insanity and responsibility. Here we have a simple question to be asked and answered. Any of us, without any special expertise, it would seem, would be able to answer the question. The lawyer himself is probably in the best position to answer and determine whether or not the particular individual is able to communicate the kind of information that is necessary to effectively aid and assist in his defense and understand the proceedings against him.

If the behavioral scientist is the grave digger, then the lawyer, through his relatively passive and placid role, is the pallbearer. The incantation is played through the righteousness and dignity that only courts can muster. Following the ritual, the incompetent individual is buried and lost in the labyrinth of hospital systems. Indeed, he is at the crossroad—not prisoner, not patient, but someone in between, unable to get help, someone without a definite status. The hospital staff experience him as an unnecessary burden, not a good patient, but a person who is there under duress, unwilling to cooperate and participate in treatment. Frequently, the hospital staff's attitude is such that it makes it impossible for even a cooperative offender-patient to benefit from the milieu treatment. The staff are put in a bind as well. If they do treat him, to what end? To rehabilitate him to stand trial and then possibly face imprisonment is not a task to which many treators aspire. The individual hospitalized as a result of a competency hearing is in quite a different position from the person acquitted by reason of insanity and then hospitalized. When the individual has been acquitted he no longer is an offender-patient. It is easier to view him as a patient with expectations that through treatment he can begin to lead a productive, responsible life. The person found incompetent to stand trial has the worst of all worlds. His fate has not been decided. He is detailed and committed to a place which is supposed to provide help, but which views him with suspicion, distrust, and fear.

In the past, individuals who suicided were punished or were punished further by unholy interment—burial at a crossroad without distinctive marking. I do not mean to suggest that pleading incompetency to stand trial is suicidal, yet it does not get the individual very far. If not a dead end, such commitments most often turn out to be a long delay. This delay may actually deprive the individual of needed treatment as well as cause delays in the legal system.

Some study (Lipsitt, 1971) has been given to the application of objective measures to determine competency. These efforts are worthwhile but do not solve the problem. Behavioral scientists, as well as lawyers, need to be made aware of the actual consequences of a finding of incompetency and the little utilitarian value of such a proceeding. Application of behavioral science technology in the legal arena should be limited to the dispositional phase of the legal process and not at those points in the proceedings which deal with legal responsibility and purely legal issues. Since the question of competency is basically a jurisdictional question and not dispositional, the behavioral scientist's role could be eliminated. Responsibility for the competency proceeding needs to be returned to the appropriate keepers of that trust. This is a question the lawyer must answer. Only the lawyer knows whether or not his client is able to assist, cooperate, and understand the legal issues. Lawyers, in turn, must avoid using the competency issue as a maneuvering dilatory device and, instead, face the problem squarely. The legal profession must no longer support and encourage attorneys in this avoidance. To do so makes a mockery of two systems, each of which in its own way is able to serve the offender-patient.

REFERENCES

Commonwealth v. Harrison. 173 N.E. 2d 87 342 Mass. 279. 1961.

Dusky v. U. S. 362 U. S. 402. 1960.

Lipsitt, P. D.: Competency for Trial: a Screening Instrument. *Am J Psychiatr,* *128:*137, 1971.

McGarry, L. A.: Competency for Trial and Due Process via the State Hospital. *Am J Psychiatr, 122:*623, 1965.

Menninger, Karl A.: *The Crime of Punishment.* New York, Viking, 1968.

Robey, A.: Criteria for Competency to Stand Trial: A Checklist for Psychiatrists. *Am J Psychiatr, 122:*616, 1965.

Scheidemandel, Patricia L. and Kanno, C. K.: *The Mentally Ill Offender.* Baltimore, Garamond/Pridemark, 1969.

Szasz, Thomas: *Law, Liberty, and Psychiatry: An Inquiry into the Social Uses of Mental Health Practices.* New York, Macmillan, 1963.

U. S. v. Chisholm. C. C. 149 F. 284. 1904.

The Dilemma of Competency for Trial and Mental Illness

Paul D. Lipsitt

Under statutory provisions in all states a court may request an opinion from a state mental hospital about whether a person accused of a crime possesses the required mental capacity to be tried. The common-law standard for such capacity includes an understanding of the nature and object of the proceedings against him, an ability to comprehend his own circumstances in reference to these proceedings, and an ability to communicate with his attorneys so that they can aid him in the development of his defense.

A recent decision of the Supreme Judicial Court of Massachusetts could lead to radical changes in the pretrial commitment procedures to mental hospitals of persons accused of crimes. In the case of *Commonwealth v. Druken*(1) the defendant was initially tried and found guilty of breaking and entering, as well as assault. He received a two-year sentence after the Bridgewater State Hospital had determined that he was competent to stand trial. On appeal to the Superior Court, the defendant was again sent to Bridgewater, and was this time determined to be incompetent after the customary procedure of observation and report to the court by the medical director. As a result, he would have been indefinitely committed until such time as he was determined to be fit for trial.

The case was appealed to the Supreme Judicial Court on the grounds that Druken had been improperly committed to a mental hospital. The high court held that a person who has been committed to a mental institution after a determination that he is incompetent for trial must receive the same safeguards against his loss of freedom that he would receive if he were involuntarily hospitalized as a mentally ill person. To provide an accused person with less would be to deprive him of his constitutional rights under the Fourteenth Amendment.

In this case, after the observation period for the determination of competency, a hearing was held to determine if the defendant should be indefinitely committed. The statute states that if there is a finding of insanity, a report of the prisoner's mental condition is to be made to the "court or judge issuing the warrant or commitment . . . with the recommendation that the prisoner be committed as an insane person."(2)

The confusion caused by the intermingling of issues of competency, insanity and mental illness in the statutes, as well as a dearth of reference to competency definition and criteria, has been reflected in psychiatric reports and court rulings. Although, the only legal rationale for a criminal commitment before trial is on the basis of competency to stand trial, cases are frequently disposed of through indefinite commitment on the basis of mental illness or dangerousness.

It is at this point that the status of the defendant may subtly shift from an issue of competency to one of mental illness for commitment purposes. To be committed involuntarily, a mentally ill person must be ". . . subjected to a disease, psychosis, neurosis, or character disorder which renders him so deficient in judgment or emotional control that he is in danger of causing physical harm to himself or to others, or the wanton destruction of valuable property, or is likely to conduct himself in a manner which clearly violates the established laws, ordinances, conventions or morals of the community."(3)

In the Druken case, the court reasoned that, although there may be justification for committing a person for an observation period to determine his fitness for trial, it was unconscionably alien to the rights of the defendant to be indefinitely committed under criminal status merely because he had been accused of an offense for which he had not been tried and found guilty. Therefore, the court held that he should be entitled to the stringent safeguards provided for persons involuntarily committed civilly to a mental institution. These procedures are spelled out in other sections of the statute dealing with the hospitalization of such persons.(4) Two physicians are required to certify that the accused is mentally ill. The certifying physician can hold no office or appointment in the institution to which the person has been committed other than in an advisory capacity, and where practicable, one of the physicians should be board-certified in psychiatry. There is also provision for periodic review of the case when there has been a civil commitment to Bridgewater. The civil procedure is in marked contrast to that in competency proceedings, where there is no periodic review, and certification is by the medical director of Bridgewater or a member of the medical staff.

Providing these legal safeguards for the person who is committed as mentally ill and incompetent is certainly commendable. However, it is hoped that the addition of the safeguards designed for the mentally ill will not cloud the issue that the immediate purpose of his hospitalization and treatment is to attain a level of mental competency to allow him to function as a defendant in a criminal proceeding. When he reaches this level, he may still be mentally ill in a clinical sense. Nevertheless, he should be released back to court to defend himself.

As a result of the Druken decision, it will be even more important to develop a functional test of competency so that the legal issue of whether a person is competent to stand trial can be resolved. It is neither good law nor good therapy for an accused person to be held in legal limbo if he is competent, yet mentally ill.

REFERENCES

(1) *Commonwealth v. Druken*, 254 NE 2d 779
(2) Mass GL Ch 123, Section 105
(3) Mass GL Ch 123, Section 1
(4) Mass GL Ch 123, Sections 51, 51A and 53

The Insanity Defense

Alan A. Stone

A mountain of scholarly work exists on the insanity defense, and yet, as one sensible commentator noted, the annual judicial utterances of not guilty by reason of insanity are rarer than the annual incidence of poisonous snake bites in Manhattan.(1) In New York State during the decade of the sixties there were only 11 successful cases of not guilty by reason of insanity.(2) Despite the rarity of the tangible event the outpouring of scholarship continues. Recently, there has been a spate of critical writings suggesting the abrogation of the insanity defense.(3) Former President Nixon proposed that the traditional insanity defenses be done away with in the federal courts so as to curb unconscionable abuse of the insanity defense by criminals.(4)

Why does such a rare event achieve such academic and political significance? One important answer, I believe, is that the insanity defense touches on ultimate social values and beliefs. In its application to particular cases, it purports to draw a line between those who are morally responsible and those who are not,(5) those who are blameworthy and those who are not,(6) those who have free will and those who do not,(7) those who should be punished and those who should not,(8) and those who can be deterred and those who cannot.(9) The nature of such distinctions has every reason to claim the attention of philosophers, lawyers, behavioral scientists, theologians, and others interested in man and law. It is more difficult to understand, however, why it should so trouble those concerned with the practical problems of administering the criminal justice system.

Perhaps it is merely the possibility of such line drawing which explains why the insanity defense, although rarely invoked and less often successful, is still a political issue which inflames the public imagination. A society which feels itself increasingly unable to cope with crime might well consider such a distinction as a crack in the dike of law, order, and justice. And a society ever less able to maintain a consensus of personal values may fear the fact that, as Lord Devlin has asserted, "the concept of illness expands continually at the expense of the concept of moral responsibility".(10)

Rejection of the insanity defense, however, comes from all sectors of the political spectrum. It is attacked on one side because it excuses too many,(11) and on the other because it excuses too few.(12) One abolitionist claims that it is unfair because it is only available to the rich.(13) Another claims it is applied only to the poor and minorities as a stigmatizing weapon of oppression.(14) Former President Nixon is concerned that the insanity defense allows dangerous criminals to go free,(15) while others argue that the blameless mentally ill are confined longer than criminals.(16) Whatever their reasons, a growing list of noteworthy persons are calling for the abolition of the insanity defense: The American Psychiatric Association,(17) Lady Barbara Wooton,(18) Professor H. L. A. Hart,(19) Professor Norval Morris,(20) Dr. Thomas Szasz,(21) former President Richard Nixon,(22) Dr. Karl Menninger,(23) and Chief Justice Joseph Weintraub of New Jersey.(24)

One of the most interesting questions now being asked, particularly by Goldstein(25) and Morris(26) is: Why do we have the insanity defense? Professor Morris and Judge Weintraub seem to agree that its historic purpose has been to avoid capital punishment. History suggests that there is some truth in that theory.(27) After all, the 18th and 19th century Anglo-American system of law had hundreds of capital offenses, and it may well be that compassion and reason together balked at condemning to death for a mild but capital crime those who were clearly mad at the time of the offense.(28) Hadfield, whose case was one of the turning points in the English law, for example, had a serious war injury, and the jury was encouraged to feel his exposed brain before deciding whether to execute him for shooting at and missing the King.(29)

If one examines the cases rather than the law of insanity, one develops the impression that the function of the insanity defense in the 19th century was to exclude that minimal group of criminal offenders who were by all the prevailing standards mad; that is, mad to the man on the street. Psychiatric testimony might be necessary to do it up right, but psychiatric wisdom was not essential.

Legal formulas that would define those rare persons were introduced, but history suggests that those formulas meant different things at different

times, and like the psychiatric testimony they were perhaps less important
for the ultimate decision than the lawyers thought. The most famous
insanity decision is *M'Naghten*(30) but the legal test was formulated after
the trial, and of course he killed the wrong man. Had he killed the Prime
Minister, his fate might well have been different no matter what the
psychiatrists said, or the legal test indicated. Equally, had Hadfield killed
the King, instead of missing, palpating his brain might have been less
convincing to the jury.

The 20th century brought the deterministic theories of psychoanalysis
and sociology into the courtroom. Efforts were made to expand the
concept, broader legal tests of insanity were called for and at last arrived
in full measure in the *Durham* test.(31)

Why was the gigantic step taken? Was it because Judge David
Bazelon, who announced it, had an interest in psychiatry and
psychoanalysis? Certainly that is true, but the legal test of insanity was
being stretched in various ways in jurisdictions all over the country.(32)

Judge Bazelon has in retrospect suggested that his reason for expanding the test was to let the psychiatrist come into court and explain to
the jury, that microcosm of the community, how this person came to
commit this offense. That is, the psychiatric profession was to be given the
widest possible scope for injecting their "causal" wisdom into the court's
deliberation. But a painful series of Bazelon(32) decisions make it clear
how little wisdom was thus afforded. It is too easy to suggest that this was
because the particular psychiatrists were inadequate; they may well have
been. It is also easy to conclude that psychiatrists have no wisdom. I think
there is a more important question, however; namely, why would the
court want to understand? What difference would that make?

Justice Weintraub, in a remarkable decision, deals with psychiatric
testimony which meets all of Judge Bazelon's humanistic criteria.
Weintraub writes about that testimony as follows:

> Now this is interesting, and I will not quarrel with any of it. But
> the question is whether it has anything to do with the crime of
> murder. I think it does not. It seems clear to me that the
> psychiatric view expounded by Dr. . . is simply irreconcilable
> with the basic thesis of our criminal law, for while the law
> requires proof of an evil-meaning mind, this psychiatric thesis
> denies there is any such thing.(34)

Chief Justice Weintraub is quite right; indeed, none of the social or
behavioral sciences of the 20th century have a theory of an evil-meaning
mind.(35) Freud, 50 years ago, recognized that a psychoanalyst could not

generate a theory of responsibility. He wrote:

> The physician will leave it to the jurist to construct for social purposes a responsibility that is artificially limited to the (psychoanalytic construct of the ego). It is notorious that the greatest difficulties are encountered by the attempts to derive from (the psychoanalytic constructs) practical consequences which are not in contradiction to human feelings.(36)

Human feeling demands that people be held responsible for their acts. Freud thus anticipates former President Nixon's reaction to an expanded insanity defense. Nor have the jurists been able to construct anything better than the good Dr. Freud. Indeed, the limited function of the insanity defense over the centuries reflects those human feelings. Dean Abraham Goldstein of Yale Law School, author of a marvelous analysis of the insanity defense, reaches a similar conclusion:

> The real problem has been to find a formula that keeps the exception closely attuned to what the public can accept.(37)

Professor Joseph Goldstein, in a remarkably bitter attack(38) on the Brawner decision,(39) which terminated the expanded insanity defense of *Durham*, reiterates his view that:

> Neither legislative report, nor judicial opinion, nor scholarly comment criticizing or proposing formulations of the insanity defense has faced the crucial question: What is the purpose of the defense in the criminal process? or: What need for an exception to criminal liability is being met and what objectives of the criminal law are being reinforced by the defense?(40)

I am quite sure that many authors (Wooton,(41) Hart,(42) Szasz,(43) and others), believe they have answered those questions, and one can only conclude that Goldstein finds their answers unsatisfactory. His own recommendations are, as Dershowitz points out,(44) compatible with former President Nixon's; both believe that the findings which lead to an insanity defense should aim instead at the traditional requisite legal elements of the crime; e.g., specific intent.(45) Former President Nixon presumably believes that will lead to less abuse, less going scot-free. Professor Goldstein believes that it would and should lead to more people for the first time going scot-free; i.e., the result would be the same as in a successful defense of self-defense.(46) Professor Goldstein emphasizes that a finding of insanity now leads to involuntary confinement and is retributive.(47)

My own answer to Professor Goldstein's questions is that they are misdirected. The insanity defense is critical only to the criminal law itself. Its purpose is to insure that the criminal law has moral authority.

The Brawner court states the basic premise as follows:

> The concept of "belief in freedom of the human will and a consequent ability and duty of the normal individual to choose between good and evil" is a core concept that is "universal and persistent in mature systems of law" (*Morrissette* v. *U.S.* 342 U.S. 246, 250, 1952). Criminal responsibility is assessed when through "free will" a man elects to do evil.(48)

And a few sentences later: "The concept of lack of 'free will' is both the root of origin of the insanity defense and the line of its growth".(49)

Professor Goldstein, commenting on this section of the Brawner decision, states: "The court mistakenly equates the proposal to abolish the insanity defense with a proposal to eliminate free will. . .".(50) But the court may be inadvertently closer to the truth than is Professor Goldstein. The Brawner court recognizes that the criminal law stands or falls on the premise of free will. But what is a court to do when it confronts a case so bizarre and so incongruous that all the premises of criminal law, including free will, seem inappropriate? Should the court simply grit its teeth and go on? The court is then in that ludicrous position of the American tourist who assumes that if he speaks English loud enough, the foreigners will understand him. If so, the criminal law risks demeaning itself, risks demonstrating that its language is not universal, its moral comprehension not encompassing. How much wiser for the criminal law instead to have an escape hatch, not only to avoid embarrassment, but also because by obverse implication every other defendant does have free will. Thus, the insanity defense is in every sense the exception that proves the rule. It allows the court to treat every other defendant as someone who chose "between good and evil."

The basic problem in criminal law has been to keep the insanity defense an exception in the face of the determinist ideology which dominates the intellectual tradition of the 20th century. The sociology of crime and delinquency may be deterministic, the behaviorism which monopolizes the field of correction may be deterministic, but the criminal law is not. Those who have tried to expand the insanity defense forced the criminal law to confront its ideological isolation. Judge Weintraub recognized that fact in the decision quoted earlier. He wrote:

> The law's conception, resting as it does upon an undemonstrable view of man, is of course vulnerable. But those who attack it cannot offer a view which is demonstrably more authentic. They can tear down the edifice, but have nothing better to replace it.(51)

The importance of the insanity defense is that it is an ideological battleground, but it takes some deciphering to identify which side the combatants are on. Former President Nixon and Professor Goldstein seem to be pointing in the same direction when they question the need for a separate insanity defense. But the former hopes to exclude determinist ideology by getting rid of the insanity defense where that offensive ideology intrudes, while the latter wants to free the determinist ideology from the limiting constraints of the insanity defense and allow it to wash over the entire criminal law.

It is important to consider what the goals of this ideological struggle are. Judge Bazelon is the jurist who comes closest to answering that question for the determinists. In *Brawner* he wrote that the jury should be instructed that: "A defendant is not responsible if at the time of his unlawful conduct his mental or emotional processes or behavior controls were impaired to such an extent that he cannot justly be held responsible for his act.(52)

Here as elsewhere in Judge Bazelon's writings(53) it seems that the goal is to transform the trial into a morality play in which the community (the jury) rediscovers the meaning of justice. Justice Weintraub and others believe it would seem that justice resides in the existing system.

PSYCHIATRIC PARTICIPATION IN THE INSANITY DEFENSE

The two sides of this argument are reflected in many opposing opinions written by Judge Bazelon and then Judge, now Chief Justice Burger of the Supreme Court. There is, however, an entirely different and practical problem which has led to confusion and led these worthies to argue about other problems of the insanity defense; namely, the medical model of illness and the role of the psychiatrist. The psychiatrist, or in his earlier incarnation, the alienist, was traditionally asked by the court to determine (a) whether the defendant was mentally ill and (b) whether that mental illness was such that the defendant lacked criminal responsibility.

Historically the answer to the first question was thought by the psychiatrists to be affirmative if the defendant was psychotic. Although witnesses are capable of disagreeing about whether a given defendant is or is not psychotic, those disagreements are not directly predicated on the degree of the experts' adherence to determinism. The answer to the second question, however, asks the psychiatrist to construct a relationship between a diagnosis and the thoughts and behavior which accompanied it. That relationship does touch on causal theories and therefore the psychiatrist knowingly or not will introduce his own version of determinism.

Many psychiatrists, however, compressed these two questions. Thus, if the answer to the first was psychotic, the answer to the the second was not responsible and if not psychotic, then responsible. That compression again led to considerable dissatisfaction from both sides, the traditionalists arguing that someone could be psychotic, but criminally responsible, and the expansionists arguing that there were nonpsychotic defendants who should be found not guilty by reason of insanity. It is important to realize that both sides were asking the witness to embark on causal explanations which would inevitably rest on deterministic assumptions repugnant to criminal law.

Judge Bazelon's *Durham* decision was read by psychiatrists as they had read the earlier legal tests except that they felt they were no longer confined to an initial diagnosis of psychosis. *Durham* states: "An accused is not criminally responsible if this unlawful act was the product of mental disease or mental defect".(54)

Unfortunately, the *Durham* decision failed to define mental disease or defect, and in the current state of the psychiatric art it is rare that any criminal defendant examined by a psychiatrist will escape being labeled with some diagnosis.

The question immediately arose: Does any diagnosis mean the defendant has a mental disease or defect? Since most of the psychiatric testimony which comes to Judge Bazelon's court originates in Washington's St. Elizabeth's Hospital, it fell first to that psychiatric staff (or so they thought) to cope with this problem. Their first solution was apparently similar to the administrative practice utilized in the Armed Forces where the general policy was to consider psychoses and neuroses grounds for medical separation (mental disease or defect), and character and personality disorders grounds for nonmedical administrative separation (no mental disease or defect). This meant that the diagnosis of sociopath, listed under character disorder and a common result of psychiatric examination of accused criminals, would rule the defendant sane.(55) This result equalled the irony of the *M'Naghten* case. The M'Naghten rule was formulated only after the trial when the judges were called on the carpet by the House of Lords. Most experts agree that M'Naghten himself did not meet the standards which bear his name. In

Durham's case the diagnosis was sociopath, and given the subsequent interpretation, he, too, would have failed to meet the standard which bears his name.

The problem of the interpretation of the phrase mental disease or defect came to a head in the two *Blocker* cases. Blocker killed his common law wife, was tried, pleaded insanity, was diagnosed as a sociopath, found not insane, and was found guilty of murder. But less than 1 month later the St. Elizabeth's staff reversed their position and at another man's trial stated that sociopath was a mental disease or defect. Blocker's lawyer appealed on this basis and was granted a new trial. This sudden reversal of psychiatric opinion and its dramatic impact on the legal process provoked serious criticism. Judge Burger angrily stated: "These terms mean in any given case whatever the expert witnesses say they mean. . . . No rule of law can possibly be sound or workable which is dependent upon the terms of another discipline whose members are in profound diagreement about what those terms mean." Judge Burger concluded: "We tacitly conceded the power of St. Elizabeth's Hospital staff to alter drastically the scope of a rule of law by a 'week-end' change in nomenclature which was without any scientific basis." In a later decision he charged St. Elizabeth's staff with changing "its labels" for the purpose of bringing the maximum number of defendants under the protective umbrella."(57)

As I have said, Judge Bazelon hoped that at the very least *Durham's* broad definitions, if they accomplished nothing else, would allow psychiatrists latitude to tell the whole story of the patient rather than testify piecemeal within the stricter confines of the older tests.

This hope was dashed. Psychiatrists quickly responded to *Durham* by providing a conclusory diagnosis and attesting that this was in fact a mental disease or defect. The court responded to this tendency first in *Carter* v. *U. S.*, "Unexplained medical labels are not enough."(58) Then again, in *Lyles* v. *U. S.*,(59) it said, "If psychiatrists are inclined to testify in medical conclusions, the lawyers should seek to elicit by examination testimony which is meaningful to the jury."

In 1962 Judge Burger warned that *Durham* was supposed "to open the inquiry to the widest possible scope of medical testimony, but in case after case we have tended to narrow the inquiry rigidly to the magic words 'disease' and 'product'."(60) Judge Bazelon, too, was worried and growing less and less enchanted with psychiatrists in the courtroom. In *Rollerson* v. *U. S.* he added his own warning: "The frequent failure to adequately explain and support expert psychiatric opinion threatens the administration of the insanity defense in the District of Columbia".(61) This warning failed to achieve what was desired, and perhaps in desperation Judge Bazelon wrote yet another decision on the subject. This time he himself composed an explanatory set of instructions to psychiatric witnesses which was to accompany all orders requiring mental examinations. These instructions were also to be read aloud in court before the first expert testified.

> As an expert witness, you may, if you wish and if you feel you can, give your opinion about whether the defendant suffered from a mental disease or defect. You may then explain how defendant's disease or defect relates to his alleged offense, that is, how the development, adaptation and functioning of defendant's behavioral processes may have influenced his conduct. This explanation should be so complete that the jury will have a basis for an informed judgment on whether the alleged crime was a "product" of his mental disease or defect. But it will not be necessary for you to express an opinion on whether the alleged crime was a "product" of a mental disease or defect and you will not be asked to do so.
>
> What is desired in the courtroom is the kind of opinion you would give to a family which brought one of its members to your clinic and asked for your diagnosis of his mental condition and a description of how his condition would be likely to influence his conduct. Insofar as counsel's questions permit you should testify in this manner.

Professor Goldstein suggests that nothing in fact was learned from the two decades of *Durham* because the court had never stated what it wanted to learn. Yet Judge Bazelon's decisions suggested he had hoped to learn whether psychiatry and social science could relate condition to conduct. That explanatory relationship is based not on the medical model of disease as Judge Bazelon seems to suggest, but on the deterministic causal theories of behavior current in psychiatry which have little to offer the moral decisionmaker. Jerome Hall recognized this aspect of *Durham* at the outset, he wrote . . . "the emphasis of the Durham test is on the question of causation . . .".(63) Psychiatry failed Judge Bazelon because like all of the social and behavioral sciences it lacks a concept of an evil-meaning mind as a cause, and I might add it also lacks a concept of what is good and right.

The legal test of insanity which replaced *Durham* was similar to that of the American Law Institute. That test and the other common tests are included as an appendix to this chapter. None of these tests solve any of the problems I have discussed; indeed, if Rita Simon, who studied jury deliberation is correct, the tests make little difference. The jury based on the human feelings Freud spoke of seems to come to its own conclusion.(63a)

CODA

In the foregoing discussion, I have said that the insanity defense is the contradictory juncture between a deterministic modern theory of the causes of action, and an enduring free-will theory of the morality of action. I conclude that the contradiction is insoluble, because the epistemological structures rise on different foundations.

It is worth a moment, however, to examine the way some scholars have tried to seek an escape from the dilemma by another route than the insanity defense; namely, a notion of partial responsibility and a more general, more subtle mitigating defense.

Proposals to this end may be seen as occurring along a continuum. First, and least revolutionary, is what Goldstein has called the "trend toward subjective liability."(64) Under this notion, the defense's subjective state may mitigate both the offense charged and the sentence. For example, more than a dozen States now acknowledge partial responsibility for intoxication in murder cases; many permit proof of heat of passion, provocation, self-defense, and so on.(65) The Model Penal Code generalizes this tendency, permitting a reduction in a homicide charge from murder to nonreckless manslaughter if "committed under the influence of extreme mental or emotional disturbance for which there is reasonable explanation or excuse."(66) The Code is doubly subjective in that it requires the excuse be evaluated "from the viewpoint of a person in the actor's situation under the circumstances as he believed them to be."(67)

But this is a situational and not a personal exculpation, and it is not a purely subjective standard in that it weighs not what the defendant did feel, but what a (normal) person in his position and his beliefs as to the facts would have felt. The effects of physical injury, drugs, or emotional grief are to be considered—but many other factors may not be. A second more radical standard along the continuum would also take into consideration the peculiar personal characteristics of the person: his intelligence, excitability, and capacity to control his acts. The so-called *Wells-Gorshen* doctrine developed in California but now embodied in a few States' statutes permits such factors to be considered and to result in a finding of partial responsibility—but only insofar as they negate the "capacity of the accused to form the specific intent essential to constitute a crime.(68) Or, as the Model Penal Code puts it, as "relevant to prove the defendant did or did not have a state of mind which is an essential element of the offense."(69)

If one examines these two formulas in the context of my dualistic analysis, it is as though they seek to balance deterministic data against free will in a special sense. Deterministic data are to be used not to explain why he did it but why his free will was compromised.

A third, still more radical model of partial responsibility could be posed. It would be extremely eclectic as to its factual triggers or sources and subtle or graded as to its results. That is to say, the jury could seek to mitigate punishments for persons on the basis of any number of factors which predisposed them to commit antisocial acts, reduced their capacity to conform their behavior, or made them less blameworthy. Mitigation might be appropriate not only for those with mental disorders, impaired behavior controls, but also for those who were reared in subgroups of different morals, or who had hostile or abusive parents, etc.

Whether or not it would be a moral achievement for the legal system to accommodate itself to a coherent doctrine of diminished responsibility based on all relevant grounds, it seems a distant possibility. So we are returned to the criterion of mental illness as one which, if not ethically or scientifically unique as a determinant of behavior, is at least one with a tradition of recognition and some popular sense of legitimacy.

APPENDIX: THE MAJOR VARIANTS OF THE INSANITY DEFENSE

1. *The M'Naghten Test*

   (*Daniel M'Naghten's* Case, 10 C.&F. 200,210–211, 8 Eng. Rep. 718,722–723 [1843]).

   Every man is to be presumed to be sane, and . . . to establish a defense on the ground of insanity, it must be clearly proved that, at the time of the committing of the act, the party accused was labouring under such a defect of reason, from disease of the mind, as not to know the nature and quality of the act he was doing; or if he did know it, that he did not know he was doing what was wrong.

This is now the sole test in fewer than half the States, but is one of the standards in most jurisdictions.

2. *The Irresistible Impulse Test*

   A. (*Parsons* v. *State*, 2 So. 854, 866–67 [Ala. 1887]).

   Did he know right from wrong, as applied to the particular act in question?. . . . If he did have such knowledge, he may nevertheless not be legally responsible if the two following conditions concur: (1) If, by reason of the duress of such mental disease, he had so far lost the power to choose between the right and wrong, and to avoid doing the act in question, as that his free agency was at the time destroyed; (2) and if, at the same time, the alleged crime was so connected with such mental disease, in the relation of cause and effect, as to have been the product of it solely. (Note: Most jurisdictions drop the key word "solely" from this formulation.)

B. (*Davis* v. *United States*, 165 U.S. 373, 378 [1897] [The Federal Rule]).

(The accused is to be classed as insane if) though conscious of (the nature of his act) and able to distinguish right from wrong,. . . yet his will, by which I mean the governing power of his mind, has been otherwise than voluntarily so completely destroyed that his actions are not subject to it, but are beyond his control.

The irresistible impulse test is nowhere relied on as the sole test, and has been rejected by 22 States, England, and Canada. However, it is used in conjunction with the M'Naghten test in an increasing number of jurisdictions, now about 15.

3. *The Durham Test*

(*Durham* v. *United States*, 214 F. 2D862, 874–875. [D.C. Cir. 1954]).

An accused is not criminally responsible if his unlawful act was the product of mental disease or mental defect . . . We use 'disease' in the sense of a condition which is considered capable of either improving or deteriorating. We use 'defect' in the sense of a condition which is not considered capable of either improving or deteriorating and which may be either congenital, or the result of injury, or the residual effect of a physical or mental disease.

The *Durham* rule, which originated in the Court of Appeals for the District of Columbia, has since been specifically rejected there. *United States* v. *Brawner*, 471 F. 2d 969 (D.C. Cir. 1972). It has, however, been adopted by statute in Maine and the Virgin Islands. The New Hampshire test most resembles *Durham*, but its basic intent is to allow the jury to formulate the insanity standard.

4. *The American Law Institute (ALI) Test*

(American Law Institute, Model Penal Code, Proposed Official Draft sec.4.01 [1962] [First presented in 1955]).

1. A person is not responsible for criminal conduct if at the time of such conduct as a result of mental disease or defect he lacks substantial capacity either to appreciate the criminality of his conduct or to conform his conduct to the requirements of law.

2. As noted in the Article, the terms "mental disease or defect" do not include an abnormality manifested only by repeated criminal or otherwise antisocial conduct.

As of 1971, the ALI test has been adopted by statute in seven States, and by decision in three more. On the Federal level, six circuit courts of appeal have adopted the test as is, and two others have made minor modifications.

NOTES

(1) Cohen, Review of A. Goldstein, Insanity Defense, 13 *Contemp. Psych.* 386 (1968).

(2) N.Y.U. Colloquium, 1 *J. Psychiat. and Law* 297 (1973).

(3) H. L. A. Hart, *The Morality of the Criminal Law*, (Jerusalem: Magnes Press, 1964); T. S. Szasz, *Law, Liberty and Psychiatry* (New York: The Macmillan Co., 1963); S. L. Halleck, *Psychiatry and the Dilemmas of Crime* (New York: Harper and Row, 1967).

(4) Derschowitz, Abolishing the Insanity Defense: The Most Significant Feature of the Administrations Proposed Criminal Code—An Essay, 9 *Crim. L. Bull.* 435 (1973).

(5) Hart, *supra* note 3.

(6) *Durham* v. *U.S.*, 214 F.2d 862, 876 (D.C. Cir. 1954).

(7) *Brawner* v. *U.S.*, 471 F.2d 969 (D.C. Cir. 1972).

(8) Royal Commission on Capital Punishment 1949–53, report CMD No. 8932 at 98 (1953).

(9) *The King* v. *Porter*, 55 *Commw. L. Rev.* 182, 186 (Austl. 1936).

(10) P. Devlin, *The Enforcement Of Morals* (London: Oxford University Press, 1959), p. 17.

(11) Dershowitz, *supra* note 4.

(12) Criminal Responsibility and Psychiatric Expert Testimony, Group for the Advancement of Psychiatry, Report 5, 1954; Waelder, Psychiatry and the Problem of Criminal Responsibility, 101 *U. Pa. L. Rev.* 378 (1952).

(13) Halleck, *supra* note 3.

(14) T. Szasz, *Psychiatric Justice* New York: Macmillan Co., 1965).

(15) Dershowitz, *supra* note 4.

(16) Katz and Goldstein, Abolish the Insanity Defense—Why Not? 72 *Yale L.J.* 853 (1963).

(17) This is their fall-back position in their amicus brief in *Brawner*. Cited in: Stone, Law and Psychiatry, 1 *Psychiatric Annals* 22 (1971).

(18) B. Wooton, *Crime and the Criminal Law* (London: Stevens and Sons, 1963).

(19) Hart, *supra* note 3.

(20) Morris, The Dangerous Criminal, 41 *So. Cal. L. Rev.* 514 (1968).

(21) Szasz, *supra* note 3.

(22) Dershowitz, *supra* note 4.

(23) K. Menninger, *The Crime of Punishment* (New York: Viking Compass, 1968).

(24) Weintraub, *Annual Judicial Conference*, 37 F.R.D. 365 (1964).

(25) Goldstein, The Brawner Rule, 1973 *Washington U. L. Q.* 126.

(26) *Morris, supra* note 20.

(27) N. Walker, *Crime and Insanity in England*, Vol. I (Edinburgh: Edinburgh University Press, 1968).

(28) *Cf.* Consultant's Report on Criminal Responsibility, section 503, p. 251, Working Papers of the National Commission on Reform of Federal Criminal Laws, 1970, U.S. Government Printing Office, Wash., D.C.

(29) Walker, *supra* note 27.

(30) *Id.*

(31) *Durham* v. *U.S.*, 214 F2d 862 (D.C. Cir. 1954).

(32) A. Goldstein, *The Insanity Defense* (New Haven: Yale University Press, 1967).

(33) Stone, *supra* note 17.

(34) J. Katz, J. Goldstein, and A. Dershowitz, *Psychoanalysis, Psychiatry And Law* (New York: Free Press, 1967), p. 362.

(35) Consultant's Report on Criminal Responsibility, *supra* note 28.

(36) S. Freud, *Moral Responsibility for the Content of Dreams* (1923) (London: Hogarth Press, 1961) Standard ed.

(37) Goldstein, *supra* note 32 at 90.

(38) Goldstein, *supra*, note 25.

(39) *Brawner* v. *U.S.*, *supra*, note 7, at 986.

(40) Goldstein, *supra*, note 25 at 127.

(41) Wooton, *supra*, note 18.

(42) Hart, *supra*, note 3.

(43) Szasz, *supra*, note 3.

(44) Dershowitz, *supra*, note 4.

(45) Consultant's Report, *supra*, note 28.

(46) Goldstein, *supra*, note 25.

(47) Katz and Goldstein, *supra*, note 16.

(48) *Brawner* v. *U.S.*, *supra*, note 7, at 985.

(49) *Id.*, at 986.

(50) Goldstein, *supra*, note 25.

(51) Katz et al., *supra*, note 34 at 362.

(52) *Brawner* v. *U.S.*, *supra*, note 7, at 1032.

(53) Stone, *supra*, note 17.

(54) *Durham* v. *U.S.*, *supra*, note 6 at 874, 875.

(55) Cf., *Briscoe* v. *U.S.*, 248 F2d 640, 644 n.6 (D.C. Cir. 1957).

(56) *Blocker* v. *U.S.*, 288 F2d 853, 859–61 (D.C. Cir. 1961).

(57) *Campbell* v. *U.S.*, 307 F2d 597, 612 (D.C. Cir. 1962).

(58) *Carter* v. *U.S.*, 252 F2d 608, 615 (D.C. Cir. 1957).

(59) *Lyles* v. *U.S.*, 254 F2d 725 (D.C. Cir. 1957).

(60) *Frigillana* v. *U.S.*, 302 F2d 670 (D.C. Cir. 1962).

(61) *Rollerson* v. *U.S.*, 343 F2d 269, 272 (D.C. Cir. 1964).

(62) Appendix to *Washington* v. *U.S.*, 390 F2d 457 (1967).

(63) Hall, Psychiatry and Criminal Responsibility, 65 *Yale L. J.* 761, 780 (1956).

(63a) R. Simon, *The Jury and the Defense of Insanity* Boston: Little, Brown, 1967).

(64) Goldstein, *supra*, note 32 at 191.

(65) *Id.*, at 194–199.

(66) American Law Institute Model Penal Code sec. 201.3, Tent. Draft No. 9 (1959).

(67) *Id.*

(68) *See, People* v. *Wells*, 202 P2d 53, 62–63 (Cal. 1949) *cert. denied* 337 U.S. 919; *People* v. *Gorshen*, 336 P2d 492, 503 (Cal. 1959).

(69) ALI Model Penal Code, *supra*, note 66.

IV.

Psychiatric
Assessments

Introduction

Since the beginning of organized communal living, societies have sought to develop effective methods for dealing with the identification and management of their deviant members. American society, concerned with individual freedom and constitutional safeguards of the rights of citizens, has established conditions under which an individual's freedom may be limited for the benefit and welfare of the community. These conditions emphasize two justifications for placing restrictions on an individual's liberty: to protect society from the individual and to protect the individual from oneself. In both justifications, the individual's potential dangerousness to oneself or others is crucial. Throughout the history of corrections and mental health care, these two kinds of dangerousness have been cited most often as the basis for detention.

Unfortunately, considerable evidence in the professional literature indicates that psychiatrists and jurists do not agree on when an individual is dangerous to society or to oneself. Disagreement also exists among courts of law in different states as to what constitutes dangerousness. In many states, laws concerning sexual crimes are focused upon the "sexual psychopath" or "sexually dangerous person." Many of these statutes appear to have been formulated upon the implicit assumption that all individuals who exhibit any type of sexual disturbance are potentially dangerous to society.

Some of the difficulties of defining dangerousness emerge in hearings to review release applications from mental hospitals and in habeas corpus proceedings when an inmate challenges the right of the institution to continue commitment. Two questions seem to be fundamental: 1. What specific kinds of behavior are serious enough to be considered dangerous? 2. Concerning a return to the community, what degree of positive prognosis is sufficient to allow release under supervision? If conclusive and definitive answers could be supplied for both questions, the potential dangerousness of the criminal offender would be as controversial as it is.

Katz and Goldstein (1960) suggested that dangerous behavior might be construed to apply to: 1. only a crime for which an insanity defense was successfully raised; 2. all crimes; 3. only felonious crimes; 4. only crimes for which maximum sentence is authorized; 5. only crimes categorized as violent; 6. only crimes which inflict physical or psychological harm upon the victim, regardless of whether the harm is repairable or irreparable; 7. any conduct, even if not labeled criminal, categorized as violent, harmful, or threatening; 8. any conduct which may provoke violent retaliatory acts; 9. any physical violence toward oneself; 10. any combination of these categories. Any of these categories, together or separately, leave much to be desired in terms of a practical definition of dangerous behavior. Concerning the eighth category, a person might conceivably provoke a violent retaliatory act like a serious stabbing from another person simply by name-calling. However, a court of law would probably not incarcerate the name-caller as a dangerous offender.

According to Abraham Goldstein (1967), even the Model Penal Code, which addresses itself to the dangerous offender, fails to provide a workable definition of dangerousness. *The Challenge of Crime in a Free Society*, written by the President's Commission on Law Enforcement and the Administration of Justice (1967), alludes to the need for identifying dangerous or habitual offenders who pose a serious threat to the community. The Report includes as dangerous offenders ". . . those whose personal instability is so gross as to erupt periodically in violent and assaultive behavior, and those individuals whose long-term exposure to criminal influences has produced a thoroughgoing commitment to criminal values that is resistive of superficial efforts to effect change." Apparently the Commission recognized the current superficial level of treatment with the dangerous offender, although it did not detail a very satisfactory definition of what constitutes a typology of dangerousness.

EVALUATION AND PREDICTION

More than any other professional group, psychiatrists have come to be identified as experts who can predict dangerousness. Frederick (1974) claims that psychiatrists have inherited their reputation as experts "because of the aura associated with the medical profession" and because psychiatrists have not discouraged the enhancement of their reputation:

Psychiatrists have been willing actors in a fulsome drama with an expanding proscenium and a proliferating cast. The fact that judges and other members of the legal profession encourage this state of affairs has provided an additional stimulus for psychiatrists to don the mantle of predictor, even though the justification for that image remains unwarranted.

Psychiatrists have criticized psychiatric predictions of dangerousness for their lack of reliability. Rubin (1972) and Rappeport and his colleagues (1967) have stressed the inaccuracy of predictions of dangerousness by psychiatrists and have noted that psychiatrists have regularly permitted themselves to be cast in the role of predictor. In defense of psychiatry, Halleck (1967) observed that "the most a psychiatrist can say is that he has had considerable experience in dealing with disturbed people who commit dangerous acts, that he has been designated by society to diagnose and treat such individuals, and that his skill in treating dangerous behavior in those diagnosed as mentally ill has generally been appreciated."

Psychologists can derive little comfort from the questionable record of their colleagues in psychiatry. When Megargee (1970) conducted a detailed review of the use of psychological tests in the prediction of violence, he concluded:

> Thus far no structured or projective test scale has been devised which, when used alone, will predict violence in the individual case in a satisfactory manner. Indeed, none has been developed which will adequately postdict, let alone predict, violent behavior.

Frederick (1974) adds that the record of psychologists in other areas of clinical prediction is something less than impressive.

BASE RATES AND FALSE POSITIVES

A fundamental problem in the prediction of dangerous or violent behavior is caused by the fact that acts of violence have a low base rate. Therefore, as various empirical studies have demonstrated, prediction tables tend to produce overprediction. That is, when predictions of rare events (those with low base rates) are attempted, the result—in statistical terms—is the problem of *false positives*. When a predictive approach is used that employs a high cutting point—for example, an accuracy rate of 95 out of 100—the number of false positives which would result (5 out of 100) is unacceptably high. Stone (1975) uses the following example to demonstrate the problem:

> Assume that one person out of a thousand will kill. Assume also an exceptionally accurate test is created which differentiates with 95 percent effectiveness those who will kill from those who will not. If 100,000 people were tested, out of the 100 who would kill, 95 would be isolated. Unfortunately, out of the 99,900 who would not kill, 4,995 people would also be isolated as potential killers.

The 4,995 people—the false positives—are the innocent victims of the test. As Stone observes, any test which yields an accuracy level on prediction of 95 percent possesses, by the standards of behavioral science, an extraordinarily high cutting point. In mental health, a realistic estimate of 60–70 percent would result in intolerably high rates of false positives.

Saleem A. Shah's selection makes the observation that some of the professional literature concerning the problems of prediction appeared more than twenty years ago. Recently, Wenk and his co-workers (Wenk and Emrich, 1972; Wenk, Robison, and Smith, 1972) have summarized some very relevant empirical studies involving statistical cutting rates within the context of criminal justice, rather than of mental health. On the basis of a violence prediction scale devised to predict parole violation by the commission of violent acts, the California Department of Corrections conducted a study that yielded eighty-six percent false positives. Another study conducted by the California Youth Authority produced ninety-five percent false positives. It is difficult to understand— and more difficult to justify—the ignorance of these and related findings demonstrated by many so-called "experts" who appear in court to testify on the dangerousness of various types of social deviants.

DANGEROUSNESS AND THE MENTALLY ILL

Halleck (1967) has stated: "Since dangerous behavior is likely to be unreasonable behavior, the dangerous offender will frequently be a person who has previously demonstrated unreasonable behavior that may have been defined as mental illness." The assumption that dangerousness to self and to others is a characteristic typically associated with mental illness has failed to receive conclusive support in empirical research. Studies as early as 1922 found that patients in public mental hospitals had post-discharge arrest rates that were lower than those of the general population. Recent studies (Durbin et al, 1977; Giovannoni and Gurel, 1967; Rappeport and Lassen, 1965, 1966; Zitrin et al, 1976) have indicated that arrest rates for ex-hospital patients tend to equal or exceed arrest rates for the general population. However, Thornberry's (1978) survey of the literature indicated that estimates of dangerousness range from 0.7 to 4.7 percent and "these rates certainly cannot be considered substantial." By totaling the number of patients and the number of offenses reported in these studies, Thornberry demonstrates that of the 18.7 percent of ex-mental patients arrested, only 2.9 percent were rearrested for offenses against a person. Consequently, fewer than five persons in a hundred who have been released from a mental institution are likely to be dangerous to themselves or others.

A "natural experiment" to test predictions of dangerousness evolved from the U.S. Supreme Court decision in *Baxstrom v. Herold* (1966). Because Johnny Baxstrom had been moved to Dannemora State Hospital in New York—an institution for the criminally insane—after the expiration of his maximum criminal sentence, he was adjudged by the Court to have been denied equal protection under the law. The statutory procedures under which Baxstrom was committed civilly to Dannemora allowed for retention of prisoners who were considered mentally ill upon expiration of their sentences.

As a result of the Baxstrom decision, almost a thousand patients were transferred from hospitals for the criminally insane to civil hospitals for the mentally ill during the period from 1966 to 1970. The transfer provided a "natural experiment" to test predictions of dangerousness among a population for whom the risk of potential violence was perceived as high enough to justify maximum security confinement.

Four and a half years after the 1966 court order, only 2.7 of the Baxstrom patients had been returned to hospitals for the criminally insane. Frederick (1974) observed that "no single factor or set of factors appeared which would differentiate significantly between the latter group and other Baxstrom patients. From a representative sample of 246 patients surveyed in 1970, approximately half were in the community and 17 percent had been arrested at some point in time." Nevertheless, less than 1 percent had been remanded to a correctional facility.

DANGEROUS OFFENDER STATUTES

Basically two types of statutes concern themselves with the dangerous offender. The first is generally referred to as the repeated or habitual offender statute; it provides for increased length of sentence with each successive offense. Most states, according to Guttmacher have this kind of statute, although there is considerable reaction against the use of them because the statutes fail to allow the courts enough discretion in sentencing.

The second kind of statute concerning the dangerous offender is the sexual psychopath law, which is included among the statutes of approximately twenty-five states. A great deal of opposition to these laws has been expressed because of the lack of discrimination among types of sex offenders. "I have always been opposed to such legislation," states Guttmacher (1963) "because there are some persons who, though they commit sexual offenses, are not true sexual deviants and therefore should not be considered. . . . furthermore, many offenses which from a legal point of view must be deemed nonsexual are basically sexual." For example, cases involving arson, burglary, and assault frequently are felt to have a sexual origin.

The complex legal problems posed by laws involving sexual offenders present immense difficulties, generally because of lack of diagnostic and treatment facilities. In reviewing his experiences with the sexual psychopath statutes, Robitscher (1966) states: "In some ways, the fate of a criminal in a prison may be superior to that of an adjudged psychopath in a hospital. For this reason, when an individual transgresses the criminal code, he has a right to be treated as a criminal." In reality, the sexual psychopath seldom receives the treatment provided for many nonsexual offenders. As Guttmacher implies, it would seem more realistic to include serious sex offenders with the general group of dangerous offenders than to isolate them. For treatment of serious sex offenders and disposition of their cases, grouping them with dangerous offenders would be practical, provided that sufficient treatment was available.

REFERENCES

Baxstrom v. Herold, 383 U.S. 107; 86 S. Ct. 760 (1966)

Durbin, J. R., Pasewark, R. A., and Albers, D. "Crime and Mental Illness: A Study of Arrest Rates in a Rural State." *American Journal of Psychiatry*, 1977, 134, 80–83.

Frederick, C. J. "Dangerousness and Disturbed Behavior." Paper presented before the Law and Socialization Committee in Division 9, A.P.A., September 2, 1974, New Orleans, Louisiana.

Giovannoni, J. M., and Gurel, L. "Socially Disruptive Behavior of Ex-Mental Patients." *Archives of General Psychiatry*, 1967, 17, 146–153.

Goldstein, A. S. *The Insanity Defense*. New Haven, Connecticut: Yale University Press, 1967.

Guttmacher, M. S. "Dangerous Offenders." *Crime and Delinquency*, 1963, 9, 381–390.

Halleck, S. *Psychiatry and the Dilemmas of Crime*. New York: Harper and Row, 1967.

Katz, J., and Goldstein, J. Dangerousness and Mental Illness. *Journal of Nervous and Mental Disease*, 1960, 131, 404–413.

Megargee, E. "The Prediction of Violence with Psychological Tests." In C. D.

Spielberger (Ed.), *Current Topics in Clinical and Community Psychology.* New York: Academic Press, 1970.

President's Commission on Law Enforcement and Administration of Justice. *The Challenge of Crime in a Free Society.* Washington, D.C.: U.S. Government Printing Office, 1967.

Rappeport, J. R., and Lassen, G. "Dangerousness—Arrest Rate Comparisons of Discharged Mental Patients and the General Populations." *American Journal of Psychiatry*, 1965, 121, 776–783.

Rappeport, J. R., and Lassen, G. "The Dangerousness of Female Patients: A Comparison of Arrest Rates of Discharged Psychiatric Patients and the General Population." *American Journal of Psychiatry*, 1966, 123, 413–419.

Robitscher, J. B. *Pursuit of Agreement: Psychiatry and the Law.* Philadelphia: Lippincott, 1966.

Rubin, B. "Prediction of Dangerousness in Mentally Ill Criminals." *Archives of General Psychiatry*, 1972, 27, 397–407.

Stone, A. A. *Mental Health and Law: A System in Transition.* Washington, D.C.: U.S. Government Printing Office, 1975.

Thornberry, T. B. "Community Followup and Dangerous Mental Patients." In C. J. Frederick (Ed.), *Dangerous Behavior: A Problem in Law and Mental Health.* Washington, D.C.: U.S. Government Printing Office, 1978.

Wenk, E. A., and Emrich, R. L. "Assaultive Youth: An Exploratory Study of the Assaultive Experience and Assaultive Potential of California Youth Authority Wards." *Journal of Research in Crime and Delinquency*, 1972, 9, 171–196.

Wenk, E. A., Robison, J. O., and Smith, G. W. "Can Violence Be Predicted?" *Crime and Delinquency*, 1972, 18, 393–402.

Zitrin, A., Hardesty, A. S., and Burdock, E. T. "Crime and Violence among Mental Patients. *American Journal of Psychiatry*, 1976, 133, 142–149.

Psychiatry and the Presumption of Expertise: Flipping Coins in the Courtroom

Bruce J. Ennis and Thomas R. Litwack

A critical aspect of the civil commitment process is the extraordinary influence psychiatrists exert in the determination of who shall be involuntarily hospitalized. At commitment hearings, psychiatrists are permitted and even encouraged to offer their opinions on the ultimate issues—is the prospective patient "mentally ill," or "dangerous," or "in need of care and treatment?" Psychiatrists are also allowed to describe the potential patient using technical terminology and psychiatric diagnoses. Judges and juries, believing that psychiatrists are *experts*, usually defer to their judgments and recommendations.(1)

In many states persons who are not considered physically dangerous to themselves or others can be hospitalized involuntarily, even without judicial proceedings, if two psychiatrists certify that the prospective patient is "mentally ill" and in need of treatment.(2) No state authorizes two laymen—a grocer and a clerk for example—to hospitalize a neighbor simply because the laymen believe he or she is mentally ill and in need of treatment. This extraordinary power is given to psychiatrists but not to laymen because legislators and judges assume that psychiatrists are uniquely qualified to determine when an individual requires hospitalization.

This assumption of expertise rests upon two further assumptions: that psychiatrists are able to reach conclusions that are *reliable*, that is, that other psychiatrists would agree with those conclusions; and that those conclusions are *valid*, that is, that they accurately reflect reality.

Unfortunately, judges and legislators are not aware of the enormous and relatively consistent body of professional literature questioning the reliability and validity of psychiatric evaluations and predictions.

In this article we examine the assumptions that psychiatrists are "expert" at resolving the issues relevant to a civil commitment proceeding and that psychiatric opinions and terminology assist the judge or jury in reaching accurate and humane decisions.(3) Based upon our reading of the professional literature, we have concluded that 1. there is no evidence warranting the assumption that psychiatrists can accurately determine who is "dangerous"; 2. there is little or no evidence that psychiatrists are more "expert" in making the predictions relevant to civil commitment than laymen; 3. "expert" judgments made by psychiatrists are not sufficiently reliable and valid to justify nonjudicial hospitalization based on such judgments; 4. the constitutional rights of individuals are seriously prejudiced by the admissibility of psychiatric terminology, diagnoses, and predictions, especially those of "dangerous" behavior; and therefore 5. courts should limit testimony by psychiatrists to descriptive statements and should exclude psychiatric diagnoses, judgments, and predictions.(4)

In short, we believe there is no evidence that psychiatric opinions and terminology clarify rather than confuse the issues in a civil commitment proceeding, and there is good reason to believe that judges and juries could function quite adequately in a civil commitment proceeding without "expert" opinion testimony.

THE PROFESSIONAL LITERATURE

"Reliability" does not have a precise meaning,(5) but as used herein it refers to the probability or frequency of agreement when two or more independent observers answer the same question (for example, what is Mr. Smith's diagnosis? Is Smith dangerous?) If representative pairs of psychiatrists, interviewing a representative sample of prospective patients, usually agree that each individual is or is not "dangerous," the judgment of "dangerousness" is said to be reliable. Conversely, if pairs of psychiatrists would not usually agree whether such individuals are dangerous, that judgment is said to be unreliable.(6)

"Validity," on the other hand, refers not to how likely psychiatrists are to agree about a particular judgment but to how *accurate* their judgments are. If every psychiatrist in the world agrees that Smith would commit a dangerous act if released from the hospital, that judgment would be 100 percent reliable. But if Smith were released and does not commit a dangerous act, the judgment would be invalid. Similarly, psychiatric judgments of "dangerousness" would be generally reliable if most observers would agree whether or not given individuals are dangerous, yet generally invalid if those judgments usually would be wrong.

Even though the validity of psychiatric judgments is of primary importance, we are interested in their reliability as well. For psychiatric judgments are likely to be no more valid, and probably less valid, than they are reliable. For example, if predictions of dangerousness are 50 percent reliable there is only one chance in two that a second psychiatrist would agree with a first that Smith is "dangerous." If psychiatrists cannot generally agree whether Smith is dangerous, we cannot be confident about the accuracy of any individual prediction that Smith is dangerous. Smith is either dangerous or not dangerous, schizophrenic or not schizophrenic. When psychiatrists disagree, when their judgments are unreliable, it is evident that at least some of them are wrong. The more likely psychiatrists are to disagree, the greater is the likelihood that an individual judgment is invalid. The reliability of a judgment also assumes major significance because reliability is usually easier to ascertain then validity. If validity studies are not available, examination of the reliability of psychiatric judgments provides a basis for estimating the upper limits of validity.

It should also be noted, before we proceed to review the literature, that the ultimate question is *not* whether psychiatric judgments are *at all* valid, but whether they are sufficiently valid to meet the traditional criteria for the admissibility of "expert," conclusory testimony and, in a civil commitment context, whether they are sufficiently valid to permit involuntary deprivations of liberty based on such judgments without violating the constitutional rights of prospective patients.

Thus, if psychiatric predictions and opinions are no more valid than those of laymen such conclusions should not be admissible, if similar conclusions by laymen would not be admissible—and certainly they should not be accorded any special weight. Special weight should be given only to the opinions of a witness who can demonstrate two things: that he uses techniques and knowledge not available to laymen to arrive at his conclusions; and that the application of these techniques results in judgments that are significantly more valid than the judgments laymen otherwise would reach.(7)

In other words, a judgment about another person's mental condition or propensity to engage in dangerous behavior should not be deferred to as an expert judgment simply because it is made by a person who happens to be a psychiatrist. Before a psychiatrist's conclusory judgment can be considered an admissible expert judgment—much less worthy of special attention—the psychiatrist must employ techniques and apply knowledge that have been shown to produce substantially more reliable and valid results than could the techniques and knowledge available to laymen. It has been assumed that something in the education, training, experience, and techniques of psychiatrists makes their judgments more reliable and more valid than those judgments would be in the absence of such education, training, experience, and techniques. That assumption may be incorrect.

But even if psychiatric judgments were somewhat more valid than those of laymen, we will argue that they should nevertheless be inadmissible in civil commitment hearings. As we will demonstrate, the results of other "scientific" methods such as polygraph examinations provide far more valid judgments than those of psychiatrists but generally have been excluded from the courtroom as insufficiently trustworthy to justify denial of important rights. Psychiatric judgments, though less valid, are generally admissible. This article questions whether such a policy is rational or constitutional.

THE RELIABILITY OF PSYCHIATRIC JUDGMENTS

Theoretically, there are at least four kinds of psychiatric judgments that may be relevant in a civil commitment proceeding: is the prospective patient "mentally ill;" is he dangerous; does his condition require or justify involuntary hospitalization and treatment; will involuntary hospitalization and treatment cure or benefit the prospective patient? How often do psychiatrists agree or disagree in their answers to these four questions? Or, phrased differently, how reliable are their judgments in each of these four areas?

There are several studies of the reliability of psychiatric diagnosis and we will discuss those studies in a moment. But there are almost no studies of the reliability of psychiatric judgments in the remaining three areas. Accordingly, we will be concerned almost exclusively with the reliability of psychiatric diagnoses.

It is necessary to preface our discussion with a brief discription of basic diagnostic terminology. Studies usually focus upon the reliability of certain broad diagnostic categories: the organic psychoses, the functional psychoses, the neuroses, the character disorders, and, in some studies, "normality."

Patients are described as "psychotic" by the official diagnostic manual of the American Psychiatric Association when:

> their mental functioning is sufficiently impaired to interfere grossly with their capacity to meet the ordinary demands of life. The impairment may result from a serious distortion in their capacity to recognize reality. Hallucinations and delusions, for example, may distort their perceptions. Alterations of mood may

be so profound that the patient's capacity to respond appropriately is grossly impaired. Deficits in perception, language and memory may be so severe that the patient's capacity for mental grasp of his situation is effectively lost.(8)

There are two major subtypes of psychosis: the organic and the functional. An organic psychosis has a known psysiological cause; a functional psychosis does not.

"Neurosis" refers to a condition in which there is no loss of reality testing, but the individual nevertheless suffers from considerable experienced anxiety or from one of many "symptoms," such as compulsive behavior or some type of phobia. The term "symptom" refers to some form of behavior or emotional state which the individual himself finds to be debilitating and which he experiences as foreign to his basic personality.

The diagnosis of "character disorder," now more commonly referred to as "personality disorder," refers to deeply ingrained, maladaptive, and self-defeating—but nonpsychotic—patterns of behavior. For example, character disorders include impulsive behavior such as alcoholism or drug dependence, anti-social behavior, or personality characteristics that severely interfere with social relationships, such as chronic, undue suspiciousness or excessive shyness. Unlike the neuroses which are characterized by relatively specific and episodic symptoms, the character disorders are much more generalized self-defeating patterns of behavior.

A diagnosis of "normal" can best be defined as the absence of any identifiable psychosis, neurosis, or character disorder.

Within each broad diagnostic category are subcategories, and there are subcategories within the subcategories. For example, the three major subcategories of functional psychosis are schizophrenia, the affective psychoses, and the paranoid states; while within the subcategory of schizophrenia there are several subtypes including the simple type, the catatonic type, the paranoid type, the hebephrenic type, and others. The following official definition of schizophrenia illustrates the breadth of this diagnostic category:

> [Schizophrenia] includes a group of disorders manifested by characteristic disturbances of thinking, mood and behavior. Disturbances in thinking are marked by alterations of concept formation which may lead to misinterpretations of reality and sometimes to delusions and hallucinations, which frequently appear psychologically self-protective. Corollary mood changes include ambivalent, constricted and inappropriate emotional responsiveness and loss of empathy with others. Behavior may be

withdrawn, regressive and bizarre. The schizophrenics, in which the mental status is attributable primarily to a *thought* disorder are to be distinguished from the *mood affective illnesses* . . . which are dominated by a *mood* disorder. The *Paranoid states* . . . are distinguished from schizophrenia by the narrowness of their distortions of reality and by the absence of other psychotic symptoms . . . .(9)

The literature indicates that psychiatric diagnoses using these categories are not very reliable. According to Ziskin, "the most common research findings indicate that, on the average, one cannot expect to find agreement in more than about 60% of cases between two psychiatrists."(10) The chances of a second psychiatrist agreeing with the diagnosis of a first psychiatrist "are barely better than 50–50; or stated differently, there is about as much chance that a different expert would come to some different conclusion as there is that the other would agree."(11)

Actually, as we shall see, the reliability of psychiatric judgments of specific diagnostic categories (schizophrenia, paranoid type, depressive reaction, passive-aggressive personality, and so on) is even lower— somewhere in the neighborhood of 40 percent. In other words, if a first psychiatrist testifies that a prospective patient suffers from involutional melancholia or some other specific, nonorganic diagnosis, it is more likely than not that a second psychiatrist would disagree.

In an early study Ash measured the diagnostic agreement between two or three psychiatrists who jointly interviewed 52 patients in a psychiatric clinic.(12) The three psychiatrists agreed on specific diagnoses in only 21 percent of the cases, and totally disagreed in 31 percent. When asked whether a patient fit into one of the more general categories of psychopathology (mental deficiency, character disorder, psychosis, neurosis, and normal) pairs of psychiatrists agreed from 58 to 67 percent of the time, and the trio of psychiatrists agreed only 46 percent of the time. The Ash study suggests that specific psychiatric diagnoses (such as hysterical neurosis, or psychotic depression) are hardly reliable at all, and that broader categories are of limited reliability.(13) Ash found that only in 3 of 22 cases did all three psychiatrists agree that the patient was "pathologically abnormal."(14)

Schmidt and Fonda conducted a study that obtained somewhat more positive results.(15) Each of 427 state hospital patients was diagnosed by pairs of psychiatrists (a psychiatric resident and a chief psychiatrist) under realistic conditions, using the then standard diagnostic system. They found that: a) the diagnosis of organic psychosis was made very reliably (92 percent of the patients diagnosed as "organic" by the chief psychiatrists were also diagnosed as such by the residents); b) the diagnosis of nonorganic psychosis was fairly reliable (80 percent agreement); and c) the diagnosis of nonpsychotic disturbances was moderately reliable (71 percent agreement).

However, agreement as to the major subtype of each of these three categories (11 subtypes in all) was obtained in only about 50 percent of the cases and was almost absent in cases of nonsociopathic, nonpsychotic disturbances. For example, the clinicians could agree whether a nonorganic psychosis was "involutional," "affective," or "schizophrenic" in only 47 percent of the cases.

Norris compared the diagnoses given 6,263 patients at an observation unit and then again a few weeks later at a mental institution. The overall rate of agreement was only 60 percent. Yet, when organic cases—about which there was substantial agreement—were excluded, the rate of agreement on the existence and nature of neuroses and character disorders dropped to 54 percent and 43 percent, respectively. This low level of agreement occurred despite the hospital diagnostician's knowledge of the original diagnosis, which would tend to increase the incidence of diagnostic agreement.(16)

Beck and his co-workers designed their research to correct the flaws of previous studies.(17) Instead of measuring actual diagnostic reliability, they examined psychiatric judgments under conditions designed to discern the potential reliability of diagnosis.(18) Nevertheless, even under such reliability-maximizing conditions they found the average percentage of agreement for specific diagnoses was only 54 percent (ranging from 33 to 61 percent between different pairs of psychiatrists) and that regarding one important patient characteristic, the severity of depression, there was only 59 percent agreement. When only the major divisions of psychosis, neurosis, and character disorder were used to classify patients, the rate of agreement was 70 percent.

Studies of reliability conducted under such controlled conditions produce higher rates of diagnostic reliability than are likely to be obtained in actual psychiatric practice. There the lack of controls means that such factors as inexperienced or incompetent psychiatrists, particularized interviewing techniques and conditions, definitional ambiguities and biases, semantic differences, and so on all contribute to lower diagnostic reliability. As a result, Beck's study suggests the maximum reliability obtainable at the present time. Beck noted that the rate of agreement regarding particular diagnoses in actual practice is likely to be between 32 and 42 percent.

As we have seen, broad diagnostic categories are more reliable than specific diagnostic categories.(19) But in many instances even a broad diagnosis can be quite unreliable. In one study, for example, 43 experienced psychiatrists diagnosed an individual after viewing a filmed interview. They could not even agree whether the individual was or was not psychotic; 17 psychiatrists thought he was, and the other 26 believed he was not.(20)

Mehlman used a different technique to study diagnostic reliability, and yet produced findings similar to the studies already discussed.(21) Psychiatrists in a mental hospital were randomly assigned patients for diagnosis. Since the assignments were random, any major differences in the *frequency* with which the psychiatrists arrived at particular diagnoses would tend to indicate the idiosyncratic nature of their judgments. In fact, the differences in the frequency of diagnoses made by the psychiatrists were significantly greater than would be statistically probable by chance, suggesting that the test participants did indeed display personal preferences for specific diagnoses. This, of course, would reduce the chance of their agreeing in any given case.

Another study using a similar methodology considered the diagnoses assigned to female patients who were randomly assigned to each of three wards.(22) Independent investigation confirmed that the patients did not differ from ward to ward in socio-economic characteristics. The percentage of patients diagnosed as schizophrenic varied among wards from 23 to 36 percent; those diagnosed as neurotic from 30 to 45 percent; and those diagnosed as having a character disorder from 12 to 22 percent. (These differences were all statistically significant. In other words, there was less than one chance in 20 that they were due to chance differences in patient assignment.) Moreover, on one ward which had three different chief psychiatrists over a two-year period the percentage of cases diagnosed as schizophrenic varied from 22 percent under one psychiatrist to 67 under another; similarly, the percentage diagnosed as character disorder varied from 15 to 56 percent even though there was every reason to believe that, as a group, there were no differences in patient populations during the tenure of each psychiatrist.

In a lengthy review, Zubin surveyed the major studies of diagnostic reliability conducted before 1968, including, but not limited to, those of Ash, Schmidt and Fonda, Beck, Norris, Mehlman, and Pasamanick.(23) He concluded that:

> [T]he degree of overall agreement between different observers with regard to specific diagnoses is too low for individual diagnosis. The overall agreement on general categories of diagnosis, although somewhat higher [64–84 percent], still leaves much to be desired. The evidence for low agreement across specific diagnostic categories is all the more surprising since, for

the most part, the observers in any one study were usually quite similar in orientation, training, and background.(24)

Additional studies suggest that other types of diagnosis are also unreliable. In one experiment, 27 experienced psychiatrists, all members of a hospital faculty, used a standardized set of 565 statements to rate a patient presented to them in a half-hour filmed interview.(25) The psychiatrists " . . . were unable to agree as to a patient's diagnosis, prognosis, psychodynamics, the causes of her problems, the feelings she was consciously experiencing or the feelings that were latent (unconscious)."(26) The author, noting massive disagreement, concluded that:

> [A]rt far outweighs science when experts in the field of psychiatry try to say what they have discovered in another person. . . . Practitioners of the art disagree with each much more than is commonly recognized . . . . Psychiatrists seem to find sufficient strength and self-confidence in consensual validation deriving from what they assume to be and view as shared expert opinion. ("The men who are expert in the field would agree with my judgment."). The findings reported here *categorically contradict* such a belief.(27)

In a study by Rickles and others, apparently nonpsychotic patients were rated by psychiatrists on an 8-point scale of psychopathology. The reliability of psychopathology ratings among even experienced psychiatrists was found to be quite low, approaching zero.(28)

Nor are psychiatrists very adept at distinguishing between depressed and nondepressed patients. In 1959:

> . . . a Philadelphia psychiatrist and leading depression researcher . . . found himself disturbed by what he called "the low reliability of psychiatric diagnoses of depression." As an experiment he had two skilled psychiatrists diagnose a selected sample of 20 hospital patients. There was a somewhat embarrassing result: Both psychiatrists labeled six of the patients as depressed, but they did not choose the same six.(29)

It is important to understand that psychiatric judgments are not only unreliable with respect to the ultimate diagnoses, but lack consistency even in the perception of the presence, nature, and severity of symptoms. In a study already mentioned above where 17 psychiatrists out of 43 diagnosed a patient as psychotic after all 43 had observed the same film interview, the experimenters concluded that the disagreements were not due solely to differing diagnostic preferences.(30) Rather, those psychiatrists who reached a diagnosis of schizophrenia saw both different and more severe symptoms than other diagnosticians. In the case of another film interview presented by the same experimenters, the differences in diagnostic labels were attributable to disagreements about the level of the patient's apathy and the degree of his distortion of reality, variables that are crucial to the differentiation of psychosis from neurosis. These clinicians were observing the same interview rather than conducting independent examinations; thus, the degree of consistency should have been higher than it would be in actual practice.

Rosensweig observed the same phenomenon after studying the reliability of psychiatric perceptions under very controlled conditions: experienced psychiatrists all observed the same interview (conducted by one of them) of chronic, hospitalized patients.(31) Nevertheless, there was only moderate agreement among them regarding the presence or degree of a large variety of symptoms.

The preceding studies conclude that psychiatric judgments are not very reliable.(32) But psychiatrists and judges act as if they were. Pasamanick and his colleagues, after citing other studies which indicate that "psychiatric diagnosis is at present so unreliable as to merit very serious questions when classifying, treating and studying patient behavior and outcome,"(33) report that despite the unreliability of diagnosis, the length of hospitalization and the types of treatment received are significantly different for patients with different diagnoses.(34) In other words, differences in diagnosis are not merely semantic quibbles. Conceivably patients with one diagnosis might be discharged or given only tranquilizing medication while similar patients, because they have been given a different diagnosis, might be hospitalized and subjected to shock therapy.(35)

Given the demonstrable unreliability of psychiatric diagnoses, however, it seems obvious to us that the decision to deprive another person of his or her liberty, or freedom of choice, should never turn upon that individual's psychiatric diagnosis.

THE VALIDITY OF PSYCHIATRIC JUDGMENTS

It may be useful to note again that there are at least four kinds of psychiatric judgments that may be relevant in a civil commitment proceeding: is the prospective patient "mentally ill;" is he "dangerous;" does his condition require involuntary hospitalization and treatment; and will involuntary hospitalization and treatment "cure" or benefit the prospective patient? There are very few studies of the validity of psychiatric judgments in the first, third and fourth areas. There are more studies of the validity of psychiatric judgments of dangerousness. We will discuss those studies in a moment.

First, however, it bears repeating that reliability and validity are not synonymous. A particular judgment is valid if it accurately describes or predicts that which it is intended to describe or predict.(36)

THE VALIDITY OF DIAGNOSES

Although there are comparatively few studies of the validity of psychiatric diagnoses, the studies discussed above which indicate that such diagnoses are of limited reliability also suggest that they may be of limited validity. And the rate of validity may depend on the use to which these judgments are put. For example, a diagnosis of psychosis may accurately describe qualities the diagnostician *perceived* in a patient; it may less accurately describe qualities the patient objectively manifested; and it may predict with no accuracy at all whether the patient is dangerous, requires hospitalization, or will benefit from treatment.(37)

Ziskin reviewed the literature through 1969 and concluded that

> there are few studies providing a scientific basis for drawing conclusions about the validity of diagnosis in general and virtually none in areas concerning their validity for any legally relevant issues, except parole.(38)

Nevertheless, the few studies that do exist suggest that diagnostic validity is quite low.

In a comprehensive research project, Nathan and his co-workers compared the diagnoses given to hospital patients with the symptoms and behaviors recorded by the diagnosticians themselves, thus avoiding the issue of whether a particular symptom or behavior was indeed present.(39) The authors sought to determine whether the diagnoses followed logically and consistently from the recorded perceptions of behavior, in other words, whether the diagnoses followed the relatively standardized rules for making evaluative judgments based on the presence or absence of various symptoms and behaviors. Even under these controlled conditions the authors found that diagnoses had only limited validity. They discovered that the diagnosis of psychosis generally was arrived at only when the examiner had recorded the presence of one or more of a small group of symptoms—such as hallucinations, delusions, lack of reality testing, disordered thought processes, or autistic behavior—that are associated with psychosis. On the other hand, more specific diagnoses (such as paranoid schizophrenia or hysterical neurosis) were applied even when the examiner had not recorded evidence of one or more symptoms or behaviors supposedly associated with that specific diagnosis. In short, most specific diagnoses do not accurately describe even those symptoms perceived by the examiner, to say nothing of the actual symptoms exhibited by the patient.(40)

In another study of diagnostic validity Goldsmith and Mandell selected 34 relatively complete psychodynamic formulations from 336 inpatient records of a psychiatric hospital.(41) The formulations described the patients' history, emotions, and motivations in some detail. Each patient originally had been designated as falling within one of seven diagnoses. Psychiatrists and laymen then were asked to study the formulations and to predict the assigned diagnoses. The objective was to determine the extent to which the symptoms and behavior identified in the formulations would enable test participants to reach the same diagnoses. The authors found that the psychiatrists predicted the assigned diagnoses only slightly more often than chance would dictate. More important, there was no significant difference in the accuracy of the diagnostic predictions made by the psychiatrists and those made by laymen. Since diagnoses are supposed to reflect overt behavior, the study suggests that psychiatrists cannot validly predict behavior from their understanding of the patient's emotional and motivational structure and history.

That psychiatric diagnoses are often invalid is perhaps best demonstrated by studies in which previously diagnosed patients were carefully reevaluated and rediagnosed—leading to the discovery that the initial diagnoses were *usually* wrong. In one study, for example, 26 consecutive patients who had been admitted to an inpatient psychiatric unit of a general hospital with a diagnosis of "acute schizophrenia" were carefully reexamined to determine whether the individuals *indeed* met the clinical criteria for the diagnosis of acute schizophrenia. Only *one* of the 26 patients in fact met the criteria; the 25 other patients were all reclassified with a non-schizophrenic diagnosis.(42)

THE VALIDITY OF PREDICTIONS OF DANGEROUSNESS

Perhaps the most important judgment psychiatrists make is whether or not an individual is "dangerous:"

> [A]pproximately 50,000 mentally ill persons per year are predicted to be dangerous and preventively detained. . . . In addition, about 5% . . . of the total mental . . . hospital population of the United States . . . are kept in maximum

security	sections	on	assessment	of	their	potential
dangerousness.(43)

There is evidence that the perception of dangerousness is the single most important determinant of judicial decisions to commit individuals or to release patients requesting discharge from a hospital.(44) Psychiatrists commonly testify at civil commitment proceedings that a given individual is "dangerous" to himself or others. How valid are these predictions? First let us consider the research results on dangerousness to others.

In early 1969 Dershowitz reviewed the few studies in the literature on the prediction of anti-social conduct and concluded:

> . . . that psychiatrists are rather inaccurate predictors—inaccurate in an absolute sense—and even less accurate when compared with other professionals, such as psychologists, social workers and correctional officials and when compared to actuarial devices, such as prediction or experience tables. Even more significant for legal purposes, it seems that psychiatrists are particularly prone to one type of error—overprediction. They tend to predict antisocial conduct in many instances when it would not, in fact, occur. Indeed, our research suggests that for every correct psychiatric prediction of violence, there are numerous erroneous predictions. That is, among every group of inmates presently confined on the basis of psychiatric predictions of violence, there are only a few who would, and many more who would not, actually engage in such conduct if released.(45)

Perhaps the most striking evidence supporting Dershowitz's conclusions comes from the study of the results of "Operation Baxstrom" involving 969 prisoner-patients in New York State who were affected by the Supreme Court's decision in *Baxstrom v. Herold*.(46) The Court held that those persons remaining in Department of Corrections hospitals after their prison terms had expired must be released, and committed civilly, if at all. Each of the 969 patients had been detained in maximum-security hospitals because psychiatrists determined that they were mentally ill and too dangerous for release or even for transfer to civil hospitals. Nevertheless, one year after the patients were transferred to civil hospitals, 147 had been discharged to the community and the 702 who remained were found to present no special problems to the hospital staff. Only 7 patients were found to be so difficult to manage or so dangerous as to require recommitment to a Department of Corrections hospital.(47) Several years later, 27 percent of the patients were living in the community, only 9 had been convicted of a crime (only 2 of felonies), and only 3 percent were in a

correctional facility or hospital for the criminally insane.(48)
As one of the authors has written elsewhere:

> In statistical terms, Operation Baxstrom tells us that psychiatric
> predictions are incredibly inaccurate. In human terms, it tells us
> that but for a Supreme Court decision, nearly 1,000 human
> beings would have lived much of their lives behind bars, without
> grounds privileges, without home visits, without even the limited
> amenities available to civil patients, all because a few psy-
> chiatrists, in their considered opinion, thought they were dan-
> gerous and no one asked for proof.(49)

Another recent study,(50) described by one observer as "the most
extensive study to date on the prediction . . . of dangerousness in criminal
offenders,"(51) confirms the lesson of *Baxstrom*. A team of at least five
mental health professionals, including two or more psychiatrists, was
asked to conduct unusually thorough clinical examinations of individuals
who had been convicted previously of serious assaultive crimes (often
sexual in nature), assigned to special treatment programs after conviction,
and who were then eligible for release. Based upon the examinations,
extensive case histories, and the results of psychological tests, the team
attempted to predict which individuals again would commit assaultive
crimes if released. These predictions of dangerousness were made prior to
the court hearings at which the ultimate release decisions were made. Of
49 patients considered by the evaluating team to be dangerous and
therefore not recommended for release, but who nevertheless were
released after a court hearing, 65 percent had not been found to have
committed a violent crime within five years of returning to the community. In other words, two-thirds of those released despite predictions of
dangerousness by the professional team did not in fact turn out to be
dangerous.(52)
Furthermore, as the authors of this study note:

> The difficulty involved in predicting dangerousness is im-
> measurably increased when the subject has never actually per-
> formed an assaultive act. . . . We submit that to properly assess
> indications of *possible* dangerousness in the absence of an actual
> instance of dangerous acting out requires the highest degree of
> psychiatric expertise and may well exceed the present limits of our
> knowledge. . . . *No one can predict dangerous behavior in an*
> *individual with no history of dangerous acting out.*(53)

One psychiatrist has noted that there is no empirical support for the belief that psychiatrists can predict dangerous behavior.(54) To the contrary, even with "the most careful, painstaking, laborious, and lengthy clinical approach to the prediction of dangerousness, false positives may be at a minimum of 60 to 70%.(55) In other words, even under controlled conditions, at least 60 to 70 percent of the people whom psychiatrists judge to be dangerous may, in fact, be harmless. Similarly another psychiatrist acknowledges that psychiatrists "cannot predict with even reasonable certainty that an individual will be dangerous to himself or others."(56)

Still another study found that only five of 1,630 parolees (.31 percent, or less than one-third of one percent) identified by the California Department of Corrections at the time of release as "Potentially Aggressive" (based on a history of aggressive behavior and psychiatric predictions) actually committed known violent crimes after release, as compared with .28 percent of those parolees (17 of 6,082) who were not predicted to be potentially aggressive.(57) On the basis of their studies and review of the literature, the authors concluded that, even for individuals known to have committed a violent act,

> The best prediction available today . . . is that any particular member of that set *will not* become violent . . . . There has been no successful attempt to identify, within either of the offender groups, a sub-class whose members have a greater-than-even chance of engaging again in an assaultive act.(58)

They also add that:

> Confidence in the ability to predict violence serves to legitimate intrusive types of social control. Our demonstration of the *futility* of such prediction should have consequences as great for the protection of individual liberty as the demonstration of the *utility* of violence prediction would have for the protection of society.(59)

Monahan summarized his review of the most recent literature on the prediction of violence as follows:

> The conclusion to emerge most strikingly from these studies is the great degree to which violence is overpredicted . . . . Of those predicted to be dangerous, between 65% and 95% are false positives—people who will not, in fact, commit a dangerous act. Indeed, the literature has been consistent on this point ever since

Pinel took the chains off the supposedly dangerous mental patients at La Bicetre in 1792, and the resulting lack of violence gave lie to the psychiatric predictions which justified their restraint. Violence is vastly overpredicted whether simple behavioral indicators are used or sophisticated multi-variate analyses are employed, and whether psychological tests are administered or thorough psychiatric examinations are performed. It is also noteworthy that the population used . . . [in recent] studies was highly selective and biased toward positive results—primarily convicted offenders, "sexual psychopaths," and adjudicated delinquents. The fact that even in these groups, with higher base-rates for violence than the general population violence cannot be validly predicted bodes very poorly for predicting violence among those who have not committed a criminal act.(60)

Finally, there is no support in the literature for the popularly held notion that the mentally ill are more dangerous, as a group, than the general population;(61) or for any belief that the presence of a psychiatric disturbance, per se, makes the prediction of violence easier and more accurate than would otherwise be the case.(62)

The studies discussed thus far are, for the most part, studies of the validity of predictions of danger to others. There are, in addition, numerous studies of the validity of predictions of danger to self. Writing in 1972, Murphy concluded that "prediction of the infrequent event of suicide is poor. It would be very much poorer in a population unselected for risk. The development of predictive tools of high accuracy has not yet been achieved, not even for populations with high risk of suicide (of which suicide attempters are but one example)."(63)

An even more recent and comprehensive review of the literature by Greenberg concludes that "a method for distinguishing persons who will suicide from those who will not with a measure of accuracy sufficiently high to permit its use in psychiatric commitments simply does not exist at present."(64)

PREDICTIONS OF THE NEED FOR TREATMENT

Psychiatrists frequently predict whether a person's condition requires hospitalization or treatment. That is, they often predict whether a person will be able to "get along" outside a hospital. Again, there are very few studies of the validity of such predictions. It is difficult to conduct such studies because once the psychiatrist predicts that the individual will not be able to get along in the community the individual is usually hospitalized, denying researchers the opportunity to determine whether the prediction was right or wrong.

In one relevant study, Rappeport, Lassen, and Gruenwald studied 73 patients who requested court hearings to obtain release from a psychiatric hospital.(65) Their psychiatrists felt they were not suitable for release. Of the 73, 26 were released by the courts—despite the objections of their psychiatrists—and 47 were remanded to the hospital. Twelve of the 47 subsequently escaped. The investigation studied the community adjustment of these 38 individuals after at least one year. Notably, 44 percent of the court-released and 42 percent of the escaped patients made a satisfactory adjustment to the community (they had not been in serious trouble with the law, had not been rehospitalized, and were caring for themselves). Of equal significance, in neither group did any serious antisocial behavior occur, although a number of the patients who did not adjust were involved in minor accidents or crimes. Since these rates of adjustment compared favorably with those obtained in studies of patients released on the recommendation of psychiatrists, and since the courts have acted contrary to the opinions of psychiatrists in what were presumably difficult cases, the investigators concluded that ". . . the courts may be considered [to have] a better prediction rate [than psychiatrists] since they released patients that otherwise would not have been released at that time."(66) The reasons for this outcome suggested by the authors—psychiatrists may have less tolerance for deviant behavior and may require greater certainty of community adjustment than judges—are discussed later.(67)

There are also a few studies that are less directly on point but are still suggestive. The details vary from study to study, but the essential points are similar. In each study individuals who had been examined in a hospital admission ward and found to require full-time hospitalization and treatment were randomly divided into two groups. One group was hospitalized and the other was treated in the community or in a day hospital on an outpatient basis. Over a substantial period of time, only a few of the community patients failed to get along in the community and had to be hospitalized. In fact, the community patients recovered faster than the hospitalized patients (and cost the state half as much money).(68)

PREDICTIONS OF THE EFFECT OF TREATMENT

Whether a prospective patient will respond favorably or unfavorably to hospitalization and treatment should be a central issue in every commitment proceeding. Unfortunately, it is not. Once again we find that there are very few studies of the validity of psychiatric predictions of the probable outcome (the "prognosis") of hospitalization and treatment.

Robbins and Guze surveyed the literature concerning the validity of clinicians' judgments of the prognosis of schizophrenic patients.(69) They found considerable variations between the predicted prognoses and the actual outcomes of treatment. In practice, patients who received a poor prognosis did poorly as infrequently as 55 percent of the time in one study and as frequently as 91 percent of the time in another. In contrast, patients with a good prognosis did well as frequently as 83 percent of the time in one study and as infrequently as 36 percent in another.(70)

Other investigations showed that psychiatrists accurately predicted the beneficial or nonbeneficial effect of electro-shock therapy for several hundred patients only 41 percent of the time.(71) In other words, their predictions would have been more valid if they had been based on the flip of a coin.

THE AMBIGUITY OF PSYCHIATRIC DIAGNOSES

The studies discussed previously indicate that psychiatrists often disagree in their judgments—especially their diagnostic judgments—and that even when they do agree those judgments—especially predictive judgments—are often wrong. Indeed, psychiatric predictions that an individual is dangerous are *usually* wrong. Furthermore, perceptions of symptoms and behavior vary dramatically among examining psychiatrists (and psychologists), and psychiatric diagnoses are sometimes pinned on individuals who have not, in fact, exhibited the symptoms supposedly associated with their diagnosis. As one authority has observed, we "can no longer take for granted the validity of any clinician's judgment."(72)

There is, however, another, very important point to be made about psychiatric diagnoses—a point that is related to the issue of validity but is also somewhat distinguishable from it: Many, if not most, psychiatric diagnoses are so broad, imprecise, and ambiguous that they are likely to convey much erroneous information about patients who are assigned such diagnoses. That is, even if a psychiatric diagnosis is "valid" to the extent that the subject of the diagnosis is exhibiting at least one of the "symptoms" preeminently associated with the diagnosis, the diagnosis may at the same time be *in*valid to the extent that the diagnosis suggests that the patient is exhibiting other symptoms which, in fact, the patient is not manifesting.

This point is dramatically illustrated by a recent study orchestrated by Rosenhan.(73) In that study eight confederates, all normal and healthy, gained admission to 12 psychiatric hospitals by complaining that they were hearing voices saying "empty," "hollow," and "thud." Otherwise, no significant falsification of "person, history, or circumstances" was made. Upon admission to the psychiatric wards, the pseudo-patients immediately ceased claiming to hear voices and simulated no other abnormal symptoms. With the exception of nervousness brought on by the circumstances of their commitment, their subsequent behavior was perfectly normal. All but one of the patients had been admitted with a diagnosis of schizophrenia, and all were discharged with a diagnosis of "schizophrenia in remission." The diagnosis was a valid indication that the pseudo-patients exhibited one of the characteristic symptoms of schizophrenia—hallucinations. However, it was not a valid indication that the pseudo-patients exhibited any of the other symptoms characteristic of schizophrenia, officially described as follows:

> . . . characteristic disturbances of thinking, mood and behavior . . . .alterations of concept formation which may lead to misinterpretation of reality and sometimes to delusions and hallucinations, which frequently appear psychologically self-protective. Corollary mood changes include ambivalent, constricted and inappropriate emotional responsiveness and loss of empathy with others. Behavior may be withdrawn, regressive, and bizarre. . . .(74)

Similarly, because psychiatric diagnoses are so broad and ambiguous—and overlapping—there is little or no relationship between diagnosis and symptomatology. Rather, as several studies have demonstrated, there is considerable overlapping of symptoms between diagnostic categories, and within a diagnostic category there is considerable variability of symptomatology.(74a) Thus, knowing what diagnostic category an individual falls into tells us little or nothing about how the individual is in fact behaving (save for the fact—if the diagnosis is at all valid—that the individual is manifesting at least one of the "symptoms" associated with the diagnosis).

In one study, Zigler and Phillips categorized almost 800 patients as falling into one of four broad diagnostic groups: schizophrenic, manic-depressive; psychoneurotic, or character disorder. The patients were also assessed for the presence or absence of major symptoms. The investigators found that there was little relationship between the diagnostic category and the likelihood of the presence, or absence, of particular symptoms. For example, the percentage of patients who were rated as "tense" varied little from category to category (from a high of 40% to a low of 32%, in fact). Even regarding those symptoms that are more particularly associated with one category or another, neither a complete nor an exclusive association was to be found. For example, 64% of the diagnosed "manic-depressives" were rated as "depressed," but 58% of the "psycho-neurotics" (and 28% of the "schizophrenics") as well. Similarly, while 35% (and only 35%) of the "schizophrenics" appeared to exhibit hallucinations, so did 12% of the "character disorders." And only 20–25% of the "schizophrenics" exhibited such classically "schizophrenic" symptoms as withdrawal, perplexity, and bizarre ideas.(75)

In sum, as Frank observed on the basis of his exhaustive review of the research literature: "save (for) perhaps the gravest kind of psychotic behavior," there are few if any correlations between diagnoses and patterns of behavior . . ." and "[t]hese data seem to point to the lack of validity of this mode of classifying behavior, and question the (usefulness) of diagnosis."(76)

WHY PSYCHIATRIC JUDGMENTS ARE UNRELIABLE

Before discussing the specific reasons why psychiatric judgments are unreliable and invalid it is necessary to recognize a more general problem: individual psychiatrists are not given any opportunity to learn from their mistakes. Goldberg, for example, points out that clinicians rarely get feedback on the accuracy of their judgments.(77) They may believe their judgments are reliable and valid, but they have no systematic way of testing that belief.(78) For "[u]nlike other specialties, psychiatry lacks adequate statistics and followups, because psychiatrists have not seriously attempted to check on their methods and results in the way other medical doctors regard as their scientific duty."(79) As a result, very little of what psychiatrists think they are able to do "can be adequately validated."(80) One psychiatrist has acknowledged that the absence of a self-corrective mechanism means that in many cases, "the diagnosis of psychosis becomes almost a matter of chance. It is dependent on the training, experience and personal philosophies of the psychiatrist who examines the [person] and the circumstances under which the [person] is examined."(81)

Although the specific reasons why psychiatric judgments and predictions are unreliable and invalid are varied, many of them can be grouped under six broad and occasionally overlapping headings: orientation and training, context, time, class and culture, personal bias, and inadequacies of the diagnostic system and ambiguity of psychiatric data. Finally, there are additional reasons for the inaccuracy of psychiatric predictions of dangerousness.

ORIENTATION AND TRAINING

It has been suggested that psychiatrists are prone to diagnose mental illness and to perceive symptoms in ambiguous behavior because they are trained in medical school that it is safer to suspect illness and be wrong, than to reject illness and be wrong.(82) In other words, "being a mental health professional may constitute a set to perceive mental illness. . . ."(83)

In addition, each school of psychiatry has a different view of what mental illness is, how it is caused, and how it should be treated. Substantial evidence suggests that psychiatric judgments are strongly influenced by these different schools of thought and training. Pasamanick, Dinitz, and Lefton, for example, inferred from their findings that:

> . . . despite their protestations that their point of view is always the individual patient, clinicians in fact may be so committed to a particular school of psychiatric thought that the patient's diagnosis and treatment is largely predetermined. Clinicians . . . may be selectively perceiving only those characteristics and attributes of their patients which are relevant to their own preconceived system of thought. As a consequence, they may be overlooking other patient characteristics which would be considered crucial by colleagues who are otherwise committed. . . .(84)

CONTEXT

If upon entering a room one notices a book in a wastebasket, it is reasonable to assume it is not a valuable book. But seeing the same book in a locked book case gives rise to an entirely different opinion as to its value. Similarly, a person dressed in normal clothing and sitting in his living room creates one impression, while the same person dressed in a hospital robe and slippers and sitting on a bench in a hospital corridor creates a much different impression. It should therefore come as no surprise to learn that diagnosis is often influenced by the setting in which a person is observed, with inpatient settings disposing clinicians toward a diagnosis of psychosis.(85)

Other factors, in addition to the place of examination and appearance of the subject, may influence diagnosis. To illustrate, the effect of "suggestion" or "set" was examined in a study in which an actor portrayed a healthy man while talking about himself in a diagnostic interview with a clinician.(86) The interview was recorded and played to groups of graduate students in clinical psychology, psychiatrists, law students, and undergraduates. Before playing the tape, however, a prestige figure—a different person for each group—told the groups that the interview was interesting because the subject "looked neurotic but actually is quite psychotic." As a control four comparable groups heard the taped interview but were given no prestige suggestion for "psychosis." After hearing the tape, the groups were asked to assign the interviewee to one of 30 specified diagnostic categories. None of the control groups diagnosed the subject as psychotic, and the majority diagnosed him as healthy. By contrast, 60 percent of the psychiatrists, 30 percent of the undergraduates, 28 percent of the psychologists, 17 percent of the law students, and 11 percent of the graduate psychology students diagnosed psychosis.(87) The authors conclude that prestige suggestion influences diagnosis, and that an initial diagnosis "may have a profound effect" upon a subsequent diagnosis by influencing "interpersonal perception, whether or not the [initial] diagnosis label refers to a disease which actually exists."(88) In other words, clinicians often perceive what they expect to perceive and the impact of suggestion on clinical perception may be profound.

In his study of pseudo-patients—in which eight sane individuals feigning one symptom of schizophrenia were admitted to various mental hospitals with that diagnosis—Rosenhan found that even though immediately after admission the pseudo-patients ceased displaying that symptom and behaved normally,

> once a person is designated abnormal, all of his other behaviors and characteristics are colored by that label. Indeed, that label is so powerful that many of the pseudo-patient's normal behaviors were overlooked entirely or profoundly misinterpreted.(89)

For example, when several of the pseudo-patients took notes of their experiences, that activity was noted in three of their records as "an aspect of their pathological behavior."(90) The purpose of Rosenhan's study was to determine whether "the salient characteristics that lead to diagnoses reside in the patients themselves or in the environment and contexts in which observers find them."(91) Although the pseudo-patients related absolutely normal life histories, Rosenhan found that "diagnoses were in no way affected by the relative health of the circumstances of a pseudo-patient's life. Rather, the reverse occurred: the perception of his circumstances was shaped entirely by the diagnosis."(92) Other studies focusing on the importance of context likewise conclude that "the initial set with which the interviewer begins the interview has considerable effect upon the outcome."(93) For example "[i]nterviewers given different sets about interviewees (*i.e.*, that interviewees are cold or warm) perceive interviewees differently—even after 30 minutes of interview time."(94)

TIME

Since even "normal" people speak and behave differently from one day to the next, it is no less natural for an allegedly mentally ill individual to appear agitated one day and composed the next. Consequently, the timing of a prospective patient's examination may substantially influence the diagnosis he or she is given. In his 1967 review of studies, Zubin found that the consistency over time of specific diagnoses of nonorganic conditions is quite low, and that even the "broad diagnostic categories appear to display a low order of consistency [about 50 percent] over time."(95) In a related study Edelman found that diagnostic impressions change by a fourth interview-therapy session about 25 percent of the time.(96) He also noted that:

> The typical procedure for establishing a diagnosis is a single unstandardized interview, the results of which may be augmented by psychological testing. An implicit assumption of this procedure is that interviewee behavior has been adequately sampled in the allotted time span and that the interviewee is sufficiently motivated to reveal all pertinent information. Yet, there are numerous studies which indicate that interviewee behavior is mediated by complex process variables suggesting that such assumptions may not always be justified.(97)

In other words, even if a patient's behavior is consistent over time, different aspects of that behavior may be observed at different times.(98)

In addition, the limited amount of time usually available for a psychiatric evaluation may combine with the psychiatrist's "set" to perceive mental illness, thus resulting in overpredictions of disturbance. For example, when there is only limited time to examine a patient who is allegedly dangerous, the psychiatrist is likely to search for, and find, signs of dangerousness such as aggressive fantasies. He is not nearly so apt, however, to be attentive to evidence of nondangerousness, such as a history of good impulse control.

CLASS AND CULTURE

There is considerable evidence that psychiatric judgments are strongly influenced by the socio-economic backgrounds of the clinician and patient. Philips and Draguns reviewed the literature from 1966 to 1969 and concluded:

. . . The influence of the client's socio-economic class in facilitating the attribution of some, and impeding the application of other, nosological designations is particularly well documented . . . [T]he findings converge in suggesting social distance as the mediating variable. Across socio-economic or other subcultural lines, the middle class diagnostician is prone to assign categories of severe psychopathology. . . .(99)

In a controlled experiment, Lee and Temerlin found that the diagnoses of psychiatric residents were highly influenced by the imagined socio-economic history of the patient (and by the perceived diagnoses of other, prestigious psychiatrists) independent of the clinical picture presented. A lower socio-economic history biased diagnosis toward greater illness and poorer prognosis.(100) Similarly, according to studies conducted by Ordway, clinicians may be influenced to conclude that lower socio-economic class individuals are dangerous because such individuals are presumed to be impulsive and therefore more prone to violence.(101)

Sexual stereotypes and biases may also color clinicians' judgments. In a study by Braverman, et al.,(102) for example, male and female clinicians described the ideally healthy woman as being "more submissive, less independent, less adventurous, more easily influenced, less aggressive, less competitive, and more excitable in minor crises"(103) than the ideally healthy man. By implication, clinicians tend to view women as somewhat disturbed when they are as independent, adventurous, aggressive, and competitive as men are or should be.(104)

Different cultural backgrounds may also have profound effects on clinicians' perceptions. In one study, 23 patients were interviewed by both British and American psychiatrists. The American psychiatrists not only reported almost twice as many symptoms per patient as did the British psychiatrists, but in addition they reported differences in the types of symptoms observed. Specifically, the Americans were much more likely to "observe" signs and/or feelings of inadequacy, dependency, and social underachievement.(106) Another study comparing the judgments of British and American psychiatrists confirmed that, as between the two groups, there is both a wide variation in diagnostic preferences, and a strong tendency to perceive the severity of a patient's symptoms differently—though there was general agreement as to which "symptoms" the patients manifested.(107) In short, "psychiatrists in both countries perceived the same groups of symptoms, but interpret [sic] them in different ways."(108) Specifically, American psychiatrists and, among the British, those who were older, tended to view patients as having more severe pathology. And a third study, in which a filmed interview was shown to British and American psychiatrists, again found that British psychiatrists see different patterns of pathology and less pathology generally—especially less severe pathology.(109)

PERSONAL BIAS

The factor which may most influence diagnosis is the clinician's own personality, value system, self-image, personal preferences, and attitudes. Raines and Rohrer, in their study of psychiatric predictions of combat officer candidate success, found that psychiatrists were predisposed to observe different personality traits in the same individual.(110) Moreover, the various traits and symptoms observed were not valued equally by the different psychiatrists. The authors concluded that:

> . . . the psychiatry decision involves not only the psychiatrist's emotional problems and defenses, but also his entire value system and probably his self-image . . . .
> This results in a greater sensitivity on the part of the psychiatrist for certain facets of the patient's personality structure, and a greater perceptual distortion . . . of other facets. . . . Once perceived, correctly or distortedly, each item is subjected to the psychiatrist's value system.(111)

In a follow-up study, the same authors discovered that psychiatrists' observations and perceptions of their patients tend to reflect their own personality structures and problems.(112) A related study concluded that the psychiatrist's personal values (such as his attitute toward the value of military service and doing one's "duty") often influence the supposedly neutral clinical judgment as to whether an individual is psychologically "fit for duty."(113)

Grosz and Grossman present evidence suggesting that the clinicians' varying personal biases may account for the significant differences in their evaluation of ambiguous and emotionally charged case history data.(114) They summarize their findings, as follows:

> . . . The more complex, ill-defined, ambiguous, unfamiliar and uninformative the data, the more strongly do the observer's set, focused attention, expectation, bias and other intra-observer conditions come into play and influence his perception, judgment, and decision. . . . The possibility exists that such judgments are less informative about the patient whom they are meant to describe than about the clinician who makes them. They may reveal the clinician's concepts of norms or his toleration of deviations compared to those of his peers, his clinical orien-

tation and attitudes toward certain aspects of the patient's history, his clinical experience and interests, and perhaps even his own background and personality.(115)

Their conclusions are borne out by others. For instance, Dickes, Simons, and Weisfogel demonstrate that the unconscious conflicts of clinicians often cause distortions in perception, and misapprehension of the patient's true condition.(116) And in the context of sanity hearings Pugh found that the ultimate determinations are strongly influenced by the personal idiosyncracies of the examining psychiatrist.(117)

Strupp found that therapists' perceptions of a patient presented in a film interview varied according to the therapist's experience and his attitude toward the patient.(118) As an illustration of the latter factor, if for some reason the therapist disliked the patient the result was often a poor prognostic evaluation. Braginsky and Braginsky suggest a possible context in which a psychiatrist might develop a dislike for a patient. Their study showed that mental health professionals view patients who express radical political views as more disturbed than patients who voice the same psychiatric complaints, but whose political views are more conventional. They also discovered that voicing criticism of the mental health profession, whether from a radical or conservative perspective, may substantially increase a patient's psychopathology in the eyes of mental health professionals, while flattering the profession tends to decrease a patient's otherwise perceived symptomatology.(119) Numerous other studies confirm that the clinician's personal values and attitudes strongly influence diagnosis and judgment.(120)

We have seen that idiosyncratic values and attitudes often influence psychiatric diagnoses and prognoses. Moreover, there is evidence that values and attitudes characteristic of psychiatrists as a group may influence other psychiatric judgments, such as the decision whether or not to release hospitalized patients. First, psychiatrists as a group may have little tolerance for deviant behavior and consequently may require a high standard of community adjustment.(121) Second, psychiatrists as a group are likely to be paternalistic and therefore relatively insensitive to considerations of civil liberty.(122) Third, psychiatrists may be susceptible to family pressures to commit.(123) Fourth, psychiatrists may have a vested interest—for example, in the patient's continued participation in an experimental treatment program—which can only be fulfilled by the patient's continued confinement.(124) Finally, psychiatrists may view poor adjustment to the hospital as a negative indicator of potential community adjustment, rather than as dissatisfaction with incarceration.(125)

INADEQUACIES OF THE DIAGNOSTIC SYSTEM

In the follow-up study to Beck,(126) Ward and his collaborators asked pairs of psychiatrists who had interviewed the same patients to discuss their conclusions in an attempt to discover why their diagnoses had differed. Two major sources of error were discerned. One source of error was inconsistency of perception among diagnosticians and assignment of different weights to the same symptoms. The largest sources of error derived from the inadequacies of the diagnostic system—the excessively fine distinctions required, the uncertain criteria for particular diagnoses, and the requirement of choosing a predominant diagnostic category when none was clearly evident.(127)

Ward's findings of inconsistent psychiatric perception are echoed in an interesting study by Strauss which shows that 1. it may often be very difficult—if not impossible—to determine whether a given individual is, or is not, experiencing hallucinations or delusions (the key diagnostic criteria of the psychoses, especially of schizophrenia) and 2. even if the person is, such phenomena should be viewed in terms of a continuum of reality distortion, rather than simply as being present or absent.(128) Of 119 acutely disturbed patients comprising Strauss' study, 74 reported experiences that were considered by the examiner to be possibly but not clearly delusional, and 41 reported experiences that were considered to be possibly but not clearly hallucinatory. Psychiatrists predisposed to observe symptoms of disorder could have interpreted these ambiguous experiences as delusions or hallucinations, which would have justified a diagnosis of psychosis or perhaps schizophrenia. But, as Strauss points out in summarizing his findings:

> [Acute psychiatric] patients describe . . . such a variety of perceptual and ideational experiences that in many cases a simple "presence" or "absence" rating would make experiences seem much more distinct than they actually were. Since it was so difficult to dichotomize ideational and perceptual aberrations into categories of hallucinations and delusions on the one hand and "normal" on the other, the concept of schizophrenia as a discrete disorder for which these symptoms are often considered diagnostic is also brought into question.(129)

Not only may the experiences described be ambiguous, but a significant ambiguity is raised by the diagnostic manual of the American Psychiatric Association—which presumably provides the basis for psychiatric diagnoses. In one part of the manual psychiatrists are instructed to diagnose as psychotic only persons whose "mental functioning is sufficiently impaired to interfere grossly with their capacity to meet the ordinary demands of life."(130) That instruction, standing alone, would suggest to laymen and to psychiatrists that almost everyone diagnosed as psychotic would meet the criteria for involuntary commitment—mentally ill and in need of care and treatment—in use in most states. In the next paragraph of the manual, however, psychiatrists are instructed that they may diagnose individuals as falling within the sub-categories of psychosis such as schizophrenic, paranoid, manic-depressive, even if the individuals "are not in fact psychotic."(131) Consequently, an assumption that an individual diagnosed as schizophrenic requires involuntary care and treatment often may be erroneous. Psychiatrists would be the first to acknowledge that millions of persons who could be diagnosed as schizophrenic do not require hospitalization. Unless one realizes that a person may fall within a subcategory of psychosis without being "in fact" psychotic, the use of diagnoses such as schizophrenia is misleading and can prejudice the prospective patient's rights.(132)

INVALID PSYCHIATRIC PREDICTIONS OF DANGEROUSNESS

While all the foregoing factors may also dispose psychiatrists to assess erroneously a patient's capacity for violence, there are additional, more particularized, reasons why psychiatric predictions of "dangerousness" are of such limited validity.

Unlike the task of formulating a diagnosis, psychiatrists are not even trained in the assessment or prediction of "dangerousness." Medical schools do not offer courses in the prediction of dangerous behavior; nor are there textbooks explaining the method and criteria by which such assessments are to be made. Rappeport, for instance, conducted a thorough research of the literature and found "no articles that could assist [psychiatrists] in any great extent in determining who might be dangerous, particularly before he commits an offense."(133) Moreover, no traits, symptoms, or conditions which are useful predictors of dangerous behavior have been identified. Rubin, looking for such "characteristics of danger," found that the literature was "sparse, disorganized, and impressionistic."(134)

Guttmacher studied 20 individuals who had been hospitalized for psychiatric reasons prior to committing a homicide.(135) After searching the hospital records and case histories for clues or common features which might have alerted the hospital staff to the patient's dangerousness, his conclusion was that it was not possible "to decipher in these cases any symptoms which they presented in common that might act as warning signs of impending catastrophe."(136)

In summary, training and experience do not enable psychiatrists adequately to predict dangerous behavior. Rather, such predictions are determined by the time and place of diagnosis, the psychiatrist's personal bias, social pressures, the class and cultures of the respective parties, and other extraneous factors. Finally, even if psychiatrists could accurately determine which persons are mentally ill, that determination would not assist them in predicting dangerousness because, as has been previously noted, there is no correlation between mental illness and dangerous behavior. To the contrary, the mentally ill may even be less dangerous than the population as a whole.(137) Moreover, dangerous behavior does not occur in a vacuum. As Guttmacher has noted, "one cannot anticipate with accuracy [the] social situations which the released . . . patient will have to meet."(138) In all probability, then, whether a person will commit a dangerous act depends in large part upon fortuitous and unpredictable events.(139)

LEGAL CONSEQUENCES AND RECOMMENDATIONS

From the preceding studies it is possible to draw the following conclusions. Psychiatric diagnoses are quite unreliable.(140) Psychiatrists are more likely to disagree than to agree about specific diagnoses such as psychotic depression, paranoid schizophrenia, or passive-aggressive personality; and while diagnoses limited to the broad categories of functional disorder are more reliable, in actual practice psychiatrists are almost as likely to disagree about such diagnoses as they are to agree. Moreover, whether or not quasi-diagnostic descriptive adjectives—such as "apathetic," "depressed," or "agitated"—are applied to particular patients appears to depend as much upon the background and ideosyncracies of the examiner as the actual behavior of the patients themselves.

The evidence that exists also suggests that psychiatric diagnoses are quite often invalid. In any event, many psychiatric diagnoses—especially the diagnostic categories of "psychosis" and "schizophrenia"—are so broad and ambiguous that one cannot know, from the diagnosis, what "symptoms" the "patient" is or is not manifesting. Even worse, psychiatric diagnoses—again, particularly the categories of "psychosis" and "schizophrenia"—often suggest the presence of symptoms and/or degrees of psychopathology that (in many cases where the diagnosis is applied) simply do not exist.

All the evidence available indicates that psychiatrists have absolutely no expertise in predicting dangerous behavior—indeed, they may be *less* accurate predictors than laymen—and that they usually err by overpredicting violence.

Finally, whether a prospective patient will be labelled psychotic or nonpsychotic, schizophrenic or nonschizophrenic, dangerous or non-dangerous, able or unable to care for himself or herself may be determined by one or more of the following factors: the theoretical orientation and methodology of the examining psychiatrist; the socio-economic and cultural background of the patient and psychiatrist; and the time, place, and circumstances of the psychiatric examination. In summary, there is good reason to believe that psychiatric judgments are not particularly reliable or valid, and that psychiatric diagnoses and predictions convey more erroneous than accurate information. The legal implications of this demonstrated psychiatric fallibility are obviously far-reaching.

PSYCHIATRIC JUDGMENTS UNDER RULES OF EVIDENCE

An exception to the ordinary rules of evidence has been created to permit experts to testify in court as to their opinions, conclusions, and judgments. With the exception of psychiatrists, witnesses are required to prove their expertise before courts will permit them to testify as experts. If that same proof were required of psychiatrists, they could not qualify as expert witnesses. Support for this proposition may be provided by analogy to the judicial treatment of polygraph results.

There is no question that psychiatric judgments are far less reliable and valid than polygraph judgments.(141) Although the evidence is still accumulating, a conservative estimate is that an experienced polygraph examiner can correctly detect truth or deception about 80 to 90 percent of the time.(142)

Despite this proven reliability and validity of polygraph tests, only a handful of state and federal trial courts have received polygraph reports in evidence, and then usually for only limited purposes.(143) Moreover, as of 1973, no appellate court had approved the admission of polygraph reports over the objection of a party.(144)

In *State v. Valdez*,(145) for example, the Supreme Court of Arizona refused, absent stipulation, to permit the use of polygraph evidence in court, even though it believed that under conservative estimates polygraph operators could correctly determine truth or deception in 75 to 80 percent of all cases (15 to 20 percent inconclusive and less than 5 percent proven error).(146) The court gave five reasons for excluding lie detector results: the possibility that extraneous qualities or characteristics of the subject might yield erroneous results; the tendency of judges and juries to treat lie detector evidence as conclusive; the lack of standardized testing procedures; the difficulty of evaluating examiner opinions; and the nonacceptance of the technique by appropriate scientific bodies.

Each of these objections provides a cogent reason also to exclude psychiatric judgments: extraneous qualities of psychiatric patients—such as their socio-economic class—may substantially influence psychiatric judgments; judges and juries usually defer to psychiatric judgments, psychiatric interview procedures are unstandardized; it is difficult for judges and juries to evaluate the validity of individual psychiatric judgments; and psychiatrists and behavioral scientists who have studied the reliability and validity of psychiatric judgments almost unanimously agree that such judgments are of low reliability and validity.

Accordingly, psychiatrists should not be permitted to testify as expert witnesses(147) until they can prove through empirical studies that their judgments are reliable and valid.(148).

PSYCHIATRIC JUDGMENTS IN CIVIL COMMITMENTS

It is our contention that psychiatric diagnoses often convey more inaccurate than accurate information about an individual, in that a diagnosis suggests that the individual manifests the range of symptoms associated with that diagnosis when, in fact, the individual may exhibit only one, or even none, of these symptoms.

For example, a diagnostic label of "psychosis" indicates that the patient so diagnosed is exhibiting—or at least was perceived by the examiner as exhibiting—at least one of five major "symptoms": hallucinations, delusions, grossly inappropriate affect, disorganized thought processes, or severely withdrawn behavior. However, apart from the very real possibility that a patient so diagnosed might not be psychotic at all,(149) there is no way of knowing, from the diagnosis alone, *which* of the symptoms the patient was exhibiting, or the degree of their severity. Moreover, the diagnosis, per se, tells us nothing about the individual's potential dangerousness, the expected duration of his or her condition, whether it can be treated, and, if so, how. Moreover, it does not purport to tell us whether the individual is friendly or unfriendly, cooperative or uncooperative, happy or depressed. In short, the diagnosis itself answers none of the questions that conceivably could be important to a judge or jury in a civil commitment proceeding.(150) Indeed, though a diagnosis of psychosis by definition indicates that an individual's "mental functioning is sufficiently impaired to interfere grossly with [his or her] capacity to meet the ordinary demands of life,"(151) that definition is essentially meaningless because "[a]ll of us [psychiatrists] know basically psychotic individuals who continue . . . to meet the ordinary demands of life and nonpsychotic individuals who fail utterly to measure up to this criterion."(152)

By way of partial illustration, one study found that only 18.5 percent of the people living in mid-Manhattan could be considered mentally healthy (free of significant symptoms of mental pathology) while almost 25 percent of the population was impaired and exhibited "mental morbidity." Individuals in the latter group were all characterized by "symptom formations that [had] halting, laming, or crippling effects on the performance of one's daily life." Most of those individuals probably could be considered "mentally ill" within the meaning of prevalent civil commitment provisions;(153) nevertheless, they were living and functioning in the community. Another study, conducted by the National Institute of Mental Health, concluded that "as many as eight million people a year may suffer depression severe enough to merit being treated by a doctor, [but only] 250,000 Americans were hospitalized for the ailment last year."(154) In other words, only three percent of all persons thought to be severely depressed required hospitalization for that condition. The rest, though depressed, were able to "get along" in the community. Accordingly, since many "psychotic" or "severely depressed" persons do not require hospitalization, those labels do not assist the trier of fact in a civil commitment proceeding in deciding whether or not to commit the prospective patient. But since diagnoses such as psychosis or schizophrenia have scare word qualities, they often misleadingly suggest to a judge or jury that the individual should be committed to a hospital.(155)

We do not suggest that psychiatrists should have no role in civil commitment hearings. We do suggest that their testimony be limited to descriptions of behavior which would exclude diagnoses, opinions, and predictions. We recognize that in many states lay witnesses are permitted to offer certain limited types of opinion testimony regarding mental condition.(156) They are permitted to do so, however, only because they lack the education or training to describe behavior in other than conclusory terms.(157) Since psychiatrists supposedly are trained to observe and describe behavior in concrete terms, there is no need for them to offer diagnoses.(158) And if an individual truly requires involuntary hospitalization, that need should be apparent from the individual's overt behavior and/or statements.

The admission of psychiatric judgments in a civil commitment proceeding denies prospective patients due process. This point, although essential, can be simply stated. Justifying the deprivation of an individual's liberty on the basis of judgments and opinions that have not been shown to be reliable and valid should be considered a violation of both substantive and procedural due process.(159) Certainly a procedure by which judges flipped coins to determine who would be committed would offend our sense of fundamental fairness. It is our contention that psychiatric judgments have not been shown to be substantially more reliable and valid.

CROSS-EXAMINATION

Since many variables other than the actual condition of an individual may influence psychiatric perceptions, descriptions, and judgments, their validity cannot be assumed. Rather, they must be examined to determine whether the data before the psychiatrist supports his or her conclusion. We have seen that psychiatric terminology often conveys misleading information, which is usually prejudicial to the prospective patient. By way of illustration, if a recommendation that an individual be hospitalized rests upon the psychiatrist's judgment that the individual is "psychotic," cross-examination might reveal that the diagnosis of psychosis in turn rests upon the presence of only one symptom—voicing delusions, for example. Since the prospective patient did not exhibit any other symptoms of psychosis, or any violent behavior or threats, commitment could be justified, if at all, only by the presence of that one symptom—delusions. Moreover, if further cross-examination indicates that the patient's beliefs were not demonstrably true, but not particularly unreasonable or uncommon,(160) exposing the psychiatrist's personal concept of "delusion" would make the limitations of his or her diagnosis apparent.(161)

Even though descriptive statements about behavior are assumed to be objective, too often they are based in substantial part on subjective judgment and opinions. For example, statements such as "the patient is apathetic," or "severely depressed" or "distorting reality" are not objective observations at all; the behavioral criteria for attaching such labels have been shown to vary substantially among psychiatrists.(162) Although it may be that any description of an individual's emotional condition involves an irreducible amount of subjectivity, that does not detract from the necessity of requiring psychiatrists to refine their descriptions. If a patient's behavior or threatened behavior is so disturbed as to require involuntary hospitalization, it should be possible to describe that behavior, or those threats, in concrete and unambiguous language.(163)

At present, most cross-examination of psychiatrists is perfunctory or nonexistent.(164) One reason is that many attorneys accept psychiatric judgments at face value, possibly because they feel incapable of challenging such judgments.(165) Another is that the prospective patient's lawyer, who usually is not present during the psychiatric examination on which the psychiatrist's judgment is based, has little information about the individual circumstances that might have influenced that judgment.

Not inconceivably, the psychiatrist might report only those portions of the prospective patient's comments and actions which would support an inference that the individual was disturbed, even though 99 percent of what he or she said and did would be entirely consistent with what we regard as normal behavior. Nor is it uncommon for psychiatrists to omit qualifying remarks, thereby making the prospective patient's statements seem more irrational than they are.(166) Understandably, the patient often does not remember what the psychiatrist has omitted or misstated, or is in no position to challenge the psychiatrist's recollection of the interview.(167) Consequently, meaningful cross-examination may not be possible unless the prospective patient's lawyer was present when his or her client was examined, and therefore knows what actually happened during the psychiatric examination.

In an analogous situation the Supreme Court has ruled that a defense lawyer must be permitted to attend and observe the circumstances of a police line-up so that his subsequent cross-examination of the identifying witness will be meaningful.(168) Following that example, a few lower courts have suggested that prospective patients be extended the right to representation at all psychiatric examinations by a lawyer, personal physician, or friend, or, in the alternative, that a tape recording or videotape of the interview be made available to them.(169) The studies collected in this article confirm the wisdom of those suggestions and the necessity for their adoption.

EXPERT WITNESSES FOR THE PROSPECTIVE PATIENT

Cross-examination may suggest the fallibility of the opposing psychiatrist and the shortcomings of the psychiatric profession. But calling to the stand a psychiatrist who disagrees with the opposing psychiatrist is an even better way of forcing judges and jurors to use their common sense. In fact, it may be the only feasible method because the so-called "independent" psychiatrist, despite claims to the contrary, does not exist.(170) Furthermore, the judgments of even "independent" psychiatrists are subject to bias and error. Accordingly, prospective patients at least should be given the opportunity to call psychiatrists who they believe are likely to agree with them that commitment is not necessary. If the prospective patient is indigent, the reasonable costs of retaining at least one psychiatrist, chosen by the prospective patient, should be borne by the state. If after examination the retained psychiatrist is not willing to testify on behalf of the prospective patient he or she will have to go to trial without favorable psychiatric testimony. Even so, we believe this procedure should be given preference over the appointment of an ostensibly "independent" psychiatrist, as is presently done in several

states.(171) If a supposedly "independent" psychiatrist testifies against
the wishes of the prospective patient, it has a devastating impact on the
minds of judges and jurors.(172)

NONJUDICIAL COMMITMENT

Our concern so far has been with the role of psychiatrists in judicial
proceedings. In many states, however, persons can be hospitalized involuntarily for months or even years without ever having appeared before
a judge or jury. Typically, a certification by two psychiatrists—or even
two physicians—that a person is mentally ill, or dangerous, or both, will
suffice to authorize involuntary hospitalization. There is no evidence that
psychiatric judgments made outside the judicial process are any more
reliable or accurate than those made in a judicial context. Consequently,
the former are just as vulnerable as the latter to the criticisms we have
raised in this article. Accordingly, involuntary hospitalization based on
medical certification without benefit of a judicial determination of the
necessity for hospitalization should no longer be permitted.

If medical certification is not abolished, it should be permitted only in
emergency situations, where the prospective patient is considered im-
minently dangerous to self or others. And medical certification should
authorize involuntary hospitalization only for the limited time necessary
to institute judicial proceedings.

INSUFFICIENT GROUNDS FOR COMMITMENT

There is no reason to believe that psychiatrists can determine who is
"mentally ill" or predict who requires involuntary care and treatment any
more reliably and accurately than they can make other diagnoses and
predictions. Given the breadth and ambiguity of these terms, and the lack
of any agreed definitions for them, such judgments are likely to be
significantly less reliable and accurate than psychiatric judgments usually
are.

At the least, therefore, no person should be involuntarily hospitalized
on the basis of a judgment that the person is "mentally ill" or in need of
care and treatment, when the only support for that judgment is the
opinion of a psychiatrist. Furthermore, we have found no evidence that
the judgment of who is "mentally ill," or who requires care and treatment, can be reliably and accurately made by anyone. In the present state
of knowledge, commitment on these grounds is of necessity a completely
arbitrary act. No person could be confined under the criminal law solely
because of a judgment that the person is a "criminal type," because that
standard is too imprecise to permit any test of the validity of the

judgment. Similarly, no person should be confined under the civil law solely because of a judgment that the person is "mentally ill" or "in need of care and treatment" because these standards are too imprecise to permit any test of the validity of such judgments.

CRITERIA FOR COMMITMENT DUE TO DANGEROUSNESS

We have seen that predictions of dangerous behavior are wrong more often than they are right even in those cases in which the subject of the prediction has actually done or threatened something dangerous in the past. And without such evidence of past dangerous behavior, predictions of dangerous behavior are even more inaccurate. These findings raise considerable doubt about the utility and constitutionality of any statute which authorizes involuntary confinement on the ground of danger to self or others. But if such confinements are to be permitted, we should at least reduce the risk of error as much as possible by insisting on evidence of an overt act, attempt, or threat of a dangerous nature in the recent past. Absent such evidence, deprivations of liberty on the ground of dangerousness should be impermissible. Finally, the meaning of "dangerousness" should be spelled out more precisely because at present ambiguity of the term encourages over-prediction. The appropriate standard should require proof that in the absence of hospitalization there is a substantial likelihood that the prospective patient would inflict major physical injury upon self or others in the near future.(173)

CONCLUSION

In 1964, Judge (now Chief Justice) Warren E. Burger wrote that psychology is, at best, an "infant among the family of science," that psychiatry and psychology cannot claim to be truly scientific, and that psychiatrists and psychologists "may be claiming too much in relation to what they really understand about the human personality and human behavior."(174) The professional literature confirms Justice Burger's intuitive judgment; psychiatrists have bitten off more than they can chew. The fault, however, is not theirs alone, for legislatures and courts, in an attempt to shift responsibility for making the determination of who shall remain free and who shall be confined, have turned to psychiatry, seeking easy answers where there are none.

Subject to constitutional limitations, the decision to deprive another human of liberty is not a psychiatric judgment but a social judgment. We shall have to decide how much we value individual freedom; how much we care about privacy and self-determination; how much deviance we can tolerate—or how much suffering. There are no "experts" to make those decisions for us.

NOTES

(1) *See, e.g.,* Cohen, *The Function of the Attorney in the Commitment of the Mentally Ill,* 44 *Texas L. Rev.* 424 (1966) [hereinafter cited as Cohen], and *The Administration of Psychiatric Justice: Theory and Practice in Arizona,* 13 *Ariz. L. Rev.* 1 (1971) (reporting the deference of judges to psychiatric opinion in civil commitment proceedings) [hereinafter cited as *Project*]; Rosenberg & McGarry, *Competency for Trial: The Making of an Expert,* 128 *Am. J. Psychiat.* 1092, 1092–95 (1972) (competency to stand trial determinations); Weihofen, *Detruding the Experts,* 1973 *Washington U. L. Quarterly* 38 (regarding sanity-insanity determinations) [hereinafter cited as *Detruding*].

(2) *See, e.g., N.Y. Mental Hygiene Law,* § 31.27 (McKinney 1973).

(3) Much of the relevant literature has been collected and analyzed in an excellent book by J. Ziskin, *Coping with Psychiatric and Psychological Testimony* [hereinafter cited as ZISKIN] (available from Law and Psychology Press, 202 South Rexford Drive, Beverly Hills, California 90212). Ziskin also concludes that

> . . . despite the ever increasing utilization of psychiatric and psychological evidence in the legal process, such evidence frequently does not meet reasonable criteria of admissibility and should not be admitted in a court of law and if admitted should be given little or no weight.

Id. at 1.

(4) Judgments by psychologists, including those based on clinical examination and those based upon psychological tests, are also of limited reliability and validity. *See* ZISKIN, *supra* note 3.

But since this article is about the civil commitment process, in which psychologists rarely participate, we are concerned primarily with an examination of the reliability and validity of judgments made by psychiatrists.

(5) *See* L. CRONBACH, *Essentials of Psychological Testing* 173–182 (3d ed. 1970) [hereinafter cited as CRONBACH].

(6) In general, the "reliability" of a judgment will depend on the sample of interviewees. In the judgment of dangerousness, for example, when the sample is of the general population, there should be considerable agreement among psychiatrists—and among laymen—because

only a small percentage of the sample would present a substantial question of dangerousness. The same should be true when the sample consists only of individuals who recently have committed violent acts and continue to express violent intentions. In the typical civil commitment proceeding, however, there is usually some evidence, but not over-whelming evidence, of dangerousness or harmlessness. An example would be an individual exhibiting delusions of persecution but having no history of violent behavior. Many individuals subject to civil commitment proceedings present such a questionable picture, especially when dangerousness-to-self is included in the concept of dangerousness. It is the reliability of predictions of "dangerousness" in these ambiguous-but-typical contexts that is in issue.

(7) *See, e.g., Carmody v. Aho* 251 Minn. 19, 86 N.W.2d 692, 695 (1957).

(8) AMERICAN PSYCHIATRIC ASSOCIATION, DSM—II: *Diagnostic and Statistical Manual of Mental Disorders* 23 (2d ed. 1968) [hereinafter cited as DSM–II]. For a general critical evaluation of DSM—II emphasizing in particular the lack of specificity and consistency in the definition of various terms contained therein, see Jackson, *The Revised Diagnostic and Statistical Manual of the American Psychiatric Association*, 127 Am. J. Psychiat. 65 (1970) [hereinafter cited as Jackson].

(9) DSM–II at 33.

(10) ZISKIN, *supra* note 3, at 123.

(11) *Id.* at 126.

(12) Ash, *The Reliability of Psychiatric Diagnosis*, 44 J. Abn. & Soc. Psych. 272 (1949) [hereinafter cited as Ash].

(13) This study utilized patients with relatively minor problems so diagnosis was more difficult than diagnosis of individuals with more serious problems would have been. *See* Zubin, *Classification of the Behavior Disorders*, 18 Ann. Rev. Psych. 373 (1967) [hereinafter cited as Zubin]. However, the psychiatrists involved jointly interviewed the patients, which should have increased the rate of agreement by reducing the variations in patient behavior and information that would occur from separate interviews. *See also* ZISKIN, *supra* note 3, ch. 4.

(14) Ash, *supra* note 12, at 275.

(15) Schmidt & Fonda, *The Reliability of Psychiatric Diagnosis: A New Look*, 52 J. Abn. & Soc. Psych. 262 (1956).

(16) V. NORRIS, *Mental Illness in London* 42–53 (Maudsley Monographs No. 6, 1959).

(17) Beck, Ward, Mendelson, Mock & Erbaugh, *Reliability of Psychiatric Diagnosis: A Study of Consistency of Clinical Judgments and Ratings*, 119 Am. J. Psychiat. 351, 352–55 (1962) [hereinafter cited as Beck, et al.].

(18) The psychiatrists were all experienced, and prior to the experiment they discussed various diagnostic categories, ironed out semantic difficulties, and reached a consensus regarding the specific criteria for each of the categories. According to the authors, considerable discussion about particular "diagnostic descriptions" contained in the official diagnostic manual was necessary to minimize differences.

(19) Beck, et. al., *supra* note 17, at 355. Though the reliability of the major diagnostic categories may appear to be fairly high, at least under "good" conditions, two caveats should be noted. First, the broader the diagnostic category, the less clearly it specifies what particular symptoms or behavior the patient manifested (much less their underlying causes). Second, such broad categorization masks great differences in the degree or severity of pathology that can exist within the categories. In short, the broader the category, the less valid or meaningful it becomes.

(20) Katz, Cole & Lowery, *Studies of the Diagnostic Process: The Influence of Symptom Perception, Past Experience, and Ethnic Background in Diagnostic Decisions*, 125 Am. J. Psychiat. 937 (1969) [hereinafter cited as Katz, Cole & Lowery]. *See also*, Copeland, Cooper, Kendall & Gourlay, *Differences in Usage of Diagnostic Labels amongst Psychiatrists in the British Isles*, 118 *British J. Psychiat.* 629 (1971) [hereinafter cited as Copeland, et al.].

It is conceivable that some of the differences in diagnoses made by psychiatrists observing such a filmed interview might be attributed to their inability to structure the interview in the way they might in their actual practice; but considering the results of other studies comparing individual interviews, and considering the additional sources of error introduced thereby, we think it likely that reliability studies based on film interviews overestimate reliability.

(21) Mehlman, *The Reliability of Psychiatric Diagnoses*, 47 J. Abn. & Soc Psych. 577 (1952).

(22) Pasamanick, Dinitz & Lefton, *Psychiatric Orientation and Its Relation to Diagnosis and Treatment in a Mental Hospital*, 116 Am. J. Psychiat. 127 (1959) [hereinafter cited as Pasamanick, et al.].

(23) Zubin, *supra* note 13.

(24) *Id*. at 383.

(25) Stoler & Geertsma, *The Consistency of Psychiatrists' Clinical Judgments*, 137 J. Nerv. Ment. Dis. 58 (1963).

(26) *Id*. at 64.

(27) *Id*. at 65 (emphasis added).

(28) Rickles, Howard, Lipman, Covi, Park & Uhlenhuth, *Differential Reliability in Rating Psychopathology and Global Improvement*, 26 J. Clin. Psychol. 320 (1970).

(29) Cherry & Cherry, *The Common Cold of Mental Ailments: Depression*, N.Y. Times, Nov. 25, 1973 (Magazine) at 38 [hereinafter cited as Cherry & Cherry].

(30) Katz, Cole & Lowery, *supra* note 20.

(31) Rosensweig, Vandenberg, Moore & Dukay, *A Study of the Reliability of the Mental Status Examination*, 117 Am. J. Psychiat. 1102, 1104–05 (1961).

(32) Even this conclusion may be too conservative. Spitzer and his collaborators have pointed out that most studies of diagnostic reliability (including those discussed herein) overrate "true" reliability by failing to correct the obtained percentage of agreement for chance agreements which may, in certain contexts, be substantial. Spitzer, Cohen, Fleiss & Endicott, *Quantification of Agreement in Psychiatric Diagnosis*, 17, Arch. Gen. Psychiat. 83, 87 (1967).

(33) Pasamanick, et al., *supra* note 22, at 127.

(34) *Id.*

(35) There are a few studies comparing the diagnostic reliability of psychologists and laymen, most of which report no significant difference. *E.g.*, Goldberg, *The Effectiveness of Clinicians' Judgments*, 23 J. Consulting Psychol. 25, 33 (1959).

(36) There are several types of validity: predictive validity, concurrent validity, content validity, and construct validity. For a general discussion of the various types, *see* CRONBACH, *supra* note 5, at 104–05.

(37) For a general discussion of the relevance of the concept of validity to psychiatric diagnoses, see Zigler & Philips, *Psychiatric Diagnosis: A Critique*, 63 J. Abn. & Soc. Psychol. 607, 612 (1961).

(38) ZISKIN, *supra* note 3, at 127–28.

(39). Nathan, Samaraveera, Andberg & Patch, *Syndromes of Psychosis and Neurosis, A Clinical Validation Study*, 19 Arch. Gen. Psychiat. 704 (1968) [hereinafter cited as Nathan, et al.].

(40) It will never be possible to assess the "validity" of psychiatric diagnoses until it is first proved that there are such things as "schizophrenia," or "manic-depressive psychosis." On the other hand, if a diagnostic label is merely a short-hand way of describing the presence of certain symptoms, then it should be possible to assess the correspondence between a diagnosis and the presence of symptoms which, by definition, are associated with that diagnosis. Thus, if "schizophrenic" persons are supposed to exhibit symptoms *X*, *Y*, and *Z*, and if a person with none of those symptoms is diagnosed as "schizophrenic," we could say that particular diagnosis is invalid. It is validity in this more limited sense with which we are concerned here. Even in this qualified sense, however, it is difficult to assess the validity of psychiatric diagnoses; first, because there is no general agreement on the irreducible minimum of symptoms

required for each diagnosis, and second, because the symptoms themselves are often so vague or subjective (poor judgment, inappropriate
affect, and so forth) that it is impossible to measure the correspondence
between such an ephemeral symptom and the diagnostic category.

(41) Goldsmith & Mandell, *The Dynamic Formulation: A Critique of
a Psychiatric Ritual*, 125 Am. J. Psychiat. 1738 (1969).

(42) Taylor, Gaztanaga, and Abrams, *Manic-Depressive Illness and
Acute Schizophrenia: A Clinical, Family History, and Treatment
Response Study*, 131 Am. J. Psychiat. 678 (1974). *See* also Taylor,
Abrams, and Gaztanaga, *Manic Depressive Illness and Schizophrenia*, 6
Comprehensive Psychiatry 91 (1975). Commenting on the prior report,
another psychiatrist has pointed out that there are significant (mis)
treatment consequences of such faulty diagnoses, and that "[t]here is an
unusual readiness to diagnose (or misdiagnose) schizophrenia in the
United States because insufficient attention is paid to the basic steps in
psychiatric history taking and examination procedures." Straker,
Editorial: *Schizophrenia and Psychiatric Diagnoses*, 131 Am J. Psychiat.
693 (1974).

(43) Rubin, *Prediction of Dangerousness In Mentally Ill Criminals*,
27 Arch. Gen. Psychiat. 397 (1972) [hereinafter cited as Rubin].

(44) Kumasaka, Stokes, & Gupta, *Criteria for Involuntary
Hospitalization*, 26 Arch. Gen. Psychiat. 399 (1972). For a general
analysis of the problems surrounding attempts to predict dangerousness
and for discussion of the concept of preventive detention, see Dershowitz,
The Law of Dangerousness: Some Fictions about Predictions, 23 J. Legal
Ed. 24 (1970); Foote, *Comments on Preventive Detention*, 23 J. Legal
Ed. 48 (1970); von Hirsch, *Prediction of Criminal Conduct and
Preventive Confinement of Convicted Persons*, 21 Buff. L. Rev. 717
(1971–72).

(45) Dershowitz, *The Psychiatrist's Power in Civil Commitment: A
Knife That Cuts Both Ways*, Psychology Today, Feb. 1969, at 47. The
author adds that:

> One reason for this overprediction is that a psychiatrist almost
> never learns about his erroneous predictions of violence—for
> predicted assailants are generally incarcerated and have little
> opportunity to prove or disprove the prediction; but he always
> learns about his erroneous predictions of nonviolence—often
> from newspaper headlines announcing the crime. This higher
> visibility of erroneous predictions of nonviolence inclines him,
> whether consciously or unconsciously, to overpredict violent
> behavior.

Id. at 47.

(46) 383 U.S. 107 (1966).

(47) Hunt & Wiley, *Operation Baxstrom After One Year*, 124 *Am. J. Psychiat.* 974 (1968). The follow up figures after one year reflect a total of less than 969 since they do not include 24 deaths, 10 transfers, 62 convalescents, and 24 miscellaneous dispositions.

(48) Steadman & Keveles, *The Community Adjustment and Criminal Activity of the Baxstrom Patients: 1966–70*, 129 *Am. J. Psychiat.* 309 (1972). The authors also provide evidence that it is difficult to predict arrests and convictions. Indeed, they suggest that reliable predictions of dangerousness cannot be made with the present state of knowledge, because there are no solid research findings regarding the factors that accurately predict dangerous behavior.

(49) Ennis, *The Rights of Mental Patients*, in *The Rights of Americans* 487 (Dorsen ed. 1970). Other studies have shown that incompetence-to-stand-trial judgments by psychiatrists often unfairly harm criminal defendants. *See* McGarry, *The Fate of Psychotic Offenders Returned For Trial*, 127 *Am. J. Psychiat.* 1181 (1971).

(50) Kozol, Boucher, & Garofalo, *The Diagnosis and Treatment of Dangerousness*, 18 *Crime & Delinquency* 371 (1972) [hereinafter cited as Kozol].

(51) Monahan, *Dangerous Offenders: A Critique of Kozol, et al.*, 19 *Crime & Delinquency* 418 (1973) (a letter from John Monahan to the Editor).

(52) Not only did Kozol's patient sample consist only of known assaultive offenders, but most of them had assaulted young victims. As the authors recognize, "the person who would assault a relatively helpless victim . . . must have an extremely strong urge to do violence." Kozol, *supra* note 50, at 378. That factor, which should increase the rate of correct prediction, is not usually present when predictions of dangerousness are made. This suggests that the high error rate of 65 percent is much lower than the rate of error that would be expected in general practice. On the other hand, the error rate of 65 percent is based on a sample of borderline cases which may not be representative of *all* the predictions of dangerousness made by these psychiatrists. A somewhat lower error rate is possible in those cases where the non-psychiatric decision-maker would agree with the psychiatrist, but of course such a lower error rate is not then attributable to any special ability of the psychiatrist.

(53) Kozol, *supra* note 50, at 384 (emphasis added). The authors note that only 8 percent of the offenders recommended for discharge (as being nondangerous) were recidivists. This suggested to them that mental health professionals may be able to predict nondangerous behavior.

However, the fact that predictions of nondangerousness were wrong only 8 percent of the time may simply be a function of the low base rate of violent behavior. That is, if 90–99 percent of any given population will not engage in violent behavior, predictions of individual nonviolence within that population will necessarily be generally accurate. *See* Monahan, *supra* note 51; Kozol, Boucher, & Garofalo, *Dangerousness*, 19 *Crime & Delinquency* 554 (1973) (a letter to the editor).

(54) Rubin, *supra* note 43, at 397–98 *citing* Kozol, Boucher, & Garofalo, The Diagnosis of Dangerousness, (a paper read to the annual meeting of the American Psychiatric Association, San Francisco, May 13, 1970).

(55) Rubin, supra note 43, at 397–98. Cocozza & Steadman, *Some Refinements in the Measurement and Prediction of Dangerous Behavior*, 131 *Am. J. Psychiat.* 1012 (1974).

(56) Usdin, *Broader Aspects of Dangerousness* in *The Clinical Evaluation of the Dangerousness of the Mentally Ill* 43 (J. Rappeport ed. 1967).

Regarding the ability of psychological tests to measure "dangerousness", *see* Megaree, *The Prediction of Violence with Psychological Tests*, in 2 *Current Topics in Clinical and Community Psychology* 97 (C. Spielberger ed. 1970) which concludes:

> Thus far no structured or projective test scale has been derived which, when used alone, will predict violence in the individual case in a satisfactory manner. Indeed, none has been developed which will adequately *post*dict, let alone *pre*dict, violent behavior.

Id. at 145.

(57) Wenk, Robison & Sineth, *Can Violence be Predicted?* 18 *Crime & Delinquency* 393 (1972).

(58) *Id.* at 394. The authors report two additional studies. In the first, a violence prediction scale was constructed from a number of seemingly relevant items, and was administered to a large number of parolees. Yet, only 14 percent of the exoffenders predicted by the instrument to be dangerous violated parole by committing a (known) violent, or potentially violent act—as compared to a 5 percent rate of violent acts for the parolees predicted to be nondangerous. In the second study, despite the use of "elaborate case histories, current measures of mental and emotional functioning, and professional diagnosis," it was found to be impossible to develop a classification scheme for identifying which of over 4,000 California Youth Authority wards on parole would commit a violent, recidivistic offense. Indeed, no single predictive criterion or 'item" was

found to produce accurate predictions in more than one out of every 20 cases.

(59) *Id.* at 402.

(60) Monahan, *The Prediction and Prevention of Violence,* in *Proceedings of The Pacific Northwest Conference on Violence and Criminal Justice* (Issaquah, Washington, Dec. 6–8, 1973) (to be published) [hereinafter cited as Monahan].

(61) *See* Gulevich & Bourne, *Mental Illness and Violence,* in *Violence and the Struggle for Existence* 309 (D. Daniels, M. Gilula, & F. Ochberg eds. 1970); and the authorities cited *infra* at note 137.

(62) The Pennsylvania Task Force on Commitment Procedures concluded that "since the capacity to predict dangerous conduct is no greater in the case of mentally ill persons than others, preventive detention is no more justified in the case of mental illness than elsewhere." *Commonwealth of Pennsylvania, Task Force in Commitment Procedures, Dept. of Public Welfare* (1972), *cited in* J. Monahan, Dangerousness and Civil Commitment 4 (Invited Testimony Before the California Assembly Select Committee on Mentally Disordered Criminal Offenders. Patton, California, Dec. 13, 1973).

(63) Murphy, *Clinical Identification of Suicidal Risk,* 27 *Arch. Gen. Psychiat.* 356, 357 (1972).

(64) Greenberg, *Involuntary Psychiatric Commitments to Prevent Suicide:* 49 *New York University Law Review* 227, 263 (1974).

(65) Rappeport, Lassen & Gruenwald, *Evaluations and Follow-up of State Hospital Patients Who Had Sanity Hearings,* 118 *Am. J. Psychiat.* 1079 (1962).

(66) *Id.* at 1083. *See also,* Zwerling & Wilder, *An Evaluation of the Applicability of the Day Hospital in Treatment of Acutely Disturbed Patients,* 2 *Israel Annals of Psychiat.* 162 (1964). *Cf.* Livermore, Malmquist, & Meehl, *On the Justifications for Civil Commitment,* 117 *U. Pa. L. Rev.* 75, 85, n.29 (1968) (regarding release or elopement against medical advice) [hereinafter cited as Livermore, et al.].

(67) See text accompanying notes 77–139.

(68) *See, e.g.,* Langsley, Pittman, Machotka & Flomenhaft, *Family Crisis Therapy Results and Implications,* 7 *Family Process* 145 (1968). A very recent study questions the assumptions underlying commitment of mentally ill persons to mental hospitals. Reding & Maguire, *Non-segregated Acute Psychiatric Admissions to General Hospitals— Continuity of Care Within the Community Hospital,* 289 *N. Eng. J. Med.* 185 (1973). Over a four-year period a total of 344 patients were admitted as psychiatric emergencies to the nonpsychiatric units of the three general hospitals of a New York County. Forty percent of the patients were diagnosed as schizophrenic or paranoid, 25 percent as depressed or suicidal, and 8 percent as personality disorders involving violent behavior

at home. Physical restraints and electroconvulsive therapy were not used. The median length of hospitalization ranged from 6.5 days for one group of patients to 8.5 days for another, compared with a median stay in psychiatric units of general hospitals in New York of 15–24 days, and in New York State Mental Hospitals of 51 days. Of the 344 admissions there was not one suicidal or homicidal attempt in over 4,000 days of acute psychiatric hospitalization. *Id.* at 187. The researchers found that "[t]he atmosphere of the nonpsychiatric general-hospital unit seemed to have a soothing or tranquilizing effect on patients with acute psychiatric illness." *Id.* The researchers concluded that "this effect is partly accounted for by a constant negative reinforcement of antisocial behavior, in contrast to what prevails in psychiatric wards, where patients are expected to exhibit disturbed behavior and where agitated behavior in one patient leads to agitation in another." *Id.* The researchers also concluded that admission of such patients to general hospitals rather than to mental hospitals "seems to shorten the length of hospitalization" and "seem[s] to offer a satisfactory and less costly alternative to the traditional forms of psychiatric hospitalization." *Id.* at 188. This study suggests that predictions that allegedly mentally ill people require commitment to a mental hospital are often erroneous.

(69) Robbins & Guze, *Establishment of Diagnostic Validity In Psychiatric Illness: Its Application to Schizophrenia*, 126 *Am. J. Psychiat.* 983 (1970).

(70) A psychiatric prognosis can be a self-fulfilling prophecy because only those patients with a good prognosis are likely to receive the aid of scarce psychotherapeutic resources.

(71) Wittman, *A Scale for Measuring Prognosis in Schizophrenic Patients*, 4 *Elgin Papers* 20–33 (1941), *cited in* ZISKIN, *supra* note 5, at 132–33; Wittman & Steinberg, *Follow-up of an Objective Evaluation of Progress In Dementia Praecox and Manic-Depressive Psychosis*, 5 *Elgin Papers* 216–27 (1944); *cited and discussed in* ZISKIN, *supra* note 3, at 132–33.

(72) Thorne, *Clinical Judgment*, in *Clinical Assessment in Counseling and Psychotherapy* 30–31 (Woody & Woody, eds., 1972). *See also* Ziskin, *supra* note 3, for a collection of a substantial body of psychiatric and psychological opinions — not studies — that psychiatric judgments, including diagnoses, are of low validity.

(73) Rosenhan, *On Being Sane in Insane Places*, 179 *Science* 250 (1973) [hereinafter cited as Rosenhan].

(74) DSM–II, *supra* note 8, at 33. Technically, of course, the diagnoses of schizophrenia were *wholly* invalid, since the confederates were not, in fact, delusional or hallucinating.

(74a) *See* Zubin, *supra* note 13. *See* also Thorne and Nathan, *The General Validity of Official Diagnostic Classifications*, 25 J. Clin. Psychol. 375 (1969).

(75) Zigler & Phillips, *Psychiatric Diagnosis and Symptomatology*, 63 J. Abnorm. & Soc. Psychol. 69 (1971).

(76) Frank, *Psychiatric Diagnosis: A Review of Research*, 81 J. Gen. Psychol. 157, 164 (1969).

(77) Goldberg, Simple Models or Simple Processes: Some Research on Clinical Judgments, 23 Am Psychol. 483, 484 (1968).

(78) *See* Chapman & Chapman, *Genesis of Popular but Erroneous Psychodiagnostic Observations*, 72 J. Abnorm. Psychol. 193 (1967).

(79) Schmideberg, *The Promise of Psychiatry: Hopes and Disillusionment*, 57 Nw. U.L. Rev. 19, 21 (1962) [hereinafter cited as Schmideberg].

(80) *Id.*

(81) Halleck, *A Critique of Current Psychiatric Roles In The Legal Process*, 1966 Wisc. L. Rev. 379, 393. *See also*, Baur, *Legal Responsibility and Mental Illness*, 57 Nw. U.L. Rev. 12, 14–17 (1962); Diamond & Louisell, *The Psychiatrist as an Expert Witness: Some Ruminations and Speculations*, 63 Mich. L. Rev. 1335, 1341 (1965) [hereinafter cited as Diamond & Louisell]; Sadoff, *Psychiatry Pleads Guilty*, 51 A.B.A.J. 48, 49 (1965); Schmideberg, *supra* note 79.

(82) E,g., Leifer, *The Competence of the Psychiatrist in the Determination of Incompetency: A Skeptical Inquiry into the Courtroom Functions of Psychiatrists*, 14 Syracuse L. Rev. 564, 573 (1963); Livermore, et. al., *supra* note 66, at 77; Shah, *Crime and Mental Illness: Some Problems in Defining and Labeling Deviant Behavior*, 57 Mental Hygiene 21 (1969); Temerlin, *Suggestion Effects in Psychiatric Diagnosis*, 147 J. Nerv. Ment. Dis. 349 (1968).

(83) Temerlin, *Diagnostic Bias in Community Mental Health*, 6 Community Mental Health J. 110, 115 (1970) [hereinafter cited as Temerlin].

(84) Pasamanick, et al., *supra* note 22, at 131. *See also* Grosz & Grossman, *The Sources of Observer Variation and Bias in Clinical Judgments: I. The Item of Psychiatric History*, 138 J. Nerv. Ment. Dis. 105, 111 (1964); Nathan, *Thirty-two Observers and One Patient: A Study of Diagnostic Reliability*, 25 J. Clin. Psychol. 9 (1969). For evidence that ideas about the same diagnostic category may vary significantly with the diagnostician's professional identity, theoretical orientation, and employment setting, see Fitzgibbons & Shearn, *Concepts of Schizophrenia Among Mental Health Professionals*, 38 J. Consult. & Clin. Psychol. 288 (1972).

(85) *See, e.g.*, Babigian, Gardner, Miles & Romano, *Diagnostic Consistency and Change in a Follow-up Study of 1215 Patients*, 121 Am. J. Psychiat. 895 (1965).

(86) Temerlin, *supra* note 83.

(87) The interesting differences among the groups in the percentage of psychotic diagnoses are doubtless due to a number of different factors. One such factor might be the perception of the prestige figure; the law students, for example, may have felt the criminal law professor assigned as their prestige figure was speaking outside his area of expertise when he suggested the subject was psychotic.

The important finding for our purposes is that while some members of every group, especially the psychiatrists, made diagnoses of psychosis, none of the comparable control groups did so.

(88) Temerlin, *supra* note 83, at 116.

(89) Rosenhan, *supra* note 73, at 253.

(90) *Id.*

(91) *Id.* at 251.

(92) *Id.* at 253.

(93) Huguenard, Sager & Ferguson, *Interview Time, Interview Set, and Interview Outcome*, 31 *Percept. & Mot. Skills*, 831, 834 (1970).

(94) *Id.* at 834–36. *See also* Asch, *Forming Impressions of Personality*, 41 *J. Abnorm. & Soc. Psychol.* 258 (1946).

(95) Zubin, *supra* note 13, at 386.

(96) Edelman, *Intra-therapist Diagnostic Reliability*, 25 *J. Clin. Psychol.* 394 (1969).

(97) *Id.* at 395.

(98) *See* Ward, Beck, Mendelson, Mock & Erbaugh, *The Psychiatric Nomenclature: Reasons for Disagreement*, 7 *Arch. Gen. Psychiat.* 198 (1962) [hereinafter cited as Ward, et al.].

(99) Phillips & Draguns, *Classification of the Behavior Disorders*, 22 *Ann. Rev. Psychol.* 447, 467 (1971).

(100) Lee & Temerlin, *Social Class, Diagnosis, and Prognosis for Psychotherapy.* 7 *Psychotherapy: Theory, Research & Prac.* 181 (1970). *See also* Garfield, Weiss & Pollack, *Effects of the Child's Social Class on School Counselor's Decision Making*, 20 *J. Counsel. Psychol.* 166 (1973); Harrison, McDermott, Wilson & Schrager, *Social Class and Mental Illness in Children: Chance of Treatment*, 13 *Arch. Gen. Psychiat.* 411 (1965); Harrison, McDermott & Showerman, *Social Status and Child Psychiatric Practice: The Influence of the Clinician's Socio-Economic Origin*, 127 *Am. J. Psychiat.* 652 (1970); Routh & King, *Social Class Bias in Clinical Judgment*, 38 *J. Consult. & Clin. Psychol.* 202 (1972); Stein, Greene & Stone, *Therapists' Attitude as Influenced by A-B Therapist Type, Patient Diagnosis, and Social Class*, 39 *J. Consult. & Clin. Psychol.*

301 (1972). For the effect of race and sex see Allon, *Sex, Race, Socio-Economic Status, Social Mobility, and Process-Reactive Ratings of Schizophrenics,* 153 *J. Nerv. Ment. Dis.* 343 (1971); Gross, Herbert, Knatterud & Donner, *The Effect of Race and Sex on the Variation of Diagnosis and Disposition in a Psychiatric Emergency Room,* 148 *J. Nerv. Ment. Dis.* 638 (1969). Similar findings have been obtained in the studies of the influence of clinician bias on psychological test interpretation. *See, e.g.,* Haase, *The Role of Socio-economic Class in Examiner Bias,* in *Mental Health of the Poor* 241–47 (F. Riessman, J. Cohen, and A. Pearl, eds. 1964); Levy & Kahn, *Interpreter Bias on the Rorschach Test as a Function of Patient's Socio-economic Status,* 34 *J. Proj. Techs. Pers. Assessment* 106 (1970); Trachtman, *Socio-economic Class Bias in Rorschach Diagnosis: Contributing Psychological Attributes of the Clinician,* 35 *J. Pers. Assessment* 229 (1971).

(101) Ordway, *Experiences in Evaluating Dangerousness in Private Practice and in a Court Clinic,* in *The Clinical Evaluation of the Dangerousness of the Mentally Ill* 35 (J. Rappeport, ed. 1967).

(102) Broverman, Broverman, Clarkson, Rosenkrantz & Vogel, *Sex-role Stereotypes and Clinical Judgments of Mental Health,* 34 *J. Consult. and Clinical Psychol.* 1 (1970).

(103) *Id.,* at 5.

(104) *See* also Nowacki & Poe, *The Concept of Mental Health as Related to Sex of Person Perceived,* 40 *J. Consult. and Clinical Psychol.* 160 (1973); Chessler, *Women and Madness* (1972).

(106) Sandifer, Hordern, Timbury & Green, *Similarities and Differences in Patient Evaluation by U.S. and U.K. Psychiatrists,* 126 *Am. J. Psychiat.* 206 (1969) [hereinafter cited as Sandifer].

(107) Copeland, et al., *supra* note 20. The formal definition of "schizophrenia" is no different in Britain than in the United States, but American psychiatrists are apparently willing to attach the label to a much greater range and variety of individuals than are British psychiatrists. See Kendell, Cooper, Gourlay, Copeland, Sharpe & Garland, *The Diagnostic Criteria of American and British Psychiatrists,* 25 *Arch. Gen. Psychiat.* 123 (1971).

(108) Copeland, et al., *supra* note 20, at 635.

(109) Katz, Cole & Lowery, *supra* note 20.

(110) *See* Raines & Rohrer, *supra* note 12.

(111) *Id.* at 732–33.

(112) Raines & Rohrer, *The Operational Matrix of Psychiatric Practice II: Variability in Psychiatric Impression and the Projection Hypothesis,* 117 *Am. J. Psychiat.* 133 (1960). *See also* Rosenzweig, Vandenberg, Moore, & Duhay, *A Study of the Reliability of the Mental Status Examination,* 117 *Am. J. Psychiat.* 1102 (1961) (different in-

terviewers elicit significantly different aspects of a patient's personality).

(113) Sullivan, *Influence of Personal Values on Psychiatric Judgment: A Military Example*, 152 J. Nerv. Ment. Dis. 193 (1971).

(114) Grosz & Grossman, *The Sources of Observer Variation and Bias in Clinical Judgments: 1. The Item of Psychiatric History*, 138 J. Nerv. Ment. Dis. 105, 111 (1964).

(115) *Id.*

(116) Dickes, Simons & Weisfogel, *Difficulties in Diagnosis Introduced by Unconscious Factors Present in the Interviewer*, 44 Psychiat. Quar. 55 (1970).

(117) Pugh, *The Insanity Defense in Operation: A Practicing Psychiatrist Views* Durham *and* Browner, 1973 Wash. U.L.Q. 87.

(118) Strupp, *The Psychotherapist's Contribution to the Treatment Process*, 3 Behav. Sci. 34 (1958). *See also* Wallach & Strupp, *Psychotherapist's Clinical Judgments and Attitude Toward Patients*, 24 J. Clin. & Consult. Psychol. 316 (1960), (showing that high motivation for treatment, independent of the degree of "pathology," predisposes clinicians to like patients better and, in turn, to attribute a more favorable prognosis to them. Individuals who disagree with their psychiatrist's perception of their needs—including the need for hospitalization—will be considered more disturbed than if they agree with the psychiatrist's judgment).

(119) Braginsky & Braginsky, *Psychologists: High Priests of the Middle Class*, Psychol. Today, Dec. 1973, at 15, 139. Thus, patients who voice dissatisfaction with hospitalization and the treatment they are receiving are likely to be perceived as sicker than originally thought, and more in need of hospitalization—a classic Catch-22 situation. See also note 118, *supra*.

(120) *See, e.g.*, Mehlman, *The Reliability of Psychiatric Diagnosis*, 47 J. Abnorm. & Soc. Psychol. 577 (1952); Pasamanick, et al., *supra* note 22.

(121) There is evidence that psychiatrists have a lower "tolerance" for abnormal behavior than other professionals (lawyers, in particular). Brown, *Lawyers and Psychiatrists in the Court: Afterword*, 32 Md. L. Rev. 36, 39 (1972). It is likely that many psychiatrists would characterize certain behavior as dangerous which laymen, including judges and juries, would not.

(122) An attitudinal survey of California psychiatrists suggests that since most of them are confident that their clinical judgments provide an adequate basis for civil commitment, they are impatient with legal, civil libertarian limitations on the implementation of such judgments. *See ENKI Research Institute, A Study of California's New Mental Health Law* 210–11, (ENKI Corp., California 1972).

(123) Familial and administrative pressures often and significantly may influence both psychiatric decisions regarding the need for hospitalization and the supposedly independent evaluation of emotional impairment. For empirical evidence of this see Greenley, *Alternative Views of the Psychiatrist's Role*, 20 *Social Problems* 252 (1972). His data also suggest that psychiatrists often claim to base their ultimate decision solely on the patient's condition when, in fact, it is the product of outside pressures as well. *See also* Wilde, *Decision Making in a Psychiatric Screening Agency*, 9 *J. Health & Soc. Behavior* 215 (1968). *But cf.* Gove, *Who is Hospitalized: A Critical Review of Some Sociological Studies of Mental Illness*, 11 *J. Health & Soc. Behavior* 294 (1970).

(124) *See*, e.g., *Law's Labor Lost*, 40 *Psychiat. Quar.* 150, 156 (1966) (Editorial comment).

(125) See note 119 *supra*, and accompanying text.

(126) Beck, et al., *supra* note 17.

(127) Ward, et al., *supra* note 98. A third source of error, which was relatively unimportant in the Beck study where the interviews were held only minutes apart, was the inconsistency of patient behavior between different interviews. Under more typical conditions, other sources of unreliability would also play a role: inexperienced or incompetent diagnosticians, language and cultural differences between clinicians and patients, the effect of different clinical settings, differences in diagnostic preferences, differences in the time available for evaluation, psychiatric biases, and so forth. *Cf.* Smith, *A Model for Psychiatric Diagnosis*, 14 *Arch. Gen. Psychiat.* 521 (1966).

(128) Strauss, *Hallucinations and Delusions as Points on Continua Function*, 21 *Arch. Gen. Psychiat.* 581 (1969) [hereinafter cited as Strauss].

(129) *Id.* at 586. *See also* Freedman, *Various Etiologies of the Schizophrenic Syndrome*, 19 *Dis. Nerv. Syst.* 1 (1958); Opler, *Schizophrenia and Culture*, 197 *Sci. Amer.* 103 (1957); Strauss, *Diagnostic Models and the Nature of Psychiatric Disorder*, 29 *Arch. Gen. Psychiat.* 445 (1973).

Based on his data, Strauss suggests three reasons why reported experiences may often be difficult to classify as delusional or nondelusional, hallucinatory or nonhallucinatory (that is, psychotic or nonpsychotic). First, it is often difficult to discern just how much a patient (who, for example, feels guilty for causing someone's death, or feels that he or she is a burden to others) is, or is not, distorting reality. Second, an evaluation of the patient's psychopathology may be colored by an awareness—or lack thereof—of certain factors in a patient's history or environment. For example, the psychiatric and diagnostic implications of a belief that "the devil is trying to influence me" may be difficult to evaluate if the patient has had fundamentalist religious training, and it may likewise be difficult to evaluate, or to characterize as psychotic or nonpsychotic "experiences such as that of a woman who heard the neighbors talking about her through the walls of her cheaply built apartment." Strauss, *supra* note 128, at 583. Third, it may not be clear just how rigidly or strongly the patient adheres to his or her belief in the distorted ideas or perceptions he or she may be experiencing, however fleetingly. Strauss concludes as follows:

> It might be both more accurate and more useful to conceptualize hallucinations and delusions as points on continua of function and to conceptualize schizophrenia similarly as representing a point or points on continua of function. The suggested parameters of these continua of function are: the degree of a patient's conviction of the objective reality of a bizarre experience, the degree of direct cultural or stimulus determinants of an experience; the amount of time spent preoccupied with the experience; and the degree of implausibility of an experience.

Strauss, *supra* note 128, at 586.

(130) DSM–II, *supra* note 8, at 23.

(131) *Id.*

(132) To complicate the issue further, psychistrists often diagnose individuals as psychotic whether or not they are able to care for themselves in the community. In practice, a person may appear to exhibit one of the five classical symptoms of psychosis—hallucinations, delusions, lack of reality testing, disordered thought processes, or severely withdrawn behavior—and therefore will be diagnosed as psychotic, even though the symptoms are not so extensive or debilitating as to require involuntary care and treatment. *See* Nathan, et al., *supra* note 39, at 711–14. See also note 153 *infra*, and accompanying text.

(133) Rappeport, Lassen & Hay, *A Review of the Literature on the Dangerousness of the Mentally Ill*, in *The Clinical Evaluation of the Dangerousness of the Mentally Ill*, 72, 79 (J. Rappeport ed. 1967).

(134) Rubin, *supra* note 43, at 399.

(135) Guttmacher, *A Review of Cases Seen by a Court Psychiatrist*, in *The Clinical Evaluation of the Dangerousness of the Mentally Ill*, 17 (J. Rappeport ed. 1967).

(136) *Id.* at 27.

(137) See notes 61 and 62 *supra*. Additional empirical studies supporting this proposition are described in Ennis, *Civil Liberties and Mental Illness*, 7 Crim. Law Bull. 101 (1971).

(138) Guttmacher, *supra* note 135, at 27.

(139) Monahan has suggested that research, resources, and energy should be shifted from the so-far futile attempt to identify violence-prone persons to the identification and modification of situations conducive to violence.

> . . . Such a change in tack might lead to appreciable gains in preventive efficiency (it could hardly do worse than current efforts at person identification), and would obviate the seemingly insurmountable problem of unjustly intervening in the lives of innumerable false positives.
>
> Ultimately, it may be possible to classify both persons and environments in a typology of violence. One might then predict with some validity that a person of a given type will commit a violent act if he remains in one type of environment, yet will remain non-violent if placed in another situational context.

Monahan, *supra* note 60, at 18 (paging of prepublication draft).

(140) An exception to this statement is the diagnosis of organic psychosis, which is apparently reliable about 80–90 percent of the time.

(141) *See generally,* Ziskin, *supra* note 3, at 5–6; Collier, *Again, the Truth Machines,* N.Y. *Times,* Nov. 25, 1973, (Magazine) at 35 [hereinafter cited as Collier]; Inbau & Reid, *The Lie-Detector Technique: A Reliable and Valuable Investigative Aid,* 50 A.B.A.J. 470 (1964); Shattuck, Brown & Carlson, *The Lie Detector as a Surveillance Device,* ACLU Reports (Feb. 1973); Note, *Problems Remaining For the 'Generally Accepted' Polygraph,* 53 Boston U.L. Rev. 375 (1973); Note, *Hypnosis, Truth Drugs, and the Polygraph: An Analysis of their Use and Acceptance by the Courts,* 21 U. Fla. L. Rev. 541 (1969); and Annot., *Physiological or Psychological Truth and Deception Tests,* 23 A.L.R.2d 1306 (1952).

(142) One study by polygraph enthusiasts claims that 94 percent of all subjects can be tested accurately, with less than 1 percent error. *E.g.*, J. Reid & Inbau, *Truth and Deception: The Polygraph ("Lie Detector") Technique* 234 (1966). Another study claims to have achieved definite results 95.6 percent of the time with only three known errors out of 4,093 reports. F. Inbau, *Lie Detection and Criminal Interrogation* (1968). Two experimental studies using students reported that a polygraph examiner could correctly identify 100 percent of all "innocent" students, and 88 to 94 percent of all "guilty" students. Davidson, *Validity of the Guilty Knowledge Technique: The Effects of Motivation,* 52 J. Appl. Psychol. 62 (1968); Lykken, *The GSR in the Detection of Guilt,* 43 J. Appl. Psychol. 385 (1959). One of the more carefully controlled studies concluded that polygraph operators accurately can determine truth or deception in 87.75 percent of all cases. Hovarth & Reid. *The Reliability of Polygraph Examiner Diagnosis of Truth and Deception,* 62 J. Crim. Law

Crimin. & P. S. 276 (1971) [hereinafter cited as Hovarth & Reid].

(143) Those cases are discussed in Comment, *Pinocchio's New Nose*, 48 *N.Y.U.L. Rev.* 339 (1973) [hereinafter cited as *Pinocchio*]; Note, *The Emergence of the Polygraph at Trial*, 73 *Colum. L. Rev.* 1120 (1973).

(144) *See* the cases and authorities cited in *Pinocchio*, *supra* note 143, at 341 n.16.

(145) 91 Ariz. 274, 371 P.2d 894 (1962).

(146)*Id.* at 282, 371 P.2d at 900.

(147) Psychologists have often not been permitted to testify as experts absent "a showing of at least a semblance of scientific acceptance of the psychologist's ability to formulate a dependable conclusion under all of the circumstances of the case." *People v. Spigno*, 156 Cal. App. 2d 279, 288, 319 P.2d 458, 463 (1957). At least it is required that "he can substantiate [his findings] by evidence that would be acceptable to recognized specialists in the same field." *State v. Padilla*, 66 N.M. 289, 298, 347 P.2d 312, 318 (1959). *See also Jenkins v. United States*, 307 F.2d 637 (D.C. Cir. 1962).

These standards are hardly rigorous but they are more rigorous than the standards applied to psychiatrists, who need only show that they are psychiatrists. Yet psychologists may well be more accurate in their judgments than psychiatrists. At the least their test results are subject to direct inspection by other experts. *See generally* Lassen, *The Psychologist as an Expert Witness in Assessing Mental Disease or Defect*, 50 A.B.A.J. 239 (1964); Levine, *The Psychologist as Expert Witness in "Psychiatric" Questions*, 20 *Clev. St. L. Rev.* 379 (1971); Comment, *The Psychologist as an Expert Witness*, 15 *Kans. L. Rev.* 88 (1966).

We do not suggest that judgments made by psychologists are sufficiently reliable and valid to qualify psychologists as "experts" in civil commitment cases. They probably are not. See ZISKIN, supra note 3. We do suggest, however, that if psychiatrists were required to make the same minimal showing of expertise that often is required of psychologists before offering certain conclusions—for instance, that a prospective patient is dangerous—such conclusions would not be admissible. There is, for example, not even a semblance of scientific evidence to substantiate any psychiatrist's claim that he or she accurately can predict violent behavior, especially in the absence of a recent overt act of violence.

(148) Objective, rather than subjective, validation is the central premise of the scientific method. One example of the law's insistence on objective rather than subjective validation is the recent flood of court decisions requiring employers to prove, through objective studies, that the tests used to discriminate among job applicants actually measure the applicants' qualifications for the job. *E.g., Griggs v. Duke Power Co.*, 401 U.S. 424 (1971); *Chance v. Bd. of Examiners*, 458 F.2d 1167 (2d Cir.

1972); *Vulcan Society v. Civil Service Comm.*, 360 F. Supp. 1265
S.D.N.Y. 1973). Those decisions, in turn, rely upon the Equal Employment Opportunity Commission's Guidelines on Employee Selection
Procedures, 29 C.F.R. § 1607 *et seq.*, which require "empirical
evidence," based on "studies," that a test is valid. *Id.* at § 1607.5(a).

(149) *See* texts accompanying notes 39–40 and 128–129 *supra.*

(150) *See, e.g., Washington v. United States*, 390 F.2d 444, 454
(D.C. Cir. 1967):

> . . . it does not help a jury of laymen to be told of a diagnosis
> limited to the esoteric and swiftly changing vocabulary of
> psychiatry. Every technical description ought to be "translated"
> in terms of "what I mean by this," followed by a down-to-earth
> concrete explanation in terms which convey meaning to laymen.
> A psychiatrist who gives a jury a diagnosis, for example, of
> "psychoneurotic reaction, obsessive compulsive type" and fails to
> explain fully what this means, would contribute more to society if
> he were permitted to stay at his hospital post taking care of
> patients.

We suggest that no diagnosis should be admissible. If the psychiatrist is
required to detail the evidence supporting the diagnosis, no legitimate
purpose is served by admitting the diagnosis. The policy reasons which led
that court to restrict psychiatric testimony in the context of an insanity
defense are even more compelling in the context of a civil commitment
proceeding. In the insanity trial, there will always be psychiatrists
testifying on both sides of the issue, thus making it clear to the jury that
psychiatry is not an exact science. In the typical civil commitment
proceeding, however, one or more psychiatrists will testify in favor of
commitment, and no psychiatrists will testify in opposition. The insanity
trial is usually sufficiently long to enable a conscientious lawyer to cross-
examine an opposing psychiatrist at length on the reliability and validity
of his judgments. That can be an educational process for a jury. The civil
commitment hearing, on the other hand, usually lasts only a few minutes
providing no realistic opportunity for the patient's lawyer to probe the
biases and fallibility of the opposing psychiatrist. The insanity defense is
almost always tried before a jury. Civil commitment hearings are almost
always before a judge. And there is some reason to believe that juries are
more distrustful of psychiatric testimony than are judges. Psychiatric
testimony in a civil commitment proceeding is likely to be more
speculative and less accurate than psychiatric testimony in an insanity
defense trial because in the latter the psychiatrist is simply asked to tell us
whether in the past a specific dangerous act, committed in known circumstances, was or was not the product of mental disease or defect. In a
civil commitment proceeding the psychiatrist is called upon to predict

whether in the future, in unknown circumstances, the patient will or will not commit some unspecified dangerous act, and to predict, in addition, whether that act will be the product of self-defense, mental disease or defect, justified anger, accident, a simple criminal act caused by economic need, a desire for revenge, and so on. Moreover, it is difficult to understand why a psychiatrist is often not permitted to testify as a defense witness in a criminal trial that the defendant did not have certain propensities, but is permitted to testify in a civil commitment proceeding that the prospective patient does have those propensities. *See State v. Sinott*, 24 N.J. 408, 132 A.2d 298 (1957); 43 N.J. Super. 1, 127 A.2d 424, 429 (1956) (opinion of the court below in the same case). *See also United States v. Brawner*, 471 F.2d 969, 1006 (D.C. Cir. 1972); *State v. Bromley*, 72 Wash. 2d 150, 432 P.2d 568, (1967). *But cf. People v. Jones*, 42 Cal. 2d 219, 266 P.2d 38 (1954). *See also* Weihofen, *Detruding, supra* note 1 (the author concludes that: "The main reason for the abandonment [in *Brawner*] of the rule in *Durham v. United States* [214 F.2d 862 (D.C. Cir. 1954)] was to escape the undue dominance by the experts in determing a defendant's mental responsibility.") *Washington* and *Brawner*, in short, recognize the importance of requiring psychiatric witnesses to state the bases of their conclusions if the rightful role of the trier of fact is to be preserved.

There is a substantial body of psychiatric opinion fully in agreement with the view expressed here that psychiatric diagnoses are essentially meaningless, yet potentially prejudicial to the rights of prospective patients. *See, e.g.*, Baur, *Legal Responsibility and Mental Illness*, 57 *Nw. U.L. Rev.* 12 (1962); Diamond & Louisell, *The Psychiatrist as an Expert Witness: Some Ruminations and Speculations*, 63 *Mich. L. Rev.* 1335 (1965); Halleck, *A Critique of Current Psychiatric Roles in the Legal Process*, 1966 *Wis. L. Rev.* 379 (1966); Sadoff, *Psychiatry Pleads Guilty*, 51 *A.B.A.J.* 48 (1965).

(151) DSM—II, *supra* note 8.

(152) Jackson, *supra* note 8, at 69.

(153) A. Srole, T. Langner, S. Michael, M. Opler & T. Rennie, *Mental Illness in the Metropolis—The Midtown Manhattan Study* 138 (1962). The term "mental illness," which appears in most commitment statutes, is not a psychiatric term and is not even used in DSM—II. Most psychiatrists would not suggest that a person who could be diagnosed as "mentally disordered" under DSM—II should be considered "mentally ill" within the meaning of the commitment statutes. However, the vagueness of the term "mental illness" would permit a psychiatrist to term anyone diagnosible under DSM—II as "mentally ill." And, even within the confines of DMS—II, a psychiatrist could say that if an individual is diagnosible under DSM—II, his mental functioning is "disturbed."

DSM—II, *supra* note 8, at 39. According to Srole's data over 80 percent of the population of mid-Manhattan probably could be described as "mentally disturbed" within the meaning of DSM—II. Persons who are impotent or who have tension headaches may be diagnosed as mentally disordered under DSM—II if "emotional factors play a causative role," as could persons whose behavior is characterized by "pouting, procrastination, intentional inefficiency, or stubborness," or by "excessive concern with conformity and adherence to standards of conscience." DSM—II, *supra* note 8, at 43–44, 47. Accordingly, even though most people in the United States could be described as mentally disturbed within the meaning of DSM—II, that term, when applied to a prospective patient in a commitment hearing, is likely to convey a more sinister impression to a judge or jury.

(154) Cherry & Cherry, *supra* note 29, at 38.

(155) For a radical critique of the entire diagnostic process, viewing the "diagnostic act" itself as a means of social control, see Miller, *The Latent Social Functions of Psychiatric Diagnoses*, 14 J. *Offender Therapy* 148 (1970). *See also* Kaplan, *Civil Commitment "As You Like It,"* A Critique of the Psychiatric Approach to Crime and Correction, 23 *Law & Contemp. Prob.* 650 (1958); Schmideberg, *Socio-legal Consequences of the Diagnostic Act*, 14 J. *Offender Therapy* 157 (1970).

An eminent federal judge, with extensive experience in forensic psychiatry, has concluded that psychiatric judgments are not very reliable, and offer little assistance to judge or jury. Bazelon, *Psychiatrists and the Adversary Process*, 230 *Scientific American* 18 (1974). Moreover, Judge Bazelon frequently "had occasion to find psychiatrists making decisions for motives and under pressures from outside their professional role." *Id.* at 22.

(156) *E.g., United States v. Pickett*, 470 F.2d 1255 (D.C. Cir. 1972); *State v. Corley*, 108 Ariz. 240, 495 P.2d 470 (1972); Wigmore, *Evidence* §§ 1933, 1938 (3d ed. 1940); C.J.S. *Evidence*, § 548 (1964). Laymen, for example, may testify that an individual seemed "off his rocker" or "crazy" or "out of touch with reality."

(157) *E.g.,* Wigmore, *supra* note 156, at § 1934.

(158) We recognize that in some instances it is difficult to distinguish between opinions and descriptive statements—*e.g.,* the patient is "depressed," "withdrawn," or "apathetic." But most diagnoses, and all predictions, do not suffer from this difficulty and should never be received in evidence.

(159) The due process and equal protection clauses have been held applicable to civil commitment proceedings. *E.g., McNeil v. Director, Patuxent Institution*, 407 U.S. 245 (1972); *Specht v. Patterson*, 386 U.S. 605 (1967); *Baxstrom v. Herold*, 383 U.S. 107 (1966). *See also Jackson v.*

Indiana, 406 U.S. 715 (1972); *Humphrey v. Cady,* 405 U.S. 504 (1972); *O'Connor v. Donaldson,* 422 U.S. 563 (1975).

(160) See notes 128–29 *supra,* and the accompanying text.

(161) *See, e.g., Specht v. Patterson,* 386 U.S. 605 (1967); *United States v. Bohle,* 445 F.2d 54, (7th Cir. 1971). In the latter, the court observed of psychiatry:

> We are dealing with a field of science in which there are many variables and one in which opinions must perforce be based upon many subjective factors requiring judgment evaluation. Here particularly the party to be confronted by such an opinion should have the full opportunity of cross-examination.

Id. at 65.

(162) See Beck, et al., *supra* note 17; Katz, Cole, & Lowery, *supra* note 20; Copeland, et al., *supra* note 20, Sandifer, et al., *supra* note 106. Katz, Cole and Lowery termed this phenomenon a "problem of varying subjective thresholds." *Supra* note 20, at 945.

(163) If there is to be civil commitment, there is no legitimate basis for civil commitment other than recent overt acts, attempts, or threats of overt acts. Any other basis for commitment necessarily involves judgments and predictions which psychiatrists are unable to make reliably and accurately. It follows that hospital records containing diagnoses, opinions, ambiguous descriptions, predictions, or any other ambiguous, nonfactual information, about which observers might well differ should not be admissible in evidence over the patient's objection, especially if the author of the entry is not available for cross-examination. *See United States v. Bohle,* 445 F.2d 54 (7th Cir. 1971); *Lyles v. United States,* 254 F.2d 725 (D.C. Cir. 1957); *New York Life Ins. Co. v. Taylor,* 147 F.2d 297 (D.C. Cir. 1945); *State v. McGregor,* 82 R.I. 437, 111 A.2d 231 (1955). *But cf. People v. Kohlmeyer,* 284 N.Y. 366, 31 N.E.2d 490 (Ct. of Appeals, 1940). Whether even unambiguous, factual statements contained in hospital records should be admissible depends upon the purpose for which such statements are admitted. For example, records of the medication prescribed for the patient might be admissible if offered only to show that such medication was given; they should not be admissible if offered to suggest that the patient was so disturbed as to require that medication.

(164) *See, e.g.,* Cohen, and *Project, supra* note 1.

(165) For examples of more adequate cross-examination *See* ZISKIN, *supra* note 3, Kumasaka and Gupta, *Lawyers and Psychiatrists in the Court: Issues on Civil Commitment,* 32 *Md. L. Rev.* 6 (1972).

(166) For a specific example, *see* Ennis, *Mental Illness,* in *1969–1970 Annual Survey of American Law* 29, 37–40.

(167) *Id.* Often, such interviews are conducted while the patient is agitated about being deprived of liberty, or is under the influence of various medications—circumstances which do not promote ease of recollection.

(168) *United States v. Wade*, 388 U.S. 218 (1967). See also, *Gilbert v. California*, 388 U.S. 263 (1967). The rule in *Wade* subsequently was limited to indicted or formally charged defendants. *Kirby v. Illinois*, 406 U.S. 682 (1972). On the other hand, since involuntary psychiatric interviews are a form of "custodial interrogation," *Miranda v. Arizona*, 384 U.S. 436 (1966), would support, by analogy, the right of a lawyer to be present at the psychiatric examination of his client.

(169) *E.g.*, *Thornton v. Corcoran*, 407 F.2d 695 (D.C. Cir. 1969); *Lessard v. Schmidt*, 349 F. Supp. 1078 (E.D. Wis. 1972), *vacated on other grounds sub nom. Schmidt v. Lessard*, 414 U.S. 473 (1974).

(170) See Diamond, *The Fallacy of the Impartial Expert*, 3 Arch. Crim. Psychodynamics 221 (1959).

(171) In *In re* Gannon, 123 N.J.S. 104, 301 A.2d 493 (Somerset Co. Ct. 1973), the court ruled that "in a commitment proceeding due process of law includes the right to an independent psychiatric examination" at state expense. That decision was based on the court's finding "that psychiatrists differ very definitely in their evaluations and diagnoses of mental illness. In a commitment proceeding . . . the right to counsel is of little value without a concurrent right to an independent psychiatric examination."

(172) Frequently, the "independent" psychiatrist is, or has been, a staff colleague of the psychiatrist or psychiatrists recommending hospitalization.

(173) If the recommendations contained in this Section are adopted, the number of persons subject to involuntary hospitalization would be substantially diminished. Some persons would still be subject to involuntary hospitalization, but only upon evidence of overt acts or threats, the proof of which would not require subjective opinions or judgments. If a person truly requires involuntary hospitalization, there should be abundant and unambiguous evidence of that, and hence no need for opinions and predictions.

(174) Burger, *Psychiatrists, Lawyers, and the Courts*, 28 *Fed. Prob.* 3, 7 (1964). *See also O'Connor v Donaldson*, 422 U.S. 563 (1975) (Burger, C.J. concurring).

Dangerousness: A Paradigm for Exploring Some Issues in Law and Psychology

Saleem A. Shah

There have been a number of developments in recent years which indicate closer research and professional interactions between the fields of law and psychology. The law continues to reflect increasing interest in the contributions of the behavioral and social sciences, and empirical legal research has flourished; judicial opinions frequently reference psychological and other related research, and collaborative research, teaching, and consultative endeavors involving legal scholars and social scientists have become quite common. And, as a more widely visible indication that the substantive area of "law and psychology" has indeed achieved notable recognition within the discipline, the year 1976 saw, for the first time, a chapter in the *Annual Review of Psychology* addressed to the topic of psychology and law (Tapp, 1976).

With these developments as background, this article focuses on the phenomenon of "dangerousness" as it is addressed by our legal and social institutions, as well as on the role and potential contributions of psychology and other behavioral and social sciences to this important subject. The topic of "dangerousness" serves as a paradigm illustrating broader issues pertaining to interactions between law and psychology. The present issues also extend well beyond the domain of law and psychology.

DEFINITIONAL ISSUES

It has been suggested that dangerousness, like beauty, lies in the eye of the beholder. Certainly, the term is rather vague and appears often to receive surplus meanings. As used in this article, *dangerousness* refers to a propensity (i.e., an increased likelihood when compared with others) to engage in dangerous behavior. *Dangerous behavior* refers to acts that are characterized by the application of or the overt threat of force and that are likely to result in injury to other persons. This also defines violent behavior and, in this article, the two are considered synonymous.

This usage is very close to the usual dictionary meaning of the word *dangerous*, but it certainly does not approach the specificity typically required of operational research definitions. Nonetheless, my concern here is not with research definitions as such but with the broader range of behaviors and events that the law, for its purposes, subsumes under this rubric. More precisely, acts that commonly are defined as *crimes of violence* exemplify the behaviors of major concern in the foregoing definition. The core behaviors or offenses of concern to the law are probably represented in the Uniform Crime Reports of the FBI (Kelley, 1976). Violent crimes include murder, aggravated assault, forcible rape, and robbery. Along with these offense categories would also be included the so-called inchoate crimes, that is, attempts to commit violent crimes.

One could go well beyond this core category of dangerous acts to include, for example, all crimes involving assault and battery, arson, kidnapping, extortion, all serious felonies, all crimes, and even harmful and threatening acts that may not be criminal (see, e.g., Goldstein & Katz, 1960). However, as the definition is broadened, general agreement tends to decrease and problems of unreliability and vagueness increase. In the final analysis, such definitions relate closely to social values, cultural norms, and the political processes whereby a society arrives at broad policy decisions.

There are several points in the criminal justice and mental health systems at which questions about an individual's dangerousness are addressed:

1. Decisions concerning bail, or release on personal recognizance, for persons accused of crimes, including the level at which bail is to be set.

2. Decisions concerning the waiver to adult courts of juveniles charged with serious crimes.

3. Sentencing decisions following criminal convictions, including decisions about release on conditions of probation.

4. Decisions pertaining to work-release and furlough programs for incarcerated offenders.

5. Parole and other conditional release decisions for offenders.

6. Decisions pertaining to the commitment and release of "sexual psychopaths," "sexually dangerous persons," "defective delinquents," and the like.

7. Determinations of dangerousness for all indicted felony defendants found incompetent to stand trial (e.g., in New York State.(1))

8. Decisions pertaining to the special handling of and transfer to special prisons of offenders who are disruptive in regular prisons.

9. Commitment of drug addicts (because of fears that they will commit violent crimes to support their drug habit).

10. Decisions concerning the emergency and longer term involuntary commitment of mentally ill persons considered to pose a "danger to self or others."

11. Decisions regarding the "conditional" and "unconditional" release of involuntarily confined mental patients.

12. Decisions concerning the hospitalization (on grounds of continued mental disorder and dangerousness) of persons acquitted by reason of insanity.

13. Decisions regarding the transfer to security hospitals of mental patients found to be too difficult or dangerous to be handled in regular civil mental hospitals.

14. Decisions concerning the invocation of special legal proceedings or sentencing provisions for "habitual" and "dangerous" offenders.

15. Decisions concerning the likelihood of continued dangerousness of persons convicted of capital crimes, as a basis for determinations pertaining to the use of the death sentence.(2)

Even though the above list is already rather long, some other situations also occur in the areas of family and health law where decisions are based on judgments of the likelihood of harm and danger to others, for example, the quarantine of persons with certain communicable diseases and the placement under guardianship of battered and abused children who are judged to be at risk from their parents or guardians.

Despite the very serious consequences that can follow for individuals officially designated dangerous, it is astonishing to note the frequent absence of clear and specific definitions and criteria in laws pertaining to the commitment and release of the mentally ill and of persons handled via "sexual psychopath" laws and related statutes. While *dangerousness* as used in laws and regulations is clearly a *legal* term requiring determination by courts, such crucial determinations are often actually made by mental health "experts" as a function of judicial default (see, e.g., Shah, 1974; Wexler & Scoville, 1971).

For example, involuntary commitments of the mentally ill using criteria of "dangerousness to self or others" affect literally thousands of persons each year. In 1972, 41.8% of all inpatient admissions to state and county mental hospitals were involuntary; this involved a total of 169,032 admissions (National Institute of Mental Health, 1974). It must be noted, however, that many patients would have had more than one admission during that calendar year; also, the legal criterion of "dangerous to self or others" would have applied to some unknown proportion of all the involuntary admissions. Of course, the above figure does not include involuntary admissions to psychiatric services of general hospitals, private psychiatric facilities, VA hospitals, community mental health centers, and residential psychiatric facilities for children.

Despite the number of persons affected, the laws that authorize involuntary commitments provide glaring illustrations of circularity and vagueness in their definitions of mental illness and dangerousness (see, e.g., Shah, 1977). In recent years, challenges to these laws, based in part on issues of vague definitions and criteria, have been successful, and several such laws have been found unconstitutional. As a result, several markedly improved revisions have been enacted during the last few years, and more precise definitions and stricter decision rules are increasingly evident (see, e.g., Shah, 1977).

Judicial definitions (in contrast to statutory definitions) of dangerousness have been similarly vague in the past, and very loose and elastic interpretations have been quite typical. For example, in 1960, the court in *Overholser v. Russell*(3) held that competent evidence that the individual may commit *any criminal act* was sufficient to indicate his dangerousness to the community. (The specific concern was about Russell's "check-writing proclivity.") However, in the past few years some impressive improvements in judicial definitions and interpretations have been made.

In 1966, in *Millard v. Cameron*,(4) a case of indecent exposure handled via the District of Columbia's sexual psychopath law, the U.S. Court of Appeals ruled that "dangerous conduct be not merely repulsive or repugnant but must have a *serious* effect on the viewer" (emphasis added). Two years later, the same appellate court stated in *Millard v. Harris*(5) that the possible harm from the patient's exhibitionism to "very seclusive, withdrawn, shy, sensitive" women was insufficient in regard to the "limits on the extent to which the law can sweep the streets clear of all possible sources of occasional distress to such women." The court also provided an analytic framework for assessing dangerousness which has received wide attention:

Predictions of dangerousness, whether under the Sexual

Psychopath Act or in some other context, require determinations of several sorts: the type of conduct in which the individual may engage; the likelihood or probability that he will in fact indulge in that conduct; and the effect such conduct if engaged in will have on others. Depending on the sort of conduct and effect feared, these variables may also require further refinement. (p. 973)

In 1969, in *Cross v. Harris*,(6) the U.S. Court of Appeals elaborated further on its earlier analysis in *Millard* and noted that a "finding of 'dangerousness' must be based on a high probability of substantial injury." Referring to the analytic framework provided earlier in *Millard v. Harris*, Chief Judge David Bazelon pointed out,

Without some such framework, "dangerous" could readily become a term of art describing anyone whom we would, all things considered, prefer not to encounter on the streets. We did not suppose that Congress had used "dangerous" in any such Pickwickian sense. (p. 1099)

The analytic framework and reasoning provided in the aforementioned cases have been cited widely by other courts. Recently, in *State v. Krol*,(7) the Supreme Court of New Jersey provided a rather detailed and important opinion:

Dangerous conduct is not identical with criminal conduct. Dangerous conduct involves not merely violation of social norms enforced by criminal sanctions, but significant physical or psychological injury to persons or substantial destruction of property. Persons are not to be indefinitely incarcerated because they present a risk of future conduct which is merely socially undesirable. (p. 301)

Thus, while it is evident that impressive strides have been made toward general judicial applications of more precise and narrowly constructed legal definitions of dangerousness, there is no guarantee that the "law in practice" will conform closely to the "law on the books."

SOME CONCEPTUAL ISSUES

A major problem in efforts to assess, predict, prevent, and change dangerous behavior is the manner in which such behavior is conceptualized. Behavior—whether defined as dangerous, friendly, constructive, or antisocial—is often viewed as stemming largely if not entirely from *within* the person; that is, it is viewed as a stable and fairly consistent characteristic of the individual. Stated differently, behavior is viewed as being determined largely by the individual's personality. Thus, the assumption is often made that samples of "dangerous" behavior are fairly typical of the individual and are likely to be displayed in other situations as well. Hence, through a conceptual short-cut, certain aspects of the individual's *behavior* are initially defined as dangerous, and then the *individual himself* comes to be viewed and labeled as dangerous. This, of course, can be quite misleading inasmuch as violent and dangerous acts tend to be relatively infrequent, occur in rather specific interpersonal and situational contexts, may be state-dependent (e.g., under the influence of alcohol or other drugs), and may not be very representative of the individual's more typical behavior.

However, a person-oriented conceptualization of behavior (whether based on personality-trait or psychodynamic notions) appears to be fairly common among mental health professionals, especially those working in the fields of forensic psychology and psychiatry. The basic assumptions of the law and of most lawyers and judges also seem to have this "person-focused" perspective on behavior.

There is, however, a tradition in psychology that has emphasized the importance of situational and environmental influences on behavior (see, e.g., Kantor, 1924, 1926; Lewin, 1935; Lewin, Lippitt, & White, 1939). Several other theoretical perspectives are also relevant in this regard—ranging from social learning theory (e.g., Bandura, 1971; Bandura & Walters, 1963; Patterson, 1971; Rotter, 1954), to developments in ecological psychology (e.g., Barker, 1968), to more recent innovations referred to as environmental psychology (e.g., Proshansky, Ittelson, & Rivlin, 1970; Wohlwill, 1970). During the past decade there has been a major resurgence in the area of personality and social psychology of the longstanding interest in examining person *and* situational variables, especially the specific *interactions* of these sets of variables in determining behavior. An impressive body of research, conceptual and theoretical developments, and debates have taken place in this lively and promising area (see, e.g., Bem & Allen, 1974; Bowers, 1973; Ekehammar, 1974; Endler & Hunt, 1968; Endler & Magnusson, 1976; Mischel, 1968, 1973, 1977; Moos, 1973).

Various characteristics of the environment exert considerable influence on the form, frequency, magnitude, and nature of the likely behaviors. Such situational factors may evoke or provoke certain behaviors and may also have inhibiting or suppressive effects on other behaviors. Thus, efforts to understand, assess, predict, prevent, and change dangerous behaviors must consider the effects of setting and situational factors as well as the interactions between these and the characteristics of the individual. Evidence strongly indicates that the particular classes of settings and situations must be taken into account far more carefully than they have been in the past (e.g., Bem & Allen, 1974; Mischel, 1973).

Just as individuals vary with respect to the range and types of behaviors they are likely to show in particular situations and also across certain situations, similarly, complex social settings also vary in the degree to which they prescribe and limit the range of expected and acceptable behaviors for persons in particular roles and situations. Thus, Mischel (1973) has suggested a number of cognitive, social-learning, person-related variables that influence how the individual perceives, constructs, and responds to the environment. Similarly, Bowers (1973) points out that "situations are as much a function of the person as the person's behavior is a function of the situation" (p. 327). In the same vein, Pervin (1977) notes that personality is coming to be seen as expressing both stability and change, and that it is the *pattern* of stability and change in relation to specific situations that needs greater attention.

In sum, it would be accurate to say that the interactional conceptualization of behavior discussed in this section has yet to have a significant impact on the actual day-to-day practices in the fields of juvenile and criminal justice and of forensic psychiatry and psychology.

SOME CLINICAL ISSUES

As noted above, there are several points in the criminal justice and mental health systems at which questions about an individual's dangerousness are often raised. In almost every instance, a major and even critical consideration in such decisions pertains to judgments about the person's future dangerousness. And, it appears that the law has for many decades assumed that reasonably reliable and accurate predictions have been made, or at least are possible. In actuality, however, there exists a rather convincing body of literature that points to the considerable technical difficulties in attempting to predict events with very low base rates. Invariably, such predictions are accompanied by rather huge rates of "false positive" errors; that is, the great majority of the persons predicted as likely to engage in future violent behavior will *not* display such behavior (see, e.g., Cocozza & Steadman, 1976; Fagin, 1976; Megargee, 1976; Monahan, 1975; Monahan, 1976).

Some of the literature relevant to this problem appeared more than 20 years ago (e.g., Meehl, 1954; Meehl & Rosen, 1955; Rosen 1954). Other empirical studies have appeared more recently (e.g., Kozol, Boucher, & Garofalo, 1972; Wenk & Emrich, 1972; Wenk, Robison, & Smith, 1972).

In addition, follow-up studies of "criminally insane" and "dangerous" patients released as a result of major court rulings have also provided evidence for the high rates of the "false positive" errors made by mental health professionals in predicting dangerousness (Hunt & Wiley, 1968; Jacoby, 1976; Steadman & Cocozza, 1974; White, Krumholz, & Fink, 1969; Thornberry & Jacoby, 1976). It must be noted, however, that in these decision-making situations there exist strong social and political pressures that demand certain types of decision rules, namely, "better safe than sorry" (Scheff, 1963; Shah, 1969). There are strong negative reactions by the community to errors associated with the *release* of dangerous persons but relatively little concern about errors leading to unnecessary confinement.

In addition to the problems noted above, there are also some systematic sources of error in clinical assessments that have implications for issues of dangerousness: illusory correlations, and ignoring statistical rules in making predictive judgments.

ILLUSORY CORRELATIONS

Chapman and Chapman (1967, 1969) demonstrated the occurrence of "illusory correlations," that is, "the report by an observer of a correlation between two classes of events which in reality are not correlated, or are correlated to a lesser extent than reported, or are correlated in the opposite direction than that which is reported" (Chapman & Chapman, 1967, p. 194).

Popular and even stereotyped association connections were shown to be one such source of systematic error(8) in observed correlations between symptom statements and features of projective test protocols (viz., projective drawings and the Rorschach Inkblot Test). Not only were both novice and experienced clinicians subject to such errors, but even persons without any psychological training displayed precisely the same types of error. On projective drawings (Draw-a-Person Test) and the Rorschach Inkblot Test, the clinical significance of certain test "signs" was found to correspond to the rated associative strength between certain symptoms and test features, rather than to the *actual* occurrence of such relationships. For example, emphasis on the eyes in the figure drawings was consistently associated with suspiciousness and paranoia, and Rorschach responses pertaining to the buttocks were consistently associated with male homosexuality. These illusory correlations demonstrated remarkable persistence even in the face of negative evidence provided in the experiments.

Golding and Rorer (1971), in a modification of Chapman and Chapman's Rorschach study, replicated the illusory correlation phenomenon. Similar results have been demonstrated by Starr and Katkin (1969) using the Incomplete Sentences Blank and by Sweetland (1972) with regard to assessments of the degree of "dangerousness" and "nondangerousness" reflected in various personality characteristics. Sweetland's findings suggest that widely held social stereotypes appear to be present, among psychiatrists and members of the general public, with respect to personality characteristics that supposedly are and are not associated with the likelihood of dangerous behavior.

STATISTICAL RULES IN PREDICTIVE JUDGMENTS

This section began with a discussion of the factors that lead to huge rates of "false positive" errors when efforts are made to predict events with very low base rates. In addition to the problems inherent in attempting to predict low-base-rate events, there are other factors that appear further to complicate and even to exacerbate such errors.

A sizeable body of literature has accumulated on the topic of predictions and judgments made under conditions of uncertainty. In contrast to earlier work which assumed that, by and large, people formed and also revised their judgments in an orderly fashion and in keeping with normative statistical principles, more recent studies suggest that people tend very often to rely on some simple intuitive heuristics or strategies that serve to reduce the complexity of the task (see, e.g., Ajzen, 1977; Kahneman & Tversky, 1973; Tversky & Kahneman, 1974).

Thus, Kahneman and Tversky (1973) have demonstrated that, rather commonly, people do not rely on statistical principles in making judgments but use a limited number of heuristics that sometimes result in reasonable judgments and other times lead to severe and systematic errors. For example, one judgmental heuristic commonly used pertains to *representativeness*. This refers to the tendency to predict the outcome that appears to be most representative of the available evidence. In many situations, representative outcomes are certainly more likely than others. However, since this is not always the case, particularly when relatively infrequent and situation-specific events are involved, systematic errors are likely to be made. Moreover, factors such as the prior probabilities of the outcome (i.e., the base expectancies) and the reliability of the available evidence must be considered with respect to the likelihood of the expected outcome.

For example, a fundamental rule of statistical prediction is that expected accuracy must control the relative weights assigned to the specific evidence being used for predictions (e.g., various clinical indices and "signs") and to the prior information (the base rates). As the expected accuracy of the prediction decreases (in situations where the base rates are very low and the available evidence not very reliable), the predictions should shift closer to the base rates. For example, if only 10% of a particular group are expected to engage in future violent behavior on the basis of prior probabilities (base rates), and if the specific evidence concerning the predictions is of poor reliability (e.g., clinical assessments and certain psychological test indices), then the predictions should remain very close to the base rates. The greater they move away from the base rates under the above conditions, the greater will be the probability of error. (See also Tversky & Kahneman, 1974.)

Experiments conducted by Kahneman and Tversky (1973) demonstrated, nevertheless, that individuals engaged in predictive tasks very commonly disregard information concerning prior probability when some specific current information is provided. There is a tendency instead to resort to the "representativeness" heuristic, even to an extent that involves gross departures from the prior probabilities. Thus, Kahneman and Tversky (1973) observed,

> Evidently, people respond differently when given no specific evidence and when given worthless evidence. When no specific evidence is given, the prior probabilities are properly utilized; when worthless specific evidence is given, prior probabilities are ignored.   (p. 242)

Another judgmental heuristic discussed by Tversky and Kahneman (1974) is *availability*. This refers to the situation in which people assess the frequency of a class or the probability of an event by the ease with which instances or occurrences of the event can be recalled. These authors note that availability can be a useful clue for assessing the frequency or probability of an event, since instances of more frequent events will tend to be recalled more readily than infrequent events. However, various other factors affect "availability" and can lead to bias and errors. For example, particular events may have greater saliency, will more readily be recalled (e.g., patients released from a security hospital who later engaged in violent or other serious crimes), and therefore may *appear* to be more frequent than is actually the case. And, as noted earlier, the social contingencies affecting predictions of dangerousness tend to ensure that the *availability* of instances of "false negative" errors (even though very infrequent) will have great salience and will be considered in a manner inconsistent with that indicated by information about the base rates.

Inspired by the work of Kahneman and Tversky, Nisbett and Borgida (1975) demonstrated that subjects tended to neglect information about behavioral base rates in a given population when they were asked to predict (or explain) the behavior of an individual drawn from that population. This tendency would appear to have much relevance for the clinical situations in which assessments of dangerousness are often made. Focus upon the particular individual being evaluated would tend to push into the background available information about the population from which the examinee had been drawn.

More recently, Ajzen (1977) examined the plausibility of yet another, or possibly alternative, cognitive strategy or heuristic that may explain the effects of base rate and other information on predictions. Ajzen suggests that, especially in the case of judgments concerning human behavior and its effects, people often rely on their intuitive understanding of factors that seem to *cause* the event in question. Such a judgmental strategy has been termed the *causality* heuristic.

Using this heuristic, people appear to look for factors that cause the behavior in question, and information that is perceived as providing evidence concerning the presence or absence of such causal factors is likely to influence the predictions. Other information, even though important in reference to normative principles of statistical prediction, will tend to be ignored if it appears to have no causal significance.

Applying this discussion to the typical clinical situations pertaining to predictions of dangerousness, one can envision much concern focused on the particular individual being examined, on his psychopathology, on the psychodynamic factors that presumably led to ("caused") past violent acts, and on the continued presence of those factors, which are believed to increase the likelihood of recurrence of similar acts. Thus, despite information about the low base rates of such acts, the use of the aforementioned judgmental heuristics, as well as the many other features of the assessment situation, all seem to combine in rather predictable fashion to increase "false positive" errors.

The basic point here is that the systematic errors discussed above do not relate just to careless clinical practices. Rather, my point is that some of these errors appear to be inherent in the very nature and social context of the judgmental task, and they are very much influenced by powerful social contingencies which, in particular situations, implicitly or even explicitly direct that "false positive" errors are much to be preferred over "false negative" errors. Nevertheless, greater awareness of and sensitivity to the aforementioned systematic errors, and related training efforts, should help both to distinguish the technical difficulties of the predictive task from the social pressures and to develop procedures that make more effective use of normative statistical principles in efforts to reduce the error rates.

A final relevant topic needs to be mentioned. Development and utilization of actuarial or statistical approaches to prediction remain neglected despite the considerable evidence for the relative superiority of such approaches over purely clinical ones (see, e.g., Goldberg, 1968; Livermore, Malmquist, & Meehl, 1968; Meehl, 1965; Pankoff & Roberts, 1968; Sawyer, 1966). Although one would not have reason to expect markedly improved accuracy in predicting very infrequent events, there would most certainly be vastly improved reliability and consistency in such decisions. Moreover, there is no reason why information provided by actuarial tables and similar devices could not be combined with specifically identified and empirically tested clinical information and also with explicit considerations of particular setting and situational factors. Systematic follow-up and feedback regarding the decisional outcomes would allow periodic revisions designed to improve overall predictive accuracy (see, e.g., Burnham, 1975; Goldberg, 1970; Gottfredson, 1975; Gottfredson, Wilkins, Hoffman, & Singer, 1974). As Elstein (1976) recently noted, the fundamental value of the actuarial approach is not in the insistence on quantification. Rather, it is in an insistence that decision rules can be made explicit and that it is most desirable to make them so. Not only would this approach facilitate the teaching of novice clinicians and evaluators, but it would greatly improve the reliability of such judgments.

Given the many sources of differences between various decision makers, increased use of actuarial approaches would provide greater consistency and uniformity in decisions based upon explicitly stated criteria and rules. Thus, even though there would continue to be difficulties in predicting events with very low base rates, at the very least we could achieve greater "equity" and "fairness" by ensuring that individuals are treated more equally as compared to others who are sufficiently similar in terms of the characteristics and criteria used for the decision (Wilkins, 1975, 1976).

SOME PUBLIC POLICY DILEMMAS

This section addresses issues of broader social relevance impinging directly on some vexing societal concerns. My purpose in addressing these issues is to focus attention on these phenomena from the perspective of those socially disadvantaged groups in our society who typically have little influence on public policies but who often bear the heaviest brunt of the consequences associated with certain policies and practices with respect to criminal violence.

VALUES, POWER, AND DANGEROUSNESS

There are markedly different societal and governmental responses to varying types and sources of danger to the community. And the defining, labeling, and handling of dangerous behaviors and situations are very much influenced by the dominant values and power structures that exist in a society. For example, social deviants labeled "mentally ill" have for several hundred years in the Anglo-American experience aroused much societal apprehension and been major targets for preventive confinement (Dershowitz, 1974a, 1974b). Yet many other categories of persons and groups who have quite glaringly demonstrated their dangerousness to society (e.g., repeated drunken drivers and offenders with three or more convictions for violent and other serious crimes) do not seem to evoke similar concerns, nor are they as readily subjected to indeterminate and preventive confinement in order to protect the community (Shah, 1974, 1975).

Moreover, it is indeed ironic that our society tends to focus attention on the dangerous acts of particular individuals (especially the mentally ill) while tolerating and overlooking the *social conditions* and *practices* that pose serious hazards to the health, safety, and physical well-being of literally millions of citizens each year (e.g., industrial practices and working conditions which result in many disabling and even fatal occupational diseases). For example, the *President's Report on Occupational Safety and Health* (1972) estimated that total deaths annually from job-related injuries amounted to over 14,000, with an estimated 2.2 million disabling injuries. The incidence of occupational disease is less well known, but estimates have pointed to "at least 390,000 new cases of disabling occupational diseases each year" (*President's Report on Occupational Safety and Health*, 1972, p. 111). It was also estimated in this report that there may be as many as 100,000 deaths per year from occupationally caused diseases. (See also Greene, 1974; Hunter, 1970; Schanche, 1974.)

Obviously, not all nor perhaps even the majority of the above-mentioned industrial and occupation-related deaths, diseases, and disabling injuries can be avoided. The basic point, however, is to note the remarkably different societal and governmental responses to different types and sources of danger to the community. It seems very difficult for lawmakers to establish effective controls when powerful groups and interests are involved. And even when regulations and established safety standards do exist for occupational safety and health, enforcement practices and sanctions reflect remarkable tolerance and "kid gloves" treatment of these powerful groups (see, e.g., Brodeur, 1974; Franklin, 1969; Geis & Meier, in press; Page & O'Brien, 1973; Scott, 1974).

LIBERTARIAN IDEOLOGIES AND VICTIMIZATION RATES

The dangerousness issue is made even more complex when we look at the impact on those societal groups most affected by such behaviors. Basic notions of social justice and fairness require that the burdens and costs of crime—especially with respect to victimization from crimes of violence—should be borne more evenly by the population (see, e.g., Rawls, 1972). Yet, there is considerable and longstanding evidence that the poor and otherwise socially disadvantaged pay a disproportionately heavy price.

Relevant data from the *National Crime Panel Survey Report* (1976) with respect to crimes of personal violence indicate that poor individuals (in families with annual incomes below $3,000) have victimization rates *more than double* those of the affluent (annual family income of $25,000 and above). The rates of victimization (per 1,000 persons aged 12 and over) were 54.3 for the poor and 25.3 for the affluent.

Additional information has been collected by the National Center for Health Statistics on rates for deaths by homicide (Klebba, 1975). These data show that exceptionally high rates are experienced by young males in the category "other than white," which is 89% black. For example, in 1972 the *age-adjusted* rates(9) for deaths by homicide (per 100,000 population) were 10.3 for all groups, 16.8 for all males, 8.2 for white males, and *83.1* for males "other than white." For the same year, the *age-specific* homicide rates(10) (again per 100,000 population) for these "other than white" males in the age groups 15–19, 20–24, and 25–29 were 55.5, 152.7, and 172.1, respectively. Klebba (1975) further points out that the age group 15–29 accounted in 1973 for fully 40.1% of all the victims of homicide and 59.3% of all those arrested for homicide.

Along the same lines, Bennett, Kleitman, and Larson (cited in Wilson, 1975) studied murder rates in various cities and found that the increase in murder rates during the 1960s was *ten times greater* than would have been expected on the basis of the changing age structure of the population alone. If the murder rate remains constant at present levels, then a child born in 1974 in Detroit, for example, and living there all his life, has 1 chance in 35 of being murdered. Most at risk are young black males living in central-city areas.

The above type of data indicate that very serious attention needs to be given to the social inequity of a situation where heavy costs in lives and serious injuries resulting from crimes of violence are disproportionately borne by the socially disadvantaged. These social groups typically have limited influence on public policies and limited options and resources for avoiding or preventing their "high risk" status for criminal victimization, for example, by moving away from high-crime inner-city areas.

A number of different surveys have sought to elicit perceptions of personal safety in various neighborhoods. Questions have typically taken the form "How safe do you feel or would you feel being out alone in your neighborhood during the (day/night)?" Or, "Is there any area right around here—that is, within a mile—where you would be afraid to walk alone at night?" National trend data from 1965 to 1974 indicate a slight increase in the percentage (from 34 to 45) of persons who responded affirmatively to the second form of the question (Hindelang, Dunn, Sutton, & Aumick, 1976). In 1972, for example, a question about fear of walking alone at night elicited the following percentage difference: 58% of the women and 20% of the men questioned were afraid to walk alone at night in their own neighborhoods; persons over 50 years of age were much more fearful than younger persons; nonwhites were more likely to report being afraid; and persons residing in large metropolitan areas were much more likely to report such fears than persons from rural areas— 53% versus 24% (Hindelang et al., 1976, Tables 2.4 through 2.10, especially Table 2.8).

There seems to be insufficient realization that to the extent that literally millions of citizens are afraid to use public streets in the evenings, markedly restrict their social interactions and activities in their own neighborhoods, and live with high levels of fear and apprehension, their "civil liberties" have seriously been infringed. Moreover, since the government is not able to provide better protection to its citizens, basic notions of equity require that more adequate and effective victim-compensation and restitution programs be instituted (see, generally, Edelhertz, 1975; Edelhertz & Geis, 1974; Geis, 1975; Schafer, 1970, 1975).

Obviously, behavioral and social scientists cannot resolve such public policy issues nor the fundamentally moral and political questions inherent in these and many related social problems. They can, however, study these phenomena in efforts to spotlight them for public and governmental attention and to provide the empirical evidence which could, hopefully, help to guide and to revise public policies. It also seems that, in the development of public policies with respect to these social problems, the political power of influential social groups needs to be balanced by a more concerned awareness of the greater risks of life and limb experienced by socially disadvantaged groups. The inequities inherent in such situations are strikingly at odds with the principle of "justice as fairness" (Rawls, 1972).

DANGEROUS AND HABITUAL OFFENDERS

In rather marked contrast to public policies and practices that tend to make highly questionable assumptions about the dangerousness of the mentally ill as a group, there is abundant evidence to indicate that recidivistic offenders account for a disproportionate amount of all crimes leading to arrests. Of course, not all arrests lead to convictions. But the concern here is with the prevalence of violent crimes in the community and not just with convictions. Victims remain just as surely robbed, raped, and murdered even though the accused defendants may not be convicted—or even apprehended.

The most recent, published, official data indicate that there were 1,026,284 crimes of violence reported to the police in 1975, or about 481.5 per 100,000 persons (Kelley, 1976). Data available from the national panel samples of the joint Law Enforcement Assistance Administration and Bureau of Census Victimization Surveys indicate that nonreporting rates for rape, personal robbery, and aggravated assault were 44%, 46%, and 44%, respectively. The nonreporting for business robbery, in contrast, was only 10% (Hindelang, 1977).(11)

Thus, as contrasted with the legal, constitutional, and policy questions discussed earlier with respect to the use of preventive confinement of the mentally ill on the basis of unreliable and inaccurate predictions of dangerousness, we are now concerned with individuals at the extreme other end of the continuum—serious recidivistic offenders. In the case of this latter group, violent and other serious crimes have repeatedly been manifested. The major policy question that arises is, At what point does the *demonstrated* danger become glaring enough to justify special efforts to protect the community from further harm at the hands of serious recidivistic offenders?

Wolfgang, Figlio, and Sellin (1972) conducted a birth-cohort study that involved almost 10,000 boys in Philadelphia. These investigators found that about one third (3,475) of the boys had had at least one officially recorded contact with the police; but almost half of these boys showed no further police contacts. However, a very small proportion of the total cohort (6%), and a small proportion also of those who had had police contacts (18%), were charged with five or more offenses. This group of 627 chronic offenders accounted for fully 71% of the homicides committed by the entire cohort, 77% of the rapes, 70% of the robberies, and 69% of the aggravated assaults.

Similarly, a study in New York City found that while only 2% of all persons arrested had been previously arrested for homicide, fully 40% of all those arrested for homicide had previous arrests for a violent crime, and 30.5% for felonious assaults (Shinnar & Shinnar, 1975).

The PROMIS Research Project (1977) in the District of Columbia has analyzed data pertaining to all arrests between January 1, 1971 and August 31, 1975; information was available regarding rearrests, reprosecutions, and reconvictions involving 45,575 criminal defendants. It was found that persons who were repeatedly arrested, prosecuted, and convicted accounted for a disproportionately large share of the "street crime." Thus, if a defendant had five or more arrests prior to the current arrest, the probability of subsequent arrest began to approach certainty

(PROMIS Research Project, 1977). This study also found that defendants who had committed previous violent crimes (i.e., homicide, assault, sexual assault, and robbery) had the highest proportion of rearrests for violent crimes. (See also Petersilia, Greenwood, & Lavin, 1977.(12))

The foregoing findings are rather troubling. The fundamental values of our society require that we lean over backwards to protect the rights of persons accused of crimes. Very explicit decision rules are also provided in order to avoid the risk of erroneous convictions. We say that we would rather let nine guilty persons go free than convict a single innocent person. But a related policy consideration pertains to the risks of crime victimization that the community, and especially the socially disadvantaged sectors, suffers at the hands of individuals who repeatedly endanger society.

The situation with regard to the handling of chronic and recidivistic offenders provides an interesting contrast with policies and practices that are regularly used to involuntarily confine the mentally ill on the grounds of "dangerousness to others," even though they may have committed no serious or violent criminal acts (see, e.g., Levine, 1977; Schwitzgebel, 1977; Shah, 1977; Wexler & Scoville, 1971).

If indeed the community is to be protected from those who have amply *documented* their dangerousness, it seems evident that more realistic and readily usable measures of social defense should be provided and consistently applied. For example, the severity of the prescribed sanctions could well be reduced (e.g., from 10 down to 3 or 5 years of confinement), but the *certainty* of sanctions needs markedly to be increased (see, e.g., Petersilia, Greenwood, & Lavin, 1977; Shinnar & Shinnar, 1975; Wilson, 1975). Moreover, a wide range of social defense alternatives, other than incapacitation through imprisonment, should also be available—for example, weekend confinement, community work programs, and very close supervision in the community. The use of such less drastic alternatives, while *also* providing suitable protection for the community, will of course require markedly increased public expenditures.

DILEMMAS OF PREVENTIVE CONFINEMENT

The terms *preventive confinement* and, especially, pretrial *preventive detention* are highly charged and evoke strong emotions in our society. Perhaps for this reason, there has not been much open and forthright discussion of the relevant issues.

Dershowitz (1973, 1974a) suggests that prevention, as an element in criminal justice, should be conceptualized as a continuum on which three points can be located: pure prevention, in which confinement requires no prior act (e.g., the internment of Japanese-Americans during World War II and the involuntary commitment, on police-power grounds, of the mentally ill); confinement based on suspicion of a prior act but without a criminal conviction (e.g., as provided by some of the "sexual psychopath" statutes); and confinement based on proof of a prior act, but which exceeds the duration normally associated with a criminal conviction for that act (e.g., the Maryland Defective Delinquent Act—just recently repealed—and various "habitual" and "dangerous" offender laws).

Dershowitz (1974a, 1974b) points out that almost all organized societies appear to have employed some mechanism such as preventive confinement for the purpose of incapacitating persons who are perceived to be dangerous but who cannot be convicted for a past offense. He argues, however, that the more a society circumscribes the formal criminal process with very tight safeguards that make criminal convictions difficult, the greater is the likelihood that many dangerous persons will manage to benefit from these safeguards. Such developments then give rise to the perceived need for other alternatives.

In our society, invocation of therapeutic objectives and the labeling of some legal procedures as "civil" (rather than criminal) have allowed great leeway for the uses of preventive confinement. Thus, by resorting to legal word games and verbal gymnastics, that which we would not and could not do to persons convicted of serious crimes and judged to be deserving of punishment, we manage to do quite readily to those designated as the recipients of our benevolence. Dershowitz (1973) has remarked that "the invocation of this talismanic word [civil] has erased a veritable bill of rights" (p. 1296). The unwillingness of our society, especially our legal system, to address the issues of preventive confinement in a more forthright fashion leads to policies and practices that are as inconsistent as they are hypocritical.

SOME OVERARCHING ISSUES

It should be evident that many of the topics discussed here raise numerous research, professional, and public policy questions that go well beyond the topic of dangerousness. Moreover, these issues are by no means the sole concern of the fields of law and psychology. In this final section I shall touch on potential roles and responsibilities for psychology and other behavioral and social sciences with respect to legal structures and processes in our society.

First, the preceding discussion emphasizes the importance of studying complex social phenomena from a broad and preferably interdisciplinary perspective. Many of the questions that truly concern both law and psychology will require some degree of interdisciplinary conceptualization. At the very least, questions need to be formulated in light of the social, legal, and related contexts in which the phenomena occur. This does not mean that psychologists or other social scientists cannot or should not study various law-related topics without involving legal scholars. Rather, it is only essential that the purposes and practices, as well as the relationship between the two, be clearly understood for any given law and legal process.

Let me illustrate. There is at times a tendency on the part of some social scientists to look down on various legal practices, for example, a trial. It is said that this ostensible "search for the truth" is conducted in a rather "unscientific" manner. Such comments reflect disciplinary parochialism, that is, the evaluating of some practice or procedure in another area from the perspective of one's own discipline or focus of interest. The above criticism of a trial suggests that such critics may not appreciate that the trial of an issue of fact is *not* a scientific exercise. Rather, it is a very practical procedure for the management of doubt. Its major purpose is to settle disputes in a manner designed to promote general perceptions of fairness and justice and to reduce conflict.

In short, when social scientists wish to contribute to refinements of legal doctrines and processes, and also to understand the effects of legal processes on other aspects of social behavior, the relevant knowledge base should include some understanding of the social and functional aspects of the process.

If psychologists wish to help in ameliorating various social problems in our society, the need for broad interdisciplinary perspectives becomes even greater. As Katkin, Bullington, and Levine (1974) have pointed out, the effective resolution of complex social problems requires their understanding from a range of perspectives. Thus, a critical need is to ensure that research oriented toward the understanding and amelioration of social problems includes in its basic conceptualization and formulation the perspectives of those in society charged with the responsibility for dealing with the problems (Coleman, 1972; Shah, 1976). There is, therefore, a need for the development of "exoteric" knowledge, rather than just the esoteric or discipline-related knowledge that is created more readily (Churchman, 1977).

Second, behavioral and social scientists need to focus more attention on the development of empirical data that could be of assistance in the examination and testing of the various behavioral assumptions underlying legal doctrines, concepts, and procedures (see, e.g., Tapp, 1976). For example, civil commitment laws for the mentally ill make the assumption (with regard to police-power commitments) that the mentally ill constitute the most dangerous group in our society (Shah, 1975, 1977). Yet, as noted earlier, there is rather glaring evidence that several other groups in society are far more demonstrably dangerous, namely, drunken drivers and serious recidivistic offenders.

Third, it seems rather essential to develop better linkages between laws and the making and unmaking of public policies, and sound empirical findings. Although the empirical soundness of underlying assumptions is not the only consideration in regard to the formulation of laws and other public policies, we should at least try to ensure that major policies are not based on myths and stereotypes—especially when they place certain segments of society at a disadvantage.

In a notable contribution several years ago, Kalven (1968) made a rather important point:

> On the one hand, it is simplistic to urge that because law makes factual assumptions, there should be a one-to-one linking and testing of the underlying social facts, an endless dropping of empirical footnotes to points of law. On the other hand, it is nonsense to say that better documentation of fact cannot ever be relevant to law because the final business of law is not truth but political preference. (p. 67)

This distinguished legal scholar and empirical researcher also commented on the criticism by some lawyers more than 20 years ago concerning the reliance by the U.S. Supreme Court on social science evidence in its decision in *Brown v. Board of Education.*(13) The essential point of the major critics was that there are some value judgments in law that are of such fundamental importance that they can only be trivialized if social science or other such evidence is sought for their support. That is, given conflicting research findings and the typical arguments about the design of the studies and interpretation of the results, legal critics maintained that such fundamental decisions about the constitutional rights of blacks and other Americans cannot be allowed to rest on such shaky social science foundations (Kalven, 1968).

Finally, more attention should be given to "user oriented" information dissemination in order to facilitate utilization of research relevant to social problems. It would be accurate to say that in very large measure, scientific and professional publication efforts relate to the career contingencies of the authors, and the items are directed primarily to their peers. However, scientific and professional publications do *not* address the needs of policymakers and agency administrators who should have easy and readily understandable access to important new findings and developments in their areas of concern.

What seems to be needed is a series of "state of the art" publications, addressing major, current, and developing social issues to which psychology has some relevant and useful knowledge to contribute. Careful attention should be given to assure that essentially ideological beliefs and preferences are not asserted under the trappings of science. These publications should be prepared in a style and format suitable for the specific intended audiences (viz., policymakers and the general public) and should provide a carefully balanced and critical appraisal of the state of current knowledge as well as suggested implications for contemplated policy options. Such items prepared and published by professional associations should *not* be used for any disciplinary or professional ax grinding.

CONCLUSION

Under the topic of "dangerousness"—its definition, conceptualization, and handling—a fairly broad array of issues and questions have been raised. This topic, as well as many others at the psychology-law interface, requires broader frames of reference for its study, basic social accountability in terms of addressing the needs and problems of the larger society and not remaining preoccupied solely with the concerns of the discipline, and the use of notions of equity and fairness in evaluating existing policies and practices against the basic values that our society claims to cherish.

Finally, the manner in which our society defines and handles various forms of dangerousness provides vivid illustration of the need to work toward greater equity and fairness in societal policies and practices. Groups with power and influence, and certain social conditions and practices, do *not* evoke sufficient concerns about their dangerousness. It is also much easier to deal with more focused concerns about dangerous individuals than to address larger aspects of some socially troublesome ideologies and economic interests. Thus, the social and political problems of dealing more effectively with the profusion of firearms in our society, for example, and with the considerable use and abuse of beverage alcohol—both of which factors relate to the nature and frequency of violent acts—remain the topics of endless debates. Moreover, despite the degree to which we claim to value life and to cherish civil liberties, such sensitivities do not seem to extend sufficiently to also consider the rights of citizens placed at high risks of criminal victimization.

In the final analysis, perhaps a basic challenge for psychology in its interactions with legal and social process is to bring relevant knowledge and skills to bear on major social inequities so that the policies and practices in our society can more truly "comport with the deepest notions of what is fair and right and just."(14)

REFERENCES

Ajzen, I. Intuitive Theories of Events and the Effects of Base-Rate Information on Prediction. *Journal of Personality and Social Psychology*, 1977, 35, 303–314.

Bandura, A. Social Learning Theory of Aggression. In J. F. Knutson (Ed.), *The Control of Aggression: Implications from Basic Research.* Chicago: Aldine, 1971.

Bandura, A., & Walters, R. *Social Learning and Personality Development.* New York: Holt, Rinehart & Winston, 1963.

Barker, R. *Ecological Psychology: Concepts and Methods for Studying the Environment of Human Behavior.* Palo Alto, Calif.: Stanford University Press, 1968.

Bem, D., & Allen, A. On Predicting Some of the People Some of the Time: The Search for Cross-situational Consistencies in Behavior. *Psychological Review*, 1974, *81*, 506–520.

Bowers, K. S. Situationism in Psychology: An Analysis and Critique. *Psychological Review*, 1973, *80*, 307–336.

Brodeur, P. *Expendable Americans.* New York: Viking Press, 1974.

Burnham, F. W. Modern Decision Theory and Corrections. In D. M. Gottfredson (Ed.), *Decision-making in the Criminal Justice System: Essays and Reviews.* Washington, D.C.: U.S. Government Printing Office, 1975.

Chapman, L. J., & Chapman, J. P. Genesis of Popular but Erroneous Psychodiagnostic Observations. *Journal of Abnormal Psychology*, 1967, 72, 193–204.

Chapman, L. J., & Chapman, J. P. Illusory Correlations as an Obstacle to the Use of Valid Psychodiagnostic Signs. *Journal of Abnormal Psychology*, 1969, 74, 271–280.

Churchman, C. W. Towards a Holistic Approach. In R. A. Scribner & R. A. Chalk (Eds.), *Adapting Science to Social Needs* (AAAS Conference proceedings). Washington, D.C.: American Association for the Advancement of Science, 1977.

Cocozza, J. J., & Steadman, H. J. The Failure of Psychiatric Predictions of Dangerousness: Clear and Convincing Evidence. *Rutgers Law Review*, 1976, 29, 1084–1101.

Coleman, J. *Policy Research in the Social-Sciences.* Morristown, N.J.: General Learning Press, 1972.

Dershowitz, A. M. Preventive Confinement: A Suggested Framework for Constitutional Analysis. *Texas Law Review*, 1973, *51*, 1277–1324.

Dershowitz, A. M. The Origins of Preventive Confinement in Anglo-American Law, Part I. *University of Cincinnati Law Review*, 1974, 43, 1–60. (a)

Dershowitz, A. M. The Origins of Preventive Confinement in Anglo-American Law, Part II. *University of Cincinnati Law Review*, 1974, 43, 781–846. (b)

Edelhertz, H. Compensating Victims of Violent Crimes. In D. Chappell & J. Monahan (Eds.), *Violence and Criminal Justice.* Lexington, Mass.: Lexington Books, 1975.

Edelhertz, H., & Geis, G. *Public Compensation to Victims of Crime.* New York: Praeger, 1974.

Ekehammar, B. Interactionism in Personality from a Historical Perspective. *Psychological Bulletin*, 1974, *81*, 1026–1048.

Elstein, A. S. Clinical Judgment: Psychological Research and Medical Practice. *Science*, 1976, *194*, 696–700.

Endler, N. S., & Hunt, J. M. S-R Inventories of Hostility and Comparisons of the Proportions of Variance from Persons, Responses, and Situations for Hostility and Anxiousness. *Journal of Personality and Social Psychology*, 1968, *9*, 309–315.

Endler, N. S., & Magnusson, D. Toward an Interactional Psychology of Personality. *Psychological Bulletin*, 1976, *83*, 956–974.

Fagin, A. The Policy Implications of Predictive Decision-making: "Likelihood" and "Dangerousness" in Civil Commitment Proceedings. *Public Policy*, 1976, *24*, 491–528.

Franklin, B. A. The Scandal of Death and Injury in the Mines. *New York Times Magazine*, March 30, 1969.

Geis, G. Victims of Crimes of Violence and the Criminal Justice System. In D. Chappell & J. Monahan (Eds.), *Violence and Criminal Justice*. Lexington, Mass.: Lexington Books, 1975.

Geis, G., & Meier, R. *White-collar Crime: Offenses in Business, Politics, and the Professions*. New York: Free Press, in press.

Goldberg, L. Seer over Sign: The First "Good" Example? *Journal of Experimental Research in Personality*, 1968, *3*, 168–171.

Goldberg, L. Man versus Model of Man: A Rationale, plus Some Evidence for a Method of Improving on Clinical Inferences. *Psychological Bulletin*, 1970, *73*, 422–432.

Golding, S. L., & Rorer, L. G. "Illusory Correlation" and the Learning of Clinical Judgment. *Oregon Research Institute Research Bulletin*, 1971, *11*, 10.

Goldstein, J., & Katz, J. Dangerousness and Mental Illness. *Yale Law Journal*, 1960, *70*, 225–239.

Gottfredson, D. M. *Decision-making in the Criminal Justice System: Reviews and Essays* [Crime and Delinquency Issues, National Institute of Mental Health, DHEW Publication No. (ADM) 75–238]. Washington, D.C.: U.S. Government Printing Office, 1975.

Gottfredson, D. M., Wilkins, L. T., Hoffman, P. B., & Singer, S. M. *The Utilization of Experience in Parole Decision-making* (Summary Report, National Institute of Law Enforcement and Criminal Justice). Washington, D.C.: U.S. Government Printing Office, 1974.

Greene, W. Life vs. Livelihood. *The New York Times Magazine*, Nov. 24, 1974, pp. 95–98; 104–105.

Hindelang, M. J. Personal Communication, April 10, 1977. (Information to appear in the forthcoming *Sourcebook of Criminal Justice Statistics—1977*, to be published by the U.S. Government Printing Office.)

Hindelang, M. J., Dunn, C. S., Sutton, L. P., & Aumick, A. L. *Sourcebook of Criminal Justice Statistics—1975*. Washington, D.C.: U.S. Government Printing Office, 1976.

Hunt, R., & Wiley, E. Operation Baxstrom after One Year. *American Journal of Psychiatry*, 1968, *124*, 974–978.

Hunter, D. *The Diseases of Occupation*. London: English Universities Press, 1970.

Jacoby, J. E. The Dangerousness of the Criminally Insane. Unpublished doctoral dissertation, University of Pennsylvania, 1976.

Kahneman, D., & Tversky, A. On the Psychology of Prediction. *Psychological Review*, 1973, *80*, 237–251.

Kalven, H. The Quest for the Middle Range: Empirical Inquiry and Legal Policy. In G. C. Hazard (Ed.), *Law in a Changing America*. Englewood Cliffs, N.J.:

Prentice-Hall, 1968.

Kantor, J. R. *Principles of Psychology* (Vol. 1). Bloomington, Ill.: Principia Press, 1924.

Kantor, J. R. *Principles of Psychology* (Vol. 2). Bloomington, Ill.: Principia Press, 1926.

Katkin, D., Bullington, B., & Levine, M. Above and Beyond the Best Interests of the Child: An Inquiry into the Relationship between Social Science and Social Action. *Law & Society Review,* 1974, 8, 669–687.

Kelley, C. *Crime in the United States—1975* (Uniform Crime Reports). Washington, D.C.: U.S. Government Printing Office, 1976.

Klebba, A. J. Homicide Trends in the United States, 1900–74. *Public Health Reports,* 1975, 90, 195–204.

Kozol, H., Boucher, R., & Garofalo, R. The Diagnosis and Treatment of Dangerousness. *Crime and Delinquency,* 1972, 18, 371–392.

Levine, D. The Concept of Dangerousness: Criticism and Compromise. In B. D. Sales (Ed.), *Psychology in the Legal Process: Vol. 1. The Criminal Justice System,* New York: Plenum, 1977.

Lewin, K. *A Dynamic Theory of Personality.* New York: McGraw-Hill, 1935.

Lewin, K., Lippitt, R., & White, R. Patterns of Aggressive Behavior in Experimentally Created "Social Climate." *Journal of Social Psychology,* 1939, 10, 271–299.

Livermore, J. M., Malmquist, C. P., & Meehl, P. E. On the Justifications for Civil Commitment. *University of Pennsylvania Law Review,* 1968, 117, 75–96.

Meehl. P. E. *Clinical vs. Statistical Prediction.* Minneapolis: University of Minnesota Press, 1954.

Meehl, P. E. Seer over Sign: The First Good Example. *Journal of Experimental Research in Personality,* 1965, 1, 27–32.

Meehl, P. E., & Rosen, A. Antecedent Probability and the Efficiency of Psychometric Signs, Patterns, or Cutting Scores. *Psychological Bulletin,* 1955, 52, 194–216.

Megargee, E. I. The Prediction of Dangerous Behavior. *Criminal Justice and Behavior,* 1976, 3, 3–22.

Mischel, W. *Personality and Behavior.* New York: Wiley, 1968.

Mischel, W. Toward a Cognitive Social Learning Reconceptualization of Personality. *Psychological Review,* 1973, 80, 252–283.

Mischel, W. On the Future of Personality Measurement. *American Psychologist,* 1977, 32, 246–254.

Monahan, J. *The Prediction of Violent Criminal Behavior: A Methodological Critique and Prospectus.* Paper prepared for the Panel on Research on Deterrent and Incapacitative Effects, National Academy of Sciences, Washington, D.C., June 1976.

Monahan, J. The Prediction of Violence. In D. Chappell & J. Monahan (Eds.), *Violence and Criminal Justice.* Lexington, Mass.: Lexington Books, 1975.

Moos, R. H. Conceptualizations of Human Environments. *American Psychologist,* 1973, 28, 652–665.

National Crime Panel Survey Report. Criminal Victimization in the United States. A Comparison of 1973 and 1974 Findings (Law Enforcement Assistance Administration). Washington, D.C.: U.S. Government Printing Office, 1976.

National Institute of Mental Health. *Legal Status of Inpatient Admissions to State and County Mental Hospitals, United States 1972* (Statistical Note 105).

Rockville, Md.: Author, 1974. [DHEW Publication No. (ADM) 74–6].

Nisbett, R. E., & Borgida, E. Attribution and the Psychology of Prediction. *Journal of Personality and Social Psychology*, 1975, *32*, 932–943.

Page, J. A., & O'Brien, M. *Bitter Wages*. New York: Grossman, 1973.

Pankoff, L. D., & Roberts, H. V. Bayesian Synthesis of Clinical and Statistical Prediction. *Psychological Bulletin*, 1968, *70*, 762–773.

Patterson, G. R. *Families. Applications of Social Learning to Family Life*. Champaign, Ill.: Research Press, 1971.

Pervin, L. The Representative Design of Person-situation Research. In D. Magnusson & N. S. Endler (Eds.), *Personality at the Crossroads: Current Issues in Interactional Psychology*. Hillsdale, N.J.: Erlbaum, 1977.

Petersilia, J., Greenwood, P. W., & Lavin, M. *Criminal Careers of Habitual Felons*. Santa Monica, Calif.: Rand Corporation, August 1977.

President's Report on Occupational Safety and Health. Washington, D.C.: U.S. Government Printing Office, 1972.

PROMIS Research Project. *Highlights of Interim Findings and Implications* (Publication 1). Washington, D.C.: Institute for Law and Social Research, 1977.

PROMIS Research Project. *Curbing the Repeat Offender: A Strategy for Prosecutors* (Publication 3). Washington, D.C.: Institute for Law and Social Research, 1977.

Proshansky, H. M., Ittelson, W. H., & Rivlin, L. G. The Influence of the Physical Environment on Behavior: Some Basic Assumptions. In H. M. Proshansky, W. H. Ittelson, & L. G. Rivlin (Eds.), *Environmental Psychology: Man and His Physical Setting*. New York: Holt, Rinehart & Winston, 1970.

Rawls, J. *A Theory of Justice*. Cambridge, Mass.: Harvard University Press, 1972.

Rosen, A. Detection of Suicidal Patients: An Example of Some Limitations in the Prediction of Infrequent Events. *Journal of Consulting Psychology*, 1954, *18*, 397–403.

Rotter, J. B. *Social Learning and Clinical Psychology*. Englewood Cliffs, N.J.: Prentice-Hall, 1954.

Sawyer, J. Measurement and Prediction, Clinical and Statistical. *Psychological Bulletin*, 1966, *66*, 178–200.

Schafer, S. *Compensation and Restitution to Victims of Crime*. Montclair, N.J.: Patterson Smith, 1970.

Schafer, S. The Proper Role of a Victim-compensation System. *Crime and Delinquency*, 1975, *21*, 45–49.

Schanche, D. A. Vinyl Chloride: Time Bomb on the Production Line. *Today's Health*, 1974, *52*, 16–19; 70–72.

Scheff, T. J. Decision Rules, Types of Error and Their Consequences in Medical Diagnosis. *Behavioral Science*, 1963, *8*, 97–107.

Schwitzgebel, R. K. Professional Accountability in the Treatment and Release of Dangerous Persons. In B. D. Sales (Ed.), *Perspectives in Law and Psychology: Vol. 1. The Criminal Justice System*. New York: Plenum, 1977.

Scott, R. *Muscle and Blood*. New York: E. P. Dutton, 1974.

Shah, S. A. Crime and Mental Illness: Some Problems in Defining and Labeling Deviant Behavior. *Mental Hygiene*, 1969, *53*, 21–33.

Shah, S. A. Some Interactions of Law and Mental Health in the Handling of Social Deviance. *Catholic University Law Review*, 1974, *23*, 674–719.

Shah, S. A. Dangerousness and Civil Commitment of the Mentally Ill: Some Public Policy Considerations. *American Journal of Psychiatry*, 1975, *132*,

501–505.

Shah, S. A. Some Issues Pertaining to the Dissemination and Utilization of Criminological Research. In *Evaluation Research in Criminal Justice*, proceedings of a conference convened by the United Nations Social Defense Research Institute, Rome, January 1976.

Shah, S. A. Dangerousness: Some Definitional, Conceptual, and Public Policy Issues. In B. D. Sales (Ed.), *Perspectives in Law and Psychology: Vol. 1. The Criminal Justice System*. New York: Plenum, 1977.

Shinnar, R., & Shinnar, S. The Effects of the Criminal Justice System on the Control of Crime: A Quantitative Approach. *Law & Society Review*, 1975, *9*, 581–611.

Starr, B. J., & Katkin, E. S. The Clinician as an Aberrant Actuary: Illusory Correlation and the Incomplete Sentences Blank. *Journal of Abnormal Psychology*, 1969, *74*, 670–675.

Steadman, H. J., & Cocozza, J. J. *Careers of the Criminally Insane*. Lexington, Mass.: Lexington Books, 1974.

Sweetland, J. P. "Illusory Correlation" and the Estimation of "Dangerous" Behavior (Doctoral dissertation, Indiana University, 1972). *Dissertation Abstracts International*, 1973, *33*, 3963B–3964B. (University Microfilms No. 73-4076, 150)

Tapp, J. L. Psychology and the Law: An Overture. *Annual Review of Psychology*, 1976, *27*, 359–404.

Thornberry, T. P., & Jacoby, J. E. *The Social Adjustment of the Released Criminally Insane Offender*. Paper presented at the meeting of the American Society of Criminology, Tucson, Arizona, November 1976.

Tversky, A., & Kahneman, D. Judgment under Uncertainty: Heuristics and Biases. *Science*, 1974, *185*, 1124–1131.

Wenk, E. A., & Emrich, R. L. Assaultive Youth: An Exploratory Study of the Assaultive Experience and Assaultive Potential of California Youth Authority Wards. *Journal of Research in Crime and Delinquency*, 1972, *9*, 171–196.

Wenk, E. A., Robison, J. O., & Smith, G. W. Can Violence Be Predicted? *Crime and Delinquency*, 1972, *18*, 393–402.

Wexler, D. B., & Scoville, S. E. The Administration of Psychiatric Justice: Theory and Practice in Arizona. *Arizona Law Review*, 1971, *13*, 1–259.

White, L., Krumholz, W. V., & Fink, L. The Adjustment of Criminally Insane Patients to a Civil Mental Hospital. *Mental Hygiene*, 1969, *53*, 34–40.

Wilkins, L. T. Perspectives on Court Decision-making. In D. M. Gottfredson (Ed.), *Decision-making in the Criminal Justice System: Reviews and Essays* [DHEW Publication No. (ADM) 75-238]. Washington, D.C.: U.S. Government Printing Office, 1975.

Wilkins, L. T. Equity and Republican Justice. *Annals of the American Academy of Political and Social Science*, 1976, *423*, 152–161.

Wilson, J. Q. *Thinking about Crime*. New York: Basic Books, 1975.

Wohlwill, J. The Emerging Discipline of Environmental Psychology. *American Psychologist*, 1970, *25*, 303–312.

Wolfgang, M. E., Figlio, R. M., & Sellin, T. *Delinquency in a Birth Cohort*. Chicago: University of Chicago Press, 1972.

NOTES

(1) Section 730.50 of New York State's Criminal Procedure Law

mandates a determination of dangerousness for all indicted felony defendants found incompetent to stand trial.

(2) Texas Code of Criminal Procedure, Article 37.071, effective June 14, 1973. Section (b)(2) includes the phrase "whether there is a probability that the defendant would commit criminal acts of violence that would constitute a continuing threat to society" (p. 278).

(3) *Overholser v. Russell*, 283 F.2d 195 (1960).

(4) *Millard v. Cameron*, 373 F.2d 468 (1966).

(5) *Millard v. Harris*, 406 F.2d 964 (1968).

(6) *Cross v. Harris*, 418 F.2d 1095 (1969).

(7) *State v. Krol*, 344 A.2d 289 (1975).

(8) The expression *systematic errors* is used, following Chapman and Chapman (1967), to refer to reliable sources of inaccuracy in certain assessment and prediction tasks.

(9) The "age-adjusted" rate is a single rate derived by taking the age-specific rate (see footnote 10), multiplying by a standard (the total population of the United States for 1940), adding all the hypothetical deaths that would have taken place using this standard, then dividing by the 1940 population, and finally multiplying by a factor K—using a K of 1,000 in computing for all deaths and a K of 100,000 for any specific cause of death.

(10) The "age-specific" rate refers to the number of deaths to persons in a population of a given age group, divided by the total number of persons in the population in that age group, and then multiplied by a factor K (using a K of 1,000 when computing for all deaths and a K of 100,000 for any specific cause of death).

(11) Note that one should not compare the victim survey data directly with the Uniform Crime Reports, since there are a number of definitional and counting rule differences between the two data sources. For example, the Uniform Crime Reports would count a robbery with multiple victims as one robbery, but the Census Victimization Surveys would count the number of victims involved.

(12) This is a rather interesting study of a sample of 49 felons at a medium-security prison who had at least one conviction of armed robbery and who had served at least one previous prison term. The study data were derived from in-depth personal interviews and official criminal justice records. This sample of 49 offenders reported a total of 10,500 crimes, or an average of 214 per offender. Given a criminal career averaging about 20 years (with about half this time spent in prison), each offender committed an average of about 20 major felonies per year. When self-reported crimes were compared with the official data, only 12% of the reported crimes were found to have resulted in a recorded arrest. Two

broad categories of offenders emerged from the sample: the *intensives* (who saw themselves as criminals and went about their crimes in a purposeful manner) and the *intermittents* (who were less likely to see themselves as criminals and whose crimes were less frequent but more recklessly committed). The *intensives* tended to commit several crimes a month but were arrested for only about 5% of their crimes. The *intermittents* had a generally lower frequency of crimes but were much more likely to be arrested.

(13) *Brown v. Board of Education*, 347 U.S. 483 (1954).

(14) Justice Felix Frankfurter in his dissenting opinion in *Solesbee v. Blakcom*, 339 U.S. 9, 16 (1950).

V.

**Psychiatric Disorders
and
Criminality**

Introduction

In Part I some of the problems involved in applying psychiatric and psychological concepts to the interpretation of criminal behavior were discussed. One of the major assumptions of the intrapsychic or "internal-sickness" model of criminality, as Brodsky (1972) has observed, is that "the commission of a crime is indicative of the offender's psychological maladjustment and of his underlying need for professional psychological attention." Halleck (1965) in his historical review of American psychiatry and the criminal, stated that the criminal offender has been a source of interest to the psychiatrist

> . . . because he bears many startling resemblances to those we call mentally ill. When incarcerated (and sometimes before) the offender proved to be a miserable, unhappy person who could be observed to suffer in the same way as the mental patient. Psychoanalytic psychiatry taught us that those psychological mechanisms which produced neurotic suffering were also operant in individuals who demonstrated criminal behavior. These observations fostered psychiatry's hopes of contributing to the understanding and alteration of criminal behavior.

The shortcomings of the approach of criminality-as-illness were thoroughly explored in the selections by Saleem A. Shah and David E. Silber.

The selections in Part V are concerned with a different but related issue: the distribution and frequency of psychiatric or psychological disorders among criminal offenders. The problem is not the application of the medical model to criminal behavior *per se*, but the incidence of disorders that may have no direct causal relationship with the nature and seriousness of the observed criminal offense or offenses.

Research on the incidence of psychiatric disorders in a population of offenders is subject to a great many methodological problems. Early reports of an impressionistic type (Abrahamsen, 1952; Karpman, 1949) stressed the presence of *some* kind of psychopathology in *all* criminals and regarded the "normal offender" as a myth. In the absence of any reasonable constraints on observation, these early reports are of little or no value. Consequently, the contention by Barnes and Teeters (1959) that "the criminal class as a whole (including those not apprehended and arrested as well as those arrested and convicted) is certainly as intelligent and stable, mentally and emotionally, as the general population" is also difficult to evaluate.

Personality comparisons by testing between delinquent populations and control groups of non-delinquents were reviewed by Schuessler and Cressey (1950). These sociological researchers noted that only 47 (or 42%) of the 113 studies they examined were able to differentiate successfully between the two populations. Waldo and Dinitz (1967) reported significant differences in the predicted directions in 47 of 56 objective tests, 6 of 8 performance tests, and 19 out of 30 projective tests. The most successful instrument used was the Minnesota Multiphasic Personality Inventory (M.M.P.I.), which successfully differentiated between groups in 28 of 29 studies reviewed. Seventy-six of the 94 studies reviewed by Waldo and Dinitz reported significant differences between populations; 70 of these studies found significant differences in the directions predicted. Waldo and Dinitz caution, however, against uncritical acceptance of these results, especially when the M.M.P.I. was used.

Brodsky (1972) has provided a tabular summary of studies involving psychiatric evaluations of offenders from 1918 to 1970. As shown by the information reported in Table 1, the reported range of psychotic disturbance was narrow, between 1% and 2% of the population that was assessed. Because of the large time span involved, useful comparisons are difficult to make between studies.

Research on the incidence of psychiatric disorders in a population of offenders is subject to some severe methodological and conceptual difficulties. Diagnostic categories and procedures are markedly dissimilar from study to study; populations differ greatly in terms of key demographic and life history variables, statutory offense definitions, and prior criminal records. Finally, comparative information on control subjects is usually not provided. As Tappan (1960) observed, "Figures on psychoneurosis and psychopathic personality are too variable, as are the

Studies of Psychiatric Evaluations of Offenders

Source	Population	Diagnosis	Percent
Glueck (1918)	608 Sing Sing Prisoners	Psychotic or mentally deteriorated	12.0
		Normal	41.0
		Mentally retarded	28.1
Overholser (1935)	5,000 felons under Briggs Law in Mass.	Abnormal	15.0
		Normal	85.0
Bromberg & Thompson (1937)	9,958 offenders before Court of General Sessions, New York City	Psychotic	1.5
		Psychoneurotic	6.9
		Psychopathic personalities	6.9
		Feebleminded	2.4
		Normal or mild personality defects	82.3
Schilder (1940)	Convicted felons, Court of General Sessions of New York City	Psychotic	1.6
		Neurotic	4.2
		Psychopathic personalities	7.3
		Feebleminded	3.1
		Normal	83.8
Banay (1941)	Sing Sing prisoners	Psychotic	1.0
		Emotionally immature	20.0
		Psychopathic	17.0
		Normal	62.0
Poindexter (1955)	100 problem inmates	Mentally ill	20.0
		Normal	80.0
Schlessinger & Blau (1957)	500 typical prisoners	Character and behavior disorders	85.0
		Normal	15.0
Shands (1958)	1720 North Carolina felon admissions to Central Prison	Psychotic	3.5
		Personality disorder	55.8
		Psychoneurotic	3.9
		Sociopathic personality	7.0
		Other	5.3
		No psychiatric disorder	4.7
		Transient personality disorder	19.8
Brodsky (1970)	32,511 military prisoners	Character and behavior disorders	77.1
		No psychiatric disease	21.3
		Miscellaneous disorders	1.6

concepts themselves, to offer much insight into the prevalence of these disorders among criminals."

Brodsky (1972) identifies what is undoubtedly the most significant of all limitations on the interpretation of studies of psychiatric disorders in offenders:

> They all deal with groups of persons who have gone through criminal justice proceedings. There may well be reason to believe that this experience swells the magnitude of existing psychological difficulties and perhaps plants new ones where few had taken root.

Brodsky quotes Schuessler and Cressey on the difficulties of testing for psychiatric disorders in offenders: "the results of this method do not indicate whether criminal behavior is the result of a certain personality trait or whether the trait is the result of criminal experiences."

REFERENCES

Abrahamsen, D. *Who are the Guilty?* New York: Rinehart, 1952.

Barnes, H. E., and Teeters, N. K. *New Horizons in Criminology.* Englewood Cliffs, New Jersey: Prentice-Hall, 1959.

Brodsky, S. L. (Ed.), *Psychologists in the Criminal Justice System.* Washington, D.C.: American Psychological Association, 1972.

Halleck, S. *Psychiatry and the Dilemmas of Crime.* New York: Harper and Row, 1967.

Karpman, B. Criminality, Insanity and the Law. *Journal of Criminal Law and Criminology,* 1949, 39, 584–605.

Schuessler, K. F., and Cressey, D. R. Personality Characteristics of Criminals. *American Journal of Sociology,* 1950, 56, 476–484.

Tappan, P. W. *Crime, Justice and Correction.* New York: McGraw-Hill, 1960.

Waldo, G., and Dinitz, S. Personality Characteristics of Criminals. *Journal of Research in Crime and Delinquency,* 1967, 3, 1–20.

Forensic Psychiatry:
Diagnosis And
Criminal Responsibility

Fritz A. Henn, Marijan Herjanic, and Robert H. Vanderpearl

This study examines the likelihood of a given psychiatric illness resulting in criminal or violent behavior. It also documents the response of one forensic service to the question of criminal responsibility. In viewing the interface between psychiatry and law, questions concerning the association between psychiatric illnesses, dangerousness, and criminal responsibility are among those most frequently asked. The data we present partially answer the first of these questions in a statistical sense, but are not useful in making predictions concerning a given individual. In this area, we feel that psychiatry has limited ability; as stated by the American Psychiatric Association's Task Force on Violence, "Such judgments (concerning an individual) are fundamentally of very low reliability" (16, p. 2).

The question of responsibility *vis-a-vis* mental illness is answered not scientifically, but philosophically. In general, we can demonstrate how this problem has been dealt with at the Malcolm Bliss Mental Health Center Forensic Service. The issues concerning insanity and competency and the consequence of such judgments before the court reflect the attitude of society as a whole and, as such, are a proper area for legislative definition. What psychiatry can offer is the best information concerning the influence of various mental illnesses on behavior, the expected results of treatment, and an advocacy of the patient's needs consistent with a responsible view of society' requirements.

METHODS

One thousand one hundred ninety-five patients referred to the Forensic Service at Malcolm Bliss Mental Health Center in St. Louis, Missouri between 1952 and 1973 were included in the study. The records were reviewed by the authors, and a questionnaire including criminal charges, diagnosis, referral source, outcome, and demographic variables was completed. The information was coded, punched on computer cards, and processed.

RESULTS

The relationship between the psychiatric diagnosis and the type of crime is presented in Tables 1, 2, and 4. There are more crimes than defendants, as up to two charges were recorded for each patient. Tables 1 and 2 correlate the charges with the principal diagnosis reported to the court for each defendant. To simplify already complicated tables, in Tables 1 through 4, "schizophrenia" includes also patients diagnosed as schizoaffective (16 patients) and probable schizophrenia (30 patients). "Personality disorders" consist of two thirds antisocial personality and about one third other personality disorders. "Alcoholism and drug abuse" consist of three fourths alcoholics and one fourth drug abusers, and "other diagnoses" include sexual deviation, epilepsy, neurosis, and various medical diagnoses.

Homicide is included among "crimes against persons." It is listed separately also, being the most serious charge a defendant could be accused of and proportionately most likely to be referred for psychiatric evaluation. The differences in the proportions of the types of crime for various diagnostic groups are not striking (Tables 1 and 2). Referrals of defendants without psychiatric illness involve crimes against persons to a greater degree than other diagnostic categories, which is a reflection on the criteria for referral and index of suspicion of those responsible for referrals. Among persons with serious psychiatric illnesses which may lead to a defense of insanity (schizophrenia, affective disorder, organic brain syndrome, and mental retardation), schizophrenics and patients with affective disorders are charged with fewer sexual offenses and more crimes against the public, whereas those with organic brain syndrome or mental retardation are charged with more sexual offenses(14). The "other" category, for the most part, is composed of medical complications found in the defendants.

About one quarter of the patients seen in the Forensic Service [313] received an additional psychiatric diagnosis, the most common of which was alcoholism. In Table 3, the secondary diagnoses are listed in order of

TABLE 1. Distribution of diagnosis vs. type of crime

Diagnosis	N	Homicide	Crimes Against Persons [a]	Sex Offenses	Crimes Against Property [b]	Crimes Against Public	No. of Offenses (Total 100%)
		%	%	%	%	%	
Schizophrenia	217	11	33	14	27	26	241
Affective disorders	60	12	32	5	32	31	75
Organic brain syndrome	92	14	42	23	14	21	100
Mental retardation	85	12	32	28	20	20	94
Alcoholism and drug abuse	87	13	33	23	25	19	97
Personality disorder	454	9	32	16	31	21	543
Other diagnosis	129	12	29	40	16	15	147
No psychiatric illness	71	25	49	25	17	9	89
Total patients	1195	12	34	20	25	21	1386

[a]Includes homicide, robbery, and assault.
[b]Includes burglary, larceny, auto theft, arson, and fraud.
[c]Includes all offenses.

TABLE 2. Distribution of types of crime vs. diagnosis

Type of Crime	Schizophrenia	Affective Disorder	Organic Brain Syndrome	Mental Retardation	Alcohol and Drug Abuse	Personality Disorder	Other	No Illness	Total No. of Offenses [a] (100%)
	%	%	%	%	%	%	%	%	
Homicide	16	6	8	7	8	30	11	14	160
Crimes against persons [b]	17	5	10	6	7	37	9	9	469
Sex crimes	12	1	8	10	8	32	21	8	277
Crimes against property [c]	18	7	4	5	7	48	7	4	349
Crimes against public	22	8	7	6	6	40	8	3	291
Total offenses	17	5	7	7	7	39	11	7	1386

[a] Includes all offenses.
[b] Includes homicide, robbery, and assault.
[c] Includes burglary, larceny, auto theft, arson, forgery, and fraud.

frequency. It should be noted that those secondary diagnoses most often seen—alcoholism, drug abuse, mental retardation, epilepsy, and sexual deviations—do not include psychiatric illness commonly giving rise to psychotic states. When primary diagnoses are examined for the number of secondary diagnoses in each group, it is found that over half of the diagnoses of organic brain syndrome are complicated by other problems, the majority of which involve alcohol abuse. In general, alcohol problems dominate complicating conditions seen in all diagnostic categories, however, they appear to play a much smaller role in defendants with

TABLE 3. Secondary diagnosis (1195 cases)

Diagnosis	No.	Diagnosis	No.
Alcoholism	97	Personality disorders	12
Drug addiction	39	Undiagnosed	12
Mental retardation	29	Depression	5
Epilepsy	28	Neurosis (hysterical, anxiety)	3
Sexual deviation	24	Schizophrenia	2
Other	24	Probable schizophrenia	2
Antisocial personality	21	Mania	1
Organic brain syndrome	15	Schizoaffective disorder	0

schizophrenic illnesses than with other primary diagnoses. An inter-relationship between drug and alcohol abuse and antisocial personality is also evident in our sample, for in both forms of chemical dependency antisocial personality is the most frequently seen secondary diagnosis.

Table 4 takes this into consideration, including both first and second diagnoses. The sum of each row is more than 100 percent because each individual diagnosis, first or second, was counted separately. A comparison between Tables 2 and 4 will reveal the influence of secondary diagnoses. As expected, the largest difference is observed in the group, "alcohol and drug abuse." There are some deviations from the average worthy of note. Schizophrenics are least likely to be charged with forgery or fraud, whereas for affective disorder, this is the most common charge. Patients suffering from organic brain syndrome are most likely to be charged with assault. Mentally retarded patients are more frequently charged with arson, whereas this same charge is relatively infrequent for those with personality disorders. As expected, "others," which includes the diagnosis of sexual deviation, are charged more often with sexual crimes, and defendants with no psychiatric illness are charged more often with homicide.

Pretrial examinations resulted in reports to the court concerning the sanity of the defendants and their competence to stand trial. "Insane" refers to the opinion of the psychiatrist regarding the defendant's sanity at the time he committed the criminal act, whereas "incompetent" denotes

TABLE 4. Individual patients charged with type of crimes [a] vs. all diagnoses [b]

Type of Crime	Schizo-phrenia	Affective Disorder	Organic Brain Syndrome	Mental Retar-dation	Alcohol and Drug Abuse	Person-ality Disorder	Other	No Illness	No. of Individual Patients Charged with Crimes (100%)
	%	%	%	%	%	%	%	%	
Homicide	17	6	10	6	15	32	17	13	158
Robbery	15	5	3	8	20	50	17	9	156
Assault	22	6	17	9	22	37	15	5	150
Total crimes against persons 1, 2, 3	18	6	10	10	19	39	16	9	464
Sex crimes	12	2	10	12	15	34	32	8	239
Burglary	21	4	5	8	21	50	14	5	171
Larceny and auto theft	21	10	3	7	17	48	11	2	87
Arson	10	6	8	16	16	25	12	6	49
Forgery and fraud	6	14	8	4	20	56	8	2	50
Total crimes against property 5, 6, 7, 8	18	8	6	9	20	49	13	4	431
Total crimes against public	23	5	8	9	19	45	16	32	272
Total 1st and 2nd diagnosis	15	4	7	8	15	32	15	5	1508

[a]Includes first and second charge. Individuals charged with two counts of the same crime included only once.
[b]Diagnoses include first and second.
[c]Total of a row is more than 100 percent because some individual patients have more than one diagnosis.

the opinion that the defendant is too ill to stand trial. Significant changes in these reports occurred with regard to competency, especially in the case of defendants suffering from chronic psychosis. The proportion of the defendants judged incompetent to stand trial, while insane at the time of the crime, has decreased over the years(15). Tables 5 and 6 present the relationship between diagnosis and types of crime on one side, and competency to stand trial and insanity on the other. As expected, there are more patients thought to be insane than those incompetent to stand

TABLE 5. Relationship among competency, sanity, and diagnosis [a]

Diagnosis	No.	Incompetent	Insane
		%	%
Schizophrenia	217	48	71
Affective disorder	60	38	55
Organic brain syndrome	92	41	54
Mental retardation	85	21	33
Alcohol and drug abuse	87	1	5
Personality disorders	454	1	2
Other diagnoses	129	12	16
No psychiatric illness	71		

[a]First diagnosis only.

TABLE 6. Relationship among competency, sanity, and crimes [a]

Type of Crime	No.	Incompetent	Insane
		%	%
Homicide	158	20	27
Crimes against persons	433	18	28
Sex crimes	229	12	16
Crimes against property	314	17	25
Crimes against public	219	20	26

[a]Includes first crime only.
[b]Includes homicide, robbery, and assault.
[c]Includes burglary, larceny, auto theft, arson, forgery, and fraud.

trial. Schizophrenia is the leading cause of both insanity and incompetency, followed by organic brain syndrome. The relatively low proportion of incompetent or insane defendants with mental retardation reflects the fact that the diagnosis was quantitated as mild, moderate, or severe, with the majority being mildly retarded. There is no substantial difference in the proportion of incompetent or insane defendants, depending on the type of crime (Table 5), with the exception of sex crimes, which have considerably lower rates.

DISCUSSION

The question of an association between psychiatric disorders and criminality has been studied in a variety of populations. Although it is impossible to gather a truly representative sample at any point in the criminal process, from the commission of the criminal act to the parole of defendants, it is possible to approach the question from several vantage points. A systematic investigation of 223 male criminals in prison or on parole in the state of Missouri(10) has shown that serious psychiatric illness is rare among convicted criminals. Among them, there were none with a diagnosis of affective disorder, two (< 1 per cent) with schizophrenia, one (< 1 per cent) with organic brain syndrome, and 16 with mental deficiency, only one of whom was considered to have a degree of intellectual impairment sufficiently great to preclude a normal self-sufficient life in the community. Fifty-two per cent of the subjects had received a psychiatric diagnosis. Most frequent by far was alcoholism. The study had included defendants from a wider area in the state of Missouri than our study. Considering this and the fact that some defendants with a diagnosis of serious psychiatric illness in our own study were judged as competent and sane, we feel justified to conclude that practically all defendants with serious psychiatric illness were included in our sample and that our results may serve as a base from which to calculate frequencies with which patients with serious psychiatric illnesses (schizophrenia, affective disorders, organic brain syndrome, and mental retardation) get involved in criminal activities, especially when serious crimes are involved. In the case of a patient with an obvious psychiatric illness, minor charges may have been dropped.

To be able to estimate the involvement of psychiatrically ill patients in criminal offenses, the chance has to be high for both discovering the criminal offense and the existing mental illness(12). These conditions are met only for homicides where: practically all crimes are discovered; about 80 per cent of crimes are solved(23); and proportionally the highest number of arrested defendants were sent for psychiatric evaluation(13). There were 1927 persons arrested for homicide in St. Louis between 1964 and 1973, inclusive. During the same time period, 19 of those defendants were found to suffer from schizophrenia, schizo-affective disorder, or probable schizophrenia, giving an incidence of 0.98 per cent. The estimated rate for schizophrenia among defendants charged with homicide is very near the estimated prevalence of this illness in an urban, racially mixed population(18,19). The estimated rates for other serious illnesses are: affective disorders (in all cases, depression), an incidence of 0.36 per cent; organic brain syndromes, 0.52 per cent incidence; and mental retardation, 0.47 per cent incidence. These are considerably lower rates than expected in the general population. The total estimated rate for all major psychiatric illnesses is 2.33 per cent. This is similar to that found by Hafner and Boker(12) of 2.97 per cent for the proportion of defendants involved in violent assaults suffering from a serious psychiatric illness.

The finding that between 2 and 3 per cent of offenders charged with violent crimes suffer from a serious psychiatric illness in both our study and the German investigation suggests that the prevalence of mental illness among violent criminal offenders and the general population is roughly comparable, with mental illness in fact being found somewhat less among offenders than in the general population. This is in agreement with a series of older studies(1, 7, 20), the most complete(7) of which reported an arrest rate for mental patients about one fourth of that found for the general population. This contrasts with the more recent reports of Zitrin *et al.*(23), Rappeport and Lessen(21), and Giovannoni and Gurel(8). In these studies, attempts were made to calculate arrest rates for psychiatric patients and some were found to be higher than those found in the general population. The latter two studies are suspect because of a lack of correlation of diagnosis with arrest rate. The number of violent offenses in both studies was very small, allowing contributions by a few antisocial or alcoholic offenders to skew the results. The recent work of Zitrin *et al.*(24) follows 867 patients admitted to Bellevue Hospital in New York from July 1969 through June 1970. This study found that 10 per cent of patients receiving a diagnosis of schizophrenia had been arrested between 1968 and 1972. The arrest rate for murder and robbery is no higher than that found in the general population living in the area of the hospital; however, the rates for rape, assault, and burglary are higher. This study does not give criteria for diagnosis. Indications are that a large proportion of the patients diagnosed as schizophrenic charged with violent acts (N = 42) had considerable alcohol abuse (52 arrests for intoxication among these 42 individuals). Guze *et al.*(11) found that alcoholism, drug abuse, and antisocial personality were the features of arrests in a psychiatric clinic population. This suggests that alcoholism, rather than schizophrenia, may account for the arrest rate found by Zitrin *et al.*(24). It appears from our data that there is no evidence that psychotic patients commit serious crimes against persons or sexual crimes with greater frequency than the general population. Patients with affective illness definitely commit such crimes less frequently.

Comparing the diagnostic breakdown of our study with that found in other forensic services illustrates the role of the law in defining the population of defendants sent for psychiatric evaluation. In those areas in which misdemeanors and minor offenses result frequently in involvement of the criminal justice system, forensic services are dominated by schizophrenics(2,4,24). In services involving predominantly felons, such as ours, the proportion of defendants with personality disorders, predominantly antisocial, dominates(5,9). One exception to this generalization involves the high proportion of schizophrenic patients reported by Jablon(15) from Philadelphia.

The data on secondary diagnoses demonstrate the influence of alcohol and drug abuse on serious criminal activities. The proportion of these defendants charged with crimes against persons, sexual offenses, or crimes against property is exceeded only by defendants with a personality disorder (mainly antisocial personality). The recent findings of Tinklenberg *et al.*(22) on the role of alcohol and Seconal in violent offenses coupled with our data on the use of alcohol and drugs in a psychiatric population suggest that this may be the single most important factor in the genesis of violent crimes.

The questions of competency to stand trial and the insanity plea are complex and fraught with disagreement. The history of English and American criminal law points out that culpability is considered an essential factor in invoking the criminal law justice system(3). Although this is the primary factor in keeping the insanity defense, the issue of competency involves more, for the finding of incompetency eliminates the right to trial and an indefinite commitment to a mental hospital may be substituted. Recent efforts to define criteria for incompetency to stand trial(16) suggest that the diagnosis of psychosis in itself is no bar to competency. Our Forensic Service, which operates under Missouri law using McNaughten criteria, followed a practice of active treatment in the most recent time interval studied. Active treatment of psychiatrically ill defendants accounts for the dramatic rise from less than 17 per cent to more than 65 per cent of insane defendants being found competent to stand trial. Those defendants not responding to treatment and found incompetent without the probability of responding should be considered as candidates for civil commitment as suggested by *Jackson vs Indiana (406,* US 715, 1972). Examining the disparity within the proportion of insane and incompetent defendants in each diagnostic category, as expected, we find that the differences were smallest in organic illness (organic brain syndrome and mental retardation). In spite of the fact that psychosis is only rarely a cause of serious criminal activity, there are cases in which this is so. For these individuals, the question of criminal responsibility is valid, and by rejecting the involvement of psychiatry in these exceptional cases, one would eliminate all rehabilitative elements from the criminal justice system and substitute forces protective of society but punitive to the individual. At the same time, psychiatrists must sharply reject the utilization of criminal commitment as an easier alternative to getting the mentally ill involved in treatment, as may have happened subsequent to the Lanterman-Petris-Short Act in California(17). Such misuse of the competency procedures invites the extremes of either utilization of psychiatric facilities for control of political and social dissidents or the elimination of the commitment option, resulting in unnecessary failure to treat a treatable group of criminal defendants.

NOTES

(1) Ashley, M. C. Outcome of 1000 Cases Paroled from the Middletown State Hospital, State Hosp. Q. (N.Y.), 8: 64–70, 1922.

(2) Bearcroft, J. S. A Comparison of Psychiatric Admissions from Prison and Other Sources. *Br. J. Psychiatry, 112:* 581–587, 1966.

(3) Becker, L. E. Durham Revisited: Psychiatry and the Problem of Crime. *Psychiatr. Ann.*, 3: 17–49, 1973.

(4) Binns, J. K., Carlisle, J., Nimmo, D., Park, R. H., and Todd. N. A. Remanded in Custody for Psychiatric Examination. *Br. J. Psychiatry,* 115: 1133–1139, 1969.

(5) Binns, J. K., Carlisle, J., Nimmo D., Park, R. H., and Todd, N. A. Remanded in Hospital for Psychiatric Examination. *Br. J. Psychiatry,* 115: 1125–1132, 1969.

(6) Brill, H., and Malzberg, B. Statistical Report Based on the Arrest Record of 5.354 Male Expatients Released from New York State Mental Hospitals during the Period 1946–48. *Ment. Hosp. Serv. Suppl. Am. Psychiatr. Soc.*, 153: August, 1962.

(7) Cohen, L. H., and Freeman, H. How Dangerous to the Community Are State Hospital Patients? *Conn. Med.*, 9: 697–700, 1945.

(8) Giovannoni, J. M., and Gurel, L. Socially Disruptive Behavior of Ex-mental Patients. *Arch. Gen. Psychiatry*, 17: 146–153, 1967.

(9) Greenland, C., and Rosenblatt, E. Remands for Psychiatric Examination in Ontario 1969–70. *Can. Psychiatr. Assoc. J.*, 17: 397–401, 1972.

(10) Guze, S. B., Tuason, V. B., Gatfield, P. D., *et al.* Psychiatric Illness and Crime with Particular Reference to Alcoholism: A Study of 223 Criminals. *J. Nerv. Ment. Dis.*, 134: 512–521, 1962.

(11) Guze, S. B., Woodruff. R. A., and Clayton, P. J. Psychiatric Disorders and Criminality. *J. A. M. A.*, 227: 641–642, 1974.

(12) Hafner, H., and Boker, W. Mentally Disordered Violent Offenders. *Soc. Psychiatry*, 8: 220–229, 1973.

(13) Henn, F. A., Herjanic, M., and Vanderpearl, R. H. Forensic Psychiatry Anatomy of a Service. in preparation.

(14) Henn, F. A., Herjanic, M., and Vanderpearl, R. H. Forensic Psychiatry: Profiles of Sexual Offenders. *Am. J. Psychiatry.* In press, 1975.

(15) Jablon, N., Sadoff, R., and Heller, M. A Unique Forensic Diagnostic Hospital. *Am. J. Psychiatry*, 126: 1663–1667, 1970.

(16) Lion, J., and Kenefick, D. Clinical Aspects of the Violent individual. *Task Force Report,* p. 2 American Psychiatric Association, Washington, D.C., 1974.

(17) McGarry, A. L., and Curran, W. J. Competency to Stand Trial and Mental Illness. *Crime and Delinquency Issues Monograph.* National Institutes of Health Center for Studies of Crime and Delinquency. Bethesda, Maryland, 1972.

(18) Norris, V. *Mental Illness in London, Maudsley Monograph No. 6.* Chapman and Hall, London, 1959.

(19) Pasamanick, B., Lemkau, P. V., Roberts, D. W., and Krueger, D. E. A Survey of Mental Disease in an Urban Population. I. Prevalence by Age, Sex, and Severity of Impairment. *Am. J. Public Health,* 47: 923-931, 1957.

(20) Pollock, H. M. Is the Paroled Patient a Menace to the Community? Psychiatr. Q., 12: 236-244, 1938.

(21) Rappeport, J. R., and Lassen, G. Dangerousness—Arrest Rate Comparisons of Discharged Patients and the General Population. *Am. J. Psychiatry,* 121: 776-783, 1965.

(22) Tinklenberg, J. R., Murphy, P. L., Murphy, P., Darley, C. F., Roth, W. T., and Kopell, B. S. Drug Involvement in Criminal Assaults by Adolescents. *Arch. Gen. Psychiatry,* 30: 685-689, 1974.

(23) Uniform Crime Reports for the United States, 1973, Document 2701-00012. United States Government Printing Office, Washington, D.C.

(24) Zitrin, A., Hardesty, A., Burdock, E., and Drossman, A. Crime and Violence among Mental Patients. *Sci. Proc. of the 128th Annual Meeting of the American Psychiatric Association, Abs.,* 142: 140-141, 1975.

Criminality and Psychiatric Disorders

Samuel B. Guze, Donald W. Goodwin, and J. Bruce Crane

The widespread concern over the apparently increasing crime rate needs no documentation. The extent of criminal behavior may be suggested by the following quotation from the 1967 report entitled *The Challenge of Crime in a Free Society* of the President's Commission on Law Enforcement and Administration of Justice. "In the United States today, one boy in six is referred to the juvenile court. A Commission survey shows that in 1965 more than two million Americans were received in prisons or juvenile training schools, or placed on probation." The report estimates that the annual cost of crime in the United States is about 21 billion dollars, of which about 4.2 billion dollars are for public expenditures such as police, courts, and prisons.

The role of psychiatry in understanding and modifying this extensive and costly criminal behavior is not clear and is a subject of controversy. Since 1959, the senior author, with the help of many colleagues, has been trying to characterize and measure the associations between criminality and psychiatric disorders.(18) This long-term investigation began with a systematic psychiatric and social study of a consecutive series of 223 convicted male felons (121 parolees and 102 "flat-timers"). The goal as originally stated was "to determine the prevalence and kinds of psychiatric disorders in such a population, and to note any possible associations . . . between psychiatric illness, family history, parental home experience, delinquency, and crime history, and school, job, military, and marital histories."(1)

The original study of the convicted criminals was supplemented by interviews with relatives about the index subjects, systematic and comprehensive criminal recidivism data after three years of follow-up, an analysis of the parole experience of the 121 parolees in the original sample during a period of more than three years of parole, and an extensive psychiatric study of first-degree relatives carried out three to five years after the original examination of the index criminals. A great deal of social, medical, and psychiatric data has been accumulated and analyzed, but for purposes of this paper the following conclusions are relevant. Sociopathy, alcoholism, and drug addiction were the only psychiatric disorders found more frequently among the index subjects than in the general population. The only psychiatric disorders seen more frequently among their first-degree relatives than in the general population were sociopathy, alcoholism, drug addiction, and hysteria. The first three were found chiefly in the male relatives, and hysteria was found only in the female relatives. Whether among the index subjects or among their relatives, sociopathy, alcoholism, and drug addiction were frequently seen in the same individual.

These results have great practical consequences. The absence of an increased prevalence of schizophrenia, manic-depressive disease, or organic brain syndromes raises questions about the adequacy or relevance of many discussions concerning psychiatric illness and criminal responsibility, since such discussions usually exclude from consideration sociopathy, alcoholism, and drug addiction. When increased prevalence rates for schizophrenia, manic-depressive disease, and organic brain syndromes were not found in the original sample, it seemed appropriate to ask whether some cases of these conditions were in fact incorrectly diagnosed sociopathy, alcoholism, or drug addiction. The absence of increased prevalence rates for the first three disorders among the first-degree relatives indicated that this was probably not so. Nevertheless, one of the reasons for carrying out the present follow-up study of the index subjects was to determine the validity of the original diagnoses.

METHOD

The follow-up interviews were conducted between July 1967 and October 1968. The interviewers at follow-up, while familiar with the results of the study up to that point, did not know the individual diagnoses of the men, nor did they consult the original interview record until after the follow-up interview had been completed. The follow-up interviews were conducted in our hospital, in other psychiatric and general hospitals, in private homes, in jails, in places of work, at airports, in hotel rooms, and, in a few cases, via long-distance telephone. Men were located and interviewed in nearly one-half the states from New Hampshire to California and from Florida to Washington. When each subject was contacted, he was reminded of the original interview, and his cooperation was solicited for the follow-up interview. Each individual was reimbursed for his time, in addition to any travel expenses he might have incurred, receiving $10 if he came to a place convenient to the interviewer or $5 if the interview was conducted at the subject's home. A few subjects receive $20 because of special circumstances.

Research assistants kept a detailed log of the search for each individual, noting all contacts with the subject, his friends, relatives, employers, police, etc. Any comments, suggestions, descriptions, or other information obtained from these sources were recorded. All kinds of records were gathered: police, prison, parole, hospital, clinic, private physician, vital statistics, military service, insurance, etc. Whenever possible, wives of the men were also systematically interviewed. The results of these interviews will be presented elsewhere.

The same structured interview was used as in the original study. It included a history of current and past illnesses and injuries; a description of all hospitalizations and operations; and a detailed symptom inventory designed to elicit the manifestations of anxiety neurosis, hysteria, obsessional neurosis, schizophrenia, manic-depressive disease, organic brain syndrome, alcoholism, drug dependency, sociopathy, and homosexuality. In addition, a detailed family history of psychiatric difficulties and a history of parental home experience were obtained. The interview also included sections dealing with school history, job history, marital history, military experiences, and police troubles. Specific inquiry was also made about suicide attempts. A mental status examination concluded the interview. Specific criteria were provided for scoring individual items. In general, these criteria selected symptoms or features that appeared to be medically significant because they required treatment or interfered with the subject's normal life.

DIAGNOSTIC CRITERIA

The diagnostic criteria were the same as those used in the original study with some slight modifications as noted below.

The general definition of anxiety neurosis for this study was taken from Wheeler et al.(9) Subjects were included in this category if they met one of the following criteria: 1. they presented a history of recurrent nervousness plus either dyspnea or palpitation; 2. they presented a history of both recurrent dyspnea and palpitation; or 3. they presented a history of recurrent anxiety attacks. In addition, such symptoms had to occur in the absence of exertion, overtly frightening experiences such as near accidents, or evidence of cardiac or chest disease. Anxiety symptoms in patients with hysteria, obsessional neurosis, schizophrenia, or manic-depressive disease (see below) would not lead to a separate diagnosis of anxiety neurosis. Such symptoms in subjects with organic brain syndrome, alcoholism, drug dependency, sociopathy, or homosexuality (see below) would lead to an additional diagnosis of anxiety neurosis.

The general definition of hysteria for this study was from Purtell et al.(10) The specific criteria of Perley and Guze(11) were used. To receive a diagnosis of hysteria, the following criteria had to be met. 1. The patient had to present a dramatic or complicated medical history beginning before the age of 35. 2. The patient had to report at least 25 of the following symptoms distributed among at least nine of these ten groups of symptoms: group 1—feeling sickly for most of life, headache; group 2—blindness, paralysis, anesthesia, aphonia, fits or convulsions, unconsciousness, amnesia, deafness, hallucinations (in the absence of a psychosis), or urinary retention; group 3—fatigue, lump in the throat, fainting spells, visual blurring, weakness or dysuria: group 4—breathing difficulty, palpitation, anxiety attacks, chest pain, or dizziness; group 5—anorexia, weight loss, marked fluctuations in weight, nausea, abdominal bloating, food intolerances, diarrhea, or constipation: group 6—abdominal pain or vomiting; group 7—dysmenorrhea, menstrual irregularity, including amenorrhea for at least two months, or excessive menstrual bleeding; group 8—sexual indifference, sexual frigidity, dyspareunia, other sexual difficulties, hospitalization for hyperemesis gravidarum, or vomiting for all nine months of pregnancy; group 9—back pain, joint pain, extremity pain, burning pains of the sexual organs, mouth, or rectum, or other bodily pains: and group 10—nervousness, fears, depressed feelings, need to quit work or inability to carry on regular duties because of feeling sick, crying easily, feeling life was hopeless, thinking a good deal about dying, wanting to die, thinking of suicide, or suicide attempts 3. No other diagnosis could be made to explain the symptoms.

The diagnostic criteria for obsessional neurosis were similar to those of Pollitt.(12) In order to receive this diagnosis, a subject had to report an obsession, defined as a recurrent or persistent idea, thought, image, feeling, impulse, or movement, which is accompanied by a sense of subjective compulsion and a desire to resist it, the vent being recognized by the individual as foreign to his personality or nature ("ego-alien"). An obsessional neurosis would be one in which such obsessional symptoms were the dominant feature of the case. Subjects with so-called obsessional personality patterns but without specific obsessions and subjects whose obsessions were secondary to schizophrenia or manic-depressive disease would be excluded from this diagnostic group.

The diagnosis of schizophrenia was used as described by Langfeldt(13) and Stephens et al(14) to refer to a chronic, frequently progressive disorder characterized by an insidious onset, poor prepsychotic adjustment, prominent delusions or hallucinations, severe disability in interpersonal relationships and job performance, minimal, if any, affective symptoms, and a clear sensorium.

The diagnosis of manic-depressive disease was used for all primary affective disorders (primary depressions and manias). The specific criteria of Cassidy et al were followed.(15) In order to receive this diagnosis a subject had to report 1. a mood change including any of the following: blue, worried, discouraged, depressed, anxious, low, high, scared, fearful, angry, afraid, gloomy, hopeless, despondent, "don't care," happy, "never better," "tops," empty or disgusted; 2. at least six of the following ten symptoms: thinking slow; poor appetite; constipation; insomnia; feeling tired; loss of concentration; suicidal ideas; weight loss; decreased sex interest; agitation manifested by wringing hands, pacing, over-talkativeness, press of complaints; 3. an episode of illness arising without preexisting psychiatric difficulties or symptoms, eg, without preexisting anxiety neurosis, hysteria, alcoholism, schizophrenia, etc. If such preexisting illnesses existed, the affective disturbance was considered to be secondary and the subject was grouped under the primary disorder.

The diagnosis of organic brain syndrome was used to include disorders characterized by evidence of significant memory impairment and disorientation. Slight memory impairment in subjects over age 60 was ignored.

Our interview included many of the symptoms of alcoholism emphasized by Jellinek.(16) In order to receive a diagnosis of alcoholism, symptoms in at least three of the following four groups were required. Group 1 included: 1. tremors or any manifestations of delirium tremens, or a history of cirrhosis; 2. impotence associated with drinking; 3. alcoholic "blackout"; 4. alcoholic binges or benders. Group 2 included: 1. subject had not been able to stop drinking when he wanted to stop; 2. subject tried to control drinking by allowing himself to drink only under certain circumstances such as only after 5 PM, or only on weekends, or only with other people; 3. drinking before breakfast; 4. drinking non-beverage forms of alcohol. Group 3 included: 1. arrests for drinking; 2. traffic difficulties associated with drinking; 3. trouble at work because of drinking; 4. fighting associated with drinking. Group 4 included: 1. subject felt he drank too much; 2. family objected to his drinking; 3. other people objected to his drinking; 4. he lost friends because of drinking; 5. he felt guilty about his drinking.

In the original study,(1) the criteria for alcoholism included items concerning frequency and quantity of drinking. Further experience indicated that the reliability and validity of the data concerning frequency or quantity of drinking were hard to establish. On reviewing the 96 index cases who received the diagnosis of alcoholism, it was found that items dealing with frequency and quantity of drinking could be omitted without affecting the diagnosis. Such items, therefore, were excluded from consideration in subsequent alcoholism diagnoses.

A diagnosis of questionable alcoholism was made when there was a drinking problem, but the specific criteria for the diagnosis of alcoholism were not fulfilled: eg, if a subject reported three or more symptoms but these were limited to two groups, or if a subject reported such striking symptoms as binges and job troubles.

The diagnosis for drug dependency was used to include subjects who reported withdrawal symptoms, hospitalization for addiction, or recurrent and prolonged use of drugs. A diagnosis of questionable drug dependency was used when the history was uncertain but drug dependency was strongly suspected. (We use the diagnosis drug dependency instead of drug addiction in keeping with the recently revised diagnostic classification of the American Psychiatric Association.)

The diagnosis for sociopathy was made if at least two of the following five manifestations were present in addition to a history of police trouble (other than traffic offenses): a history of excessive fighting, school delinquency, a poor job record, a period of wanderlust, or being a runaway. If any of the individual diagnostic criteria were scored as questionable, the subject received a diagnosis of questionable sociopathy. For the wives, a history of prostitution could be substituted for one of the five manifestations.

The diagnosis of homosexuality was used for subjects who indicated recurrent or persistent homosexual experiences. In addition, any overt homosexual experience reported by the subject was scored for separate analysis.

If a subject was thought to be ill or reported a number of possible psychiatric symptoms and yet failed to fit into any of the above diagnostic categories, he was placed in the group of undiagnosed disorders.

All the interviews and other data were reviewed by the senior author to assure uniformity of recording and scoring. Pertinent data from the follow-up, from the original study, and from various records were scored and coded for machine and computer analysis. This report will deal only with the psychiatric diagnoses. Other results will be described in subsequent publications.

RESULTS

There were 223 men in the original sample. Of these, we were able to locate 209 or 94%. The other 14 men, or 6%, could not be found. Among the 209 located men were 5 who had died, 2 who were abroad, 26 who refused to be interviewed or who were so uncooperative that we considered them as refusals, and 176 who were personally interviewed.

The dead men had died an average of three years after the initial interview. Their average age at death was 48 with a range of 21 to 81. Two were Negro. Two were married and one was a widower, having murdered his wife as the index crime. At the original interview, each had received the diagnoses of sociopathy and alcoholism. Two were definite alcoholics and three were questionable cases. No other diagnoses had been made. At least two of the men had been involved in another felony subsequent to the original study. The causes of death, obtained from their death certificates, were: cancer of the liver with cirrhosis, bullet wound of heart, bronchopneumonia, auto accident, and stab wound of the heart. Thus, three died a violent death and a fourth probably from liver complications of alcoholism.

Of the two men who were abroad, one was with the army in Vietnam and the other had been deported to Frankfurt, Germany. We were thus not able to interview these men.

The 176 men whom we interviewed represented 79% of the original sample of 87% of those located alive in the United States.

Table 1 presents the diagnoses made at the time of the first interview for the 176 men interviewed at follow-up as well as the diagnoses made originally for the entire sample of 223 men. It is apparent that the subjects we interviewed at follow-up did not differ from the full sample in the distribution of psychiatric diagnoses. In addition, none of the men who refused to be interviewed was in a psychiatric hospital or, so far as could be determined, was receiving psychiatric treatment at the time of contact. We were able to interview similar proportions of parolees and "flat-timers," 77% of the former and 81% of the latter. When the success of follow-up is compared by race, we find that we interviewed 77% of the white subjects and 85% of the Negro subjects. None of these differences between the interviewed subjects and the total sample is statistically significant, and we may thus conclude that psychiatric illness, criminal classification, and race did not determine which men we were able to interview.

Table 1 also presents the diagnoses made at follow-up, at both interviews, and at either interview for the 176 men who were followed and interviewed. It is clear that there was some inconsistency of diagnosis between the two examinations, but the distribution of diagnoses at

TABLE 1. Psychiatric Diagnoses

Diagnosis	Diagnosis At Original Interview Full Sample No. = 223 %	Men Seen At Follow-up No. = 176 Diagnosis At Original Interview %	Diagnosis At Follow-up Interview %	Diagnosis At Both Interviews %	Diagnosis At Either Interview %
Anxiety neurosis	12	12	9	2	17
Hysteria	0	0	0	0	0
Obsessional neurosis	0	0	0	0	0
Schizophrenia	1	1	1	<1	2
Manic depressive disease	0	0	0	0	0
Organic brain syndrome	<1	0	2	0	2
Sociopathy					
Definite	79	78	56	52	81
Questionable	0	0	4	0	4
Total	79	78	60		
Either				56	81
Alcoholism					
Definite	43	43	39	26	56
Questionable	11	12	15	<1	26
Total	54	55	54		
Either				40	67
Drug Dependency					
Definite	5	7	9	5	11
Questionable	0	0	4	0	4
Total	5	7	13		
Either				6	14
Homosexuality					
Ever	8	10	14	6	18
Significant	<1	<1	0	0	<1
Undiagnosed	<1	0	5	0	5

follow-up was similar to that at the initial study. Again, the principal psychiatric disorders seen were sociopathy, alcoholism, and drug dependency. The results of the two interviews indicate that sociopathy was present in from 56% to 81% of the men, alcoholism in from 40% to 67%, and drug dependency in from 6% to 14%.

Anxiety neurosis was seen in from 2% to 17%, but no cases of obsessional neurosis or hysteria were found.

Three subjects received the diagnosis of schizophrenia at least once. The two men who received this diagnosis originally were both studied at follow-up. One man received this diagnosis at each interview, another only at the first, and third man only at follow-up. On the basis of all the information available at follow-up, the second man probably suffered from a schizophreniform reaction associated with the illicit use of drugs that cleared completely before follow-up. The third man was somewhat paranoid at the time of the first interview, but this was not considered significant. By the time of follow-up, however, it was apparent that the original paranoid ideas were the beginnings of a chronic delusional disorder.

No subject received the diagnosis of manic-depressive disease at either time of study. At follow-up, three subjects reported a history of at least one episode of significant depression. These were considered secondary depressions since each man received the diagnoses of sociopathy and alcoholism at both interviews; one of these men also received the diagnoses of anxiety neurosis and organic brain syndrome at follow-up.

The one man with organic brain syndrome at the original interview was not followed. Three other men received the diagnosis of organic brain syndrome at follow-up. One was described in the previous paragraph. The second also received the diagnoses of sociopathy and epilepsy at both interviews. The third was considered a sociopath at both interviews and a questionable alcoholic at follow-up.

The percentage of men describing any homosexual experience was between 6 and 18, but the only man who was originally considered to be significantly homosexual denied any homosexuality at follow-up.

There was one subject with an undiagnosed psychiatric disorder in the original study. He was not among the men seen at follow-up. Eight men received this diagnosis at follow-up, though for five of them, it was in addition to definite diagnoses of both sociopathy and alcoholism. Four of the eight men reported a history of a chronic anxiety neurosis-like disorder without the diagnostic cardiorespiratory symptoms. Two other men reported depressions that did not meet the diagnostic criteria. They required medical attention, though only one saw a psychiatrist. This man (with diagnoses of sociopathy and alcoholism at both interviews) had received electric convulsive therapy (ECT) as a psychiatric inpatient. A seventh man complained only of mild palpitation but had been in group psychotherapy for several years. The last man was in a psychiatric hospital with symptoms suggesting schizophrenia, but was considered undiagnosed because of a history of excessive amphetamine use. It was not possible to rule out an amphetamine psychosis.

There were four diagnoses made frequently enough both originally and at follow-up to permit an analysis of the consistency of diagnosis: sociopathy, alcoholism, drug dependency, and anxiety neurosis. In addition, a history of any homosexual experiences was also obtained often enough for such analysis. The patterns of each diagnosis are presented in Table 2.

Of those originally diagnosed sociopathy, 72% continued to receive this diagnosis (definite or questionable) at follow-up, while 18% of those who did not receive this diagnosis originally received it at follow-up. For alcoholism (adding definite and questionable cases) the corresponding figures were 74% and 28%; for drug dependency, 90% and 8%; for anxiety neurosis, 29% and 6%; and for any homosexuality, 59% and 9%.

COMMENT

The results of the follow-up have confirmed the conclusions from the original study and from the family study. Sociopathy, alcoholism, and drug dependency are the principal psychiatric disorders found in association with criminality (defined as being convicted of a felony). Schizophrenia, manic-depressive disease, and organic brain syndromes apparently are not seen more frequently in a group of criminals than in the general population. The neuroses, with the possible exception of an increased prevalence of hysteria among the female relatives, do not show any apparent association with criminality. Neither does homosexuality.

The high rates for sociopathy, alcoholism, and drug dependency are striking. One problem in this investigation is that it has not been possible to study a control group from the general population, matching individuals for age, race, socioeconomic, and other factors. The study of first-degree male relatives, however, did provide a control group similar in many ways to the index subjects. Increased prevalence rates for sociopathy, alcoholism, and drug dependency were found among these relatives,(7) but the rates were lower than those found in the index subjects. Population surveys(17–21) using similar diagnostic criteria have found much lower prevalence rates for these disorders in the general population than were found in the index subjects or their first-degree relatives.

The low prevalence of schizophrenia and manic-depressive disease warrant additional comment. Possibly these conditions may be more

TABLE 2. Patterns of diagnoses among the 176 men studied at follow-up

Diagnosis at Original Interview	Diagnosis at Follow-up Interview	Sociopathy %	Alcoholism %	Drug Dependency %	Anxiety Neurosis %	Homosexuality Ever %
Definite	Definite	52	26	5	3	6
Definite	Questionable	4	7	1	<1	
Definite	None	22	10	<1	8	4
Questionable	Definite		7			
Questionable	Questionable		<1			
Questionable	None		4			
None	Definite	3	6	5	5	8
None	Questionable	<1	7	3		
None	None	19	33	86	83	82

common in certain circumstances or in association with particular crimes; for example, manic-depressive disease may be more common in cases of murder followed by suicide.(22) But these illnesses play only a small role in association with general criminality. In fact, even if we add together the cases in which any consideration was given to the diagnosis of schizophrenia or depression, and include all cases missed in the original selection procedure,(2) the maximum combined prevalence for these disorders would be about 7%. This combined prevalence is not very different from that expected in the general population.

The two interviews showed a prevalence rate for anxiety neuroses ranging between 2% and 17%. If the correct figure is 17%, it would suggest an increased prevalence of anxiety neurosis. The inconsistency in diagnosis between the two interviews, however, should be noted. Only 2% received this diagnosis at both interviews, although the prevalence rates at each interview were similar: 12% at the first interview and 9% at the follow-up interview. The inconsistency may be due to the fact that many of the symptoms reported in the first interview were so mild and transient that they were more likely to be forgotten by the subjects or misunderstood by the interviewers than were symptoms of sociopathy, alcoholism, and drug dependency. At any rate, the absence of an increased prevalence of anxiety neurosis in the first-degree relatives compared to the general population(7) suggests that the prevalence of 9% at follow-up among the index subjects may be close to the correct figure. This value is within the range reported for the general population in studies using similar diagnostic criteria.(9,23)

Only one man was ever considered to be significantly homosexual. Eighteen percent of the men, at least at one interview, reported one or more homosexual experiences. Since the men at follow-up were generally in their mid-30's and had completed little more than eight years of school, the figure of 18% varies little from that reported by Kinsey et al. These authors report for such men an incidence of homosexual experience of between 22% and 24%.(24) In view of the widespread belief that homosexual practices are common in prison, it is worth noting that many of the subjects reporting homosexual experiences insisted they had occurred only outside of prison.

The conclusions of our study are strengthened by the special features of the over-all investigation. The original sample was selected without psychiatric bias; a consecutive series of cases was studied in a systematic way; the diagnoses were made in accordance with specific criteria; and the diagnoses were validated by family and follow-up studies. While many discussions about criminality and psychiatric illness are predicated upon a presumed frequent association between crime and schizophrenia, there are no known published studies of *unselected* criminals studied in a systematic way, using explicit diagnostic criteria validated by follow-up or family study, that indicate such an association. In fact, Kloek in a recent paper,(25) reviewing his own work and that of others, concludes just as we do that the association between schizophrenia and criminality is not striking. The principal psychiatric concern in criminality, therefore, is not with schizophrenia or other psychoses, but with sociopathy, alcoholism, and drug dependency. This has obvious and important implications for any discussion of criminal responsibility, the insanity defense, rehabilitation, or psychiatric participation in the criminal process.

The variability of diagnosis between the two interviews is of particular interest. It is unlikely that this is simply the result of lying or lack of candor, since the subjects seemed remarkably candid about a wide variety of experiences, many of an unflattering nature. They talked freely about delinquent, antisocial, and criminal behavior of all kinds, including some not mentioned in the police and prison records; they told of job and marital difficulties; they gave detailed histories of parental and other familial psychopathology; and they spontaneously described personal failures of various forms. A man whose interviews contained inconsistencies concerning alcoholism, for example, might report consistent histories about drug dependency. The discrepancies probably resulted from a number of factors: failure of memory, misunderstanding of questions, interviewer differences, and, in some cases, of course, lying or denial.

Except for anxiety neurosis, most diagnoses at follow-up agreed with the original diagnosis. The finding of new cases at follow-up was predictable; obviously, further time was required for some disorders to become more evident or clear-cut. Those cases originally positive who were negative at follow-up are less easily explained. It is pertinent to emphasize that nothing we know about these men suggests the inconsistency was the result of another illness such as schizophrenia.

In a study of this nature, the method of selecting subjects is crucial. (The method for selecting the original sample permitted two loopholes through which certain categories of criminals might be lost. These categories included: 1. criminals sent directly from the courts to the state hospital for the criminally insane, and 2. criminals sent from prison to the state hospital for observation who never returned to prison. Figures for the years 1959 and 1960, during which we selected our subjects, indicate that perhaps 2% of criminals may have been missed in this fashion.(1) It is important to emphasize the fact that we studied a group of convicted felons. We can say nothing about criminals who are not apprehended, tried, and convicted. It may be that convicted criminals are more likely to be sociopaths, alcoholics, or drug abusers than those not apprehended or convicted. It may be that some men who break the law are so obviously psychiatrically ill that they are sent by the police or prosecutor directly to a mental hospital and are never brought to trial.(26) It is unclear how often this happens, but apparently it is not frequent. In addition, everyone who commits a crime is not apprehended, not all accused people are guilty, and not all guilty people are convicted. Finally, not all convicted people are guilty, though in our study few men claimed to be innocent of the crime for which they were convicted. There is no single point in the process at which it is possible to select a sample certain to be truly representative. The best that can be achieved is to have repeated studies at various points in the process of dealing with crime, carefully specifying the selection criteria and making suitable comparisons. Our investigation is one step in such an undertaking.

SUMMARY

An eight to nine year follow-up of a group of convicted felons confirmed the findings of the original investigation and of the study of their first-degree relatives that the principal psychiatric disorders associated with criminality are sociopathy, alcoholism, and drug dependency. Schizophrenia, manic-depressive disease, organic brain syndromes, the neuroses, and homosexuality are apparently not seen more frequently in criminals than in the general population. These data must influence our thinking concerning many of the important questions in the area of the law and psychiatry.

NOTES

(1) Guze, S. B., et al: Psychiatric Illness and Crime With Particular Reference to Alcoholism: A Study of 223 Criminals, *J Nerv Ment Dis* 134:512–521 (June) 1962.

(2) Guze, S. B., et al: The Drinking History: A Comparison of Reports by Subjects and their Relatives. *Quart J Study Alcohol* 24:249–260 (June) 1963.

(3) Guze, S. B., et al: A Study of Check Offenders, *Dis Nerv Syst* 24:752–754 (Dec) 1963.

(4) Guze, S. B.: A Study of Recidivism Based Upon a Follow-up of 217 Consecutive Criminals, *J Nerv Ment Dis* 138:575–580 (June) 1964.

(5) Guze, S. B.: Conversion Symptoms in Criminals, *Amer J Psychiat* 121:580–583 (Dec) 1964.

(6) Guze, S. B., and Cantwell, D.P.: Alcoholism, Parole Observations, and Criminal Recidivism: A Study of 116 Parolees, *Amer J*

Psychiat 122:436–439 (Oct) 1965.

(7) Guze, S. B., et al: Psychiatric Illness in the Families of Convicted Criminals: A Study of 519 First-Degree Relatives, *Dis Nerv Syst* 28:651–659 (Oct) 1967.

(8) Guze, S. B., et al: Delinquency, Social Maladjustment, and Crime: The Role of Alcoholism, *Dis Nerv Syst* 29:238–243 (April) 1968.

(9) Wheeler, E. O., et al: Neurocirculatory Asthenia Anxiety Neurosis, Effort Syndrome, Neurasthenia), *JAMA* 142:878–888 (March 25) 1950.

(10) Purtell, J. J.: Robins, E.; and Cohen, M. E.: Observations on Clinical Aspects of Hysteria: A Quantitative Study of 50 Hysteria Patients and 156 Control Subjects, *JAMA* 146:902–909 (July 7) 1951.

(11) Perley, M., and Guze, S. B.: Hysteria: The Stability and Usefulness of Clinical Criteria, *New Eng J Med* 266:421–426 (March 1) 1962.

(12) Pollitt, J.: Natural History of Obsessional States: A Study of 150 Cases, *Brit Med J* 1:194–198 (Jan 26) 1957.

(13) Langfeldt, G.: The Prognosis in Schizophrenia *Acta Psychiat Neurol Scand*, suppl 110, 1956.

(14) Stephens, J. H.; Astrup, C.: and Mangrum, Prognostic Factors in Recovered and Deteriorated Schizophrenics, *Amer J Psychiat* 122:1116–1120 (April) 1966.

(15) Cassidy, W. L., et al: Clinical Observations in Manic-Depressive Disease: A Quantitative Study of One Hundred Manic-Depressive Patients and Fifty Medically Sick Controls, *JAMA* 164:1535–1546 (Aug 3) 1957.

(16) Jellinek, E. M.: *The Disease Concept of Alcoholism*, New Haven Conn: Hillhouse Press, 1960.

(17) Helgason, T.: Epidemiology of Mental Disorders in Iceland, *Acta Psychiat Scand*, suppl 173, 1964.

(18) Fremming, K. H.: *The Expectation of Mental Infirmity in a Sample of the Danish Population*, Occasional Papers on Eugenics No. 7. London: Cassel & Company, Ltd., 1951.

(19) Mulford, H. A.: Drinking and Deviant Drinking, U.S.A., 1963, *Quart J Stud Alcohol* 25:634–650 (Dec) 1964.

(20) Bailey, M. B.; Haberman, P.; and Alksne, H.: The Epidemiology of Alcoholism in an Urban Residential Area, *Quart J Stud Alcohol* 26:19–40 (March) 1965.

(21) Knupfer, G.: The Epidemiology of Problem Drinking, *Amer J Public Health* 57:973–986 (June) 1967.

(22) West, D. J.: *Murder Followed by Suicide*, London: Heinemann & Cassell S Africa Pty, Ltd., Publishers, 1965.

(23) Kannel, W. B.; Dawber, T.; and Cohen, M.: The Elec-

trocardiogram in Neurocirculatory Asthenia (Anxiety Neurosis or Neurasthenia): A Study of 203 Neurocirculatory Asthenia Patients and 757 Healthy Controls in the Framingham Study, *Ann Intern Med* 49:1351–1360 (Dec) 1958.

(24) Kinsey, A. C.; Pomeroy, W. B.; and Martin, C. E.: *Sexual Behavior in the Human Male*, Philadelphia: W.B. Saunders Company, 1948.

(25) Kloek, J.: "Schizophrenia and Delinquency: The Inadequacy of Our Conceptual Framework," in de Reuck, A.V.S., and Porter, R. (eds.): *The Mentally Abnormal Offender*, A Ciba Foundation Symposium, Boston: Little, Brown & Company, 1968.

(26) Goldstein, A.: *The Insanity Defense*, New Haven, Conn: Yale University Press, 1967.

The Medical and Psychiatric Implications of Antisocial Personality (Sociopathy)

Robert A. Woodruff, Jr., Samuel B. Guze, and Paula J. Clayton

We do not yet understand the factors that produce antisocial personality (sociopathy) despite evidence to support the importance of both environmental and genetic variables(1-4). Nevertheless, it is a common condition associated with a variety of complications which may lead to medical consultation and, often, psychiatric referral. Physicians are generally aware of the social complications of sociopathy such as difficulties with the law, poor job history, and marital problems. But it may not be appreciated how often sociopaths are seen by physicians for reasons less obviously related to antisocial behavior. With this in mind we have taken the opportunity to evaluate the medical as well as psychiatric histories of sociopaths seen in our clinic to illustrate the varied reasons they have had for consulting physicians.

METHOD

The subjects of this study were taken from a series of 500 patients, new and old, who participated as index cases in a long-term follow-up and family study in process at the Washington University Psychiatric Clinic. The 500 index patients were selected to provide a cross-section of the psychiatric clinic's population. All were interviewed with a systematic, structured, research protocol containing some 500 codeable items of information. Diagnoses were made by means of checklist criteria. The diagnosis of sociopathy was defined as follows: Each patient had a history of police trouble other than traffic offenses. In addition, each patient reported at least two of the following five manifestations: a history of excessive fighting, school delinquency, a poor job record, a period of wanderlust, or being a runaway. If any of the individual diagnostic criteria was scored as questionable, the subject received a diagnosis of probable rather than definite sociopathy.

Criteria for other psychiatric diagnoses have been presented elsewhere(5,6).

DEMOGRAPHIC FINDINGS

Of the 500 patients 35 collected in our research clinic received a diagnosis of sociopathy. There were 25 patients with a diagnosis of definite sociopathy and 10 with a diagnosis of probable sociopathy. Of the 35 sociopaths 27 were men, eight were women. There were 149 non-sociopathic men and 316 non-sociopathic women. The difference in sex distribution between sociopaths and non-sociopaths was significant by chi square at the $p < 0.001$ level.

The mean age of the sociopaths was 26. The mean age of the remaining 465 patients was 37. The age difference between sociopaths and non-sociopaths was significant at the $p < 0.001$ level. It was not sex related.

Of the sociopaths 25 (71%) were white. There was no difference in race between sociopaths and the rest of the sample. Likewise, the present marital status of sociopathic subjects did not differ from the rest of the sample, except for numbers of subjects currently separated. Nine sociopaths (26%) were currently separated as compared with 39 (8%) of the remaining clinic patients ($p < 0.01$).

Of the sociopaths 26 (74%) were new cases in the clinic, as compared with 246 (53%) of the remaining clinic subjects. This difference was significant at the $p < 0.05$ level, and was independent of age.

ADDITIONAL DIAGNOSES

Twenty-two patients had an additional diagnosis of definite or probable secondary affective disorder (15 men and 7 women); 21 had an additional diagnosis of definite or probable alcoholism (15 men and six women). All but two of the eight sociopathic women had both secondary affective disorder and alcoholism. Of the 35 sociopaths, 16 had both secondary affective disorder and alcoholism. Eight had neither secondary affective disorder nor alcoholism.

Six subjects were drug dependent (five men and one woman). Four subjects received a diagnosis of hysteria (one man and three women). One man received a diagnosis of anxiety neurosis. There were three homosexuals, three subjects with undiagnosed additional disorder, one subject with organic brain syndrome, and one subject with mental retardation.

Among the 35 sociopathic patients, five received one diagnosis only; nine patients received two diagnoses; 13 patients received three diagnoses; five patients received four diagnoses; three patients received five diagnoses.

CHIEF COMPLAINTS

Table I illustrates the chief complaints reported by the 35 patients at clinic intake. Approximately one-third of the patients had chief complaints directly related to problems in behavior. Another third reported psychological chief complaints. A final third reported nonspecific complaints, or were interviewed without a chief complaint being recorded.

TABLE I. Chief complaints 35 sociopaths.

None recorded	8
Symptomatic complaints (10)	
Nervous or nerves bother me	5
Depression	1
Anxiety symptoms	1
Fear of hurting child	1
Spells	1
Stomach bothers me	1
Behavior complaints (12)	
Temper or arguments	3
Drugs	2
Drinking	2
Police trouble	1
Lying	1
School trouble	1
Stealing	1
Mother angry with patient	1
Other complaints (5)	
"I need help"	1
"I have problems"	1
"It's hard to describe"	1
"I'm tired of trying to prove myself to others"	1
"I looked at myself in the mirror and realized I'd never seen myself before"	1
	35

HOSPITALIZATIONS

The mean numbers of psychiatric hospitalizations (0.7) and total hospitalizations (2.7) for sociopaths did not differ significantly from means for the rest of the sample. Sociopaths had had as many hospitalizations despite their younger mean age. This finding was independent of the sex difference between sociopaths and non-sociopaths.

Table II lists all hospitalizations reported by the 35 sociopaths. Medical and surgical hospitalizations were more common than psychiatric hospitalizations. Surgical and traumatic hospitalizations were the most common. Hospitalizations probably related to alcohol intoxication or alcoholism were also common.

TABLE II. Hospitalizations 35 sociopaths.

Psychiatric (18 hospitalizations among
   10 subjects)

Depression or suicide attempt	6
Anxiety symptoms or "nerves"	3
Violent behavior	3
Alcoholism	2
Brain syndrome — non alcoholic	2
Type unknown	2

Medical (76 hospitalizations among 25
   subjects)

Unknown problem	22

Surgical (26)

T&A	5
Appendectomy	3
Head injury	3
Hernia repair	3
Burns	2
Lacerations	2
Trauma — unspecified — auto	2
Gunshot wounds	1
Fracture of arm	1
Tendon injury	1
Unspecified injury of foot	1
Gall bladder disease	1
Abdominal pain	1

OB-GYN (7)

Spontaneous abortion	3
D&C	2
Uterine prolapse	1
Tubal pregnancy	1

Medical (16)

Dizziness	3
Unconsciousness	2
Back pain	2
Drug overdose	2

Pneumonia	2
Spontaneous pneumothorax	1
Thyroid disease	1
Constipation	1
Duodenal ulcer	1
Pancreatitis	1
Psychiatric or medical service (5)	
Anxiety symptoms or "nerves"	3
Depression	1
Alcohol withdrawal	1
	94

INJURIES

Of the 35 sociopaths 23 (66%) reported injuries of more than minor nature; (74% of the men and 38% of the women reported such injuries). Among men, injuries were reported with significantly greater frequency (p <0.05) by sociopaths than by non-sociopaths. Approximately a third of all sociopaths had been in automobile accidents which required medical attention. Approximately a third of male sociopaths had sustained fractures of the hand or wrist, usually in fights. Other injuries reported with more than single frequency were those of the head, miscellaneous lacerations, and burns. The majority of those injuries had not resulted in hospitalization.

OTHER CLINICAL PHENOMENA

Eight of the 35 patients (four men and four women) reported one or more suicide attempts.

Thirteen of the 35 patients (eight men and five women) reported a history of 22 conversion symptoms (defined as unexplained neurologic symptoms exclusive of pain). There were four reports each of amnesia and anesthesia. There were three reports each of transitory blindness and ataxia. Also reported were unusual spells, unconscious episodes, aphonia, paralysis, and diplopia.

Anxiety attacks had occurred in approximately one-third of the sociopaths. Each patient who reported a history of anxiety attacks had also received the diagnosis of secondary affective disorder.

DISCUSSION AND SUMMARY

The complaint of a behavior problem should obviously alert any physician to the possible presence of sociopathy. Such complaints are made frequently by sociopaths, but sociopaths also come to physicians for other reasons. A past history of trauma is common among sociopathic men. Sociopathy should be part of the differential diagnosis for any male patient with a history of repeated trauma.

The frequency with which diagnoses of secondary affective disorder and alcoholism are made suggests that sociopaths often come to psychiatrists for those reasons. But previous *non-psychiatric* care is also common for affective disorder and alcoholism. Non-psychiatrists should bear this in mind.

The number of sociopathic patients new to our clinic, as compared to other patients, suggests that our contact with sociopaths is brief. Yet these patients are seen frequently by physicians. It is possible that sociopaths change physicians more rapidly than most patients. This may be the experience of all physicians, not of psychiatrists alone.

These data indicate that the complications of sociopathy are medical as well as behavioral. All physicians should be aware of the extent of the syndrome and the varied ways in which it may be presented.

NOTES

(1) Baker, D., Telfer, M.A., Richardson, C.E., and Clark, G.R.: Chromosome Errors and Antisocial Behavior. *JAMA*, 214: pp. 869–878 (Nov. 2) 1970.

(2) Gibson, H. B., and West, D. J.: Social and Intellectual Handicaps as Precursors of Early Delinquency. *Brit. J. Criminol.*, 10: pp. 21–32 (Jan.) 1970.

(3) O'Neal, P., Robins, L. N., King, L. J., and Schaefer, J.: Parental Deviance and the Genesis of Sociopathic Personality. *Amer. J. Psychiat.*, 118: pp. 1114–1123 (June) 1962.

(4) Robins, L. N.: *Deviant Children Grown Up: A Sociological and Psychiatric Study of Sociopathic Personality.* Williams and Wilkins, Baltimore, 1966.

(5) Guze, S.B., Goodwin, D.W., and Crane, J.B.: Criminality and Psychiatric Disorders. *Arch. Gen. Psychiat.*, 20:583–591 (May) 1969.

(6) Woodruff, R.A., Guze, S.B., and Clayton, P.J.: Unipolar and Bipolar Primary Affective Disorders. *Brit. J. Psychiat.*, in press.

VI.

Treating
the Criminal Offender

Introduction

The attitude of the public toward crime and criminals is deeply ambivalent. An understandable desire for vengeance and concern for the prevention of crimes, particularly heinous offenses, conflict with humanitarian impulses and liberal social philosophies. The public's ambivalence is also apparent in its views of the criminal justice system. People want the criminal justice system to rehabilitate as well as punish; to reform as well as to deter; to help as well as incapacitate the criminal offender. The deeply rooted contradictions in the public's goals and philosophies have obvious and important implications for the treatment of the criminal.

The traditional role of the criminal justice system—comprising law enforcement, prosecution, the courts, and corrections—has been the apprehension, conviction, and punishment of offenders. Despite many changes caused by social progress within the last century, the fundamental orientation of the criminal justice system is punitive. If the reform or rehabilitation of criminal offenders has become a contemporary goal of the criminal justice system, it is one that remains subordinate to the major objectives of social defense and the maintenance of public order.

Treatment usually connotes the manner in which a person or thing is handled, used, or processed. In the context of mental health, the goal of treatment or therapy is to help an individual, who has been diagnosed as emotionally disturbed or mentally ill, attain some level of adequate functioning.

Within the context of corrections, the concept of treatment has had a controversial history. Gibbons (1965) noted that "treatment is at present little more than an activity in which 'someone does something to someone else' with indeterminate or unknown results." Critics of psychotherapy might feel that Gibbons's description is equally appropriate as a characterization of many contemporary approaches in psychological treatment.

Like the orientation in mental health, the goal of correctional treatment is rehabilitative; the objective is to effect changes in the character and/or behavior of individuals who have been adjudicated delinquent or criminal in order to help them reduce or eliminate propensities toward antisocial conduct. Unfortunately, this otherwise laudable objective is expected to be pursued within an environment where punitive goals directly compete with those endorsed by the treatment.

Rehabilitative efforts in corrections have had at least two identifiable goals; they have attempted to alter the personality or behavior of the individual offender in a prosocial direction, and they have sought to improve the social conditions that are interpreted as either criminogenic or supportive of continued antisocial conduct: poverty, unemployment, racial or ethnic discrimination, and other influences conducive to social demoralization. Often regarded as novel and innovative, the current emphasis in corrections on community-based approaches and programs really constitutes a return to an orientation toward the criminal offender which antedates the nineteenth century development of the penitentiary movement in the United States.

Prisons continue to be the most visible manifestation of corrections within the criminal justice system. They are generally considered monuments to the failure of society to devise more effective and humane ways of dealing with criminals. Are they, however? Prisons today house a disproportionately high percentage of people who are socially deviant, emotionally unstable, psychologically disturbed, mentally retarded, and prone to aggression and violence as a first, rather than as a last, resort. No longer are prison populations composed primarily of nonviolent offenders. The constant search for alternatives to imprisonment has diverted into probation and other community-based correctional programs the first offenders, minor property criminals, and drug users. The criminals who are perceived as a threat to the safety of the public are left as candidates for incarceration. Consequently, modern prisons are inhabited by the highest concentration of dangerous offenders in the entire history of penology.

As a result eighty-seven stabbings and twelve inmate fatalities occurred in 1974 in one American prison, interestingly not located in the rural South. The violence occurred at San Quentin, a correctional institution in California, a state that boasts of having the most progressive correctional system in the country. In 1975, ten inmates were killed in Florida's prisons, generally in explosive outbursts of violence triggered by an argument over a bar of soap, an alleged insult, or the theft of a cigarette.

The tensions in a prison are elevated by racism. Inmates practice an informal, self-imposed segregation; whites and blacks stand in separate lines for meals, and whites, blacks, and Hispanics rarely sit together in the mess hall. White convicts with hostile attitudes towards blacks and Hispanics form together into a group, while blacks and Hispanics with anti-white biases form their own groups. The resulting groups are constantly fighting over the spoils of prison enterprises and violations of the rights and honor of each group. Such internecine strife creates potentially explosive conditions within the institution which can be ignited by a single incident.

Involvement of the New Left in American prisons during the protest years of the late 1960s and early 1970s was reflected in the demands of rioting prisoners at Attica for guarantees of "asylum and safe passage to some nonimperialist country." Eldridge Cleaver, George Jackson, Huey Newton, and Malcom X were militants who developed their political consciousness while "doing time." People with backgrounds of social and economic deprivation protested that they were "political prisoners" of a racist, capitalist system that had provided them with no alternative to a life of crime. For the protestors, "treatment" or "rehabilitation" programs were useless; for non-white inmates, participation in programs sponsored by "The Man," was roughly equivalent to collaboration with the enemy. George Jackson was contemptuous of efforts by the California prison authorities to turn him into what he called "a good nigger."

The authors of a leading textbook in corrections (Allen and Simonsen, 1978) have observed that many criminal justice practitioners tend to view any program or institution which is not punitive in its approach as "being soft" on criminals or "operating a country club for cons." They assert their belief that the implementation of an ideology of treatment does not mean coddling inmates or allowing them to administer the institution freely. In fact, they maintain that some form of treatment can be applied within the strictest and most custody-oriented institution:

> The major difference between the treatment and punishment ideologies is that in the former, offenders are assigned to the institution for a correctional program intended to prepare them for readjustment to the community, not just for punishment and confinement. There is room for punishment and for security in

the treatment approach, but little room for treatment in the punitive approach. The more humane treatment methods are intended to be used in conjunction with the employment of authority in a constructive and positive manner, but inmates must be allowed to try and to fail. Authoritarian procedures, used alone, only provide the offender with more ammunition to support a self-image as an "oppressed and impotent pawn of the power structure.

As Alberta J. Nassi (1975) emphasizes in her paper, she is very skeptical that treatment can occur within the punitive context of a state prison. She sees an almost insurmountable role conflict between treatment and custodial objectives.

BASIC ISSUES IN CORRECTIONAL TREATMENT

Treating the criminal offender involves at least three fundamental issues:

1. The rights of an offender to treatment,
2. The rights of an offender to *refuse* treatment, and
3. The ability of the criminal justice system to provide effective treatment for the criminal offender.

The right to refuse treatment might also be phrased as the "right to receive punishment rather than treatment." The first two issues raise significant questions in terms of constitutional law. The third issue involves a searching appraisal of the capabilities of contemporary correctional intervention techniques and strategies.

A series of legal decisions has affirmed on both constitutional and statutory grounds the right to treatment for individuals who have been institutionalized in mental hospitals. The right is based on civil rather than criminal proceedings (*Rouse v. Cameron*, 1966; *Donaldson v. O'Connor*, 1974; *Wyatt v. Stickney*, 1972). According to the courts, depriving an individual of freedom when the major rationale for confinement is to secure treatment for the individual involves the obligation to provide treatment. If this obligation is not met because no treatment is available, the quid pro quo for confinement has been violated, and the individual is being deprived of his liberty in violation of due process.

The relevance of the right-to-treatment arguments to the circumstances of the incarcerated felon is debatable. The rationale for confining criminal offenders is punitive rather than therapeutic, despite the conviction of many criminal justice practitioners that rehabilitation is a more defensible goal than punishment, deterrence or incapacitation. Concerning the right to treatment for juveniles, the doctrine of *parens patriae* (i.e., the juvenile court acting in the role of "kind and loving parent") implies an obligation to provide them with treatment instead of punishment. As the U.S. Supreme Court stated in the Gault decision (*in re Gault*, 1967), depriving a juvenile of rights guaranteed to adults under due process and equal protection of the law could only be justified if the informal procedures of the juvenile court operated in favor of the delinquent to secure him access to treatment.

An issue of potential significance and relevance to the incarcerated criminal offender is the supposed right to *refuse* treatment. When the treatment offered is aimed at changing the mind or thought processes of the recipient, the right to refuse treatment is based on the right to free speech in the First Amendement. The First Amendment has been interpreted to support an individual's right to "mind freedom" and "privacy of the mind." The right of any individual to have private thoughts and ideas is fundamental. The courts have been careful not to interfere in the fundamental rights of individuals except where the interference can be justified, as in the vital interest of the state. If the right to think or to have delusional thoughts is protected by the First Amendment, the use of coercive methods of treatment to change the mind would be justified when that use is in the compelling interest of the state.

Case law has held that the more experimental the treatment, the greater the responsibility of the physician to completely inform patients of possible alternatives to and consequences of that treatment. In *Mackey v. Procunier* (1973) District Appellate Court Judge Merrill addressed Mackey's contention that without his complete informed consent Mackey had been subjected to a traumatic administration of succinylcholine, a drug used in aversive therapy. An inmate of the California prison system, Mackey contended he had consented to electro-shock therapy, *not* to experimental aversive therapy. Judge Merrill wrote that if Mackey's contention was true, a serious question existed concerning "impermissible tinkering with the mental processes."

The concept of a right to a choice of punishment over treatment may seem absurd on first consideration, but a plausible argument can be framed for such a right. The right to treatment was first argued based upon statutory law rather than upon constitutional grounds; the right to a choice of punishment might be argued on a similar basis. Although it is not directly applicable to an individual diagnosed and confined as mentally ill or incompetent, the statutory interpretation is relevant to the offender like the anti-social or sociopathic individual who is criminally responsible for his conduct. The criminal could object to treatment on the grounds of the First Amendment's right to privacy of the mind and could support the objection by referring to a statutory right to punishment based on a state criminal code which designates a specific length of time in prison as punishment for the crime committed (Toomey, Allen, and Simonsen, 1974). A case referring to statutory rights has not been in the courts for a decision, but offenders sentenced to indeterminate commitments may be able to present such a case.

The most important issue in correctional treatment is whether the state, operating through the formal agencies of the criminal justice system or through the vast informal network of social service and mental health referral agencies, has the *ability* to provide effective treatment for criminal offenders. It may not matter how "effective treatment" is defined, but the objective of effective treatment must be some demonstrable or measurable decrease in antisocial conduct, particularly as indicated by a decrease in the rate of recidivism.

Charges that the rehabilitative goal of corrections had proven to be a widespread and massive failure were reported in a number of publications which received publicity in the public media. Almost inevitably, critics of treatment were quickly—and all too simplistically—labelled "hardliners," presumably to distinguish them from those who continued to advocate treatment in corrections. James Q. Wilson, author of the widely-read and much-discussed book, *Thinking about Crime* (1977), made the following assessment of correctional treatment approaches and their results:

> It does not seem to matter what form of treatment in the correctional system is attempted—whether vocational training or academic education; whether counseling inmates individually, in groups, or not at all; whether therapy is administered by social workers or psychiatrists; whether the institutional context of the treatment is custodial or benign; whether the person is placed on probation or released on parole; or whether the treatment takes place in the community or in institutions. Indeed, some forms of treatment—notably a few experiments with psychotherapy—actually produced an *increase* in the rate of recidivism.

Although exceptions can and should be raised to some of Wilson's contentions, it is difficult to fault his harsh summary judgment.

Seymour L. Halleck's paper suggests that behavior can be changed somewhat by providing an individual with new information, and group therapy techniques are particularly suitable means for helping individuals to understand their impact upon others. Subject to the same limitations set for individual therapy within the prison environment, group therapy is probably the most effective intervention in modern penology, particularly in light of the reduction in therapeutic services available to offenders. Increased use of consciousness-raising techniques not only creates new ethical issues but also helps therapists to introduce and utilize other potentially liberating interventions. Halleck discusses the applicability of psychoactive drugs and stresses the importance of continued research on biological determinants of criminal behavior. He also mentions that the type of information most readily available to prisoners tells them how to be better criminals, and he admonishes us with the caveat that not all offenders want to be rehabilitated.

At the present time, no effective way exists to treat antisocial behavior. Most of the research that has been directed toward the durable effects of behavior change has involved relatively stable, reasonably motivated, middle-class patients or clients who have voluntarily sought opportunities for therapy. However, under optimal circumstances, it has proven exceedingly difficult to gauge successful therapeutic outcomes by measures for which there is anything approaching consensus. To extrapolate from the existing research some conclusions concerning prisoners in the criminal justice system seems impossible. As Silber (1974) states, most of the prisoners in correctional institutions

> . . . are hostile, suspicious, and immature and tend to identify with subcultural values that are legally proscribed. They usually perceive their personality functioning to be acceptable. They are not, in general, likely to clamor for individual psychotherapy and usually are seen on referral. Thus, there is no strong sustained interest on the part of the prisoners themselves for treatment.

It still remains to be seen whether the individual pathology model of treatment has any relevance for minor offenders whose crimes have not yet resulted in imprisonment.

REFERENCES

Allen, H. E., and Simonsen, C. E. *Corrections in America: An Introduction.* Beverly Hills, California: Glencoe, 1978.

Donaldson v. O'Connor, 493 F. 2d 507 (5th Cir. 1974)

in re Gault, 387 U.S.; 87 S. Ct. 1428 (1967)

Mackey v. Procunier, 47 F. 2d 877 (9th Cir. 1973)

Nassi, Alberta J. "Therapy of the Absurd: A Study of Punishment and Treatment in California Prisons and the Roles of Psychiatrists and Psychologists. *Corrective and Social Psychiatry,* 1975, 21, 21–27.

Rouse v. Cameron, 373 F. 2d 451 (D.C. Cir. 1966); 125 U.S. App. D.C. 366.

Toomey, Beverly, Allen, H. E., and Simonsen, C. E. "The Right to Treatment: Professional Liabilities in the Criminal Justice and Mental Health Systems. *The Prison Journal,* 1974, 54, 43–56.

Wilson, J. Q. *Thinking about Crime.* New York: Vintage Books, 1977.

Wyatt v. Stickney, 325 F. Supp. 781 (M.D. Ala. 1971); 344 F. Supp. 373 (M.D. Ala. 1972)

Therapy of the Absurd: A Study of Punishment and Treatment in California Prisons and the Roles of Psychiatrists and Psychologists

Alberta J. Nassi

It is the intent of this inquiry to explore the treatment process in California State Prisons for Men, with particular emphasis on the roles of psychiatrists and psychologists in the prison atmosphere. The author postulates that prison is grounded in a tradition of punishment — despite stated rehabilitative aims — and that consequently, psychiatrists and psychologists who practice in this setting alter their professional standards to be more consonant with the punitive function of the prison. The question of whose agent is the psychiatrist or psychologist is at any given moment a crucial one.

HISTORICAL BACKGROUND

> The rapid development of humanism in the nineteenth century created a social climate in which psychiatry, a profession traditionally concerned with serving individuals, was encouraged to integrate its practices into a social system which punishes individuals. The resulting marriage of medical and punitive ethics has rarely been characterized by logic, consistency, or stability (Halleck, 1968:11).

The temporal continuity between Enrico Ferri's realization that "punishment should fit the individual, not the offense" (Kittrie, 1971:29) and the development of psychology and psychiatry gave impetus to the claims of behavioral scientists that the study of crime and other deviant behavior lay in their discipline. To the investigators of the matrix and the phenomena of human behavior, criminals were not all alike and should not be treated as if they were. It was, and is, argued that policies demanding uniform punishment are as obviously ineffective as administering uniform treatment to medical patients, regardless of their ailments. Inherent in the notion that crime and delinquency were not moral concerns but medical ones, was the assumption that all criminality was a manifestation of individual pathology and furthermore, that causative factors could be isolated and treated as symptoms of a medical illness. Central to this concept, was the conclusion that the criminal should not be sentenced to a fixed and unalterable punishment, but that correctional treatment required flexibility to be effective.

INDETERMINATE SENTENCE

In 1917, California pioneered the adoption of the indeterminate sentence for felony offenders. The new legislation was hailed by prison reformers because it was viewed as integral to the rehabilitative concept (Messinger, 1969). District attorneys, police officers, and correctional administrators saw in the indeterminate sentence increased latitude to imprison for longer periods criminals viewed as very dangerous. Prison administrators, in particular, embraced the indeterminate sentence as a potent instrument for inmate control (American Friends Service Committee, 1971). For psychologists and psychiatrists, the indeterminate sentence provided the adequate "flexibility" and discretion necessary to foster a "therapeutic relationship".

It is precisely this quality of indeterminancy — heralded by psychologists, psychiatrists, and others — that is the most destructive aspect of prison life. In fact, the indeterminate sentence never has been applied in a manner that parallels the medical model. The length of imprisonment has increased uniformly for most crimes. Moreover, suffering within the penal system has not decreased, but, on the contrary, it has become a form of brutality more subtle and elusive. The threat of being denied parole constantly hangs over the heads of all prisoners. Studies by Farber (1966) suggest that suffering on the part of prisoners is significantly increased by an indeterminate sentence. Most prisoners would prefer long-term fixed sentences to the indeterminate sentence to alleviate the period of worry and anxiety while they await a decision from the parole board. More recently, at a meeting of the California Psychiatrists and Psychologists Association in March, 1974, psychologists from San Quentin Prison cited the indeterminate sentence as a major contributing factor to prison violence.

ADULT AUTHORITY

The most crucial event for a prisoner is the decision to determine his sentence. The final determination of the length of the sentence and the time of parole release is the responsibility of a nine member panel known as the Adult Authority. Though the board is purported to be interdisciplinary, with the exception of a dentist, the members are drawn primarily from the ranks of law enforcement and Corrections.

Extraordinary discretionary power is lodged in the Adult Authority. The board has the power to deny parole, grant parole or set a date when parole will be granted, if certain conditions are met. The Adult Authority also may rescind the determination of a sentence after it has been made. Only recently have these powers been made subject to judicial review.

Most prisoners are convinced that there is no valid or consistent criteria operative in the sentencing hearing. Decisions appear to be arbitrary, unpredictable, and subject to political pressure (Mitford, 1972). It is precisely this quality of capriciousness that Lewin (1948) discussed as a technique to break morale through a strategy of terror — keeping the individual confused as to where he stands and just what he may expect. Indeed, frequent vacillations between severe disciplinary measures and promises of good treatment, together with spreading contradictory news, make the cognitive structure of the situation utterly incomprehensible. The individual may cease to know whether a given strategy would lead toward or away from the goal. Even those who have definite aims and are prepared to take risks will be paralyzed by severe inner conflicts in regard to what to do. Coleman (1972:8) states,

> The convict feels small, weak, and helpless much as a child who is faced with capricious and meaningless adult power. The inmate is daily encouraged, therefore, to regress to a state of dependency.

CLASSIFICATION

Classification is the initial phase of rehabilitation. It is largely through this mechanism that the prison attempts to attain the objective of reformation through individualized treatment (Cressey, 1960). Obviously, the entire process is dependant upon the original diagnosis. Yet, it is axiomatic that most prisons lack sufficient diagnostic personnel (Sutherland and Cressey, 1970). The author submits that the lack of personnel is not only indicative of the failure of diagnosis, but it is reflective of the priority of the institution.

Even when the diagnostic personnel are present, the accuracy of diagnosis is problematic. First of all, the diagnostic interview may be only five to fifteen minutes in duration, and on the basis of this interview an appraisal is made of the inmate's home life, his community life, the etiology of his criminality, and his version of the offense. Secondly, the validity of traditional psychodiagnostic techniques is seriously challenged in the prison setting. Katkin (1970:6) points out that, "the prison atmosphere is one of such severe suspicion and interpersonal instrumentality that test results indicating significant psychopathology might result from deliberate falsification or fear of negatively affecting one's parole board." Furthermore, does one interpret the fact that most inmates show psychopathic spikes on the Minnesota Multiphasic Personality Inventory to mean that only psychopaths are imptisoned? Or, is it more reasonable to assume that prison itself augements psychopathic trends in all its inmates (Zimbardo, 1971)? Indeed, Berman (1972) suggests that prison not only strengthens psychopathic trends in inmates, but in correctional officers as well. He administered a series of psychological tests to a number of correctional officer candidates and prison inmates and found the profiles to be almost identical with the inmates showing slightly less violent potential.

Also, on the basis of these brief contacts, the interviewer makes a prognosis as to the probabilities for successful rehabilitation of the offender, classifies him as to personality type, decides whether the inmate is improvable or unimprovable, and recommends a program of treatment and training. These procedures also represent a departure from the medical model because: 1. No definite relationship has ever been established between type of treatment and type of offender (Sparks, 1968). Nor, for that matter, is there any reason to believe that treatment contributes to rehabilitation. 2. Prognosis usually pivots around a prediction of dangerousness or violence which is just as scant of scientific evidence.

To a large extent, classification fails because it is in direct conflict with prison goals — custody and surveillance. Even if it were possible to diagnose an offender's needs properly and recommend a treatment strategy, the actual recommendation would be based on the custody level of the individual, the availability of space in the prison system, and the institutional requirements for manpower (Sutherland and Cressey, 1970).

TREATMENT

Treatment in prison is neither contractual nor confidential, which is another deviation from the medical paradigm. It is common knowledge that participation in treatment programs is a prerequisite for parole. The undisguised cynicism toward programming that pervades the prisoner population indicates that treatment is regarded as phony and that the motivation for participation is parole (Irwin, 1970).

California has experimented with a wide variety of therapeutic programs. Group counseling, introduced in 1955, now involves the majority of inmates. Most convicts participate in these programs out of necessity. They lack commitment and are fearful that anything meaningful revealed in the sessions might be used against them and damage any prospects for parole. As Alexander (1962:128) stated

> One cannot apply successfully all three penological principles at the same time — retaliation, intimidation, and reconstruction — as is done at present in our institutions. One cannot make the prisoner hate his authorities, fear them and at the same time expect the prisoner to trust them and accept from them advice and guidance.

Messinger (1969:285) has discussed the therapeutic model as a contribution from psychoanalysis, which "focuses attention on 'inner problems,' on talking rather than doing, and on the future as the site for practice of what has been learned." In this way, he maintains that group discussion is intended to provide cathartic relief so that hostile attitudes will be ventilated rather than acted out and, perhaps, will be modified. He sees group counseling as a vehicle to encourage inmate acceptance of restrictions and the prison regime, in general. Proposals for change are not considered, and complaints become an occasion to explain regulations and to lead the inmates to question the personal basis for dissatisfaction.

The less than orthodox use of the therapeutic model in prison is not restricted to insight therapies. Behavior therapies produce more immediate results, blend with the fundamental aims of the prison administration, and provide their specialists with indispensable roles in the prison arena. Of course, there are severe problems with any treatment approach which looks upon crime as a symptom and attempts to treat it — disregarding the interpersonal and social context. Symptom removal — based on analogies with physical medicine — assumes that the social structure has an inherent perfection (homeostasis) and that deviation from the norms is a symptom of imperfection (pathology). Consider the application of this logic by McConnell (1970:74):

> I believe that the day has come when we can combine sensory deprivation with drugs, hypnosis and astute manipulation of reward and punishment to gain almost absolute control over an

individual's behavior. It should be possible then to achieve a very rapid and highly effective type of positive brainwashing that would allow us to make dramatic changes in a person's behavior and personality. I foresee the day when we could convert the worst criminal into a decent, respectable citizen in a matter of a few months — or perhaps even less time than that. The danger is, of course, that we could also do the opposite: we could change any decent, respectable citizen into a criminal.

Finally, inasmuch as prisons systematically impose mental suffering through enforced isolation, denial of close contact with others, repression of outlet of sexuality and aggression, dependency, lack of opportunity to assume responsibility, and lack of meaningful work, the goal of therapy becomes a means to undo the deleterious effects of prison (Schnur, 1961).

WHOSE AGENT IS A PSYCHIATRIST OR PSYCHOLOGIST?

The psychiatrist and psychologist who enter the prison system may find the foundations of their approach shattered, or at least at complete loggerheads with the mission of Corrections. As a helping agent, presumably the professional regards the concern for the individual and his mental health and growth as the sine qua non of his discipline. Indeed, both the professions of psychiatry and psychology represent a tradition in which respect for individual liberties and service to the individual are primary. However, the psychiatrist or psychologist is also employed by the state, where the official policy is "protection of society" or some other vague, politically dictated desideratum. That the state's interests are invariably adverse to the offender is obvious by the fact of imprisonment or capital punishment — although some have argued that these measures are for the benefit of the offender (i.e., imprisonment to procure reformation and capital punishment to insure salvation). Katkin (1970:36) writes from his clinical experience:

> . . . what are the implications of helping an inmate adjust to living in a cage and adjusting to 20–30 more years of social isolation and sexual deprivation? Helping an inmate adjust to these conditions is helping him to become pathological by normal criteria. A psychologist adhering to the standards by which he was trained inevitably finds himself in some disagreement with the system for which he is working.

Thus, to the extent that psychiatrists and psychologists adhere to the precepts of their profession, they will have to adjust these precepts to function in harmony with the physical and social environment of the prison. Alternatively, they may attempt to reconstitute the organization and redirect its goals so that they are more consonant with their belief system. However, to the extent that the individual adjusts to the prison regime and alters the professional orientation, this orientation may become so distorted that it does not even resemble the traditions of his discipline. It is in this way, that treatment becomes indistinguishable from punishment, except by name.

The theory of cognitive dissonance provides a conceptual framework to understand how therapeutic agent will react to the wide gulf between the stated aims and actual practice of his profession in prison. Festinger (1958) wrote that two beliefs, opinions, or behaviors are dissonant with each other if they do not fit together or if they conflict. Dissonance produces discomfort and correspondingly, attempts to reduce the conflict. It follows from the theory that the psychiatrist or psychologist in prison will either alter his beliefs, opinions, or behaviors, acquire new information which will allow him to perceive the situation with less conflict, or subordinate the importance of the conflict. Most essential, if any of these attempts is to be successful, it must be met with support from either the physical or social environment.

PSYCHOLOGY OF A PENAL PSYCHIATRIST AND PSYCHOLOGIST

As a take off from the theory and on the basis of interviews with psychiatrists and psychologists at the California Medical Facility and San Quentin Prison, four modes of adaptation for penal psychiatrists and psychologists emerged as salient:

1. **The psychiatrist or psychologist ceases any pretense of treatment and becomes analogous to a custody officer.** In this capacity, the psychiatrist or psychologist carries out the orders which originate higher in the bureaucracy. Schnur (1961:306) notes that, ". . . they often outdo custody in restricting inmates." The therapeutic agent in this role is what Halleck (1971:292) termed an "institutional tranquilizer"; his main function is to keep the punishment process moving smoothly. Reducing dissonance does not occur in a vacuum, and correspondingly, prison authorities reinforce this adaptation. For example, it was reported at the meeting of California Psychiatrists and Psychologists, that the new psychiatrist to Folsom Prison was admonished by the Director of Corrections not to have illusions about conducting therapy; he was not being hired to be a therapist. According to Senior Psychologist Arthur Mattocks at the California Medical Facility, the Department of Corrections conceptualizes the role of psychologists and psychiatrists as "an extension of the spy network."

Officially, the custodial role of psychiatrists and psychologists is sanctioned by their participation on disciplinary boards and classification or screening committees, and by writing psychiatric evaluations. Certainly, there is no therapeutic foundation which justifies participation in a disciplinary hearing. Disciplinary action which results in reclassification or solitary confinement — even if couched in psychiatric terms — is punishment, not treatment. As for screening committees, psychiatrists and psychologists legitimize the decisions — although Custody and custodial criteria dominate the outcome.

A major contention among psychiatrists and psychologists is the punitive misuse of psychiatric evaluations to abet parole denials. Although a realistic appraisal of an inmate includes strengths and weaknesses, the Adult Authority often seize upon the weakness to justify and support a parole denial. Consequently, professionals conceptualize themselves as "tools of the Adult Authority," who lend status to parole decisions. While psychiatric evaluations must employ psychiatric nomenclature, none of the Adult Authority members have any training which might qualify them to understand the reports. Nonetheless, professionals continue to provide these demanded evaluations, though they consume much of their time and sanction custodial decrees. Therapists often cancel therapy sessions to write their psychiatric evaluations. Interestingly, it is not beyond the same psychiatrist, who devaluates institutional therapy, to recommend that a man remain in prison for continued treatment.

It has been fairly well documented as to how mental health professionals actualize punitive goals unofficially through the repressive use of drugs, shock treatment, behavior therapies, and psychosurgery (Opton, 1974). These modalities produce immediate results, are consonant with the goals of the prison administrators, and create indispensable roles for their practitioners in the prison arena.

At the same time that the psychiatrist or psychologist adjusts his behavior to be more consonant with the prison atmosphere, he adopts Custody's punitive attitude and their perception of the convicts. One way of justifying the adoption of punitive attitudes — thereby reducing dissonance — is to become convinced that the suffering deserve their plight (i.e., "If the inmate were innocent, he would not be in prison.") (Davis and Jones, 1960). This is what Lerner (1966) referred to as the "just world" notion, which assumes that this is an equitable world, where people reap what they deserve. The penal professional's version of the "just world" notion allows him to perceive the prisoner as "morally deficient" or "sociopathic," which is to say that he is untreatable therapeutically, so punishment is appropriate and desirable.

2. **The psychiatrist or psychologist performs routine work though it**

may be futile from a therapeutic viewpoint, given the conditions under which it is conducted. It is not unusual to hear penal psychiatrists and psychologists report that there is no therapy of any significance being conducted in prison. It is no secret that the major concern of the Department is the psychiatric evaluations and other paper work which is estimated to consume one-third to one-half of the professional's time. The average work load of a penal professional may range from 50 to 80 cases.

Capitulation through the system is reinforced with new cognitions (i.e., "If I was not here, someone less sympathetic to the inmates would be." or "It is a job; I need the money, and jobs are scarce.") Most of the professionals interviewed were in no way naive about the conflicts that the prison system presents, but they were very effective in subordinating this conflict to continue working in this setting. One way of subordinating conflict is to isolate one's role as a therapist and to deny one's role as part of the prison process. Another way of reducing conflict is to withdraw from active involvement and work as little as possible.

Although this adaptation appears more benign than the professional who obviously adopts the custodial orientation, it is more potentially explosive. Not only does the exploiter distort and misconceive his actions, but he commits further transgressions on the basis of his distorted perceptions (Berscheid, Boye, and Darley, 1968). The psychiatrist or psychologist sees himself more favorably than the would be custody officer, but he is still a ballast in the boat. Halleck (1973:30) provides a personal account of this observation:

> By participating in the punishment process, even as a healer, I loaned a certain credibility of the existing correctional system . . . In my work in prisons I did little to change an oppressive status quo. In retrospect I am inclined to believe that, although I helped a number of individuals, my presence as a non-militant, cooperative psychiatrist tended to strengthen the status quo.

3. **The psychiatrist or psychologist becomes aware of irreconcilable differences between the punitive and treatment orientations and leaves the prison for practice elsewhere.** This individual is aware of the dissonant functions that he is expected to perform in prison, but unlike the others, his attempts to relieve this dissonance have been unsuccessful. Since he could not adjust to the previous patterns, he will subsequently be eliminated, while those who can adjust stay on. This gradual process of attrition will result in a professional insulation of certain types of therapeutic agents. Not only will existing personnel make conditions difficult for nonconforming types, but in selecting personnel, only those who can "adapt" will be favored.

It was pointed out in the interviews that the attrition rate has increased in recent years. In addition, most of the psychiatrists and psychologists interviewed expressed a willingness to accept employment elsewhere. Although it was not clear whether job dissatisfaction is an index of role conflict, this is a strong possibility. Professionals indicated that dissatisfaction did not emanate from working with a felon population.

4. **The psychiatrist or psychologist forces confrontation by resisting the system.** Holding fast to his beliefs and principles, the psychiatrist or psychologist reduces his dissonance by forcing the system to be more consonant with his belief system. Although this implies an active form of resistance, several penal professionals described instances of passive resistance or nonconformity. For example, some therapists honor confidentiality and help their patients, even in defiance of institutional directives that require that illicit inmate behavior be reported. One strategy with regard to confidentiality is not to keep written files and to adhere to a "convenient lapse of memory." Other counterstrategies include writing unduly positive psychiatric evaluations, submitting psychiatric evaluations to the inmates for approval, or obtaining inmate assistance in writing the evaluation. Another unorthodox practice was confronting custodial officers in response to inmate complaints.

This subtle noncompliance is usually masked by legitimate justifications (Howard and Sommers, 1971). This strategy is especially lucrative for the individual who can continue functioning in the environment without relinquishing his beliefs. In this way, the professional's role is more or less consonant with the environment and at an equilibrium with his self identity.

Though it is comparatively rare, the prison scene is not devoid of examples of active resistance. This adaptation is highlighted in the experience of psychiatrist Frank Rundle at Soledad Prison. Rundle's first open confrontation was the result of a directive by the chief medical officer that any inmate identified as a psychiatric patient be locked in a security cell — which consisted of 24-hour a day solitary confinement, no showers, no exercise, no recreation. Rundle recalled, "I told them I could no longer be responsible for those patients — these are exactly the conditions to drive a man further into a psychosis" (Mitford, 1973:107).

The tension mounted when Rundle was subpoenaed to testify in the case of an inmate accused of killing a guard. When asked about the inmate's environment, Rundle related the horror story that is the adjustment center. When he returned to the prison, the warden decreed that Rundle have no further interaction with inmates who might become involved in court proceedings.

The denouement came shortly thereafter, when Rundle refused to release a confidential psychiatric file of a prisoner suspected of murdering a prison official. Rundle was subsequently ambushed by some 20 guards, who forcibly seized the files and escorted him to the warden's office, where he was fired. As Powelson and Bendix (1951:83) predicted, "Those who do not fit in will be eliminated."

It is the author's position that when an institution acts so as to reduce the humanity of people, its actions should be resisted not only by the victims but also by the members of the institution whose work would ordinarily contribute to the dehumanization process. What I have described in most cases is a reluctancy on the part of professionals to truly identify with the jailed at all, only their jailers. When identification with the individual breaks down, the professional has not only abandoned the *sine qua non* of his discipline but his sense of humanity.

SUMMARY AND CONCLUSIONS

Application of the medical model to the treatment of offenders assumes: crime is an outgrowth of individual pathology; the causes of crime can be isolated; criminals can be treated; and prognosis of future deviant behavior is possible. None of these assumptions have been scientifically validated, and even if they were, there is no reason to believe that the individualized treatment model would be implemented without consideration of custodial exigencies. This renders the treatment umbrella at best a gesture at window-dressing, which imputes legitimacy into an otherwise bankrupt penal system. However, the medical model is, of course, instrumental in that it enhances the public relations effort for the institution, assuages public guilt about punishment of offenders (prisoners are no longer "punished" but "treated"), and provides a more persuasive foundation for legislative and research allotment.

It has been shown that psychiatrists and psychologists, who adhere to the precepts of their profession, may find themselves in a dissonance-provoking environment, if they choose to work in the prison setting. The penal professional adapts by: assuming a role equivalent to that of a custody officer to become more consonant with the environment; going through the motions of providing treatment even if it is futile from a therapeutic viewpoint; relinquishing the job for practice elsewhere; or forcing confrontation within the system to make his role in prison more consonant with his principles as a psychiatrist or psychologist.

To avoid a compromise of the professional goals of psychiatrists and psychologists, the author proposes that dual interference by both the criminal and the therapeutic process should be prohibited. This could take several immediate forms: 1. Psychiatrists and psychologists should not sit on disciplinary boards. There is no therapeutic foundation which can justify the participation of psychiatrists and psychologists in invoking punishment. 2. Psychiatrists and psychologists should not sit on screening committees. There is no basis for professional sanctioning of custodial decisions based on security risks, custodial exigencies, institutional priorities, and other vague criteria. At best, the professional input legitimizes custodial decrees. 3. Therapy should cease to be a prerequisite for parole or linked, in any way, to term of confinement. Therapy has traditionally been offered on a contractual basis, and anything less becomes coercion. 4. Psychiatric and psychological evaluations should be abolished because they clearly violate professional ethics and undermine a therapist-patient relationship based on trust and confidentiality. In addition, it has been pointed out that these reports are interpreted by a board of men with no training in the social sciences, which is another departure from professional standards.

Along these lines, European models should be studied where punishment and treatment are conceptually segregated and the roles of judge and helper are sharply delineated (American Friends Service Committee, 1971). Imposition of imprisonment and its possible duration are questions of law to be determined by legal standards, which refers primarily to the offender's criminal act. That is, punishment fits the crime and not the individual. Furthermore, with particular application to the problem of conflict of interest, agencies that provide treatment have no power or effect upon form or duration of the prisoner's term and can serve his interests with undivided loyalty.

Finally, the author strongly recommends that psychiatrists, psychologists, and others begin to examine the issues raised in this paper. The loose definition of what is treatment has yielded an unjustified carelessness in what constitutes treatment. Regulation of the psychiatric and psychological professions is imperative. Is not that what a code of ethics is all about?

REFERENCES

Alexander, F. and H. Staub (1931) *The Criminal, The Judge, and the Public.* New York: Macmillan.

American Friends Service Committee (1971) *Struggle for Justice* New York: Hill and Wang.

Berman, A. (1971) "MMPI Characteristics of Correctional Officers." Paper presented at the meeting of the Eastern Psychological Association, New York, April, 1971.

Coleman, L. (1972) "California Prisons: The Crime of Punishment." Unpublished manuscript. Berkeley, California.

Cressey, D. (1960) "Limitations on Organization of Treatment," in *Theoretical*

Studies In Social Organization of the Prison. New York: Social Science Research Council.

Davis K. E. and E. E. Jones (1960) "Changes in Interpersonal Perception as a Means of Reducing Cognitive Dissonance." *Journal of Abnormal and Social Psychology* 61: 402–410.

Farber, M. F. (1944) "Suffering and Time Perspectives of the Prisoner." University of Iowa Studies in Child Welfare 20: 153–227.

Festinger, L., Riecker, H. W. and S. Schacter (1958) "When Prophecy Fails," in E. Maccoby, T. Newcombe, and Hartley (eds.) *Readings In Social Psychology*. New York: Holt, Rinehart, & Winston.

Halleck, S. (1968) *Psychiatric Aspects of Criminology*. Springfield, Ill.: Thomas.

Halleck, S. (1971) *Psychiatry and the Dilemmas of Crime*. Berkeley: University of California Press.

Halleck, S. (1973) *The Politics of Therapy*. New York: Science House Inc.

Howard, J. M. and R. H. Sommers (1971) "Resisting Institutional Evil from within," in N. Sanford, C. Comstock, & Associates *Sanctions for Evil*. San Francisco: Jossey-Bass.

Irwin, J. (1970) *The Felon*. Englewood Cliffs, N. J.: Prentice-Hall.

Katkin, E. (1970) "Psychological Consultation in a Maximum Security Prison: A Case History and Some Comments. Unpublished manuscript. Buffalo: State University of New York.

Kittrie, N. N. (1971) *The Right to be Different*. Baltimore: Penguin Books.

Lerner, M. J. and C. H. Simmons (1966) "Observer's Reaction to the 'Innocent Victim': Compassion or Rejection?" *Journal of Personality and Social Psychology* 4: 203–210.

Lewin, K. (1948) *Resolving Social Conflicts*. New York: Harper.

McConnell, J. V. (1970) "Criminals Can Be Brainwashed — Now." *Psychology Today* 3, 11:14–74.

Messinger, S. (1969) "Strategies of Control." Ph.D. Dissertation. Berkeley: University of California.

Mitford, J. (1972) "Kind and Usual Punishment," in B. Atkins and H. Glick (eds.) *Prisons, Protest, and Politics*. Englewood Cliffs, N. J.: Prentice-Hall.

Mitford, J. (1973) *Kind and Usual Punishment*. New York: Alfred A. Knopf.

Opton, E. M. (1974) "Psychiatric Violence against Prisoners: When Therapy Is Punishment." *Mississippi Law Journal* 45,3: 605–644.

Powelson, H. and R. Bendix (1951) "Psychiatry in Prison." *Psychiatry* 14: 73–86.

Schnur, A. (1961) "Current Practices in Correction, A Critique," in H. Toch (ed.) *Legal and Criminal Psychology*. New York: Holt, Rinehart, & Winston.

Sparks, R. F. (1968) "Types of Treatment for Types of Offenders," in *Collected Studies in Criminological Research*, Volume III. Strasbourg: Council of Europe.

Sutherland, E. H. and D. R. Cressey (1970) *Criminology*. Philadelphia: J. B. Lippincott.

Zimbardo, P. G. (1971) "The Psychological Power and Pathology of Imprisonment." Hearings before Subcommittee No. 3, House Committee on the Judiciary, 92nd Congress, Part II, Serial No. 15, October 25, 1971: 152–157.

Rehabilitation of Criminal Offenders— A Re-assessment of the Concept

Seymour L. Halleck

The American system of correctional justice fails dismally in its efforts to rehabilitate criminal offenders, and only the most naive reformers can hope that this situation will soon change. While it may now be possible for a greater number of offenders to escape the retribution or incapacitation society wishes to impose upon them, the offender who is unfortunate enough to be sentenced to prison is treated in a manner that is depressingly similar to the manner in which offenders were treated 50 years ago.

Our society's failure to rehabilitate criminals has many political and economic explanations. It is also true, however, that we have never had a clear and dispassionate idea of what we mean by rehabilitation. The term lends itself to propagandistic or pejorative uses. Some reformers insist that rehabilitation is the only legitimate goal of criminal justice, ignoring society's right to impose retribution on those who violate its laws, to use such retribution to deter potential offenders and to restrain or incapacitate those who are dangerous. Administrators of our system of correctional justice have a distressing tendency to use the term to obfuscate their critics. By constantly emphasizing rehabilitative aspects of their programs, correctional administrators are able to distract the public's attention from the harsh realities of penal treatment. "Hard liners" feel we have already invested too much time and money trying to rehabilitate criminals who should simply be punished. And finally, even some reformers, who feel that emphasis on rehabilitation often justifies repressive practices such as prolonged indeterminate confinement, have begun to question the value of rehabilitation in correctional justice.(1)

Any definition of rehabilitation must be based upon behavioral change. Society's primary goal in seeking to rehabilitate the offender is to get him to stop behaving in an illegal manner once he is freed from the restraints of prison. A more lofty goal of rehabilitation is not only to extinguish certain behaviors but to teach the offender new behaviors which are socially acceptable or socially desirable. We are not merely content to stop the offender from repeating criminal acts; we also want to make him a better citizen.

The definition of rehabilitation which says that "bad" behavior should stop and "good" behavior should take its place is primarily based on the needs of the society rather than upon the needs of the individual offender. If the definition were to be sufficient to meet the needs of both society and the offender, we would have to assume that an offender who behaves the way others want him to behave will be happy. Unfortunately, this is not always the case. The offender may find that the things that have been done to him chemically, surgically, psychologically, and socially to make him a "better" citizen have so impaired him that he is actually more miserable than he was before his treatment began. In this regard it should be noted that rehabilitation must take place through a process of intervention into the life of the patient and into the patient's environment. We do things to the patient and sometimes to those around him which we call treatment. Such treatment requires some degree of trust on the part of the offender towards those who wish to treat him. If the offender does not have some hope that treatment will leave him as happy or happier than he was before treatment, his trust and cooperation will not be forthcoming. If those who treat do not have some belief that treatment will leave the offender as happy or happier than he was before treatment, they may not be motivated to seek to rehabilitate their client.

But the ethical problem of rehabilitation has implications which go much beyond the matter of cooperation between the treater and treated. In an age when the technologies for changing behavior are becoming more precise, we have come to appreciate that even those who have violated the law have certain basic rights. There are limits to the extent to which we can legally try to change an individual's behavior, if the individual does not welcome such change. Even if the therapist or treating agency is deeply concerned with the patient's ultimate happiness or well-being, the law increasingly puts limits upon society's right to attempt alteration of the criminal's behavior without the offender consenting to such change or understanding the risk to his future well-being which may be implicit in such change. (2)

The conflict between the interest of society and the interest of the individual offender can be illustrated most powerfully by considering the "political" prisoner. Some men violate the law out of conscience or as part of a deliberate effort to change the society. If we "rehabilitated" these men and trained them to behave in a manner which the mass of citizens might find desirable, we would be negating their freedom to dissent and depriving the society of one important channel for social change. Consider, for example, the impact on our society if our prisons had succeeded in rehabilitating such convicted offenders as Henry Thoreau, Eugene Debs, Martin Luther King, or Malcolm X. These examples dramatize that the issue of rehabilitation must be considered not only in terms of our capacity to change human behavior but also in terms of under what circumstances and to what extent we should be allowed to do so.

One of the questions which penologists have debated for decades is "do we have the technical skills for changing criminal behavior and replacing it with 'desirable' behavior?" Some are skeptical that this can be done. Others acknowledge that criminal behavior can be changed but question whether such change is worth the economic effort. One of the key issues in considering rehabilitation is to make some effort to define how those behaviors labeled criminal can be changed and to describe the technologies of change with enough specificity so that their economic costs can be evaluated. This is a formidable enough task in itself, but it is only the beginning of our conceptual problem. For, even if we are convinced that we can change criminal behavior in a manner which society desires, we must consider the ethical justification for implementing such change. Each mode of therapeutic intervention must be considered not only in terms of its effectiveness, but also in terms of its ethical, political and economic implications.

CHANGING CRIMINAL BEHAVIOR

All human behavior, including criminal behavior, is determined by an individual's interaction with his environment, by who an individual is (his genetic make-up and previous experiences) and by where he is (the nature of stresses and reinforcements in his immediate environment). This oversimplified, yet accurate, conception of behavior helps to define hypotheses as to the causes of crime and more importantly suggests directions for therapeutic interventions. There are four major strategies for changing criminal behavior.

An individual's biological state may be changed. When a person is given psychoactive drugs, convulsive therapy, or is subjected to psychosurgery his brain chemistry or physiology will be altered and his behavioral responses to environmental stimuli will be altered. Many of the biological interventions currently available can drastically change behavior and can be utilized in a manner that will reduce the probability of criminal behavior. It is quite likely that in the near future we will develop even more powerful biological means of changing criminal behavior. Obviously, biological therapies can either be voluntarily accepted by the offender, or they can be imposed upon him.

The individual's environment can be changed so as to provide him with new learning experiences. In a new environment behavioral change is effected by reinforcing certain behaviors and extinguishing others. A new environment can be created either inside or outside of institutions; it can differ either partially or totally from the offender's old environment. Sometimes it is possible to devise total environments which reinforce "desirable" behavior and extinguish "undesirable" behavior. More often behavioral scientists try to change behavior by setting up limited environments in which the client is either advised or directed to change some part of his daily life. Or the client is given the opportunity to interact regularly with a therapist or counselor who provides a therapeutic climate of intimacy (in effect, a changed environment) in which new learning can take place. All of the conventional psychotherapies, individual, group and to a certain extent family, rely on the creation of a climate of trust and intimacy between therapist and client or between client and client which allows for new learning to take place. Some of the newer behavior therapies do not require intimate interpersonal relationships as part of the field in which new learning takes place, but rather an impersonal and relatively precise structuring of the client's environment.

Therapies which are based upon trust and close interpersonal relationships usually, but not always, require the client's consent. One of the interesting and ethically troubling aspects of the more precise behavior therapies is that they provide a rationale for creation of environments which can be imposed upon the client. The prison itself uses a crude form of behaviorism when it rewards certain behaviors and punishes others. But more sophisticated environments can be created by placing involuntary offenders into environments dominated by operant conditioning models such as a token economy. This is a form of treatment in which the offender may have little choice in accepting or rejecting relatively effective behavioral change. The offender may not even be aware of how his environment has been deliberately orchestrated to bring about such change. (It should be noted that behavior modification techniques can also be utilized with the client's consent. The offender can be persuaded to cooperate in a series of treatment techniques in which he voluntarily enters a certain environment or tries to change his environment in a manner which provides for new learning.)

The learning experience provided within the prison can be as powerful as those who run the prison are sophisticated enough and ruthless enough to make it. This is because the offender's captors have total control of his environment. If there were no legal or ethical restraints upon prison administrators and if they employed the principles of behaviorism with sufficient technical skill they could totally control the offender's behavior, at least while the offender was still in prison, and perhaps for a long time afterwards.

Behavior can be changed not only by changing the contingencies of reinforcement within the environment, but also by changing the nature of environmental stimuli through an increase or reduction of stress. Most maladaptive behavior is diminished when levels of environmental stress are diminished. Criminals often change their behavior when they find even temporary relief from the stresses of bigotry and poverty. They also change when the level of stress generated by their own families is moderated. The only conventional therapy that works directly at diminishing environmental stress is family therapy. But any social intervention which reduces real oppression in the offender's life is likely to reduce the probability of his repeating criminal acts.

Behavior can be changed, at least moderately, by providing people with new information. The offender may, by gaining new information about his own motivations (insight), experience change in the manner in which he perceives his environment. This change in perception may alter his responses to environmental stimuli. The offender may also gain new information or insight as to the impact he has on others. Such information will also change his motivations and perceptions. Finally, the offender can gain more information as to the nature of his environment. The manner in which such knowledge facilitates behavioral change has not been adequately conceptualized by behavioral scientists and needs some elaboration. A person who is walking in the woods and encounters a harmless snake will behave differently depending on whether he has the knowledge which allows him to discriminate between poisonous and nonpoisonous snakes. A person who is being treated badly by someone close to him but who does not know he is being treated badly may lash out at inappropriate targets. Once he perceives the source of oppression his behavior is likely to change. At a broader social level, we have seen that large groups of people such as women or Blacks have changed much of their self-punitive behavior by acquiring greater knowledge or consciousness of the oppressions which society has imposed upon them.

All of the conventional psychotherapies, individual, group, and family, are in part designed to help the individual gain greater information about himself. Group therapies are particularly suitable for helping the client to understand his impact upon others. Family therapies often provide the client with new information as to how significant figures in his life are reacting towards him. In recent years we have also seen the development of a series of consciousness-raising techniques in which behavioral change, often in the form of political activism, is facilitated by seeking to expand the awareness of oppressed people as to the sources of their misery.

For the sake of completeness, it should be noted that there is a fifth way of changing a criminal behavior, by creating an environment in which such behavior would be unlikely to take place. We can prevent an individual from committing an antisocial act within our society, temporarily, by totally incapacitating him; or permanently, by deporting him. These are well-known penological treatments. They are not included here because rehabilitation is usually defined as behavioral change which occurs and continues in what we consider to be normal society.

BEHAVIORAL TECHNOLOGY IN PRISONS

Having considered a variety of interventions which can at least theoretically change criminal behavior, it is now possible to examine the manner in which these interventions are utilized in current penology. Biological interventions are used sparsely. Psycoactive drugs are primarily utilized to control the aggressive behavior of those confined to prison. Few, if any, prisons have sophisticated enough psychiatric services to be able to diagnose and treat offenders with drugs in a manner designed to help the offender to change his behavior in a salutary manner once he has left prison.

A few years ago there was a brief resurgence of interest in psychosurgery for violent offenders suspected of having brain disorders. This practice resulted in such an enormous outcry from civil liberties groups that for all practical purposes psychosurgery in prisons is nonexistent at present. Similar considerations apply to the use of drugs as an adjunct to aversive conditioning therapy. For a time some institutions were utilizing curare-like drugs as an aversive stimulus for extinguishing "undesirable" behavior. This potentially sadistic form of treatment has also been vigorously criticized and curtailed.(3)

The major rehabilitative emphasis in modern penology is upon the total prison environment, in which it is hoped that the offender will be exposed to new learning experiences unfavorable to criminal behavior and favorable to law abiding behavior.(4) In theory, the prison environment tries to teach offenders that "crime does not pay," while at the same time teaching them new behaviors that will be so satisfying, to both offenders and society, that motivations towards antisociality will diminish. The efficiency of this process has grave shortcomings. In a society where only a tiny percentage of those who commit crimes are apprehended, convicted and imprisoned, it is hard to visualize how any form of learning, even learning based on extreme punishment, could teach offenders that "crime does not pay." Rather, the offender, through punishment, is more likely to learn the imperative of avoiding future apprehension, conviction or sentencing. He will be brutally taught that being too poor and powerless to afford the legal assistance that might keep him out of prison is highly undesirable. Even if our society could provide a system of equal justice in which most offenders did end up in prison, there would still be a question as to how much punishment would be necessary to teach those offenders that "crime does not pay." Our current system provides for an extent of punishment which far exceeds that which is necessary to teach this lesson. Public condemnation, fines, restrictions of freedom within the community or a few months of deprivation of freedom within an institution would probably teach that "crime does not pay" better than the overkill of the absurdly lengthy sentences we currently impose upon offenders. Whatever aversive conditioning to criminality itself that takes place in our penal institutions is imprecise, unscientific, and, judging by our recidivism statistics, highly ineffective. (All of this says nothing about the usefulness of punishment in deterring other offenders, which is an issue which will not be considered here.)

What does our current system of correctional justice do to teach offenders new behaviors that might help them lead satisfying and socially acceptable lives once released? Here there are a few pluses and many minuses. Some of the better prison systems do have adequate educational and vocational training programs. Almost all prison systems offer a respectable amount of spiritual guidance. Almost all of our prisons also have some type of program for rewarding inmates who demonstrate socially accepted behavior. The degree of precision involved in such programs varies. Some have relied on specific behavioral techniques such as a token economy, but such programs have recently fallen into disuse, partially on the grounds that they may be a too powerful tool for shaping behavior without the individual's consent. (There is a bitter irony here. The sadistic and sloppy behavior modification involved in traditional treatment of incarcerated offenders was rarely attacked. It was only when more precise and more powerful means of changing behavior were developed that civil libertarians became alarmed.) Other programs have tried to teach offenders desirable behavior by placing them in situations where they have few privileges and gradually granting them privileges as their behavior becomes more socially acceptable. These programs too are under legal attack on the grounds that they cruelly and inhumanely deprive the offender of basic gratifications.

Serious deficiencies are present in the efforts of modern prisons to shape behavior through either systematic or unsystematic rewards and punishments. In the first place, the incarcerated offender is living in a situation of extreme stress. A number of forces within the prison environment make it difficult for him to conform to the expectations of those in authority. Secondly, the "desirable" behavior which the institution is trying to shape may not in any way meet the needs of the offender once he is released from the institution. Prisons attempt to enforce a rigid conformity, an attitude of self-abnegation, and an exaggerated humility upon their inmates. They also teach offenders how to survive under conditions of extreme loneliness and emotional deprivation. Learning these traits may help the offender in his efforts to be released from prison, but it is unlikely that it will help him relate to people in the free world, or to learn to find a job and enjoy being productive.

Opportunities to learn how to live more adaptively in the free world through the experience of intimacy with a psychotherapist or counselor are also sorely limited in our current prisons. Nowhere in this country can the offender find the kind of individual counseling or psychotherapy that is available to the average middle-class person who seeks help. And, unfortunately, the availability of therapeutic services for the offender is getting worse, not better. If one just considers the profession of psychiatry, it must be shamefully reported that there were more psychiatrists working in prisons in the 1930s than there were in the 60s.(5) This is in spite of an enormous increase in the number of institutionalized offenders. Mental health professionals have learned, of course, that it is not easy to do counseling or psychotherapy within the walls of a prison. The offender has a problem developing trust towards a person who is an employee of the system that is determined to punish him. Even if the offender is able to have a good learning experience within the limited number of hours he is able to see his therapist or counselor, it is unlikely that these experiences can be generalized and reinforced during the major part of the offender's day which is spent in a cruel and dangerous environment.

In fairness, it must be pointed out that a certain amount of salutary learning through intimacy and through altering the contingencies of environmental reinforcement does take place in therapeutic prison groups. Group therapy is probably the most available and the most effective intervention in modern penology. Its effectiveness, however, is subject to the same limitations as individual therapy in a prison environment.

While the extent of positive learning available to offenders is limited, the possibilities of maladaptive learning in American prisons are almost unlimited. Our prisons provide a number of learning experiences which may not be directly related to whether or not the offender will later continue to commit antisocial acts but which are definitely antagonistic to developing qualities which make for happy survival in a free society. The worst aspect of the prison environment is that it teaches offenders to be fearful of intimacy. Close relationships between prison employees and offenders are discouraged, and close relationships between offenders carry the connotation of homosexuality with subsequent guilt or actual punishment. Prisons also ruthlessly suppress all manifestations of normal aggressiveness or assertiveness, qualities essential for effective survival in a competitive society. An offender who is too assertive or who is any way aggressive is punished. Finally it must be noted that the prisoner is taught to be passive and dependent. While in the institution he has practically no control over his own life and he is systematically deprived of the opportunity of making decisions. Almost every hour of his day, every work or recreational experience is structured by forces he cannot control. This kind of training in no way allows him to develop the sense of personal responsibility that is needed for effective functioning within a democratic society. As the prisoner loses his sense of autonomy he will increasingly view himself as a person who is not responsible for his subsequent behavior.

To the extent that prisons have tried to create environments which teach adaptive, non-criminal behavior they have been notoriously ineffective. The failure here is primarily related to the limitations of effective learning in a punitive environment, but it is also a by-product of the callousness and, at times, incredible naivete of those who administrate our system of correctional justice.

When the possibility of changing behavior through reducing stress in the offender's life is considered, the inadequacy of modern penology becomes even more blatant. While the offender is in prison he is deliberately exposed to a series of formidable stresses which elicit considerable psychological pain. These stresses not only require heroic adaptations to survive the prison experience, but the memories of stress are also firmly imprinted in the offender's mind and are a constant source of embitterment once he leaves prison. Furthermore, the prolonged isolation of the offender from his community usually guarantees that he will be exposed to a more stressful environment when he leaves prison than he experienced before he committed his crime. The released offender is obviously stigmatized. He is discriminated against both overtly and covertly. While in prison he has missed out on job training and job opportunities which might have enabled him to compete effectively in the free world.

In addition, he often loses many of his sources of emotional support.

When men spend years in prison there is a considerable risk that their wives will leave them. Friends forget about them or avoid them; parents or children may reject them. There are few organized programs in our prisons for helping offenders deal with these stresses. Even at the time of release from prison few efforts are made to work with the offender's family, friends, employers, or community. The paroled offender, at least in theory, has a parole agent who is supposed to help him with problems of re-entry. But the parole officer rarely has the skill, the time or the power to help reduce stress in the parolee's life. The conditions of parole may, in fact, add to the stress. When parolees are directed to live in certain places, avoid certain people, regulate their life styles, and deprive themselves of satisfactions which are available to others, such as sex and alcohol, they are likely to experience their lives as oppressive. Their situation is made even worse when they are periodically investigated by law authorities who consider parolees as prime suspects for new crimes in the community.(6)

Current efforts to alter criminal behavior by providing offenders with more information about themselves and others are also inadequate. Little insight therapy, or therapy in which the offender learns about his own motivations through an intensive therapeutic relationship, is conducted in prisons. When long-term insight-oriented psychotherapy is available, its effectiveness is limited by the harsh conditions of imprisonment. The offender exposed to a highly oppressive environment tends to view his behavior in terms of what others have done to him. So much suffering is imposed from without that it is difficult for him to gain the motivation to look within. Even if there were enough therapists to provide adequate insight therapy (which is unlikely to ever happen), it is hard to see how offenders could obtain the introspective attitude needed for such therapy unless conditions of imprisonment were drastically changed. One of the few kinds of useful information an offender does often receive in prison relates to the impact he has upon others. One good way of providing this information is through group therapy. As noted previously, group therapies in a prison setting have been one of the most effective techniques not only for helping produce more conforming behavior within the institution but also for motivating some offenders to change their behavior outside the institution.

New information that the incarcerated offender gains about the rest of the world can, in many circumstances, be a factor in diminishing the probability of future criminal behavior. The offender who learns the appropriate sources of his frustrations may lose some of his propensity to lash out at inappropriate targets. Frequently, the offender's criminal acts are, at least in part, determined by correct and oppressive attitudes and actions of other members of his family. Family therapy would seem to be a treatment of choice for many offenders. But it is almost impossible to conduct family therapy in penal institutions. Prisons are usually located in remote areas, and most families cannot afford to visit their incarcerated relatives with any regularity. Furthermore, family therapy is difficult to conduct when one member of the group is incarcerated and the others are free. The inmate fears that too much expression of his own feelings, particularly expression of anger, may discourage his loved ones from returning.

Consciousness-raising groups are not encouraged by prison administrators. When inmates learn how society has oppressed them, there is a risk that their new anger and pride will make them more difficult to manage within the prison environment. Yet much consciousness raising does go on at a covert level in many prisons. Black offenders surrounded by such a disportionate number of Black men in similar unfortunate circumstances have developed distinctly negative views of society. Both White and Black offenders are now gaining new knowledge of how the social and legal system has contributed to what they see as their victimization. They have developed a new sense of pride, have tended to blame society rather than themselves for their plight and have tried to free themselves of the self-hatred which contributes to their passivity. The overall usefulness of this new consciousness is, at this point, far from clear. It seems that some offenders have utilized their new consciousness to develop a constructive life of social activism once they leave prison. Others have been able to gain a new self-esteem that makes it easier for them to adapt to the free world. But it is also probable that many offenders who gain new information about what their society has done to them merely become embittered. Some feel justified in continuing a life of crime, and some are able to rationalize their future self-serving criminality as political action. Consciousness raising also has an impact upon other aspects of rehabilitation. On the one hand, it enables the offender to resist some of the most oppressive autonomy-destroying aspects of the prison environment. On the other hand, it also makes the offender more resistant to potentially liberating interventions, such as psychotherapy or counseling.

Finally, it must be noted that one kind of information that is always available in the prison setting relates to how to become a better criminal. Living with other convicted offenders exposes the inmate to almost unlimited sources of information as to how to engage in criminal activity and (although his teachers may not be the best), how to avoid apprehension.

WHAT COULD BE DONE

Having reviewed the depressingly inadequate manner in which our current system of penology utilizes various interventions to change criminal behavior, it is now possible to examine the manner in which the same modes of intervention could be used more effectively. Throughout this discussion, however, it will be necessary to repeatedly distinguish between "what could we do?" and "what should we do?"

In considering biological interventions, the powerful things that could be done and the ethical problems involved in doing them can be highlighted by some exaggerated examples. We could probably eliminate a good deal of repetitive criminal behavior by enforcing massive tranquilization of offenders or we could eliminate almost all repetitive criminal behavior by lobotomizing them. Hopefully, we will never get to the point of considering such interventions seriously. There will be temptations, however, to utilize drugs and surgery to control criminal behavior as more effective biological technologies are developed.(7) If we develop pharmaceutical agents which diminish aggressivity or if we develop techniques of electrode implantation in pain and pleasure centers (which can then be stimulated if the offender behaves "appropriately" or "inappropriately"), many voices even in a democratic society will call for use of these technologies as a weapon of total behavioral control. Even now we have available a drug which, if used in a Machiavellian enough fashion, could give society almost ultimate power to control criminal behavior. If we were to forcefully addict criminals to heroin and then regulate their supply of heroin contingent upon their behaving in a socially acceptable manner, society would have almost unlimited control of their behavior both in and out of prison. (To a certain extent we may be doing this with methadone right now.)

Most of the biological therapies currently available can drastically reduce the individual's capacity to enjoy a successful and happy life. If we are to consider the offender's well-being as well as society's needs, their usage must be carefully regulated. There is at this time little ethical justification for enforcing biological treatments upon nonconsenting patients. This is especially true of psychosurgery. Given the capacity of such treatment to destroy an individual's intellectual potentialities and to limit his behavioral repertoire, it should never be utilized without the offender's consent. Even if the offender should be willing to accept such a treatment, his consent should be based upon full knowledge of the dangers of the treatment and the availability of alternative treatments.

The situation with regard to psychoactive drugs is somewhat more complex. A certain number of people in any prison population exhibit manic or schizophrenic behavior which is partly influenced by some type of biological dysfunction. These people are often happier and behave more appropriately when treated with drugs such as phenothiazines and lithium. Many can avoid criminality if they use these drugs in an appropriate manner. Such drugs should, after proper psychiatric diagnosis, be available to offenders who are willing to take them. A few offenders could benefit from psychoactive drugs, but are so deranged that they lack the competency to consent to receiving such drugs. In such cases, involuntary use of these psychoactive agents might be permissible after careful psychiatric and judicial review. The guiding principle in the use of psychoactive drugs with offenders should be that they not be used to control behavior that society views as undesirable, but be used only when there is a suspected biological dysfunction and where there is good evidence that noncriminal patients with similar problems have had salutary responses to such therapy.

In the meantime, research on biological determinants of criminal behavior should continue. While most biological theories of crime are too naive to have had much influence in modern criminology, there is at least a small amount of evidence that certain criminal behavior, particularly violent behavior, may have some biological determinents.(8) If we can define these biological factors and if interventions can be found for remedying them, we may have ethical justification for using them. Further research is also needed into the relevance of biological deficits which may impair learning. A large number of offenders confined in prison appear to have had serious learning difficulties in their early school years. If we could demonstrate the relevance of dyslexia as at least a partial etiology in some forms of criminal behavior, new preventive approaches and new training techniques for younger offenders could be developed.

Intervention by creating environments in which new and socially acceptable learning takes place can be done in a far more efficient manner than we have known in the past. The data of the behavioral sciences strongly suggest that the environmental intervention involved in the conventional psychotherapies and more precise behavioral modification techniques do have some effectiveness in changing behavior that is defined as illness. They might well be equally effective in changing many forms of criminal behavior. A major question here is whether it is possible to create a therapeutic environment in prison. Far more socially useful learning could be offered if the majority of convicted offenders were treated outside of prison, in half-way houses, group homes or community clinics. Here again, society must make an ethical decision as to the extent to which it is willing to abandon its commitment to retribution. It must also decide whether it wishes to risk the possible deterrent value of incarceration in favor of the expanded rehabilitative possibilities of extramural treatment. My opinion is that the risk is overwhelmingly worth taking. Still, the issue of deterrence cannot be dismissed in a cavalier fashion. Fear of incarceration may deter at least a few white-collar criminals. Whether it deters the majority of oppressed, alienated and unreasonable men who end up in prison is more debatable. The argument over the usefulness of imprisonment as deterrence could go on endlessly. It does seem likely, however, that we could gain some real data on this issue if our society would be courageous enough to experiment with new modes of correctional practice.

Society must also consider whether it has the right to impose new learning upon offenders even if such learning takes place outside of prison. As noted previously, not all offenders want to be rehabilitated. This problem could be partially resolved by offering each convicted offender a choice of extramural treatment or incarceration. In effect we would preserve the offender's "right to punishment."

Even in the kind of system of correctional justice being considered here, there would still be the need for forceable restraint of certain offenders. Some offenders are dangerous to others. Others will not respond to treatment in an extramural setting and if they continue to commit crimes may have to be temporarily restrained. The restraining institution, however, could offer a far more therapeutic environment than that which is currently available in our prisons. If the society were willing to make the economic investment, conventional and behavioral therapies could be used within prisons far more frequently and more precisely than they are now. Academic and vocational training could be markedly expanded. Family therapies could be more extensively utilized if we were willing to provide transportation and housing for the offender's relatives. And, most important, a prison environment could be created in which values such as intimacy, assertiveness and autonomy were not massively negated. Again, some restrained offenders might not wish to be rehabilitated. These individuals, like those who reject extramural rehabilitation, could simply be restrained in a relatively benevolent environment in which no effort would be made to change their behavior.

These changes might reduce some of the environmental stress generated by the prison itself. In addition, many other kinds of environmental interventions could reduce stress in the lives of offenders once they return to the free world. One concrete intervention would be to help offenders find jobs. Another would be to provide them with adequate sustenance so as to diminish the ravages of poverty. A question arises here as to how far the society is willing to go, economically and politically, in providing special care for offenders. It might be argued that if society invested too many of its resources in trying to help those who had already committed criminal acts, rather than in alleviating stress upon those who are similarly oppressed but do not commit criminal acts, we would be discriminating against the law-abiding and perhaps even encouraging oppressed people to violate the law. Far fewer political issues are involved in another form of stress reduction, that of intervening in smaller social systems which place particular stress on the offender, such as his family. Family therapies, if expanded, could be a powerful tool towards changing criminal behavior.

(I am deliberately avoiding consideration of the extent to which criminals could be rehabilitated by drastically changing the nature of American society. Undoubtedly, a diminution in racism, economic exploitation, and social forces which create alienation would help many offenders find a non-criminal adjustment. These issues, while relevant, are beyond the scope of this paper.)

Finally, we must consider how criminal behavior might be more effectively changed through provision of new information. If use of the conventional psychotherapies were expanded as a form of re-educative intervention, many of them would be based on a concurrent effort to help the offender find new awareness of his own motivation. Much controversy exists in the behavioral sciences as to the extent to which insight facilitates behavioral change. The prevailing opinion is that insight is neither a necessary or sufficient condition of behavioral change, but that it may in certain circumstances be a powerful vector towards behavioral change.(9) We have no reason to suspect that the impact of insight upon those who behave in a criminal manner would be more or less powerful than upon those who are viewed as emotionally disturbed. The issue here is that we have never really made any sizable effort to use insight as a form of intervention in dealing with criminal behavior. Whether such an expensive intervention is practical or even possible will again be a difficult social decision. The economic issues in expanding the use of group and family therapies as a means of supplying the offender with new information are not nearly so perplexing. Group therapies are obviously more economical than individual therapies, and a powerful and useful awareness of the environment can be provided by family therapy through a relatively brief intervention.

Increased use of consciousness-expanding techniques would undoubtedly increase the probability of behavioral change but would create new ethical issues. What would happen if, instead of letting offenders develop a new consciousness of their situation through covert and anti-establishment organization, the prison system itself sought to help offenders consider the extent to which they have been victimized? It is possible to conceive of a correctional system that would help offenders learn about the social and political as well as the psychological causes of their criminality. If such learning was combined with efforts to teach legal forms of social activism, such as community organization, it might be a powerful tool for diminishing criminality. Undoubtedly, if the correctional system chose to co-opt the process of consciousness expansion now going on among offenders, it could direct the behavioral change derived from such processes in the direction of legal, rather than illegal, activism. But all of this has complex psychological and political pitfalls. It is questionable whether offenders would accept consciousness expansion from members of a social structure that is oppressing them. And it is questionable whether our society would be willing to utilize a form of therapeutic intervention that might eventually facilitate drastic changes in the society itself.

CONCLUSIONS

I have tried to show how the concept of rehabilitation must be viewed not only in terms of systematic effort to change behavior but also in terms of complex ethical, political and economic issues. Space limitations have not made it possible to explore most of the issues in depth and have led to almost complete omission of some critical issues such as the usefulness of indeterminate confinement and the gross injustices in the processes of convicting and sentencing offenders. The effort here has been to phrase questions regarding rehabilitation in a new light. It is banal and misleading to ask questions such as "does rehabilitation work?" Rather, the critical questions are first, "how can we change criminal behavior?" and second, "assuming that we know how to change criminal behavior, what ethical, political and economic restraints should limit our interventions?" The answers to the first question are not as difficult as most criminologists would have us believe. It is in our quest for finding a moral basis for rehabilitative intervention that we will encounter the greatest difficulty.

NOTES

(1) American Friends Service Committee. *Struggle for Justice—A Report on Crime and Punishment in America (6)* 1971.

(2) Halleck, S. L. Legal and Ethical Aspects of Behavior Control. *American Journal of Psychiatry.* In Press.

(3) Ennis, B. Prisoners of Psychiatry: Mental Patients, *Psychiatry and the Law.* New York: Harcourt, Brace, Jovanovich, 1972.

(4) Gilbons, D. C. *Charging the Law-Breaker*, Englewood Cliffs, N.J.: Prentice-Hall, 1965.

(5) Halleck, S. L. American Psychiatry and the Criminal: A Historical Review. *Supplement to American Journal of Psychiatry.* March, 1965.

(6) Corrections, Federal and State Parole Systems, Hearings before Subcommittee Number 3, Corrections Part VII—B Serial Number 15,

Washington, D.C.: U.S. Government Printing Office, 1972.

(7) For a brief review of some of the current technological developments see, The Mind of the Murders. *Medical World News.* New York: November 23, 1973.

(8) Mark, V. H. and Erwin, F. R. *Violence and the Brain.* New York: Harper and Row, 1970.

(9) Bandura, A. *Principle of Behavior Modification.* New York: Holt, Rinehart, and Winston, 1969.

VII.

Summaries
of Decisions
in Case Law

Introduction

The last and concluding section of this volume is comprised of forty-three abstracts of the most important legal cases related to forensic psychiatry and psychology. Most of the cases are recommended by the American Psychiatric Association as study material for the new Boards in forensic psychiatry. The abstracts are also useful to lawyers and other professionals in criminal justice. The cases have been mentioned throughout both volumes of *The Psychological Foundations of Criminal Justice*, and readers should be able to refer to these abstracts easily in this section.

The Summaries

IN RE BALLAY,
482 F.2d 648 (D.C. Cir. 1973); 157 U.S. App. D.C. 59.

Albanian-born John Ballay was committed to St. Elizabeths Hospital in Washington, D.C. After presenting himself at the White House and claiming to be a Senator from Illinois and the husband of Tricia Nixon, he tried to seek an audience with the President. On two earlier occasions that same year, 1971, he had made similar appearances—once at the U.S. Capitol and once at the White House. Ballay had no known criminal record or known record of mental illness prior to 1971. Following a hearing held before the Commission on Mental Health in July, the Commission recommended that the court commit Ballay for institutional care. Ballay asserted his right to a jury trial, was found by the jury to fall within the statutory prescription, and was admitted to St. Elizabeths Hospital. The U.S. Court of Appeals for the District of Columbia reversed the judgment on the grounds that constitutional error was committed in the trial. As the Court stated:

> John Ballay was alleged to be "mentally ill *and,* because of that illness, . . . likely to injure himself or other persons if allowed to remain at liberty . . ." The jury was instructed that it must be convinced by a *preponderance of the evidence* that both elements were present, a standard of proof which has been consistently applied by force of case law. The question is whether appellant was deprived of due process of law because the jury did not

determine, *beyond a reasonable doubt*, that he was mentally ill and consequently dangerous.

BAXSTROM v. HEROLD,
    383 U.S. 107; 86 S. Ct. 760 (1966).

Johnny Baxstrom, an inmate at Dannemora State Hospital in New York, petitioned for a writ of *habeas corpus* seeking release from the hospital, which is administered by the New York State Department of Correction. He had been convicted of assault and sentenced to prison for two years. During his incarceration, Baxstrom was certified insane by a prison physician and confined to the hospital. At the end of Baxstrom's prison sentence, the hospital sought a civil commitment, maintaining that the prisoner was still mentally ill. The Department of Mental Health found the

> petitioner unsuitable for confinement in a civil hospital. Consequently, although his custody was transferred to mental health, he was maintained in Dannemora Hospital.
>
> In New York, civil commitment requires a jury trial, and the "dangerousness" of the ill individual is a judicial determination.
>
> The United States Supreme Court, in a unanimous decision, said:

>> We hold that petitioner was denied equal protection of the laws by the statutory procedure under which a person may be civilly committed at the expiration of his penal sentence without the jury review available to all other persons civilly committed in New York. Petitioner was further denied equal protection of the laws by his civil commitment to an institution maintained by the Department of Correction beyond the expiration of his prison term without a judicial determination that he is dangerously mentally ill such as that afforded to all so committed except those, like Baxstrom, nearing the expiration of a penal sentence.
>>
>> Section 384 of the New York Correction Law prescribes the procedure for civil commitment upon the expiration of the prison term of a mentally ill person confined in Dannemora. Similar procedures are prescribed for civil commitment of all other allegedly mentally ill persons. N.Y. Mental Hygiene Law §§ 70, 72. All persons civilly committed, however, other than those committed at the expiration of a penal term, are

expressly granted the right to *de novo* review by jury trial of the question of their sanity under § 74 of the Mental Hygiene Law. Under this procedure any person dissatisfied with an order certifying him as mentally ill may demand full review by a jury of the prior determination as to his competency. If the jury returns a verdict that the person is sane, he must be immediately discharged. It follows that the State, having made this substantial review proceeding generally available on this issue, may not, consistent with the Equal Protection Clause of the Fourteenth Amendment, arbitrarily withhold it from some.

The director contended that the commitment was triggered by conviction of a crime and, thus, was a valid classification. The court said:

We find this contention untenable. Where the State has provided for a judicial proceeding to determine the dangerous propensities of all others civilly committed to an institution of the Department of Correction, it may not deny this right to a person in Baxstrom's position solely on the ground that he was nearing the expiration of a prison term. It may or may not be that Baxstrom is presently mentally ill and such a danger to others that the strict security of a Department of Correction hospital is warranted. All others receive a judicial hearing on this issue. Equal protection demands that Baxstrom receive the same.

The capriciousness of the classification employed by the State is thrown sharply into focus by the fact that the full benefit of a judicial hearing to determine dangerous tendencies is withheld only in the case of civil commitment of one awaiting expiration of penal sentence. A person with a past criminal record is presently entitled to a hearing on the question whether he is dangerously mentally ill so long as he is not in prison at the time civil commitment proceedings are instituted. Given this distinction, all semblance of rationality of the classification, purportedly based upon criminal propensities, disappears.

BLOCKER v. UNITED STATES,
288 F.2d 853 (D.C. Cir. 1961); 110 U.S. App. D.C. 41.

On April 5, 1957, in Washington, D.C., Comer Blocker shot and killed his common-law wife, Frances Hall, with whom he had had five children. Blocker had been separated from his wife for some time and had been living in Philadelphia. Prosecution showed that Blocker had purchased a shotgun in Philadelphia and had brought the gun with him to Washington, where he subsequently used it as the weapon to murder Frances Hall with two blasts. He told the arresting officer that he had come from Philadelphia to kill his girlfriend. In October of 1957, a jury in the U.S. District Court found Blocker guilty of murder in the first degree. On appeal, the Court held that giving an instruction which improperly placed the burden on the defendant of establishing his defense of insanity was reversible error, although the institution came between two instructions which properly imposed the burden on the prosecution to establish that the defendant was sane.

BOLTON v. HARRIS,
  395 F.2d 642 (D.C. Cir. 1968); 130 U.S. App. D.C. 1.

Bolton, the defendant was found not guilty by reason of insanity and sent to St. Elizabeths Hospital in Washington, D.C. Three months later he filed for *habeas corpus.* The case asked whether automatic commitment after a verdict of not guilty by reason of insanity for a period required to determine present mental condition is constitutional. The Court held that automatic commitment under these circumstances was not unconstitutional, but the Court did hold that once the observation period is over, the defendant is entitled to a judicial hearing substantially similar to those in civil commitments. The patient is entitled to periodic examinations, and if one physician believes that the patient is no longer a danger, the patient is entitled to a court hearing.

CAESAR v. MOUNTANOS,
  542 F.2d 1064 (9th Cir. 1976).

A California psychiatrist sought *habeas corpus* from a contempt adjudication for failure to respond to a court order directing him to answer questions about a former patient. The order was based on a "patient-litigant" exception to the psychotherapist-patient privilege. At issue was whether equal protection under the law provides absolute protection for the psychotherapist-patient privilege. The Court held that this privilege is not applicable when the patient places her condition in issue; patient in the case was suing for damages resulting from a car accident. The compelling interest of the state is the need to insure that truth is ascertained in its courts of law. A dissenting opinion held that the ruling in this case would restrict "relevant" information to the fact of treatment, time and length of treatment, cost of treatment, and the ultimate diagnosis, *unless* the party seeking disclosures establishes a compelling need for the production of that information.

CARTER v. GENERAL MOTORS,
    361 Mich. 577; 106 N.W. 2d 105 (1961).

This case deals with a proceeding for workmen's compensation benefits for a psychosis resulting from emotional pressure enountered in daily work by a machine operator who worked on assembly line production. Medical testimony was introduced that the operator no longer showed any symptoms of a psychosis but that he should not be employed again in production work, although he could be reemployed in some other kind of work. From an award of compensation by the Workmen's Compensation Appeal Board, the employer appealed in the nature of certiorari. The Supreme Court of Michigan held that when expert testimony indicated that a machine operator had a personality disorder and a predisposition to developing a schizophrenic process and when the operator sustained a disabling psychosis caused by emotional pressures produced by production line employment, he sustained a disability compensable under part two of the Workmen's Compensation Act. However, evidence was insufficient to sustain an award of continuing disability after all evidence of a psychosis had disappeared.

CARTER v. UNITED STATES,
    252 F.2d 608 (D.C. Cir. 1957); 102 U.S. App. D.C. 227.

The defendant, Russell E. Carter, was convicted of murder in the first degree in the U.S. District Court in Washington, D.C. He appealed the conviction. Shortly after the trial had convened, the prosecutor was informed of the death of Carter's father. The Court was recessed without sequestering the jury or admonishing them not to communicate with others or read accounts of the trial. The defense also alleged that the instructions to the jury on insanity were inadequate in that they failed to make clear that when the issue of insanity is properly raised by evidence, the burden of proof is on the government to prove sanity beyond a reasonable doubt. Instead, the defense claimed, the purport of the instructions given to the jury left jurors with a clear impression that they must reach *affirmative* conclusions of mental disease and the causal connection between the disease and the act. The U.S. Court of Appeals reversed the District Court judgment and remanded the defendant for a new trial.

DIXON v. ATTORNEY GENERAL OF PENNSYLVANIA,
  325 F.Supp. 966 (M.D. Pa. 1971).

The class action suit in this case was initiated by state hospital inmates challenging as violative of due process the constitutionality of the state's mental health statute which permitted the institutionalization of anyone who appeared to be mentally disabled and in need of care. The statute made no provision for a judicial hearing; it merely required that application be accompanied by certification by at least two physicians. In addition, no time limits were established for discharge. The Court held that a person considered for commitment is entitled to a full judicial hearing and that commitment procedures and rules should be the same in a criminal or quasi-criminal proceeding as in a civil proceeding. The patient must be given the right to confront and cross-examine witnesses. Other requirements established by the Court's decision included: right of a subject to notification that the individual is entitled to representation by counsel and that counsel can be appointed in case the individual is unable to pay for the cost of representation; subject is entitled to independent expert examination, communication with whom is privileged; evidence must be clear and convincing that the subject poses danger to himself or others of serious personal harm; burden of proof is upon the state to prove the existence of such danger; the court must specify a maximum period of time, not to exceed six months, for confinement of the individual; and the right of the subject to a transcript and full record of all proceedings and the right to appeal.

DONALDSON v. O'CONNOR,
  493 F.2d 507 (5th Cir. 1974).
O'CONNOR v. DONALDSON,
  422 U.S. 563; 95 S.Ct. 2486 (1975).

Kenneth Donaldson was involuntarily committed to a Florida state hospital for almost 15 years without receiving significant therapy. As a Christian Scientist, he refused medication and electroshock, and he received no psychiatric treatment. After release, he brought suit in United States District Court, N.D. Florida, and, in a jury trial, received $28,500 in compensatory damages and $10,000 in punitive damages from the attending physicians.

The doctors appealed, challenging these instructions given by the trial court to the jury:

You are instructed that a person who is involuntarily civilly committed to a mental hospital does have a constitutional right to receive such individual treatment as will give him a realistic opportunity to be cured or to improve his mental condition.

The purpose of involuntary hospitalization is treatment and not mere custodial care or punishment if a patient is not dangerous to himself or others. Without such treatment there is no justification, from a constitutional standpoint, for continued confinement.

The United States Court of Appeals, Fifth Circuit, affirmed the lower court that a person involuntarily committed to a state mental hospital has a constitutional right to individual treatment.

The Supreme Court decision in *Donaldson* creates a dilemma for a court dealing with civil commitments. If a court establishes jurisdiction over a person, through a finding of mental illness or juvenile delinquency, must it then determine whether or not that person is a danger to himself or others? *Donaldson* seems to say precisely that. And, if the second finding is negative, is the state precluded from institutionalizing that person for treatment?

For example, if a court finds that a teenage girl is behaving promiscuously in violation of statute, but further finds that she is not a danger to herself for others, can she be commited to an institution?

If a person is found to be mentally ill because he engages in irrational or eccentric behavior which is not dangerous, can the state institutionalize him?

The Supreme Court has not answered these questions.

DRIVER v. HINNANT,
356 F.2d 761 (4th Cir. 1966).

Joe B. Driver, a fifty-nine-year-old alcoholic from North Carolina, was first convicted of public intoxication at the age of twenty-four. Subsequently he was convicted of this offense more than two-hundred times and had spent nearly two-thirds of his life incarcerated for these infractions. In this case, while admitting the truth of the charge under a North Carolina statute, he appealed his conviction on the basis of the due process clause of the Fourteenth Amendment. His argument could be condensed into the following syllogism: Driver's alcoholism is a disease which has destroyed the power of his will to resist the constant, excessive consumption of alcohol; his appearance in public in an inebriated condition is not of his own volition but is rather a compulsion symptomatic of alcoholism; to stigmatize him as criminal for his disease constitutes cruel and unusual punishment.

Driver's plea failed in the state courts; he then unsuccessfully petitioned the Federal District Court for habeas corpus to procure release from the imprisonment ordered in his sentence. Judgment was vacated by the U.S. Court of Appeals Fourth Circuit, and Driver was ordered released from detention on the understanding that, within ten days, the state would take him into civil remedial custody. In its decision, the Court said:

> the state cannot stamp an unpretending alcoholic as a criminal if his drunken public display is involuntary as the result of disease. However, nothing we have said precludes appropriate detention of him for treatment and rehabilitation so long as he is not marked as a criminal.

DURHAM v. UNITED STATES,
214 F.2d 862 (D.C. Cir. 1954); 94 U.S. App. D.C. 228.

Monte Durham, who had a lengthy history of imprisonment and hospitalization, was convicted of housebreaking by the District Court in Washington, D.C. The only defense asserted at the trial was that Durham was of unsound mind at the time of the offense. The defendant appealed. Counsel for Durham argued that the tests for determining criminal responsibility then used in the District of Columbia (the M'Naghten rules plus irresistible impulse) were not satisfactory criteria. The Court agreed, stating:

> We find that as an exclusive criterion the right-wrong test is inadequate in that (a) it does not take sufficient account of psychic realities and scientific knowledge, and (b) it is based upon one symptom and cannot validly be applied in all circumstances. We find that the 'irresistible impulse' test is also inadequate in that it gives no recognition to mental illness characterized by brooding and reflection and so relegates acts caused by such illness to the application of the inadequate right-wrong test. We conclude that a broader test should be adopted.

The new test of criminal responsibility adopted by the Court of Appeals under Circuit Judge Bazelon held that if the defendant's unlawful act was the product of mental disease or mental defect, the defendant was not criminally responsible.

DUSKY v. UNITED STATES,
362 U.S. 402; 80 S.Ct. 788 (1960); See also 271 F.2d 385 (8th Cir.

1959).

The Court stated:

> The motion for leave to proceed *in forma pauperis* and the petition for a writ of certiorari are granted. Upon consideration of the entire record we agree with the Solicitor General that "the record in this case does not sufficiently support the findings of competency to stand trial," for to support those findings under 18 U. S. C. § 4244 the district judge "would need more information than this record presents." We also agree with the suggestion of the Solicitor General that it is not enough for the district judge to find that "the defendant [is] oriented to time and place and [has] some recollection of events," but that the "test must be whether he has sufficient present ability to consult with his lawyer with a reasonable degree of rational understanding—and whether he has a rational as well as factual understanding of the proceedings against him."
>
> In view of the doubts and ambiguities regarding the legal significance of the psychiatric testimony in this case and the resulting difficulties of retrospectively determining the petitioner's competency as of more than a year ago, we reverse the judgment of the Court of Appeals affirming the judgment of conviction, and remand the case to the District Court for a new hearing to ascertain petitioner's present competency to stand trial, and for a new trial if petitioner is found competent.

EASTER v. DISTRICT OF COLUMBIA,
361 F.2d 50 (D.C. Cir. 1966); 124 U.S. App. D.C. 33.

Defendant DeWitt Easter was convicted in the Court of General Sessions in the District of Columbia of public intoxication. The sentence was subsequently affirmed by the Court of Appeals. The U.S. Court of Appeals for the District of Columbia granted leave to appeal. It held that chronic alcoholism is a defense to a charge of public intoxication and is not itself a crime. The Court also held that expert medical and psychiatric evidence established that the defendant was a chronic alcoholic who had lost control over his use of alcoholic beverages.

IN RE GAULT,
387 U.S. 1; 87 S.Ct. 1428 (1967).

Gerald Gault, a fifteen-year-old living in Arizona, was sentenced to the "remainder of his minority" (six years) for an offense (making an obscene telephone call) for which the *maximum* penalty for an adult would have been only two months in jail. During the course of his hearings, he was deprived of most of the privileges that are granted to his adult counterparts. His appeal was heard by the United States Supreme Court. In its decision reversing the lower court's verdict, the Court affirmed the right of a juvenile to notice of the charge or charges against him; [the] right to representation by counsel; [the] privilege against self-incrimination; and rights to confrontation and cross-examination of witnesses, to a transcript of the proceedings, and to appellate review.

This case completely reshaped the direction of the juvenile justice system. It replaced the concept of *parens patriae* with that of due process and equal protection under the law. As Mr. Justice Abe Fortas stated, the informality and procedural laxity of juvenile courts were often followed by stern discipline in juvenile correctional institutions, leaving the juvenile feeling like a victim of deception.

PEOPLE OF THE STATE OF CALIFORNIA v. NICHOLAS GORSHEN,
51 Cal. 2d 716; 336 P.2d 492 (1959).

The defendant Nicholas Gorshen, a fifty-six-year-old longshoreman with a twenty year history of paranoid schizophrenia, shot and killed his foreman after having consumed a considerable quantity of sloe gin. He pleaded guilty to second degree murder and waived a jury trial. In appealing the ensuing judgment, Gorshen's counsel argued that un-contradicted psychiatric testimony, accepted by the trial court, established that the defendant did not intend to take human life or, at least, that he did not act with malice aforethought. Therefore Gorshen should be acquitted or, as a minimum of relief, his offense should be reduced to manslaughter. The California Supreme Court affirming the judgment of the lower Court, stated that in its judgment the evidence as to the objective circumstances of the killing supported all of the findings implied by the verdict. The court also asserted that the record did not support the defendant's claim that the trial court had found the defendant guilty *despite their belief* that the evidence indicated the defendant did not have the state of mind required as an element of second degree murder.

JACKSON v. INDIANA,
    406 U.S. 715, 92 S.Ct. 1845, 32 L.Ed.2d 435 (1972).

Jackson, a mentally deficient deaf mute, was accused of two robberies, was found incompetent to stand trial, and was committed to the state department of mental health until such time as the department could certify his "sanity" to the court. Medical testimony indicated that Jackson would probably never learn any communication skills, and the state had no facilities for helping him obtain those skills. He was committed under a statute carrying more lenient commitment standards and more stringent standards for release than statutes covering feeble-minded or mentally ill persons not accused of crimes.

The United States Supreme Court ruled that condemning Jackson ". . . in effect to permanent institutionalization without the showing required for commitment or the opportunity for release . . ." contained in the other statutory schemes was a denial of equal protection.

KAIMOWITZ v. MICHIGAN DEPARTMENT OF MENTAL HEALTH,
    No. 73–19434–AW Mich. Cir. Ct., Wayne Co. July 10, 1973, unreported, but text available in 1 *Mental Disability Law Rptr.* 147 (1976).

The court was asked whether "after failure of established therapies, an involuntarily confined mental patient can give legally adequate consent to an innovative or experimental surgical procedure." The Court replied that the physician must "weigh the risk to the patient against the possible benefit to be obtained by trying something new." Reiterating previous statements on First Amendment rights, the Michigan Circuit Court stated:

There is no privacy more deserving of constitutional protection than one's mind . . . Intrusion into one's intellect when one is involuntarily detained and subject to the control of institutional authorities is an intrusion into one's constitutionally protected right to privacy. If one is not protected in his thoughts, behavior, personality, and identity, then the right to privacy is meaningless.

Before a state can violate one's constitutionally protected right to privacy . . . a compelling state interest must be shown.

KREMENS v. BARTLEY,
   431 U.S. 119; 97 S.Ct. 1709 (1977).

Individuals who were between fifteen and eighteen years old were named as plaintiffs in an action challenging the constitutionality of Pennsylvania statutes governing voluntary admission and voluntary commitment of individuals eighteen years of age and younger to state mental institutions. Following certification of class, a three-judge U.S. District Court for the Eastern District of Pennsylvania held that the challenged provisions violated due process, and appeal was taken. The Supreme Court, Mr. Justice Rehnquist, held that the claims of the plaintiff were moot, in the light of recent changes in the law under which mentally ill juveniles fourteen years of age and older were, in essence, treated as adults. On the other hand, the Court found difficulties in the statute with regard to defining the members of the class it was intended to cover. The Court concluded that the issues raised were "not capable of repetition," yet they proved impossible to review. The case was remanded to the District Court for reconsideration of the class definition, exclusion of those whose claims were moot, and substitution of class representatives with valid claims.

LESSARD v. SCHMIDT,
   349 F. Supp. 1078 (E.D. Wis. 1972).

A woman, committed to a state mental hospital, brought a class action on behalf of herself and others over the age of eighteen, challenging the validity of the Wisconsin civil commitment procedures.

In declaring the procedures unconstitutional insofar as they violated various due process rights, a three-judge panel in the United States District Court, E.D. Wisconsin, had this to say about the quantum of evidence and burden of proof required in civil commitments:

> At least one court would require proof beyond a reasonable doubt on all questions relating to civil commitment. *Denton v. Commonwealth,* 383 S.W.2d 681 (Ky. 1964). In *In re Winship,* . . ., the Supreme Court held that proof beyond a reasonable doubt was required to prove every facet necessary in juvenile delinquency proceedings, noting that 'extreme caution in factfinding,' . . . is necessary because of 'the possibility that [the individual] may lose his liberty upon conviction and because of the certainty that he would be stigmatized

by the conviction.' . . . The Court reiterated its previous holding in *In re Gault* . . ., that 'civil labels and good intentions do not themselves obviate the need for criminal due process safeguards in juvenile courts, for "[a] proceeding where the issue is whether the child will be found to be 'delinquent' and subjected to the loss of his liberty for years is comparable in seriousness to a felony prosecution." ' . . . The *Winship* Court reached its conclusion despite its findings that an adjudication of delinquency 'does not deprive the child of his civil rights, and that juvenile proceedings are confidential.' . . .

The argument for a stringent standard of proof is more compelling in the case of a civil commitment in which an individual will be deprived of basic civil rights and be certainly stigmatized by the lack of confidentiality of the adjudication. We therefore hold that the state must prove beyond a reasonable doubt all facts necessary to show that an individual is mentally ill and dangerous.

IN RE LIFSCHUTZ,
2 Cal. 3d 415; 467 P. 2d 557 (1970).

Dr. Joseph E. Lifshutz, a psychiatrist practicing in California, sought a writ of habeas corpus to secure his release from custody in San Mateo County Jail, where he had been incarcerated for contempt of court. He had refused to obey a San Mateo County Superior Court order instructing him to answer questions and produce records relating to communications with a former patient. In denying Lifshutz's petition, the California Supreme Court held that no constitutional right enables a psychotherapist to assert an absolute privilege regarding all psychotherapeutic communications. The Court stated:

We do not believe the patient-psychotherapist privilege should be frozen into the rigidity of absolutism. So extreme a conclusion either harmonizes with the expressed legislative intent nor finds a clear source in constitutional law. Such an application would lock the patient into a vise which would prevent him from waiving the privilege without the psychotherapist's consent. The question whether such a ruling would have the medical merit claimed by the petitioner must be addressed to the legislature; we can find no basis for such a ruling in legal precedent or principle.

MCDONALD v. UNITED STATES,
  312 F.2d 847 (D.C. Cir. 1962); 114 U.S. App. D.C. 120

The appellant, Ernest McDonald, was convicted of manslaughter in a case involving the charge of second-degree murder for aiding and abetting his employer in the shooting of a third party named Jenkins. McDonald was sentenced to from five to fifteen years of imprisonment. In his appeal, McDonald's counsel argued that the Court's charge to the jury was defective in two respects: First, the Court failed to state that, if acquitted by reason of insanity, the appellant would be confined in a mental hospital until it was determined that he was no longer dangerous to himself or others. This kind of statement is required unless it "appears affirmatively on the record" that the defendant did not want the statement included. Second, the Court twice enumerated in its charge the alternative verdicts available to the jury, but both times it failed to include "not guilty because of insanity."

The Court of Appeals held that the evidence entitled the defendant to have the issue of mental defect submitted to the jury and that the jury should be told that a mental disease or defect includes any abnormal condition of the mind which substantially affects mental or emotional processes and substantially impairs behavior controls. The Court also held that the defendant was entitled to be instructed that if he was acquitted by reason of insanity he would be confined in a mental hospital until it was determined that he was no longer dangerous to himself or others unless he did not wish to be instructed.

MORALES v. TURMAN,
  535 F.2d 864 (5th Cir. 1976) rev'd per curiam 97 S.Ct. 1189 (1977).

This case involves an action challenging allegedly unconstitutional punitive and inhumane conditions in Texas institutions housing juvenile delinquents. A single district judge of the United States District Court for the Eastern District of Texas, 383 F.Supp.53, determined that juveniles' constitutional rights had been violated and ordered parties to submit a curative plan. The United States Court of Appeals for the Fifth Circuit vacated the decision, 535 F.2d 864, on the ground that a three-judge court should have been convened, and certiorari was granted. The Supreme Court held that the unwritten practices of juvenile institutions administered by the Texas Youth Council, challenged as unconstitutional, were not the equivalent of a statute with statewide applicability within the meaning of the three-judge court statute. Equivalency did not exist particularly when the alleged necessity of convening a three-judge court was not properly apparent until considerable factual development of the breadth and content of the administrative practices had taken place. Consequently, the single district judge properly exercised jurisdiction to decide the case, and his judgment was reviewable on the merits by the Court of Appeals.

NASON v. SUPERINTENDENT OF
BRIDGEWATER STATE HOSPITAL,
  353 Mass. 774: 233 N.E. 2d 908 (1968).

Nason was indicted for murdering his wife. In jail, he demonstrated deranged symptoms and was put in Bridgewater State Hospital, which was used for observation and secure-custody cases and did not have facilities or staff comparable to the other eleven public mental hospitals in the state. Nason petitioned for *habeas corpus*, alleging that he was being held without having been convicted of a crime and was not receiving treatment.

The Supreme Judicial Court of Massachusetts, Suffolk, said:

Cases like this present serious constitutional, legislative, and budgetary problems [.I]n comparable matters we have not failed to consider whether adequate medical and psychiatric treatment is available to persons confined in public institutions for their own and the public's protection. . . . If such treatment is not available on a reasonable, nondiscriminatory basis, there is substantial risk that constitutional requirements of equal protection of the laws will not be satisfied.

PAINTER v. BANNISTER,
  258 Iowa 1390, 140 N.W. 2d 152 (1966).

In this case, habeas corpus action was initiated by Harold Painter, father of a seven-year-old boy named Mark Wendell Painter, to regain custody of his child from the grandparents, to whom the boy had been entrusted following his mother's death two years previously. The District Court awarded custody to the father, and the grandparents appealed. The Iowa Supreme Court held that the best interests of the child required that his sixty-year-old maternal grandparents, who had provided "stable, dependable, middle-class, middlewest background," be awarded permanent custody. In refusing to return the child to his father, who had since remarried, the Court weighed the likelihood of seriously disrupting and disturbing effects on the boy's development which could result from his return to the "unstable, unconventional, arty, Bohemian, and probably intellectually stimulating" household of his father.

PATE v. ROBINSON,
  383 U.S. 375; 86 S.Ct. 836 (1966)

In 1959, Theodore Robinson was convicted of the murder of his common-law wife, Flossie May Ward; he was sentenced to life imprisonment. Being an indigent, Robinson was defended by court-appointed counsel. It was conceded at trial that Robinson shot and killed Flossie May Ward, but his counsel claimed that he was insane at the time of the shooting and raised the issue of his incompetence to stand trial. On writ of error to the Supreme Court of Illinois, it was asserted that the trial court's rejection of Robinson's claims deprived Robinson of due process of law under the Fourteenth Amendment. Robinson's conviction was affirmed. The Court found that no hearing on mental capacity to stand trial had been requested, that the evidence failed to raise sufficient doubt as to his competence to require the trial court to conduct a hearing on its own motion, and that the evidence did not raise a "reasonable doubt" as to Robinson's sanity at the time of the offense. Robinson then filed a petition for habeas corpus, which was denied without a hearing by the U.S. District Court for the Northern District of Illinois.

The Court of Appeals reversed on the ground that Robinson was convicted in an unduly hurried trial without a fair opportunity to obtain expert psychiatric testimony, and without sufficient development of the facts on the issues of Robinson's insanity when he committed the homicide and of Robinson's present incompetence. It remanded the case to the District Court with directions to appoint counsel for Robinson; to hold a hearing as to his sanity when he committed the alleged offense; and—if it found him to have been insane at that time—to order his release subject to an examination into his present mental condition. The Court of Appeals directed that the District Court should also determine in the hearing whether Robinson was denied due process by the court's failure to conduct a hearing upon his competence to stand trial; and—if it were found that his rights had been violated in this respect— that Robinson "should be ordered released, but such a release may be delayed for a reasonable time . . . to permit the State of Illinois to grant Robinson a new trial." The U.S. Supreme Court granted certiorari to resolve the difficult questions of state and federal relations posed by these rulings. The Court concluded that Robinson was constitutionally entitled to a hearing on the issue of his competence to stand trial. As the Court stated: "Since we do not think there could be a meaningful hearing on that issue at this late date, we direct that the District Court, after affording the State another opportunity to put Robinson on trial within a reasonable time, order him discharged."

POWELL v. STATE OF TEXAS,
   392 U.S. 514; 86 S.Ct. 2145 (1968).

The defendant, charged with being drunk in a public place, had presented evidence that he was a chronic alcoholic with an irresistible compulsion to drink and, once intoxicated, he had no control over his behavior. He also testified that he had had one drink the morning of the trial and no more, either because he wanted to be sober for the trial or he had no money to buy more. The lower court ruled that chronic alcoholism is not a defense to public drunkenness.

The United States Supreme Court could not agree upon an opinion, but five favored affirming the conviction for differing reasons.

Four members of the court felt the record did not support a finding of chronic alcoholism and further pointed out that the medical profession itself has no generally accepted definition or treatment for chronic alcoholism, saying:

> . . . In the first place, the record in this case is utterly inadequate to permit the sort of informed and responsible adjudication which alone can support the announcement of an important and wide-ranging new constitutional principle. We know very little about the circumstances surrounding the drinking bout which resulted in this conviction, or about Leroy Powell's drinking problem, or indeed about alcoholism itself. The trial hardly reflects the sharp legal and evidentiary clash between fully prepared adversary litigants which is traditionally expected in major constitutional cases. . . .
>
> Furthermore, the inescapable fact is that there is no agreement among members of the medical profession about what it means to say that 'alcoholism' is a 'disease.' One of the principal works in this field states that the major difficulty in articulating a 'disease concept of alcoholism' is that 'alcoholism has too many definitions and disease has practically none.' This same author concludes that *'a disease is what the medical profession recognizes as such.'* In other words, there is widespread agreement today that 'alcoholism' is a 'disease,' for the simple reason that the medical profession has concluded that it should attempt to treat those who have drinking problems. There the agreement stops. Debate rages within the medical profession as to whether 'alcoholism'

is a separate 'disease' in any meaningful bio-chemical, physiological or psychological sense, or whether it represents one peculiar manifestation in some individuals of underlying psychiatric disorders. (Emphasis in original)

This opinion noted the present futility for the court to prescribe treatment and felt that sobering up in jail was not cruel and unusual punishment.

ROBINSON *v.* CALIFORNIA,
    370 U.S. 660; 82 S.Ct. 1417 (1962).

The defendant was convicted of violation of a statute making it a criminal offense to be addicted to the use of narcotics. He was sentenced to ninety days in jail. The evidence showed that he had needle marks on his arm, the freshest being possibly three weeks old. It was agreed that he was not under the influence of drugs at the time of his arrest.

The Supreme Court found that imprisonment for the status of being a drug addict was cruel and unusual punishment. Recognizing that drug control was a legitimate state concern, the Court said:

> Such regulation, it can be assumed, could take a variety of valid forms. A State might impose criminal sanctions, for example, against the unauthorized manufacture, prescription, sale, purchase, or possession of narcotics within its borders. In the interest of discouraging the violation of such laws, or in the interest of the general health or welfare of its inhabitants, a State might establish a program of compulsory treatment for those addicted to narcotics. Such a program of treatment might require periods of involuntary confinement. And penal sanctions might be imposed for failure to comply with established compulsory treatment procedures. . . . Or a State might choose to attack the evils of narcotics traffic on broader fronts also—through public health education, for example, or by efforts to ameliorate the economic and social conditions under which those evils might be thought to flourish. In short, the range of valid choice which a State might make in this area is undoubtedly a wide one, and the wisdom of any particular choice within the allowable spectrum is not for us to decide. . . .

The statute had a fatal infirmity, the Court said, and continued:

> This statute . . . is not one which punishes a person for the use of narcotics, for their purchase, sale or possession, or for antisocial or disorderly behavior resulting from their administration. It is not a law which even purports to provide or require medical treatment. Rather, we deal with a statute which makes the 'status' of narcotic addiction a criminal offense, for which the offender may be prosecuted 'at any time before he reforms.' California has said that a person can be continuously guilty of this offense, whether or not he has ever used or possessed any narcotics within the State, and whether or not he has been guilty of any antisocial behavior there.
>
> It is unlikely that any State at this moment in history would attempt to make it a criminal offense for a person to be mentally ill, or a leper, or to be afflicted with a venereal disease. A State might determine that the general health and welfare require that the victims of these and other human afflictions be dealt with by compulsory treatment, involving quarantine, confinement, or sequestration. But, in the light of contemporary human knowledge, a law which made a criminal offense of such a disease would doubtless be universally thought to be an infliction of cruel and unusual punishment in violation of the Eighth and Fourteenth Amendments. . . .

ROUSE v. CAMERON,
  373 F.2d 451 (D.C. Cir. 1966); 125 U.S. App. D.C. 366.

The appellant, Charles C. Rouse, was arrested for having in his possession a .45 automatic and six hundred rounds of ammunition, a misdemeanor carrying a one-year sentence. Rouse was involuntarily commited to St. Elizabeths Hospital

> in Washington, D.C., for diagnosis and observation. He had been confined in the hospital for four years when he brought his *habeas corpus* petition. The lower court said its only jurisdiction was to ascertain if the patient was sane. Considering the nature of the original crime, the lower court found the risks too great to release the petitioner.
>
> On appeal, the Court of Appeals said, absent treatment, the

commitment section of the statute would be of doubtful constitutionality. The court continued:

> . . . Commitment on this basis is permissible because of its humane therapeutic goals. . . . Had appellant been found criminally responsible, he could have been confined a year, at most, however dangerous he might have been. He has been confined four years and the end is not in sight. Since this difference rests only on need for treatment, a failure to supply treatment may raise a question of due process of law. It has also been suggested that a failure to supply treatment may violate the equal protection clause. . . . Indefinite confinement without treatment of one who has been found not criminally responsible may be so inhumane as to be 'cruel and unusual punishment.'

The defendant contended a statutory right to treatment had been established and cited the 1964 Hospitalization of the Mentally Ill Act:

> A person hospitalized in a public hospital for a mental illness shall, during his hospitalization, be entitled to medical and psychiatric care and treatment. The administrator of each public hospital shall keep records detailing all medical and psychiatric care and treatment received by a person hospitalized for a mental illness and the records shall be made available, upon that person's written authorization, to his attorney or personal physician.

In looking for legislative intent, the court quoted Senator Sam Ervin who, while carrying the bill on the Senate floor, had stated that the legislation applied only to "civil hospitalization procedures." The court found this to be an ambiguous statement since no such limitation appeared in the right to treatment provision. To adopt that interpretation would raise serious equal protection questions not apparent on the face of the statute, the court said, and this contention by the defendant was disregarded.

Senator Ervin also called mere custodial care of hospitalized persons "shocking" and the right to treatment "most critical" and said:

> Several experts advanced the opinion that to deprive a person of liberty on the basis that he is in need of treatment, without supplying the needed treatment, is tantamount to a denial of due process. [The Senate bill]*** embodies provisions which will ameliorate this

problem whereas existing law makes no provisions for safeguarding this right.

PEOPLE EX REL. SCARPETTA v. SPENCE-CHAPIN ADOPTION SERVICE,
36 App. Div. 2d 254, 317 NYS 2d 298, Aff'd 28 NY 2d 185, 269 N.E. 2d 787, 321 NYS 2d 65 (1971).

This case involves the return of an out-of-wedlock infant to its natural mother after she had executed a purported surrender of the child to an authorized adoption agency. The appeal does not involve the undoing of an adoption or the return of an adopted child to its natural parents or the undoing of a surrender by the natural mother on her mere say-so. The undoing is based on a finding of fact that, for various reasons, the surrender was not by her with such stability of mind and emotion that the surrender should not be undone for improvidence. In revoking the surrender and directing the return of the child to the mother, the Court held that the mother was "motivated solely by her concern for the wellbeing of her child" and "has adequately stabilized her own relationships and has become stable enough in her own mind to warrant the return of the child to her."

SHELTON ET AL v. TUCKER ET AL,
364 U.S. 479; 81 S.Ct. 247 (1960).

This case was appealed from the U.S. District Court for the Eastern District of Arkansas. It involves an Arkansas statute which requires every teacher, as a condition of employment in a state-supported school or college, to file annually an affidavit listing without limitation every organization to which the teacher has belonged or regularly contributed within the preceding five years. Teachers in state-supported schools and colleges are not covered by a civil service system; they are hired on a year-to-year basis, and they have no job security beyond the end of each school year. The contracts of the Arkansas teachers were not renewed because the teachers refused to file the required affidavits. The court held that the Arkansas statute is invalid, because it deprives teachers from invasion by state action of their right of associational freedom protected by the due process clause of the Fourteenth Amendment. The Court stated that while there can be no doubt of the right of a state to investigate the competence and fitness of those whom it hires to teach in its schools, to compel a teacher to disclose his every associational tie is to impair one's right of free association, a right closely allied to freedom of speech and a right which, like free speech, lies at the foundation of a free society. The unlimited and indiscriminate sweep of Arkansas statute and its comprehensive interference with associational freedom go far beyond what might be justified in the exercise of the state's legitimate inquiry into the fitness and competence of its teachers.

SPECHT v. PATTERSON,
   386 U.S. 605; 87 S.Ct. 1209 (1967).

The defendant was convicted of indecent liberties under one statute, providing for a maximum ten-year sentence, and was then sentenced under another statute, the Sex Offenders Act of Colorado, to an indeterminate sentence of one day to life imprisonment. This is permissible if the trial court finds that the defendant is a danger to the public. In defendant's case, however, no sentence hearing was held. The United States Supreme Court said:

These commitment proceedings whether denominated civil or criminal are subject both to the Equal Protection Clause of the Fourteenth Amendment, as we held in *Baxstrom v. Herold*, 383 U.S. 107, and to the Due Process Clause. We hold that the requirements of due process were not satisfied here.

The court found charge under the Sex Offenders Act was a new issue and said:

Under Colorado's procedure, here challenged, the invocation of the Sex Offenders Act means the making of a new charge leading to criminal punishment. The case is not unlike those under recidivist statutes where an habitual criminal issue is 'a distinct issue' . . . on which a defendant 'must receive reasonable notice and an opportunity to be heard.' . . . Due process, in other words, requires that he be present with counsel, have an opportunity to be heard, be confronted with witnesses against him, have the right to cross-examine, and to offer evidence of his own. And there must be findings adequate to make meaningful any appeal that is allowed. The case is therefore quite unlike the Minnesota statute we considered in *Minnesota v. Probate Court*, 309 U.S. 270, where in a proceeding to have a person adjudged a 'psychopathic personality' there was a hearing where he was represented by counsel and could compel the production of witnesses on his behalf. . . . None of these procedural safeguards we have mentioned is present

under Colorado's Sex Offenders Act. We therefore hold
that it is deficient in due process as measured by the
requirements of the Fourteenth Amendment. . . .

TARASOFF v. BOARD OF REGENTS OF THE UNIVERSITY OF CALIFORNIA,
    17 Cal. 3d 425; 551 P.2d 334 (1976).

In this case, action was brought against the university regents,
psychotherapists employed by the university hospital, and campus police
to recover for the murder of the plaintiff's daughter by a psychiatric
patient. The Superior Court in Alameda County sustained demurrers
without leave to amend, and the plaintiff appealed. The Supreme Court
of California held that when a psychotherapist determines or the standards of his profession should determine that a patient presents a serious
danger of violence to another, the therapist incurs an obligation to use
reasonable care to protect intended victims against serious danger. The
discharge of obligation may require the therapist to take one or more
various steps, depending on the nature of the case. The Court further held
that, in this case, complaint could be amended on the theory of failure to
warn, to state cause of action against the therapists, to whom the patient
confided his intentions to kill plaintiffs' daughter. The Court also held
that therapists were entitled to statutory immunity from liability for
failure to bring about patient's confinement but that plaintiffs pled no
special relationship between the patient and the police defendants which
would impose upon the plaintiffs any duty to warn daughter or other
appropriate individuals. The Court finally held that the police were also
entitled to statutory immunity from liability for failure to confine the
patient.

TODD v. SUPERIOR COURT,
    68 Wash. 2d 587; 414 P.2d 605 (1966).

The Supreme Court of the state of Washington affirmed a lower court
finding that Debra Ann Todd, a thirteen-year old girl whose mother
demonstrated a disturbed mental condition which adversely affected the
child, was a dependent child as defined by a Washinton statute. The
statute permitted a finding of dependency if the child was kept in an unfit
place. School authorities, social workers, and law enforcement officers
had periodically entered petitions to have Debra Ann Todd declared a
dependent on the grounds that Mrs. Todd had steadfastly refused to
cooperate with them, had frequently withdrawn her child from
enrollment in particular schools to "fight" what she construed as a

"conspiracy" against her and her child, and had demonstrated *persecutory ideation.*

UNITED STATES v. BRAWNER,
    471 F.2d 969 (D.C. Cir. 1972); 153 U.S. App. D.C. 1.

The appellant, Archie Brawner, was convicted before the U.S. District Court in the District of Columbia of second-degree murder. The principal issues raised by his conviction relate to the appellant's defense of insanity. As a result of its deliberations, the U.S. Circuit Court of Appeals in the District of Columbia decided to adopt the American Law Institute's primary provision in its Model Penal Code: namely, that an individual is not responsible for criminal conduct if at the time of criminal conduct, as a result of mental disease or defect, the individual lacks substantial capacity to appreciate the wrongfulness of criminal conduct or to conform conduct to the requirements of the law. The terms, "mental disease or defect," incude any abnormal condition of the mind which sub-stantially affects mental or emotional processes and substantially affects mental or emotional processes and substantially impairs behavior controls. This decision overruled *Durham v. United States,* 94 U.S. App. D.C. 228; 214 F.2d 862, for trials commencing after June 23, 1972.

UNITED STATES v. CURRENS,
    290 F. 2d 751 (3d Cir. 1961).

The appellant, twenty-two-year old Donald Currens, stole a car in Mansfield Ohio, and drove it to Waterford, West Virginia, then to Pittsburgh, Pennsylvania, where he abandoned it. He was arrested in Las Vegas, Nevada, by federal officers and was later convicted of a federal offense in violation of the Dyer Act or National Motor Vehicle Theft Act. Currens had a criminal record of petty theft and a history of mental-instability which had been called, at one time or another, everything-from psychoneurotic hysterical reaction to chronic undifferentiated schizophrenia. The verdict was appealed on the grounds of insanity. In ruling on an appeal from this conviction, the U.S. Court of Appeals, Third Circuit, held that formulating a charge concerning the defendant's criminal responsibility in terms of the M'Naghten rules, based primarily on the right-wrong test was a prejudicial error. The Court recommended that the defendant was entitled to a new trial with the question of his criminal responsibility submitted on the basis of whether the jury was satisfied that, at the time of committing the prohibited act, the defend-ant, as a result of mental disease or defect, lacked substantial capacity to conform his conduct to the requirements of the law he allegedly violated.

UNITED STATES v. FREEMAN,
   357 F.2d 602 (2nd Cir. 1966).

Charles Freeman was found guilty in the U.S. District Court for the
Southern District of New York on two counts of selling narcotics. He was
sentenced to concurrent terms of five years on each count. Freeman
denied commission of the substantive offense; his principal allegation at
trial was that, at the time of the alleged sale of narcotics, he did not
possess sufficient capacity and will to be held responsible for the
criminality of his acts. In rejecting Freeman's contention, the District
Court relied on the M'Naghten rules. The U.S. Court of Appeals held that
M'Naghten rules, augmented by irresistible impulse, were unduly
restrictive as a test of criminal responsibility in the federal jurisdiction.
The Court proposed as an alternative Section 4.01 of the American Law
Institute's Model Penal Code. Section 4.01 provides that: "A person is not
responsible for criminal conduct if at the time of such conduct as a result
of mental disease or defect he lacks substantial capacity either to appreciate the wrongfulness of his conduct or to conform his conduct to the
requirements of law." Because Freeman's responsibility was determined
under the rigid standards of the M'Naghten rules, the Court of Appeals
felt that Freeman's conviction should be reversed and that the case should
be remanded for a new trial under criteria supplied by the A.L.I. Model
Penal Code. The Court added:

> . . . lest our opinion be misunderstood or distorted . . . we wish
> to make it absolutely clear that mere recidivism or narcotics
> addiction will not *of themselves* justify acquittal under the
> American Law Institute standards that we adopt today. Indeed,
> the second clause of Section 4.01 explicitly states that "the terms
> 'mental disease or defect' do not include an abnormality
> manifested only by repeated criminal or otherwise anti-social
> conduct." We approve and adopt this important caveat.

UNITED STATES EX REL SCHUSTER v. HEROLD,
   410 F.2d 1071 (2d Cir. 1969).

Roy Schuster, a New York prisoner serving a life sentence for the
murder of his wife, initiated a habeas corpus proceeding challenging the
legality of his transfer from Clinton Prison to Dannemora State Hospital,
an institution for the criminally insane. The U.S. District Court for the
Northern District of New York denied the petition, and the petitioner
appealed. The U.S. Court of Appeals, Second Circuit, held that Schuster
had been transferred without notice, hearings, or procedures accorded

civilians undergoing commitment to an institution for the criminally insane like Dannemora where Schuster was subjected to additional deprivations, hardships, and indignities. In addition, he was effectively deprived of an opportunity for parole. The Court ruled that Schuster was entitled to a hearing on the question of his sanity and to substantially all of the procedures granted to noncriminals who are involuntarily committed. Should these procedures result in the determination that Schuster was not mentally ill, the Court made the provision that he be returned to prison.

WADE v. UNITED STATES,
    426 F.2d 64 (9th Cir. 1970).

The defendant, Don Wade, was convicted of bank robbery in the U.S. District Court for the Central District of California, and he appealed the judgment. The U.S. Court of Appeals, Ninth Circuit, held that a person is not responsible for criminal conduct if at the time of such conduct, as a result of mental disease or defect, the person lacked substantial capacity either to appreciate the wrongfulness of the conduct or conform conduct to the requirements of law as stated in the A.L.I. Model Penal Code, Section 4.01. The Court, however, rejected paragraph two of the Model Penal Code, which states that "the terms 'mental disease or defect' do not include an abnormality manifested only by repeated criminal or otherwise antisocial conduct," stating that the inclusion of such an abnormality in the insanity instruction "should have little or no impact on the determination of the criminal responsibility of any mentally deranged defendant, whether psychopathic or not, since it is practically inconceivable that mental disease or defect would, in the terms of paragraph two, be manifested *only* by repeated criminal or otherwise antisocial conduct."

WASHINGTON v. UNITED STATES,
    390 F.2d 444 (D.C. Cir. 1967); 129 U.S. App. D.C. 29.

The defendant, Thomas H. Washington Jr., was convicted in the U.S. District Court for the District of Columbia of rape, robbery, and assault with a deadly weapon. His major defense was insanity. On appeal, he contended that the trial judge should have entered a judgment of acquittal by reason of insanity. The U.S. Court of Appeals held that the evidence in the case supported the finding that the defendant was not insane. Further, it stated that in an insanity case, the trial judge should limit the use of psychiatric and medical labels. The Court added that the trial judge should ensure that the meaning of terms like schizophrenia and neurosis be explained to the jury and as thoroughly as possible and that they should be explained in a way that clearly relates their relevance and meaning to the defendant and the case under consideration.

PEOPLE v. WELLS,
    33 Cal. 2d 330; 202 P.2d 53 (1949).

Wesley Robert Wells, a California prisoner serving an indeterminate sentence in Folsom State Prison, was convicted of assaulting and seriously injuring a prison guard who had proffered charges of misconduct against Wells. The Supreme Court of the State of California held that the defendant was undergoing a "life sentence" within the meaning of the statute which provided the death penalty for individuals assaulting a prison guard by means likely to produce great bodily injury. It also held that a prisoner serving an indeterminate sentence of not less than five years, when maximum term of imprisonment had not been fixed by the Adult Authority, has no valid claim to have such a sentence considered unconstitutional under the terms of the equal protection clause of the Fourteenth Amendment.

PEOPLE v. WOLFF,
    61 Cal. 2d 795; 394 P.2d 959 (1964).

The defendant, fifteen-year-old Ronald Wolff, beat and choked his mother to death after having planned the murder in order to eliminate her and get several girls to come to the house where he planned to either photograph them in the nude or rape them. Wolff was tried and convicted of first-degree murder. The judgment of the Superior Court was appealed on the ground that the California M'Naghten rules as a test of sanity were unconstitutional and deprived the defendant of due process and equal protection of the law. The California Supreme Court did not find the state's sanity test unconstitutional. However, it ruled that the evidence in the case failed to support the finding that matricide by a fifteen-year-old with a history of mental illness was murder in the first degree. It would amply sustain conviction for second-degree murder:

> The fact that we reduce the degree of the penal judgment from first to second degree murder is not to be understood as suggesting that this defendant's confinement should be in an institution maintaining any lower degree of security than for persons convicted of murder of the first degree. To the contrary, we approve of the trial court's recommendation that defendant be placed in a hospital for the criminally insane of a high security character . . .

WYATT v. STICKNEY,
325 F.Supp. 781 (M.D. Alabama N.D., 1971); 334 F.Supp. 1341 (1971); 344 F.Supp 373 (1972); 344 F.Supp 387 (1972).
WYATT v. ADERHOLT,
503 F.2d 1305 (5th Cir. 1974).

In these cases, a class action was brought to enjoin certain practices in three Alabama facilities for the mentally handicapped. In expenditure per patient, Alabama ranked fifteenth among the states. One institution housed 5,000 patients,

> including 1,500 geriatric patients and 1,000 mental retardates, who received no treatment. The United States District Court, M.D. Alabama, N.D., found that the remaining patients, who were supposed to receive treatment, did not, in fact receive *adequate* treatment. The court found this to be a violation of due process, saying:
>> The patients at Bryce Hospital, for the most part, were involuntarily committed through noncriminal procedures and without the constitutional protections that are afforded defendants in criminal proceedings. When patients are so committed for treatment purposes they unquestionably have a constitutional right to receive such individual treatment as will give each of them a realistic opportunity to be cured or to improve his or her mental condition. . . . Adequate and effective treatment is constitutionally required because, absent treatment, the hospital is transformed 'into a penitentiary where one could be held indefinitely for no convicted offense.' . . . The purpose of involuntary hospitalization for treatment purposes is *treatment* and not mere custodial care or punishment. This is the only justification, from a constitutional standpoint, that allows civil commitments to mental institutions such as Bryce. According to the evidence in this case, the failure of Bryce Hospital to supply adequate treatment is due to a lack of operating funds. The failure to provide suitable and adequate treatment to the mentally ill cannot be justified by lack of staff of facilities. . . . (Emphasis in original.)
>> There can be no legal (or moral) justification for the State of Alabama's failing to afford treatment—and adequate treatment from a medical standpoint—to the several thousand patients who have been civilly com-

mitted to Bryce's for treatment purposes. To deprive any citizen of his or her liberty upon the altruistic theory that the confinement is for humane therapeutic reasons and then fail to provide adequate treatment violates the very fundamentals of due process.

The court ordered the defendants to prepare and implement new standards for treatment and to submit the standards to the court for review within six months.

In December, 1971, the court affirmed that the patients had a constitutional right to receive such *individual* treatment as would give them a realistic opportunity to improve or be cured. The court allowed the defendants six months to set standards and fully implement a treatment program. The court found that the defendants had demonstrated good faith and deferred turning the institution over to a panel of masters.

In April, 1972, the court ordered a hearing to set standards for the care and treatment of the patients, but again deferred appointment of a master and an advisory committee.

In June, 1972, the court held the mentally ill patients and the mentally retarded patients who had joined them in the suit had been denied the right to treatment and ordered prompt institution of minimum standards of care. The court, after a hearing, found conditions had not improved and said this constituted bad faith on the part of the defendants.

The court said:

> For the present, however, defendants must realize that the prompt institution of minimum standards to ensure the provision of essential care and training for Alabama's mental retardates is mandatory and that no default can be justified by a want of operating funds. In this regard, the principles applicable to the mentally ill apply with equal force to the mentally retarded.

Bibliography

Abrahamsen, D. *The Psychology of Crime*. New York: Columbia University Press, 1966.

Abramson, M. F. "Participant Observation and Attempted Mental Health Consultation in a Public Defender Agency." *American Journal of Psychiatry*, 1971, 127(7), 964–969.

Allchin, W. H. "The Psychiatrist, the Offender, and the Community." *Med. Biol. Ill.* 1969, 19(3), 157–160.

Allen, R. C., Ferster, E., & Rubin, J. (Eds.) *Readings in Law and Psychiatry*. Baltimore, Md: Johns Hopkins Univ. Press. 1968.

Allen, R. *Mental Impairment and Legal Incompetency*. Englewood Cliffs, N.J.: Prentice-Hall, 1968.

Anderson, V. V. "Mental Disease and Delinquency." *Mental Hygiene* 3(1919), 177–198.

Arens, R. *Make Mad the Guilty: The Insanity Defense in the District of Columbia*. Springfield, Ill.: Charles C. Thomas, 1969.

Arens, R. *The Insanity Defense*. New York: Philosophical Library, 1974.

Arens, R., & Meadow, A. "Psycholinguistics and the Confession Dilemma." *Columbia Law Review*, 1956, 56, 38–46.

Balcanoff, E. J., & McGarry, A. L. "Amicus Curiae: The Role of the Psychiatrist in Pretrial Examinations." Paper presented at the 124th annual meeting of the American Psychiatric Association, Boston, Mass. May 13–17, 1968. *American Journal of Psychiatry*, 1969, 126 (3), 342–347.

Banay, R. *Mental Health in Corrective Institutions*. Proceedings of the American Prison Association New York: American Prison Association, 1941.

Barber, J. T., & Reite, M. "Crime and L.S.D.: The Insanity Plea." Paper read at the 125th anniversary meeting of the American Psychiatric Association, Miami Beach, Fla. May 5–9, 1969. *American Journal of Psychiatry*, 1968, 126(4), 531–537.

Bartholomew, A. A. "The Forensic Psychiatrist's Place in Correction." Paper presented at the fifth national conference in Perth of the Australian Crime Prevention, Correction and After-Care Council. *Aust. N.Z. J. Criminal.*, 1970, 3(2), 83–91.

Baxelon, D. L. "Psychologists in Corrections: Are They Doing Good for the Offender or Well for Themselves?" In S. L. Brodsky (Ed.), *Psychologists in the Criminal Justice System*. Marysville, Ohio: American Association of Correctional Psychologists, 1972.

Bender, L. "Psychopathic Disorders in Children." In R. M. Lindner (Ed.) *Handbook of Correctional Psychology*. New York: Philosophical Library, 1947.

Berkowitz, L. *Aggression: A Social Psychological Analysis*. New York: McGraw-Hill, 1962.

Blalock, J. "Civil Liability of Officers." *F.B.I. Enforcement Bulletin*, 1972, 41(2), 6–8, 29–30.

Binns, J. K., Carlisle, J. M., Nimmo, D. H. et. al., "Remanded in Custody for Psychiatric Examination. A Review of 83 Cases and a Comparison with Those Remanded in Hospital." *Brit. J. Psychiat.*, 1969, 115(527), 1133–1139.

Binns, J. K., Carlisle, J. M., Nimmo, D. H. et. al. "Remanded in Hospital for Psychiatric Examination. Section 54, Mental Health Act. 1960. A Review of 107 Admissions." *Brit. J. Psychiat.*, 1969, 115(527), 1125–1132.

Boruch, R. F. *Costs, Benefits and Legal Implications in Social Research*. Evanston, Ill.: Northwestern University Press, 1974.

Brodsky, S. L. *Psychologists in the Criminal Justice System*. Marysville, Ohio: American Association of Correctional Psychologists, 1972.

Brussel, J. A. *Casebook of a Crime Psychiatrist*. New York: Dell, 1968.

Bromberg, W., & Thompson, C. B. "The Relation of Psychoses, Mental Defect, and Personality to Crime. *Journal of Criminal Law*, 1937, 28, 70–89.

Burtt, M. E. *Legal Psychology*. Englewood Cliffs, N.J.: Prentice-Hall, 1931.

Buscoe, O. V. "Some Observation on Personality Disorder in a Forensic Setting." *Aust. N. Z. J. Criminol.*, 1970, 3(1), 39–44.

Campbell, D. T. "Reforms as Experiments." *American Psychologist*, 1969, 24, 409–429.

Campbell, D. T. *Qualitative Knowing in Action Research*. Paper presented as the Kurt Lewin Award Address to Division 9 (The Society for the Psychological Study of Social Issues) at the annual meeting of the American Psychological Association, New Orleans, September 1974.

Campbell, E. *Psychology Applied to Criminal Justice*. Cincinnati: Anderson, 1973.

Carmiet, B. M. et. al. "Criminal Process and Emotional Growth." In D. E. Cameron (Ed.), *International Psychiatry Clinics, Forensic Psychiatry and Child Psychiatry*. Boston: Little, Brown, 1965, (Vol. II).

Chein, I. *There Ought to Be a Law—but Why?* Paper presented at the annual meeting of the American Psychological Assocation, Chicago, September 1975.

Chesser, E. *Strange Loves: The Human Aspects of Sexual Deviance*. New York: William Morrow, 1971.

Clayton, G. *Sex and Crime*. New York: M-B Books, 1971.

Clyne, P. *Guilty but Insane*. London (?): Thomas, Nelson and Sons, 1972.

Corsini, R. "Functions of the Prison Psychologist." *Journal of Consulting Psychology*, 1945, 9, 101–104.

Cronbach, L. J. "Beyond the Two Disciplines of Scientific Psychology." *American Psychologist*, 1975, 30, 116–127.

Davidson, H. A. *Forensic Psychiatry*. New York: Ronald Press, 1952.

Davis, J. H., Bray, R. M., & Holt, R. W. "The Empirical Study of Decision Processes in Juries: A Critical Review. In J. L. Tapp & F. J. Levine (Eds.), *Law, Justice, and the Individual in Society: Psychological and Legal Issues*. New York: Holt, Rinehart & Winston, 1977.

Duffy, G. T. *Sex and Crime*. Garden City, N. Y.: Doubleday, 1965.

Eysenck, H. J. *Crime and Personality*, Boston: Houghton Mifflin, 1964.

Freud, S. "Psycho-analysis and the Ascertaining of Truth in Courts of Law. In *Clinical Papers and Papers on Technique: Collected Papers* (Vol. 2). New York: Basic Books, 1959.

Freud, S. "Some Character Types Met within Psychoanalytic Work: The Criminal out of a Sense of Guilt." In collected papers. London: Hogarth Press, 1959, (Vol. 4).

Friedlander, K. *Psychoanalytic Approach to Juvenile Delinquency*. New York: International Universities Press, 1974.

Friedman, L. M. "The Idea of Right as a Social and Legal Concept. *Journal of Social Issues*, 1971, 27, 189–198.

Friedman, L. M. "Remarks on the Future of Law and Social Science Research." *North Carolina Law Review*, 1974, 52, 1068–1078.

Friedman, L. M. *The Legal System*. New York: Russell Sage, 1975.

Friedrich, U., Erling, E. G., & Nielson, J. Chromosome Study in Forensic Psychiatric Patients. *Journal Legal Medicine*, 1971, 68(3), 138–148.

Fuller, L. L. "Human Interaction and the Law." *American Journal of Jurisprudence*, 1969a, 14, 1–36.

Fuller, L. L. *The Morality of Law*. (Rev. Ed.) New Haven: Yale University Press, 1969b.

Fuller, L. L. Some Presuppositions Shaping the Concept of "Socialization." In J. L. Tapp & F. J. Levine (Eds.), *Law, Justice, and the Individual in Society: Psychological and Legal Issues;* New York: Holt, Rinehart & Winston, 1977.

Gallatin, J. The Conceptualization of Rights: Psychological Development and Cross-national Perspectives. In R. Claude (Ed.), *Comparative Human Rights*. Baltimore: The Johns Hopkins University Press, 1975.

Glueck, B. C., Jr. "Psychodynamic Patterns in the Homosexual Sex Offender." *American Journal of Psychiatry*, 1956, 112, 584–590.

Glueck, B. *Studies in Forensic Psychiatry*. New York: Kraus, 1968.

Glueck, S., & Glueck, E. *Predicting Delinquency and Crime*. Cambridge: Harvard University Press, 1959.

Goldiamond, I. "Toward a Constructional Approach to Social Problems: Ethical and Constitutional Issues Raised by Applied Behavior Analysis." *Behaviorism*, 1974, 2, 1–84.

Goldstein, A. S. "Psychiatrists in Court: Some Perspectives on the Insanity Defense." *American Journal of Psychiatry*, 1969, 125(10), 1348–1351.

Gottfredson, D. M. "The Correctional Agency Challenge to Behavioral Science." Paper presented as part of the symposium on the role of psychology in social agency operations research, California State Psychological Association, San Francisco, December 1961.

Gough, H. G., & Peterson, D. R. "The Identification and Measurement of Predispositional Factors in Crime and Delinquency." *Journal of Consulting Psychology*, 1952, 16, 207–212.

Guze, S. B., Goodwin, D. W., & Crane, J. B. "Criminal Recidivism and Psychiatric Illness." *American Journal of Psychiatry*, 1970, 127(6), 832–835.

Haines, W. "The Future of Court Psychiatry." In R. W. Nice (Ed.), *Criminal Psychology*, New York: Philosophical Library, 1962, 268–282.

Hakeem, M. "A Critique of the Psychiatric Approach to Crime and Correction." *Law and Contemporary Problems*, 1958, 23, 650–682.

Halleck, S. L. "A Role of the Psychiatrist in Residential Treatment of the Delinquent." *Journal of Social Therapy*, 1958, 4, 1–6.

Halleck, S. L. "A Critique of Current Psychiatric Roles in the Legal Process." *Wisconsin Law Review*, 1969, 379–401.

Halleck, S. L. "The Criminal's Problem with Psychiatry." *Psychiatry,*

1959, 23(4), 409–412.

Halleck, S. L. *Psychiatry, and the Dilemmas of Crime.* New York: Harper and Row, 1967.

Halleck, S. L., and Bromberg, W. *Psychiatric Aspects of Criminology.* Springfield, Ill.: Charles C. Thomas, 1968.

Haney, C. & Zimbardo, P. G., The Socialization into Criminality: On Becoming a Prisoner and a Guard. In J. L. Tapp & F. J. Levine (Eds.), *Law, Justice, and the Individual in Society: Psychological and Legal Issues.* New York: Holt, Rinehart & Winston, 1977.

Hartman, A. A. "Social Issues and the Court Psychiatric Clinic." *Fed. Prob.* 1969, 33(3), 37–39.

Haward, L. R. C. "The Psychologists in English Criminal Law." *Journal of Forensic Psychology,* 1969, 1, 11–22.

Hayes, R. D. "Psychiatric Diagnosis and Criminal Behavior." In *Legal Medicine Annual,* 1970. Edited by C. H. Wecht, New York: Appleton-Century-Crofts. 1970, 421–450.

Healy, W. *Honesty: A Study of the Causes and Treatment of Dishonesty among Children.* Indianapolis, Ind.: Bobbs-Merrill, 1915.

Hill, D., & Watterson, D. "Electroencephalographic Studies of Psychopathic Personalities." *Journal of Neurology & Psychiatry,* 1952, 5, 47.

Hogan, R. "Theoretical Egocentrism and the Problem of Compliance." *American Psychologist,* 1975, 30, 533–540.

Hogan, R. Legal Socialization. In G. Bermant, C. Nemeth, & N. Vidmar (Eds.), *Psychology and the Law,* Lexington, Mass.: D.C. Heath, 1976.

Huffman, A. V. "Confidentiality of Doctor-patient Relationship in Relation to Court-ordered Psychotherapy." *Correct. Psychiat. J. Soc. Ther.,* 1972, 18(1), 3.

Hutchins, R. M. & Slesinger, D. "Legal Psychology." *Psychological Review,* 1929, 36, 13–26.

Irvine, L., and Brelje, T. *Law, Psychiatry and the Mentally Disordered Offender.* Vol. I. Springfield, Illinois: Charles C. Thomas, 1972.

Jacobs, F. G. *Criminal Responsibility,* New York: Humanities Press, 1971.

Jacobson, J. L., & Wert, R. D. "MMPI Profiles Associated with Outcomes of Group Psychotherapy with Prisoners." In J. N. Butcher (Ed.), MMPI: *Research Developments and Clinical Applications.* New York: McGraw-Hill, 1969.

Kalven, H., Jr. & Zeisel, H. *The American Jury.* Boston: Little, Brown, 1966.

Karpman, B. *Case Studies in the Psychopathology of Crime.* Washington, D.C.: Medical Science Press, 1933.

Karpman, B. "Criminality, Insanity, and the Law." *Journal of Criminal*

Law and Criminology, 1949, 39, 584–605.

Kelleher, M. J., & Copeland, J. R. M. "Compulsory Psychiatric Admission by the Police: A Study of the Use of Section 136." *Med. Sci. Law.*, 1972, 12(3), 220–224.

Klein, H. E., & Temerlin, M. K. "On Expert Testimony in Sanity Cases." *J. Nerv. Ment. Dis.* 1969, 149(5), 435–438.

Kohlberg, L., Kauffman, K., Scharf, P. & Hickey, J. *The Just Community Approach to Corrections: A Manual Part I.* Cambridge, Mass.: Moral Education Research Foundation, Harvard University, 1974.

Kohlberg, L., Scharf, P. & Hickey, J. "Justice Structure of the Prison. *Prison Journal*, 1971, 51, 3–14.

Koocher, G. P. (Ed.) *Children's Rights and the Mental Health Professions.* New York: Wiley-Interscience, 1976.

Ladinsky, J. *The Teaching of Law and Social Science Courses in the United States.* Working Paper No. 11, Center for Law and the Behavioral Sciences, University of Wisconsin-Madison, 1975.

Lemert, E. M. *Social Pathology: A Systematic Approach to the Theory of Sociopathic Behavior.* New York: McGraw-Hill, 1951.

Lerner, M. J. (Ed.) "The Justice Motive in Social Behavior." *Journal of Social Issues*, 1975.

Levine, E. R. "Psychologist as Expert Witness in 'Psychiatric' Questions." *Cleveland State Law Review*, 1971, 20(2), 379–389.

Lindman, T., & McIntyre, D. (Eds.), *The Mentally Disabled and the Law.* Chicago: University of Chicago Press, 1961.

Lipsitt, P. D., Lelos, D., & McGarry, A. L. "Competency for Trial: A Screening Instrument." Paper read at the 123rd annual meeting of the Am. Psychiat. Assoc. San Francisco, Calif., May 11–15, 1970. *American Journal of Psychiatry*, 1971, 128(1), 105–109.

Llewellyn, K. N. & Hoebel, E. A. *The Cheyenne Way: Conflict and Case Law in Primitive Jurisprudence.* Norman, Okla.: University of Oklahoma Press, 1941.

Loreto, G., & Rego, Barros R. "Litigant Behavior Culminating in the Homicide of a Hierarchial Superior." *Neurobiologies*, 1968, 31(4), 113–138.

Louisell, D. W., & Diamond, B. L. "Law and Psychiatry: Detente, Entent or Concomitance?" *Cornell Law Quarterly*, 1965, 50, 217–234.

Lunde, D. T. *Murder and Madness.* San Francisco: San Francisco Book Company, 1976.

MacDonald, J. M. *Psychiatry and the Criminal. A Guide to Psychiatric Examinations for the Criminal Courts.* (2nd ed.) Springfield, Ill: Charles C. Thomas, 1969.

Marshall, J. *Law and Psychology in Conflict.* New York: Bobbs-Merrill, 1966.

Mathews, A. *Mental Disability and the Law*. Chicago: American Bar Foundation, 1970.

McCord, W., & McCord, J. *Psychopathology and Delinquency*. New York: Grune & Stratton, 1956.

Meehl, P. E. "Psychology and the Criminal Law." *University of Richmond Law Review*, 1970, 5, 1–30.

Meehl, P.E. "Law and the Fireside Induction." *Journal of Social Issues*, 1971, 27, 65–100.

Megargee, E. I. The Prediction of Violence with Psychological Tests. In C. Speilberger (Ed.), *Current Topics in Clinical and Community Psychology*. New York: Academic Press, 1970.

Monahan, J. (Ed.) *Community Mental Health and the Criminal Justice System*. New York: Pergamon, 1975.

Moore, U. & Callahan, C., "Law and Learning Theory: A Study in Legal Control. *Yale Law Journal*, 1943, 53, 1–136.

Morezov, C. V., & Kalashnik, T. M. (Eds.) *Forensic Psychiatry*. New York: International Arts and Sciences Press, 1969.

Overholser, W. "Major Principles of Forensic Psychiatry." In S. Arieti, et. al. (Eds.) *American Handbook of Psychiatry*, New York: Basic Books, 1959.

Palmer, S. *Psychology of Murder*. New York: Crowell, 1966.

Parke, R. Socialization into Child Abuse: A Social Interactional Perspective. In J. L. Tapp & F. J. Levine (Eds.), *Law, Justice, and the Individual in Society: Psychological and Legal Issues*. New York: Holt, Rinehart & Winston, 1977.

Pepitone, A. *Social Psychological Perspectives in Crime and Punishment*. Paper presented at the annual meeting of the American Psychological Association, Chicago, September 1975.

Perlstein, S. *Psychiatry, the Law and Mental Health*. Dobbs Ferry, N. Y.: Oceana Press, 1967.

Peterson, D. R., Quay, H. C., & Cameron, G. R. "Personality and Background Factors in Juvenile Delinquency as Inferred from Questionnaire Responses." *Jornal of Consulting Psychology*, 1959, 23, 395–399.

Pointdexter, W. R. "Mental Illness in a State Penitentiary." *Journal of Criminal Law, Criminology and Police Science*, 1955, 45, 559–564.

Polier, W. *The Rule of Law and the Role of Psychiatry*. Baltimore: John Hopkins Press, 1968.

Powelson, H., & Bendix, A. "Psychiatry in Prison," *Psychiatry*, 1951, 14, 73–86.

Quay, H. "Personality Dimensions in Delinquent Males as Inferred from the Factor Analysis of Behavior Ratings." *Journal of Research in Crime & Delinquency*, 1964, 1, 33–37.

Rawls, J. *A Theory of Justice.* Cambridge, Mass.: Belknap, 1971.

Reckless, W. C., Dinitz, S., & Murray, E. "Self Concept as an Insulator against Delinquency." *Am. Soc. Rev.*, 1956, 21, 744–746.

Reiser, M. *The Police Department Psychologist.* Springfield, Ill.: Thomas, 1972.

Robey, A., & Brodsky, S. L. "A Bill of Rights for the Forensic Psychiatric." Paper presented at the meetings of the A.P.A., Dallas, Texas, May, 1972.

Robey, A., & Bogard, W. J. "The Complete Forensic Psychiatrist." Paper read at the 125th anniversary meeting of the American Psychiatrist Association, Miami Beach, Fla. May 5–9, 1969. *American Journal of Psychiatry*, April 1974, 29(4).

Robinson, D. N. "Therapies: A Clear and Present Danger." *American Psychologist*, 1973, 28, 129–133.

Robitscher, J. "The New Face of Legal Psychiatry." *American Journal of Psychiatry*, 1972, 129(3), 315–321.

Rollen, H. R. *The Mentally Abnormal Offender and the Law.* Oxford: Pergamon, 1969.

Roman, T. "An Ex-prisoner on Psychiatric Reporting." *Process*, 1972, 51(6), 132–136.

Rubin, S. *Psychiatry and Criminal Law.* Dobbs Ferry, New York: Oceana Publications, 1965.

Russell, D. H. "Diagnosing Offendering Patients in Massachusetts Court Clinics," *Int. J. Offender Ther.* London: 1970. Offender Therapy Series APTO Monograph.

Russell, D. H. "Children in Court: Obligations for Legal Psychiatry." *Judge Baker Guid. Center, Boston, Mass. Newsletter* 1972, 3(2), 1–15.

Russell, D. H. "From the Massachusetts Courts Clinics, U.S.A., I: A Study of Its Administration and Community Aspects." *Int. J. Offender Ther.*, 1969, 13(3), 140–147.

Russell, D. H., & Duvlin, J. M. "Massachusetts Court Clinics Statistics." July 1969 - June 1970. *Int. J. Offend. Ther.*, 1971, 15(3), 195–204.

Sabot, T. J. "The Psychiatrist and the Defense of Insanity." *Correct. Psyciat. J. Soc. Ther.*, 1972, 18(3), 32–34.

Sales, B. D. *Perspectives in Law and Psychology: The Criminal Justice System.* Volume I. New York: Plenum, 1977.

Sales, B. D. *Psychology and the Legal Process.* New York: Spectrum Books, 1977.

Sardoff, R. L. "Mental Illness and the Criminal Process: The Role of Psychiatrist." *American Bar Association Journal*, 1968, 54, 566–569.

Satten, J. "The Mind of the Offender." *Prison Journal*, 1969, 49(1), 3–5.

Scheidemandel, P. L., and Kanno, C. K. *The Mentally Ill Offender: A*

Survey of Treatment Programs. Washington, D.C.: U.S. Government Printing Office, 1975.

Schilder, P. "The Cure of Criminals and Prevention of Crime." *Journal of Criminal Psychopathology,* 1940, 2, 152.

Schonds, H. C. *A Report on an Investigation of Psychiatric Problems in Felons in the North Carolina Prison System.* Chapel Hill, North Carolina: University of North Carolina, 1958.

Schuessler, K. T., & Cressey, D. B. "Personality Characteristics of Criminals." *American Journal of Sociology,* 1950, 56, 476–484.

Schwitzgebel, R. K. "A Contractual Model for the Protection of the Rights of Institutionalized Patients. *American Psychologist,* 1975, 30, 815–820.

Shapiro, L. N. "Psychiatry in the Correctional Process." *Crime and Delinquency,* 1966, 12, 9–16.

Shapley, D. "Jury Selection: Social Scientists Gamble in an Already Loaded Game." *Science,* 1974, 185, 1033–1034, 1071.

Shuman, S. I. Why Criminal Law?: Parameters for Evaluating Objectives and Response Alternatives. In J. L. Tapp & F. J. Levine (Eds.), *Law, Justice, and the Individual in Society: Psychological and Legal Issues.* New York: Holt, Rinehart & Winston, 1977.

Silber, D. A. "Controversy Concerning the Criminal Justice System and Its Implications for the Role of Mental Health Workers." *American Psychologist,* 1974, 20(4).

Silverman, H. "Psychiatric Evidence in Criminal Law." *Criminal Law Quarterly,* 1972, 14(2), 145–171.

Spaulding, Edith R. *Experimental Study of Psychopathic Delinquent Women.* Montclair: Paterson-Smith, 1969.

Stephenson, P. S. "Factors Affecting Psychiatric Referral of Juvenile Delinquents." Division of Child Psychiatry, Department of Psychiatry, University of British Columbia, Vancouver: *Canad. J. Correct.* 1971, 1313, 274–282.

Stone, Alan. *Mental Health and the Law.* Washington, D.C.: U.S. Government Printing Office, 1975.

Sullivan, C., Grant, J. D., & Grant, M. Q. "The Development of Interpersonal Maturity: Application of Delinquency." *Psychiatry,* 1956, 20, 373–385.

Symposium, *The Use of Videotape in the Courtroom.* Provo, Utah: *Brigham Young University Law Review,* 1975.

Szasz, T. "Criminal Responsibility and Psychiatry." In H. Toch (Ed.), *Legal and Criminal Psychology.* New York: Holt, Rinehart, & Winston, 1961. 146–186.

Szasz, T. *Law, Liberty, and Psychiatry.* New York: Macmillan, 1963.

Szasz, T. "Psychiatry, Ethics, and the Criminal Law," *Columbia Law Review*, 1958, 58, 183–198.

Tanay, E. "Forensic Psychiatry in the Legal Defense of Murder." Paper presented at the plenary session of the twenty-third annual meeting of the American Academy of Forensic Sciences, Phoenix, Ariz. Feb. 23, 1971. Wayne State University, Detroit, Mich. *J. Forens. Sci.*, 1972, 16(1), 15–24.

Tapp, J. L. "Psychology and the Law: The Dilemma." *Psychology Today*, 1969, 2, 16–22.

Tapp, J. L. (Ed.) "Socialization, the Law, and Society." *Journal of Social Issues*, 1971, 27(2).

Tapp, J. L. *Cross-cultural and Developmental Dimensions of a Jurisprudence of Youth*. Working Paper No. 5, Law & Society Center, University of California, Berkeley, 1973.

Tapp, J. L. The Psychological Limits of Legality. In J. R. Pennock & J. W. Chapman (Eds.) *The Limits of Law: Nomos XV*. New York: Atherton, 1974.

Tapp, J. L. "Psychology and the Law: An Overture" In M. R. Rosenzweig & L. W. Porter (Eds.), *Annual Review of Psychology* (Vol. 27). Palo Alto, Calif.: Annual Reviews, 1976.

Tapp, J. L. & Levine, F. J. "Legal Socialization: Strategies for an Ethical Legality." *Stanford Law Review*, 1974, 27, 1–72.

Tapp, J. L. & Levine, F. J. (Eds.) *Law, Justice, and the Individual in Society: Psychological and Legal Issues*. New York: Holt, Rinehart & Winston, 1977.

Thibaut, J. & Walker, L. *Procedural Justice: A Psychological Analysis*. Hillsdale, N.J.: Lawrence Erlbaum Associates, 1975.

Thompson, G. N. *The Psychopathic Delinquent and Criminal*. Springfield: Charles C. Thomas, 1953.

Toch, H. (Ed.) *Legal and Criminal Psychology*. New York: Holt, Rinehart & Winston, 1961.

Toch, H. *Violent Men: An Inquiry into the Psychology of Violence*. Chicago: Aldine, 1969.

Waldo, G., & Dinitz, S. "Personality Characteristics of Criminals." *Journal of Research in Crime and Delinquency*, 1967, 3, 1–20.

Wattenberg, W. W. "Psychologists and Juvenile Delinquency." In H. Toch (Ed.), *Legal and Criminal Psychology*. New York: Holt, Rinehart, & Winston, 1961.

Westbury, D. G. A. "Forensic Psychiatry in Britain: Its Potentials." *Int. J. Offender Ther.*, 1969, 13(3), 1965–176.

Wexler, D. "Token and Taboo: Behavior Modification, Token Economies, and the Law." *California Law Review*, 1973, 61, 81–109.

Wheskin, F. E. "From the Massachusetts Court Clinics, U.S.A.: III,

Enforced Psychotherapy." *Int. J. Offender Ther.*, 1969, 13(3), 152–158.

Wilmer, H. A. "Murder, You Know." *Psychiatric Quarterly*, 1969, 43(3), 414–447.

Wilson, D. P. *My Six Convicts: A Psychologist's Three Years in Fort Leavenworth.* New York: Rinehart, 1951.

Woodruff, R. A., et al. *Psychiatric Diagnosis.* New York: Oxford University Press, 1974.

Zilborg, G. *The Psychology of the Criminal Act and Punishment.* New York: Harcourt Brace, 1954.

Ziskin, J. *Coping with Psychiatric and Psychology Testimony.* Beverly Hills, Calif.: Law & Psychology Press, 1970.

Index